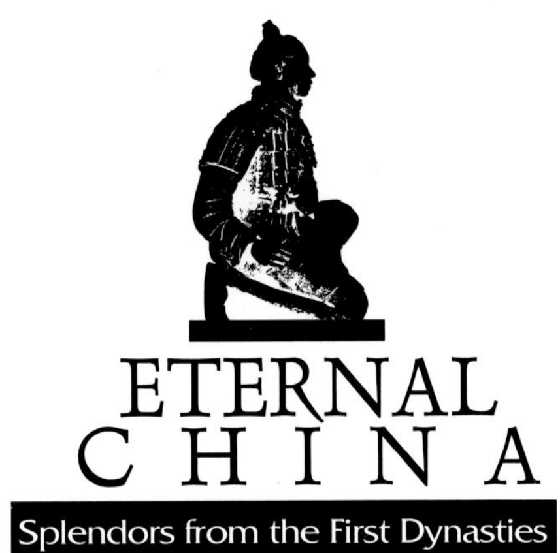

ETERNAL CHINA

Splendors from the First Dynasties

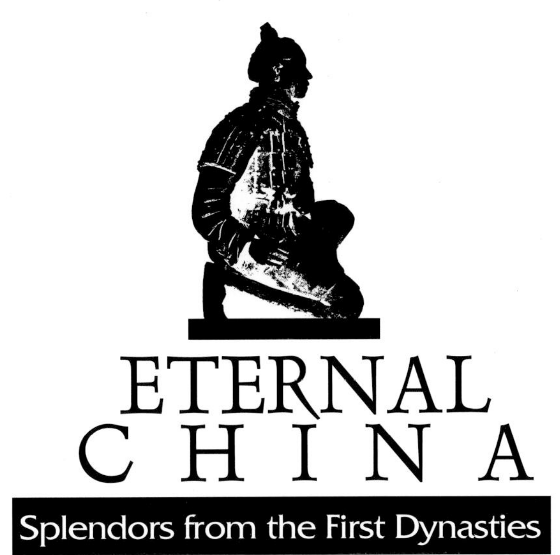

ETERNAL CHINA

Splendors from the First Dynasties

LI JIAN

editor and curator

With contributions by

Susan N. Erickson
Liu Qingzhu and Yue Hongbin
Du Jinpeng

THE DAYTON ART INSTITUTE

With the cooperation of
Administrative Bureau of Museums and
Archaeological Data of Shaanxi Province
People's Republic of China

Exhibition Schedule
The Dayton Art Institute, Ohio
7 March–7 June 1998

Santa Barbara Museum of Art, California
18 July–18 October 1998

This catalogue is published in conjunction with the exhibition of the same title, organized by The Dayton Art Institute in cooperation of the Administrative Bureau of Museums and Archaeological Data of Shaanxi Province, People's Republic of China, and the support of the Santa Barbara Museum of Art, California.

The exhibition is supported in Dayton by the General Motors Corporation, with additional support from Mrs. Virginia W. Kettering, Residence Inn by Marriott-Dayton South, Bank One, NA, United Health Care, Montgomery County, WHIO-Channel 7, *Dayton Daily News*, the Dayton Montgomery County Convention & Visitors Bureau and the National Endowment for the Arts for the exhibition tour.

The presentation of the exhibition in Santa Barbara is completely underwritten by Leslie and Paul Ridley-Tree. Additional programming is made possible by Northern Trust Bank of California.

All works in the exhibition are on loan from the museums and institutes of Shaanxi Province. The exhibition has been coordinated in Xi'an by Li Bing and Zhang Tong from the Administrative Bureau of Museums and Archaeological Data. The descriptive data of the objects have been prepared by Dang Huanying.

Published in 1998 by The Dayton Art Institute, 456 Belmonte Park North, Dayton, Ohio 45405. No part of this book may be used or reproduced in any manner without the written permission of the publisher.

First Edition
Library of Congress Catalog Card Number 98–070294
ISBN 0-937809-15-2 (paperback)

Edited by Carol Shannon and M. Kathryn Horste, Ann Arbor, MI
Designed by Jennifer Perry, The Dayton Art Institute
Photography by Wang Baoping, Xi'an
Calligraphy by Song Zhenxing, Xi'an
Color corrections by Dan Mueller
Typeset in Friz Quadrata and Delphian
Printed on 90 lb. Aero Gloss Text and 120 lb. Strobe Gloss Cover
Printed by Brown & Kroger Printing Company
Bound by Dayton Bindery Service, Inc.

Printed in the United States of America.

Cover illustration
Head of a Warrior. Qin dynasty (221–206 B.C.). Gilded bronze. Xianyang Museum. Catalogue no. 7.

Frontispiece
Qin and Han Sculpture. Calligraphy by Song Zhenxing.

Illustration on page 16
Paved road near the mausoleum of Qin Shihuang. Qin dynasty. Photo courtesy Shaanxi Museums & Archaeological Data Bureau.

Illustration on page 28
Standing Woman. Western Han dynasty. Painted earthenware. Catalogue no. 31.

Illustration on page 42
Nuwa. Eastern Han dynasty. Stone relief. Figure 3.12.

Back Cover illustration
Kneeling Archer. Qin dynasty (221-206 B.C.). Terracotta. Museum of the Qin Shihuang Terracotta Army. Catalogue no. 17.

Contents

Preface

For the promotion of cultural exchange and friendship between the American and Chinese peoples at the coming of the new century, The Dayton Art Institute and the Administrative Bureau of Museums and Archaeological Data of Shaanxi Province have cooperatively organized the exhibition *ETERNAL CHINA— Splendors from the First Dynasties* held at Dayton, Ohio in the United States. As a result of the dedication and great effort on both sides, we believe that this exhibition will be a great success and will also serve as a benchmark for future exchange, understanding, and cooperation.

The Qin-Han dynastic period is the most significant era in the development of Chinese feudal society. Even though the Qin is one of the shortest dynasties, it is still considered the most influential in Chinese history. As China's first fully unified dynasty, the Qin established for the first time the centralized sovereignty that would last for over 2,000 years. In fact, the English word "China" is derived from the pronunciation of "Qin." Secondly, the Han, Leaders of China's longest dynasty, ruled for more than four centuries. During this period, China's culture and arts experienced unprecedented development. As a result, a majority of modern day Chinese still refer to themselves as Han Chinese. Because both the Qin and Han dynasties established their capitals in present day Shaanxi province, a wealth of cultural artifacts was left behind. Along with the discovery of Qin Shihuang's terracotta army, new archaeological discoveries in Shaanxi are receiving more and more attention from both scholars and the general public. Featuring a variety of cultural and historical artifacts, many of which have been recently discovered, this exhibition possesses a high scholarly and artistic value and accurately reflects Qin-Han society. Not only will this exhibit allow the American public the enjoyment of exquisite artifacts and insight into Qin-Han history, but it will also be of great benefit to the understanding of today's culture and academia.

We sincerely offer our particular gratitude to The Dayton Art Institute for their enormous effort in organizing and hosting this exhibition. We would also like to take this opportunity to extend our best wishes for a successful exhibition tour.

Li Bin
Director of Office of Foreign Affairs
Administrative Bureau of Museums and Archaeological Data of
Shaanxi Province

祝辞

在新世纪即将来临之际，为增进中美两国人民之间的友好往来与文化交流，美国代顿艺术博物馆和陕西省文物事业管理局在美国代顿共同举办【秦汉雕塑展】。经过双方的辛勤努力，相信这次展览一定会取得圆满成功，并将是双方增进交流，加深了解，扩大合作的一个里程碑。

秦汉两朝是中国封建社会重要的发展时期。秦代是中国历史上第一个统一的封建王朝，也是中国历史上最短的王朝之一，同时也是最有影响的王朝。它所建立的中央集权制一直在中国封建社会延续了两千多年。英文 CHINA 一词即源于"秦"的发音。汉代则是中国历史上最长的朝代。它统治中国长达四个多世纪。在这一时期中国的文化和艺术得到了空前的发展，至今大多数中国人仍自称"汉族"。陕西省是秦汉立国建都之地，历史上留有极丰富的文化遗存。随著举世瞩目的秦始皇兵马俑的发现，有关陕西考古的新发现越来越受到专业人士及社会大众的关注。【秦汉雕塑展】所汇集的大量珍贵文物，许多是近年出土的，具有很高的学术和艺术价值，能够比较集中的反映秦汉时期的社会风貌。这次展览不但能使美国民众欣赏秦汉时期的精美文物，了解秦汉的历史，而且对今天的文化、学术、教育也一定会大有裨益。

值此展览开幕之际，我们特别感谢为举办这次展览而做出巨大努力的代顿艺术博馆。

祝展览获得圆满成功！

陕西省文物事业管理局
外事处 处长 李斌

Introduction

In 1974, on a stretch of scenic farmland in the central most portion of China, one of the most important, if not the most important, archaeological discoveries of all time was made. While digging for a well, farmers uncovered fragments which would lead archaeologists to the excavation of the incredible terracotta army of the dynamic and enterprising emperor, Qin Shihuang, the first emperor of the long string of China's dynasties. Qin Shihuang unified the country previously divided into six warring states, an achievement that concentrated power and authority in his hands. The emperor instituted laws and unified systems of coinage, weights, and measures. He also began construction of the Great Wall as a defensive military measure. Among his grandiose plans, the emperor was accompanied into the afterlife by an army of thousands of larger than life-size warriors, generals and horses, a tremendous tribute to the emperor buried a mile from the tomb which would enshire him at his death. Today, the Museum of the Terracotta Warriors comprises an area greater than a football stadium and is truly one of the most awe-inspiring sights that humankind has ever created.

ETERNAL CHINA is more than these legendary treasures from the Qin's army. Works of jade, bronze, gold, stone, and ceramic comprise the 115 works, which are included in the exhibition. Many of these works are traveling outside of China for the first time. In addition to the splendors from the Qin dynasty (221–206 B.C.), the Han dynasties, including the Western Han (206 B.C.–A.D. 9) and the Eastern Han (25–220 A.D.) are represented by examples of royal objects and works of extraordinary beauty. In many ways, it is a compact and concise overview of the richness that typifies these early Chinese dynasties.

ETERNAL CHINA brings to The Dayton Art Institute twelve figures from Emperor Qin's terracotta army, as well as more than one hundred other works of early Chinese art. These treasures are coming to America thanks to the generous cooperation of our colleagues in China. It has been a great pleasure, both personally and professionally, to work with Li Bin and Zhang Tong during the course of the planning and implementing this monumental endeavor.

This exhibition is dedicated to the tradition of collecting and appreciation for Chinese art at The Dayton Art institute. Since its beginning in the first decades of this century, the Art Institute and many of its most generous donors have had a profound interest in early Chinese art. The museum's founder and matriarch, Mrs. Julia Shaw Patterson Carnell, began the tradition of giving to the museum many wonderful Chinese treasures such as the highly rare and important Tang dynasty silver vase. Following in her footsteps, her son, the Honorable Jefferson Patterson, and his wife, Mary Marvin Breckinridge Patterson, continued to bestow upon the museum numerous works of art from China and all of the Far East. However, the museum's greatest patron of art of Asia has been Mrs. Virginia Kettering. As early as 1950, Mrs. Kettering and her late husband, Eugene, began to donate works from their spectacular collection to the museum. The tradition has continued steadily during the ensuing four and half decades. During the past two years alone, Mrs. Kettering has given the Art Institute more than 170 works of art, including 65 works from China, many of which are on display in the Patterson-Kettering Wing of Asian Art.

The Dayton Art Institute's curator of Asian art, Li Jian, made *ETERNAL CHINA* possible. A native of Beijing, Li Jian formulated the idea for the exhibition and shepherded it to its successful completion. Despite often working under the most arduous of circumstances, traveling countless miles in a frigid climate, and with pressing deadlines, Li Jian persevered. The result is this magnificent catalogue and the exhibition is records.

An exhibition such as this can only be undertaken by a museum with a staff as skilled and talented as ours. Credit is also due to Edward Amatore, museum's registrar, who had to navigate a maze of international red tape to pull together the logistics of this ambitious endeavor and who succeeded in obtaining NEA indemnification support. Likewise, the other members of the curatorial team, including Marianne Lorenz, Assistant Director for Collections and Programs, Dominique Vasseur, Senior Curator, and Lora Stowe, Curatorial Assistant, have made significant contributions. The display is credited to the continued ingenuity of our designer, Elroy Quenroe, of Elroy Quenroe and Associates. The installation is credited to our preparation staff headed by Joe Parsons. This publication is due to the design skills of Jennifer Perry, Art Director. She has done a masterful job for publication at the museum. Sara Weber, Director of Marketing and Communication, Heather Galecka, Communication Manager, and Jim Thornton, Assistant Director for Development, have been responsible for the marketing efforts, which virtually ensure the largest attendance for any exhibition in the history of The Dayton Art Institute.

Thanks are also due to the Art Institute's Exhibitions and Programs Committee, chaired formerly by John McCreary and now by Cheryl Garrett, for their belief in the importance of the *ETERNAL CHINA* project. The support of presidents of the

Board of Trustees, John Lombard and Ray Stickel during the three-plus years this exhibit was in the development stages has also been instrumental in its success.

This exhibition could not have been undertaken without the generous support of our sponsors: General Motors Corporation, with additional support from Residence Inn by Marriott-Dayton South, Bank One, NA, United Health Care, Montgomery County, WHIO-Channel, Dayton Daily News, and the Dayton/Montgomery County Convention & Visitors Bureau. Support has also come from the National Endowment for the Arts.

A special note of thanks is due to our colleagues in Santa Barbara. Robert Frankel, Director of the Santa Barbara Museum of Art, shared our vision and agreed very early to partner with The Dayton Art Institute. His cooperation has helped to make this effort possible.

ETERNAL CHINA links us with the past and positions us for the future. Much like orchestras that take on the project of playing Beethoven's full cycle of symphonic works over a number of seasons. Eternal China marks the beginning of an ambitious exhibition project showcasing the splendors of more than twenty centuries of Chinese art. During the next decades and a half, we will endeavor to spotlight the treasures of the dynasties which followed the Qin and Han, with works from the Tang, Song, Yuan, Ming, and Qing dynasties. We plan to build upon the foundations of our international friendship to forge a greater understanding and appreciation for the splendors of Chinese art in the years to come.

Alexander Lee Nyerges
Director
The Dayton Art Institute

Foreword

When the Santa Barbara Museum of Art opened to the public in 1941, Chinese works of art were already one of the strengths of the collection. As the Museum of Art has grown, so too has this important area of our holdings. The presentation of this important exhibition of Qin and Han sculpture from Xi'an in our community is consistent with the ongoing commitment, as envisioned by the founders of our museum, to the presentation of Chinese art.

I am grateful to Alexander Nyerges and each member of his staff at The Dayton Art Institute who have worked with their counterparts in Santa Barbara: Susan Tai, Curator of Asian Art; Cherie Summers and her staff in the Collections Management Office; Terry Atkinson, Museum Designer; Kyle Brace, Marketing Officer; and John Coplin and his crew, who constructed and installed our exhibition. Special thanks must be given to Leslie and Paul Ridley-Tree, who completely underwrote the exhibition, and to Northern Trust Bank that provided funding for programming.

This is the beginning of what we hope will be an ongoing partnership with the people of China to bring to the central coast of California more exhibitions of this quality and historical importance. We look forward to continuing and expanding the friendship that has evolved from *ETERNAL CHINA*.

Robert H. Frankel
Director
Santa Barbara Museum of Art

Lenders to the Exhibition

Museum of the Qin Shihuang Terracotta Army

秦始皇兵马俑博物馆

Shaanxi History Museum

陕西历史博物馆

Shaanxi Provincial Institute of Archaeology

陕西省考古研究所

Xianyang Museum

咸阳市博物馆

Maoling Museum

茂陵博物馆

Xi'an Institute of Cultural Relics and Archaeology

西安市文物考古研究所

Xianyang Institute of Archaeology

咸阳市考古研究所

Lintong County Museum

临潼县博物馆

Mian County Museum

勉县博物馆

Yulin Hongshixia Administrative Institute of Cultural Relics

榆林红石峡文物管理所

Acknowledgments

This exhibition and its accompanying catalogue are the result of efforts of many individuals in both China and the United States. In the fall of 1995, when Alexander Nyerges, Director, and Marianne Lorenz, Assistant Director for Collections and Programs, expressed their intention to organize a special exhibition featuring Qin-dynasty terracotta figures, my immediate thought was to consolidate the Qin and Han dynasties and to focus on the sculpture created during this period. I thank the director and the assistant director for giving me the opportunity to pursue this project. All works of art have been drawn from the collections of the institutes of Shaanxi Province. I am grateful to the lending institutions for permitting their objects to be removed from their galleries for duration of the exhibition. Arrangements for the loans were made in Xi'an by Li Bin and Zhang Tong. The descriptive data were collected from the lending institutions by Dang Huanying. I am grateful to them and their staff for their kind cooperation in all phases of the organization of this exhibition.

During the early stage of exhibition planning, Wu Hung from the University of Chicago reviewed the checklist and offered advice on the selection of objects and the catalogue. James Lally from New York and Xiaoneng Yang from the Nelson-Atkins Museum of Art provided their expertise and support. Li He from the Asian Art Museum of San Francisco and Xie Chang from the Birmingham Museum of Art shared their expertise in organizing traveling exhibitions from China. Tsing Yuan from Wright State University confirmed various issues related to the history of the Qin and Han dynasties. Ma Zhenzhi from Shaanxi History Museum, Xi'an, offered his opinion on some problematic objects. J. Heilman and his team from the Dayton Museum of Discovery, as well as Michael Portwood from the University of Minnesota, are helpful with archaeological texts and related concepts. James Robinson from the Indianapolis Museum of Art provided his support, guidance, and inspiration at various stages of this project. My former advisor, Robert Poor, encouraged me to write the catalogue at the same time when a renovation project was undertaken at The Dayton Art Institute. Thanks are also due to Jane Graham from the Indianapolis Museum of Art and Lilly Keskeys from the Freer Gallery of Art for their advice on publication issues. I express my gratitude to all these individuals for their support and generous contributions to this project.

The publication is a joint endeavor of authors from the United States and China. Thanks are due to our authors for their research and their dedication to the project. Thanks are also due to our judicious editors, Carol Shannon and Kathryn Horste. I am indebted to Geoffery Parker for his dedicated efforts in compiling the bibliography, the list of Chinese characters, and in proofreading of a great portion of the catalogue. I am also grateful to Lillian Zau, Zhang Huilin, and Zhang Huangchang from the local Chinese community for their assistance with many details. I appreciate the assistance of our museum staff from all departments. Without their contributions, this project could not have been completed. I am especially grateful to Dominique Vasseur, Lora Stowe, Kristina Sullivan and Helen Pinkney for their proofreading of the catalogue texts and their comments. I would like to express special thanks to our registrar, Edward Amatore, who worked diligently on bringing the exhibition to the United States, and our graphic designer, Jennifer Perry, who created a beautiful design for this catalogue.

Li Jian
Curator of Asian Art
The Dayton Art Institute

Chronology

Neolithic period................................ca. 5000–ca. 1600 B.C.

Shang dynasty................................ca. 1600–ca. 1050 B.C.

Zhou dynasty................................ca. 1050–256 B.C.

    Western Zhou................................ca. 1050–771 B.C.

    Eastern Zhou................................ca. 771–256 B.C.

        Spring and Autumn periods................................722–481 B.C.

        Warring States period.. 480–221 B.C.

            Pre-Qin period..383–221 B.C.

Qin dynasty......................................221–206 B.C.

Han dynasty..................................206 B.C.–A.D. 220

    Western Han dynasty.......................206 B.C.–A.D. 9

    Xin interregnum..............................9–23

    Eastern Han dynasty.........................25–220

Approximate dates of the pre-Qin rulers

Ruler	献孝惠悼昭孝庄	公公文武襄文襄	公公王王公王王	Dates
Xiangong				384–362 B.C.
Xiaogong				362–338
Huiwenwang				338–311
Daowuwang				311–307
Zhaoxianggong				307–251
Xiaowenwang				251–250
Zhuangxiangwang				250–247

Emperors of the Qin, Western Han, Xin and Eastern Han dynasties

Qin

Emperor	Name	Dates
Shihuangdi	始皇帝	246–210 B.C.
Ershihuangdi	二世皇帝	209–207

Western Han

Emperor	高惠吕文景武昭宣元成哀平孺	祖帝后帝帝帝帝帝帝帝帝帝子	Dates
Gaozu			202–195
Huidi			195–188
Empress Dowager Lü			188–180
Wendi			180–157
Jingdi			157–141
Wudi			141–87
Zhaodi			87–74
Xuandi			74–49
Yuandi			49–33
Chengdi			33–7
Aidi			7–1
Pingdi		婴	1 B.C.–A.D. 6
Ruzi Ying	孺	子	6–9

Xin

Emperor	Name	Dates
Wang Mang	王莽	9–23

Eastern Han

Emperor	光明章和殇安顺冲质桓灵献	武帝帝帝帝帝帝帝帝帝帝帝	帝	Dates
Guangwudi				25–57
Mingdi				57–75
Zhangdi				75–88
Hedi				88–106
Shangdi				106
Andi				107–125
Shundi				125–44
Chongdi				144–45
Zhidi				145–46
Huandi				146–68
Lingdi				168–89
Xiandi				189–220

Note: Unless otherwise indicated, all the dates for pre-dynastic rulers and emperors are for the periods in which they were enthroned. The pre-Qin period begins in around 383 B.C. when the Qin state relocated the capital from Yong to Liyang.

Map of the Qin Dynasty

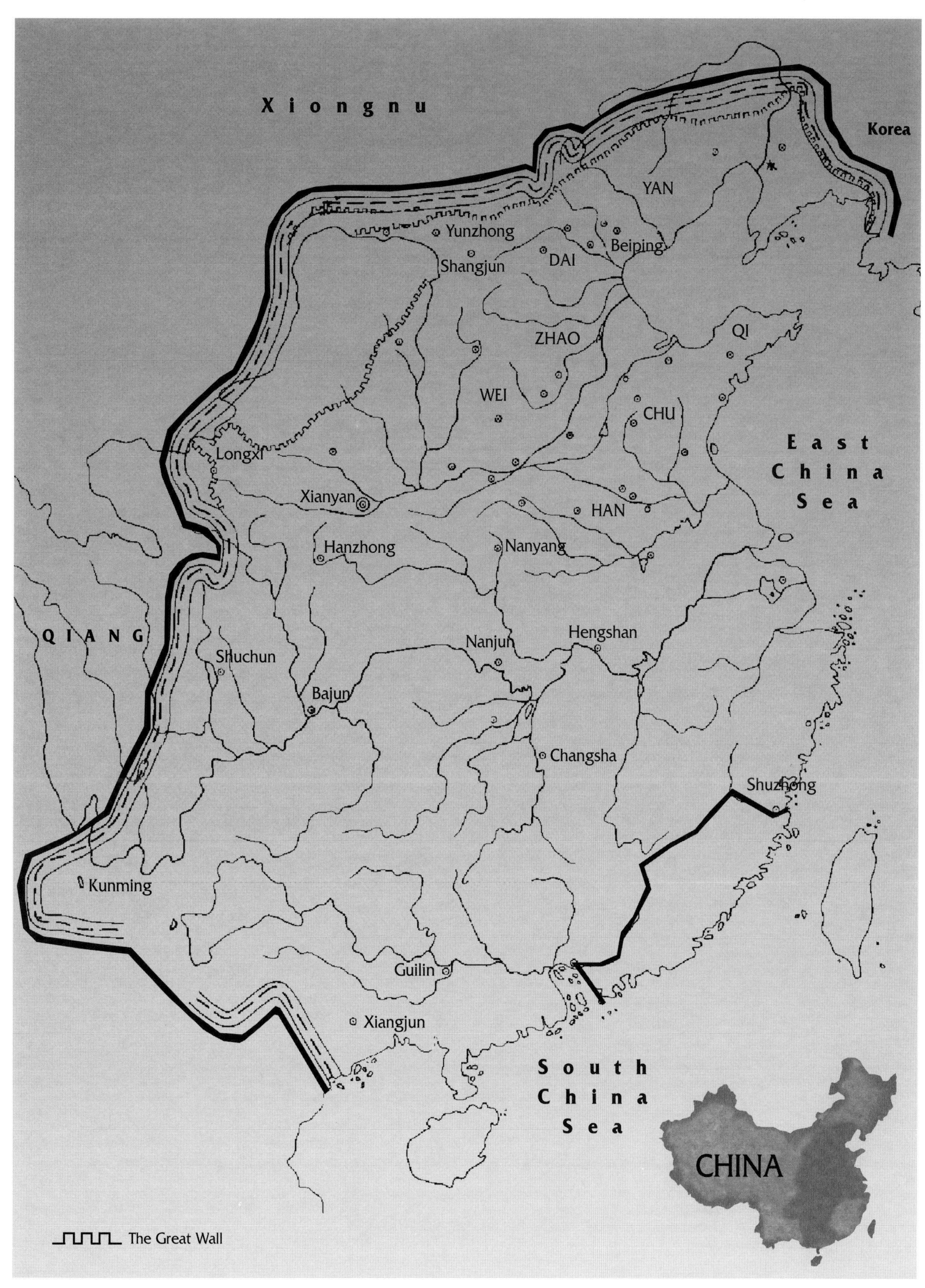

Map of the Western Han Dynasty

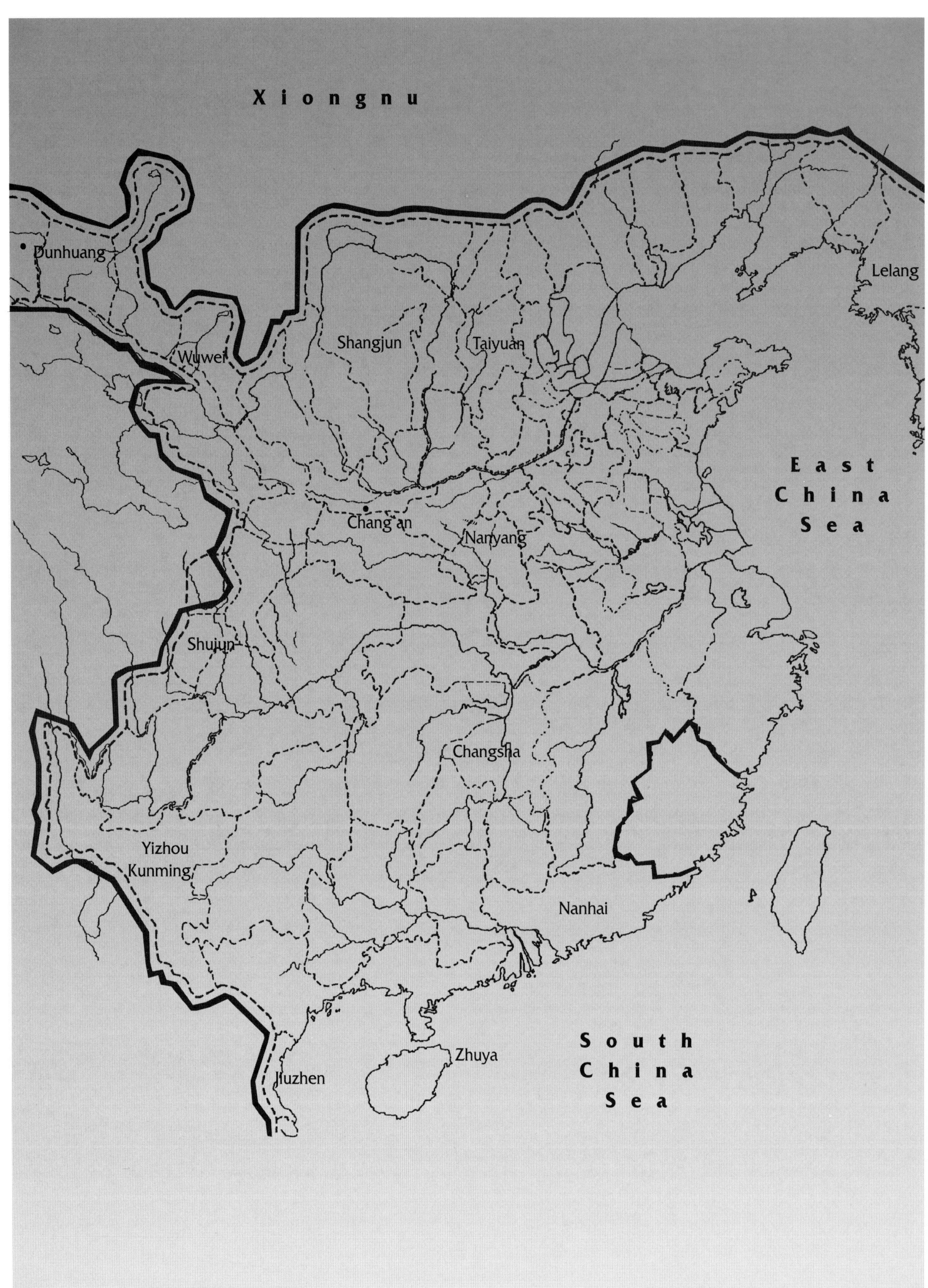

Qin and Han Cities
and Tombs

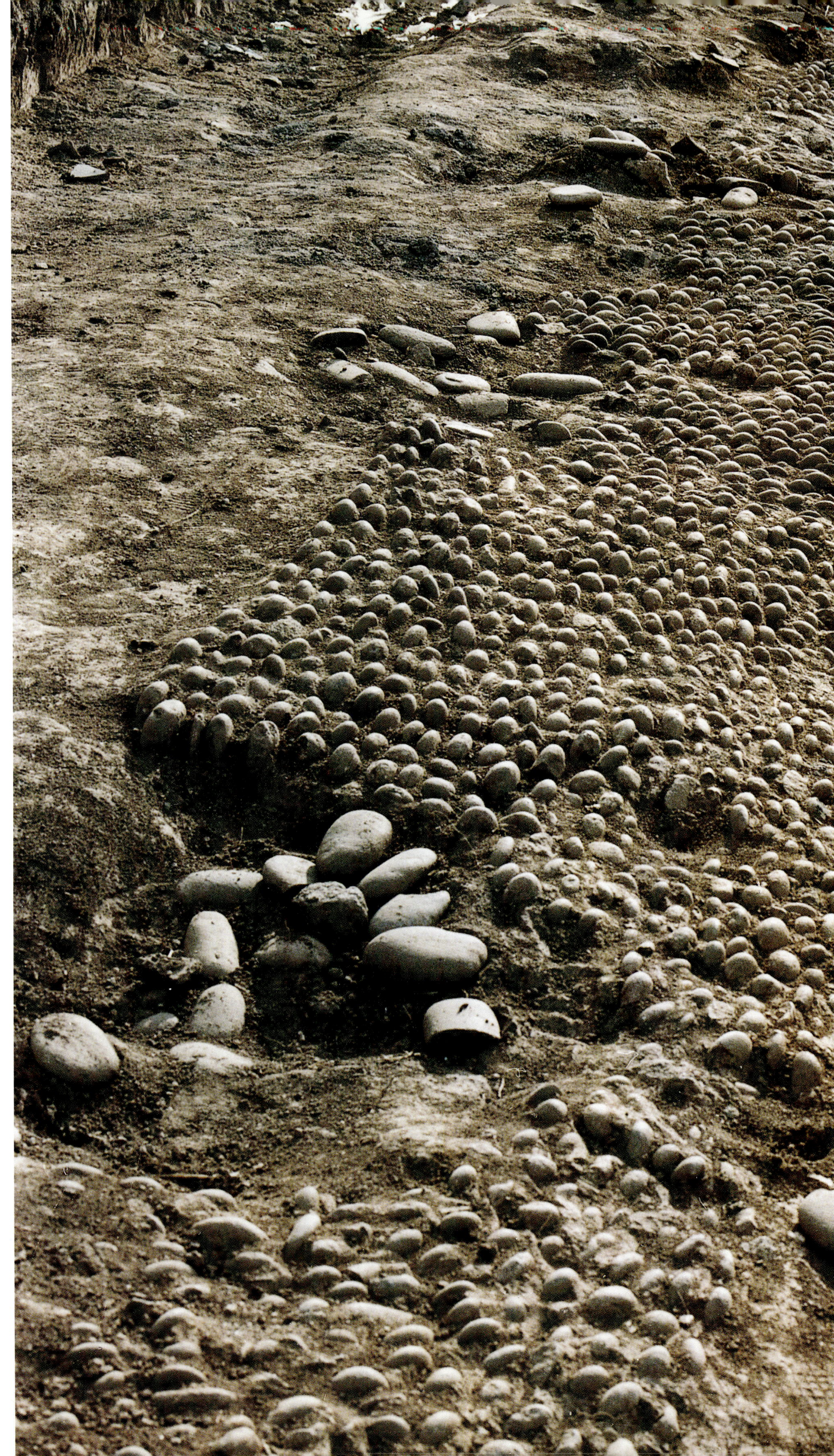

Qin and Han Cities and Tombs: Important Archaeological Discoveries from the Xi'an Region

Liu Qingzhu and Yue Hongbin
Institute of Archaeology, Chinese Academy
of Social Sciences

For centuries Qin and Han artifacts from the Xi'an area have attracted treasure hunters. Whether recovered accidentally or intentionally, many of the artifacts, usually without any archaeological data, were removed from their contexts and found their way into private and museum collections throughout the world. Organized Qin-Han archaeology in the Xi'an area began in 1933, when archaeologists from the National Beiping Academy launched an investigation, and discovered building sites of the Qin and Han periods near Xingping County and also discovered the renowned Epang Palace near Xi'an.

Significant progress was made in 1956 when a survey and excavation of Chang'an, the capital of the Western Han dynasty, was undertaken and important cultural evidence discovered. Since then, tomb sites and capitals have been surveyed, and artifacts with contextual data have been collected. The driving force undertaking these projects has been the Institute of Archaeology of the Chinese Academy of Social Sciences and the Shaanxi Provincial Institute of Archaeology. In this essay important archaeological discoveries of the Qin and Han period in the Xi'an area will be introduced within the context of cities and tombs dating from the third century B.C. to the third century A.D. The goal of this task is to promote further research and understanding of Qin-Han archaeology.

The Xi'an area encompasses modern Xi'an city, its suburban counties, and Xianyang city and its outskirts, located about thirty-five kilometers northwest of Xi'an. The Qin-Han period, the time frame discussed in this essay, consists of the pre-dynastic Qin, the Qin dynasty (221–206 B.C.), the Western Han dynasty (206 B.C.–A.D. 9), the Xin era (A.D. 9–23) and the Eastern Han dynasty (A.D. 25–220). Both the Western Han and the Xin dynasties established their capital in Chang'an, northwest of the modern city of Xi'an, and the Qin capitals of Liyang and Xianyang were also near today's Xi'an.

Archaeological Discoveries of Pre-Dynastic Qin and the Qin Periods

Cities of the Pre-Qin and the Qin Periods

During the Warring States period (480–221 B.C.), states controlled by kings and dukes scattered throughout China frequently fought with each other for territory and properties. Cities were built for defense and as bases to attack other rulers. Since the Qin state was located in the western area, which linked it to the nomadic tribes and the trade routes with the West, its economy was well developed. By the fifth century B.C., the Qin emerged as the strongest state among the seven others. The Qin's satellite cities were large, numerous, and heavily populated, especially those defensive cities built along its borders. These frontier cities were established in mountain areas and were highly militarized, while most of the Qin cities in the Xi'an area were square in layout and located near rivers. The Xi'an region was the political and cultural center of the Qin state. Consequently the cities here were constructed on a particularly large scale with an orderly layout.

Ancient Capital of Liyang

During the Warring States period, Duke Xian of Qin (r. 384–361 B.C.) and Duke Xiao of Qin (r. 361–337 B.C.) established the capital in Liyang in present day Lintong County near Xi'an. In 1964, archaeologists conducted a primary survey of the city, which was followed by a second survey and a test excavation, conducted by the Institute of Archaeology, CASS, during 1980–81.

The city was 2,500 meters long from east to west, 1,600 meters wide from north to south, and was surrounded by walls. On both the east and west walls were three gates, and two gates on both the north and south walls. There were three main east-west cross-streets and two main north-south cross-streets. In the center of the city was a building of monumental scale, while the handicraft workshops were distributed mainly over the northeast and southeast areas. Ordinary houses were comparatively dispersed, and some were scattered among the handicraft shops. The graveyard lay on the outskirts of the city. Liyang relics unearthed included a great number of bricks and tiles from the Qin to the Han dynasties, such as arched or tortoise brick tiles decorated with designs of eddies and banana leaves. Some motifs had rarely before been seen. The contents of the excavated area and its dates suggest that the greatest prosperity of the city spanned the period from the late Warring States period to the early Western Han dynasty.

Ancient Capital of Xianyang

The capital of the Qin state was relocated from Liyang to Xiangyang during the fourth century B.C., when Shang Yang

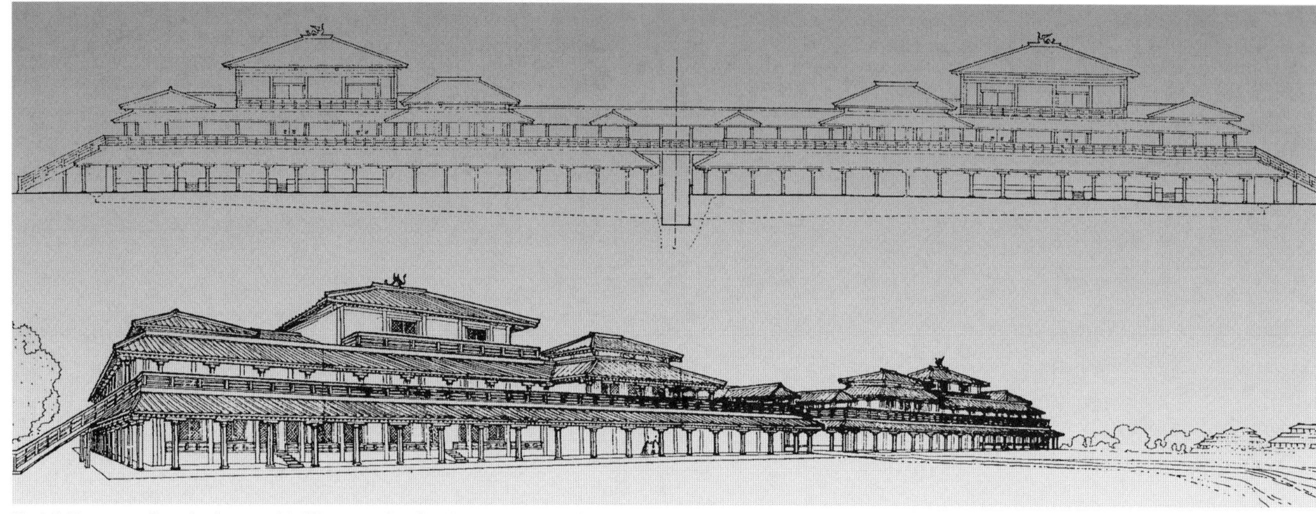

Fig.1.1. Reconstruction of palace no. 1 in Xianyang, Pre-Qin dynasty period to Qin dynasty, 4th–3rd centuries B.C.

(d. 338 B.C.), legalist of the Qin and advisor of Duke Xiao, instituted a series of political, economic, and legal reforms. From this date, Xianyang remained the capital till the end of the Qin dynasty in 221 B.C. The city, situated by the Wei River, suffered serious episodes of destruction from periodic flooding throughout its history. Its palace district, however, is comparatively well preserved. A series of ruins of large-scale palaces are scattered on a tableland of twelve square kilometers in Xianyang. Architectural bricks dating to the Qin period can be found everywhere. According to historic texts, Emperor Qin Shihuang ordered the building of architectural monuments and a series of palaces at the time of the unification of the other states. Sima Qian (145–86 B.C.), the great historian of the Western Han dynasty, recorded in the *Shi ji* that Emperor Qin Shihuang "filled his palaces with a large number of beautiful women, bronze bells and drums, captured from the other six states."[1]

The excavations and study of Xianyang have great academic significance. After the survey of capitol of the Qin and Han in 1933, archaeologists have excavated three palace sites in Xianyang. The well-preserved palace hall no. 1 was a complicated, two-story building complex set on a platform (fig. 1.1). It had eleven large and small halls for various functions, connected by winding and sloping corridors. Hollow bricks decorated with dragons, phoenixes, and geometric patterns have been found in the hallways. The floor was daubed with red paint, and the walls were decorated with colored frescoes. These frescoes are the earliest found in China and are consequently very valuable for the study of Chinese architecture and art history. Other finds in the palace area include workshops which supplied the royal court with bronzes, ironware, and ceramics. Chariot ornaments, weapons, tools of production, daily utensils, coins, and a head of a bronze figure (cat. no. 7) have also been found in the palace precinct. Of special interest is a bronze plate inscribed with an imperial edict ordering the consistency of weights and measures. According to specialists, this site most likely is the Xianyang Palace, the main palace of the Qin.

The magnificence of Xianyang is recorded in ancient literature. "In the Xianyang capital, wooden building materials were wrapped in silk and decorated with colored patterns. The floor was daubed with red paint and the walls decorated with colored frescoes. The music would continue all day and night. If you strolled the palace for a year, you still could not visit all of the grounds."[2] Unfortunately, this magnificent capital was burned by the rebelling army in the late Qin dynasty, around 206 B.C. It is said that the fire lasted three months and destroyed the once spectacular city. The Epang Palace, well-known for hiding emperors' mistresses, was also burned in the fire. In the following centuries the city was damaged repeatedly by the periodic flooding of the Wei River. These disasters have made the appearance of Xianyang an unfathomable enigma.

Suburban Palaces (ligong)

Palace complexes, built in the outskirts of Xianyang, were used as the resorts and hunting grounds of the Qin rulers. It is recorded that there were more than two hundred such palaces in the suburbs, however, their locations have not been identified. The study of these suburban palaces has recently drawn the increasing attention of scholars. New findings include the Liangshan Palace in Qian County, the Wangyi Palace in Jingyang County, and the Linguang Palace in Chunhua County. In 1992, Liu Qingzhu and Li Yufeng researched the locations and nature of a few palaces of the Qin, such as the Linguang Palace, the Zhangtai Palace, and the Shanglin Garden, as well as various ritual temples. They believe all these palaces and temples were located near Xi'an. They also believe that the large-scale ruin found in the northeast of the Yuchi may be the location of the Bushou Palace of the Qin dynasty.

Tombs of the Pre-dynastic Qin and the Qin Dynasty

During the archaeological survey in 1933, Su Bingqi and

his team discovered a group of Qin and Han dynasty tombs at Baoji, Shaanxi. This discovery is significant because it has distinguished for the first time the Qin culture from that of the Zhou with the excavated materials. During the last forty years, tombs of the pre-dynastic Qin and the Qin, constructed in various scales, have been discovered. These number in the thousands only in the Xi'an region. Studies of these tombs have been published since early 1980s, with a concentration of the excavation and research of royal tombs and mausoleums.[3]

Most tombs of the Qin state showed a continuity in the burial system practiced in the Shang-Zhou dynasties from the sixteenth century B.C. to eighth century B.C. They are mostly in the category of the square, vertical pit-tombs dug into the earth, as distinct from the tombs built with bricks and stones in central China. Generally speaking, tomb pits of the nobility were on a large scale, some being 12,000 square meters in area. Tombs of the common people, on the other hand, usually were only two square meters, merely enough to shelter the bodies. The tombs of the nobility usually were paths leading to the burial pit. Generally, the more paths a tomb had, the higher the rank of the entombed individual. A tomb with four paths, called the *ya*-shaped tomb, was typical of the nobility. The tomb with two paths is referred to as a *zhong*-shaped tomb, and one with a single path is referred to as a *jia*-shaped tomb. The tombs of low rank had only a square, vertical pit, usually without any path.

The East Mausoleums at Zhiyang

A group of tombs lies on the east bank of the Bashui River at Zhiyang in Lintong, facing the ancient capital of Liyang, about fifteen kilometers west of Xi'an. They are also known as "the East mausoleums of the Qin" because this tomb district is located to the east of another district of Qin mausoleums at Fengxiang. According to the *Shi ji* (Records of the Grand Historian), a few Qin imperial rulers and their family members had been buried at Zhiyang since the middle of the third century B.C. However, this site was seriously damaged at the end of the Qin dynasty, and its actual location has long remained a mystery.

Between 1983 and 1986 the sites of several large-scale tombs were discovered on the western side of Lishan by the archaeologists of the Shaanxi Provincial Institute of Archaeology. Four mausoleums have been identified, consisting of three *ya*-shaped tombs, five *jia*-shaped tombs, and two *zhong*-shaped tombs (fig. 1.2). The finds also included accompanying pits, attendants' tombs, and building sites, with remains of construction foundations only. Instead of using the walls as enclosures, the mausoleum made full use of the natural ravine. Only a few had moats.[4] Traditionally, a *ya*-shaped tomb was reserved exclusively for dynastic rulers. Archaeologists believe that this highest ranking tomb configu-

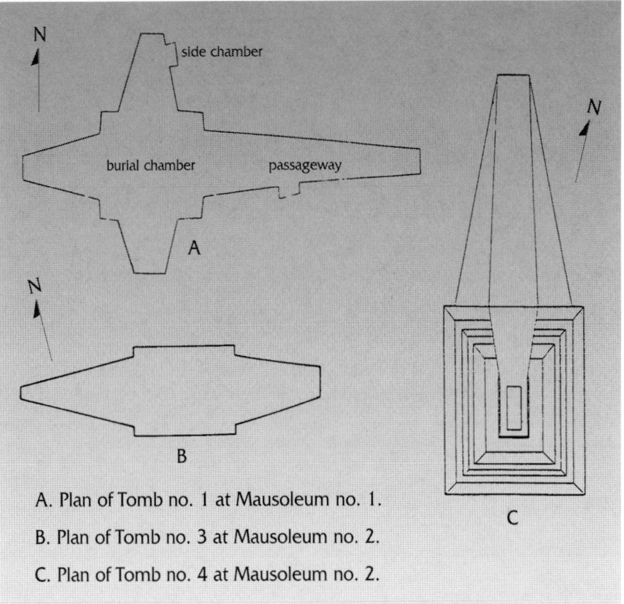

A. Plan of Tomb no. 1 at Mausoleum no. 1.

B. Plan of Tomb no. 3 at Mausoleum no. 2.

C. Plan of Tomb no. 4 at Mausoleum no. 2.

Fig. 1.2. Plans of tombs surveyed in 1986 at the East mausoleums in Zhiyang, Lintong, pre-Qin dynastic period, 3rd century B.C.

ration, found in this area, identifies tombs built for the kings of the Qin: Zhaoxiang, Xiaowen, and Zhuangxian. The appearance of this type of tomb at Zhiyang shows that an important change occurred in the Qin royal mausoleums during the third century B.C. This change indicates that the Qin rulers began to adapt the burial systems reserved for the imperial rulers of the Shang dynasty and abandoned the restriction on the burial system for the regional state rulers, practiced since the Western Zhou period.

The Qin Shihuang Mausoleum

The Qin Shihuang Mausoleum is located at the foot of the Lishan (Mount Li), Lintong. A preliminary survey of the site was conducted in the early 1960's and a more comprehensive survey started in 1974. The task was undertaken by the archaeologists of the Institute of Archaeology of Shaanxi Province, who excavated some buildings, subsidiary terracotta warriors and horses, some attendant tombs, pits, and criminals' tombs. The excavation also revealed a workshop used to make stone materials to construct the mausoleum.

The plan of the mausoleum is rectangular, with the long axis oriented north-south, and is enclosed by an inner and outer rammed wall (fig.1.3). The rammed grave mound lies south of the center, within the inner wall. It is monumental in scale, indicating its imperial majesty. The *Han shu*, written by Ban Gu (A.D. 32–92), recorded that "the height of the Qin Shihuang mound (fig. 1.4) was more than fifty *zhang*, and its girth was more than five *li*"[5] (one *zhang* is equivalent to 3.33 meters. One *li* is equivalent to 500 meters).

From 1979 to 1989, archaeologists conducted surveys of the underground palace and found that an underground wall encircled it. This walled area encompasses 180,320 square meters. In 1982, the Institute of the Physical Survey, Chinese

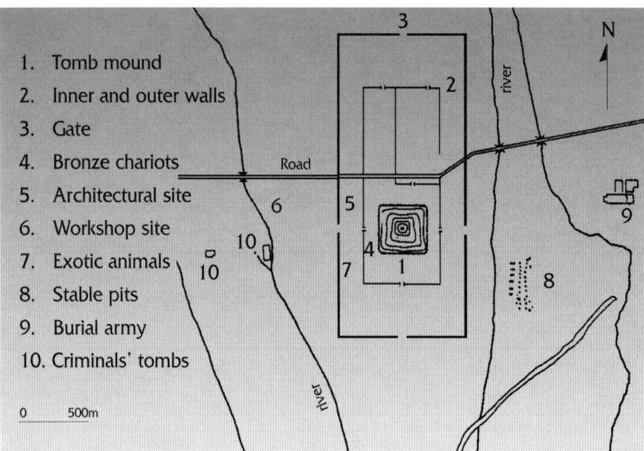

Fig. 1.3. Location and plan of the Qin Shihuang mausoleum.

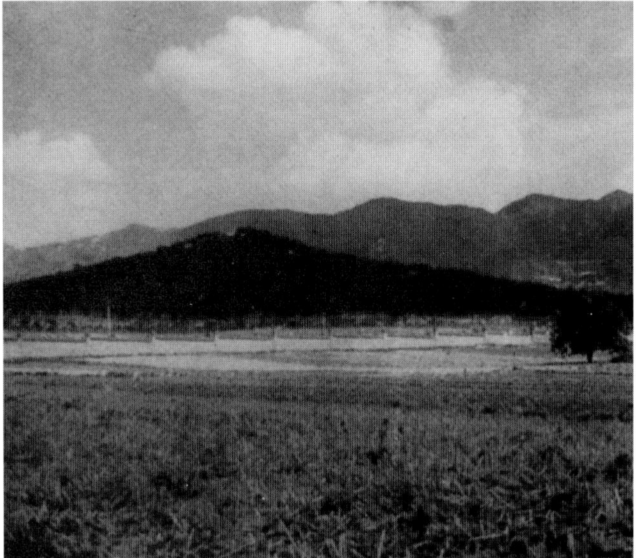

Fig. 1.4. Grave mound of the Qin Shihuang mausoleum. Qin, 209 B.C. Photo courtesy Shaanxi Museums & Archaeological Data Bureau.

Academy of Geological Sciences, conducted two experiments and found abnormal quantities of mercury in the soil of the central mound. The contaminated area is 12,000 square meters, which corresponds with historical texts. It has been recorded in the *Shi ji* that "the mercury was poured into [the chamber] to symbolize hundreds of rivers and seas."[6] A few vaulted passages leading to the underground palace have been found around the mound. It was in the western vaulted passage that archaeologists unearthed two bronze chariots in the winter of 1980. Each chariot, half the size of an actual chariot, had one driver and was pulled by four horses. The chariots, horses, and chariot drivers were all cast in bronze, and the chariots were decorated with colored drawings. They were most likely modeled after the chariots used by the emperor. This particular location perhaps was a storehouse built near the western vaulted passageway.

After Emperor Qin Shihuang unified China, he ordered more than 700,000 laborers to build his mausoleum. When the workmen dug into the earth and reached water, they used bronze to strengthen the burial chamber.[7] The treasures housed in the tomb were magnificent. No tombs from ancient times up to that date had richer treasures than did the Qin

Shihuang mausoleum.[8] Unfortunately, Xiangyu, the head of the rebelling army in the late Qin dynasty, uncovered this mausoleum and removed all the treasures. In the early Western Han dynasty, a young herdsman went into the tomb through a tunnel used by the earlier treasure hunters. Holding a torch in his hand to look for his sheep, he burnt the chamber by accident. Currently, because of the lack of techniques and funds, archaeologists cannot enter the chamber of the Qin Shihuang mausoleum. Most likely, the mystery of the underground palace will not be able to be solved in the near future.

Since 1979, archaeologists have conducted surveys and excavations of the above ground buildings in the mausoleum. They have drilled and excavated six large-scale building sites. Of these, the largest is located on the north side of the grave mound in the inner city of the mausoleum. The building is sixty-two meters in length from north to south, fifty-seven meters in width from east to west, and has a total area of 3,534 square meters. The finds include construction modules and eave tiles, as seen in figure 1.5. The other five sites are located at the western side between the two walls surrounding the mausoleum. Other objects include building materials, pottery, and pottery vessels bearing such inscriptions as *lishan*. The *lishan* is often used as a reference to the Qin Shihuang mausoleum in the *Shi ji*. The finding of artifacts with the inscription of *lishan* gives an eloquent proof of the ancient records.

Three pits containing terracotta warriors and horses have been discovered one kilometer northeast of the east outer wall of the mausoleum. Since 1976 archaeologists have excavated pit no. 3 and parts of pit nos. 1 and 2 (figs. 1.6 and 1.7). All three pits were underground buildings constructed of earth and timber. Today excavated pottery figures number more than seven thousand, including more than six hundred ceramic horses; the military chariots amount to approximately one hundred, and bronze weapons and bronze parts of the military chariots total more than nine thousand. The mixed formation of the chariots, cavalry, infantry, and crossbow-men of the Qin troops (fig. 1.8) provides an insight into Qin military strategy. As recorded in the *Sunbin binfa* by Sun Bin, a military scientist of the Warring States period, "the Qin use chariots when it is a plain, cavalrymen when fighting in steep situations, archers with crossbows when faced with disaster."[9]

In the southeast section of the mausoleum (fig. 1.3), seventeen attendants' tombs have been discovered. Of these, eight tombs have already been excavated. They contain the remains of young men and women ranging in age from twenty to thirty years. Their skeletons were mostly in disorder and might have been dismembered. Most of the accompanying objects were imperial articles with the inscription "shao fu," which in literature means "little princes" or "little princesses." According to ancient texts, after Emperor Qin Ershi, the second son of Emperor Qin Shihuang, ascended the throne, he feared his brothers and sisters would interfere with him politi-

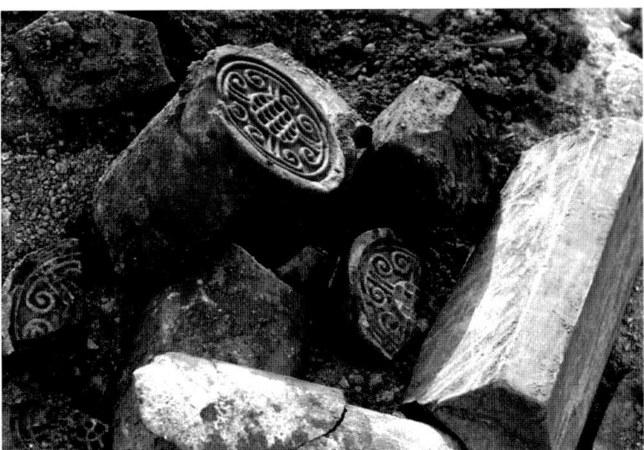

Fig. 1.5. Eave tiles and construction modules excavated from north of the Qin Shihuang mausoleum. Qin, 209 B.C. Photo courtesy Shaanxi Museums & Archaeological Data Bureau.

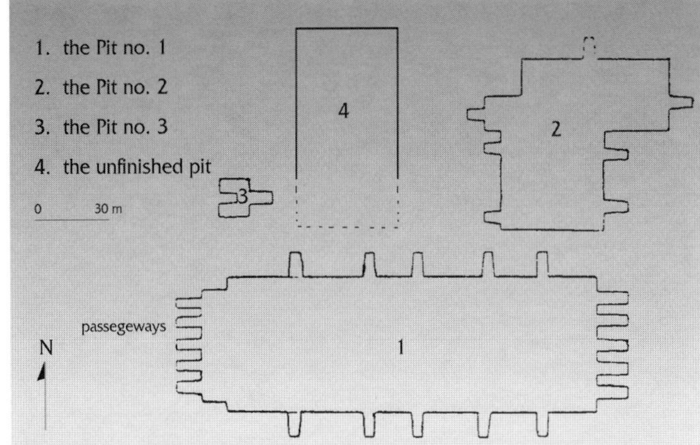

Fig. 1.6. Plan of excavation site of terracotta warriors and horses.

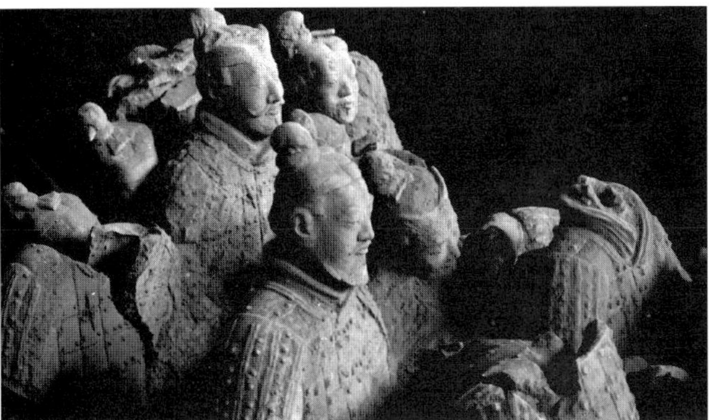

Fig. 1.7. Excavation site of terracotta chariot and infantry formation in pit no. 1. Photo courtesy Shaanxi Museums & Archaelogical Data Bureau.

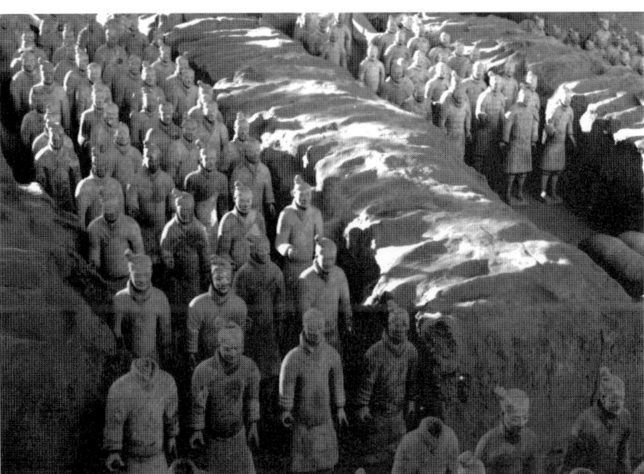

Fig. 1.8. Terracotta figures in pit 1. Qin, 209 B.C. Photo courtesy Shaanxi Museums & Archaeological Data Bureau.

ically and thus sentenced princes and ministers to death. All six princes were killed. The discovery at this site suggests that some of the bodies might be the remains of the princes and princesses executed by Qin Ershi, and others might be Qin Shihuang's close officials.

Near the attendants' tombs, more than ninety burial pits were identified, and forty of them have been excavated. Some pits contained sacrificial horses, some held pottery figures, while others had a combination of both. Similar sites have also been found outside of the western gate within the mausoleum. In addition, archaeologists found large-scale pottery kilns in the northwest of the mausoleum and its nearby villages. These kiln sites might be the imperial kilns, specifically used to make bricks, tiles, and pottery figures for large buildings and noble mausoleums.

Archaeological Discoveries of the Han Dynasty

Chang'an, located northwest of present-day Xi'an, grew to be a political, economic, and cultural center when the rulers of both the Western Han and the Xin dynasties chose it as the capital. Fourteen emperors of the Western Han lived here. After the fall of the Xin, Chang'an was destroyed in war, and it gradually became desolate when the Eastern Han authority moved its capital to Loyi, now known as Luoyang in Henan Province. Therefore, the capitol of Chang'an and the imperial mausoleums of the Western Han have become archaeological focuses in Shaanxi.

Ancient Cities of the Han Dynasty

In the late Qin dynasty, wars broke out in succession and many cities and palaces were burned by fire. Some, however, continued to grow during the Western Han dynasty. For instance, Liyang, the capital of the Western Han, was founded on the base of the capital of the Qin dynasty during the reign of Gaozu (r. 206–195 B.C.), the first emperor of the Western Han. When the capital was later moved to Chang'an because the limited space in Liyang restricted future growth, Liyang still remained the residence of retired emperors. The layouts of the cities had different characteristics according to region but were mostly square in shape, located near rivers, and with convenient traffic flow. In order to defend against the Xiongnu, nomadic people of the north, the Western Han government had built numerous frontier cities and had ordered many troops to garrison maintain passes. Most of these frontier cities later became small towns.

Chang'an exemplifies the scheme of the cities of the Western Han. The Institute of Archaeology, CASS, began a survey and excavation of Chang'an in 1956. After several decades of effort, archaeologists have identified the primary location of the city wall and gates and the layout of the city. This project continues today. The plan of this city is nearly square, orientated south and north, and surrounded on four sides by walls rammed with loess (fig.1.9). Its east wall is straight, and the other three walls are winding. There was a trench three meters in width outside the wall. The excavation also indicates there were three gates on each side of the wall, and each gate was divided into three entrance passages. Each passage was six meters wide, accommodating four Han carriages abreast.

Traffic inside the city was convenient. There are a few gates on each side of the city wall, leading to palaces and the center of the city. All the streets were straight, the longest one being Anmen, with a total length of five hundred meters. Each street was about forty-five meters wide and divided into three lanes. The middle one, called *chi dao*, with a width of twenty meters, was reserved exclusively for emperors. The two lanes on each side, with widths of twelve meters each, were used by officials and the common people. This layout exemplifies "the grand street with three passageways" as recorded in the "Western Capital Rhapsody" (Xidu fu) by Ban Gu.[10]

There were numerous, large imperial palaces inside and outside the city. The Weiyang Palace was square-shaped, about five square kilometers in area, occupying one-seventh of the whole capital. The archives and texts of the Qin dynasty were stored in the Shiqu Pavilion and the Tianlu Pavilion of the Weiyang Palace after the fall of the Qin dynasty. In the following years many important archives and texts of the Western Han were also stored in these pavilions. Unfortunately, these texts were destroyed long ago in wars, and only the ruins of the two buildings remain.

Archaeologists have surveyed and unearthed five large-scale building sites, including palace hall no. 3, which yielded tens of thousands of bone strips carved with inscriptions. Based on the texts, specialists believe that the strips were the official records of local tributes to the central government, and palace hall no. 3 could be the location of a government office in charge of the local handicraft workshops. The Changle Palace, another palace in the city, was grander than the former, with a girth about ten thousand meters. A test drilling has revealed three large building foundations. The one on the east, also called the East Hall, was constructed with stairs, courtyards, and chambers. Its monumental scale and distinguished features indicate that it might be one of the main buildings in the Changle Palace.

The armory, built around second century B.C., was situated between the Changle Palace and the Weiyang Palace in the south of the city. A rectangular rammed wall 1 1/2 meters thick enclosed it. Inside the enclosing wall there were seven storehouses. Two storehouses that have already been

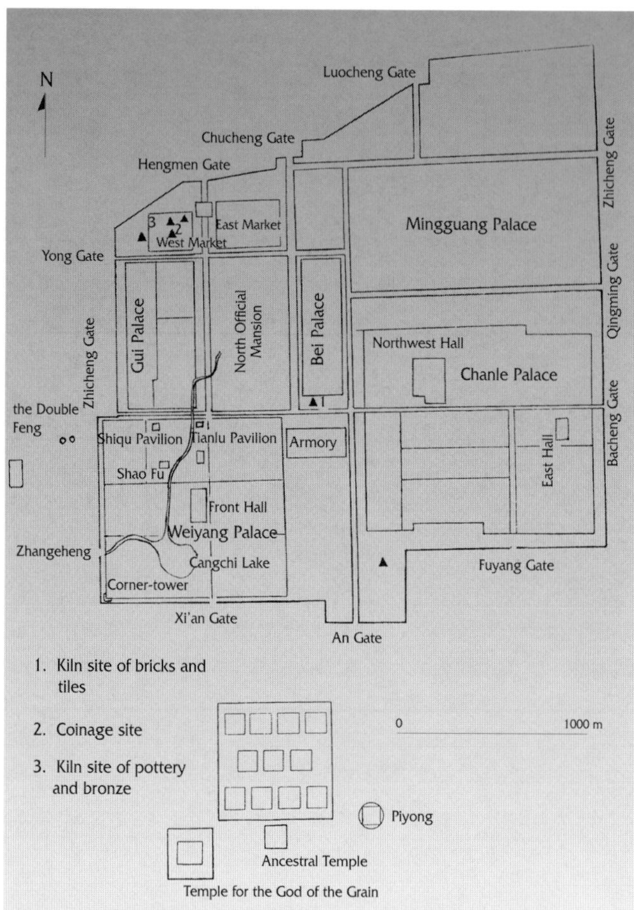

Fig. 1.9. Plan of Chang'an of the Western Han, 2nd–1st century B.C.

unearthed contained a great number of arms, such as knives, swords, spears, halberds, arrowheads, and armor. These were primarily cast in iron but some were cast in bronze. The arrangement of the pillar and charcoal found at the site suggest that the swords and spears originally lay on wooden shelves. It is believed that the armory was the ordinance depot of the Western Han and that it was destroyed along with the city gates in the battle at the end of the Xin era.

More than ten ritual sites have been discovered in the south and east suburbs of Chang'an. Only a few were constructed in the early Western Han on the building sites of the Qin. Most were built during the late Western Han. These architectural complexes were densely arranged on a grand scale. One of the most noticeable complexes was Piyong constructed in the Western Han (fig.1.10) and Jiumiao built in the Xin era. In ancient China, the ritual building was of central importance in a capital. As recorded in historical texts, emperors of the Yu era, the Xia, the Shang, and Zhou dynasties (2500 B.C.–256 B.C.) always chose the center of their capital to build ritual structures before building their capitals.[11] Any city which had ritual buildings was called "capital." One without ritual buildings was called "town."[12]

In the northwest section of the city, grand sites for making pottery, coining money, and bronze and iron casting were unearthed. Many nude pottery figures and small numbers of fragments of pottery molds, as well as single molds and reit-

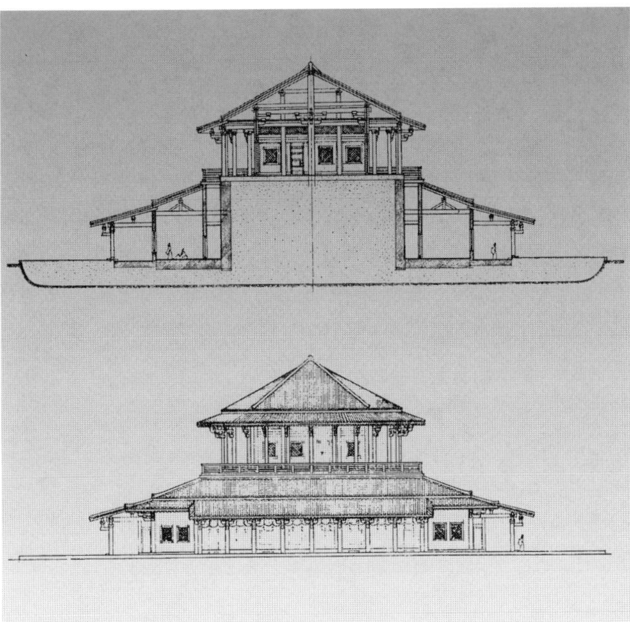

Fig. 1.10. Reconstruction and cross-section of the ritual site of Piyong, excavated in 1956 at Chang'an. Xin, A.D. 4.

erative molds for coins were unearthed. Specialists believe that these handicraft workshops were probably under the immediate control of the imperial house or the central government between the middle and late Western Han. The artifacts also include coins and their molds found at workshops in the eastern area of the city, and a group of bronzes dating to the Western Han at Sanqiao in Xi'an. All these objects suggest that there must have been large-scale workshops for making bronzes in Chang'an at the time.

Tombs of the Han Dynasty

Tombs of the nobility of the Western Han, from medium to large-scale, have been found in the Xi'an region. The tombs of the Han dynasty were usually on a larger scale than the tombs of the Qin, and used mostly hollow bricks in construction. By the Eastern Han, tombs built with bricks and stone slabs and decorated with frescos and carved designs had become prevalent, especially in provinces such as Henan, Shandong, and Sichuan. The large tombs dating to the Eastern Han are rarely seen in Shaanxi because most of the nobility followed the court when the Eastern Han dynasty moved its capital to Luoyang, Henan in the beginning of the first century A.D.

A total of eleven imperial mausoleums were constructed during the Western Han around Xi'an. Nine are located in the Xianyang tableland on the northern bank of the Wei River, and the other two lie in the southern and eastern outskirts of the city. Most of these mausoleums were built along the hills, while others were hollowed out at the base of the mountain. These mausoleums were large in scale, magnificent and majestic. The research on the imperial mausoleums of the Western Han began in 1962 with a survey of the Maoling, the

mausoleum of Emperor Wu (r. 141–87 B.C.). In the early 1980s the major effort was dedicated to Duling, the mausoleum of Emperor Xuan (r. 74–49 B.C.). Since the early 1990s significant finds have been unearthed near Yangling, the mausoleum of Emperor Jing (r. 157–141 B.C.).

The Mausoleum of Emperor Xuan (Duling)

Duling, located at Sanzhao Village in the Xi'an region, was built for Emperor Xuan, a resurgent emperor of the Western Han. During his reign, Emperor Xuan executed a series of reforms and stabilized all political and economic systems. In 49 B.C. the emperor passed away in the Weiyang Palace and was buried in Duling. From August 1982 to the summer of 1985, the Institute of Archaeology, CASS, conducted a survey and an excavation of the mausoleum and the nearby mausoleum of Empress Wang (fig. 1.11).

The plan of the mausoleum is a square with a gate in the central section of each wall (fig. 1.12). The tomb was placed in the middle of the mausoleum. The east gate is the mostly well-preserved, with its passageway paved with bricks, facing the east entrance of the tomb chamber. A palace complex for holding the memorial ceremony with an area of 20,880 square meters lies in the southeast section of the mausoleum. This palace consists of a main hall, two side halls, and other buildings, including a cellar for storage. A perfect drainage system underlies the complex. Archaeologists also unearthed three large-scale building foundations to the north and south of the mausoleum.

The mausoleum of the Empress Xiaoxuan Wang, the wife of Emperor Xuan, was built 575 meters to the southeast of the emperorís tomb. Its plan is square and has a gate in the central section of each wall. The memorial complex lies in the southwest sector of the mausoleum park, in a layout similar to that of the emperorís, yet on a smaller scale. As a result of the drilling conducted on the north, south, and east of the emperorís mausoleum, archaeologists have found a large number of accompanying pits and attendants' tombs. Two of the pits have been excavated, finding such artifacts as chariots and pottery figures (fig. 1.13). The excavation has also revealed that both sites had been plundered at earlier times, and many of the remains have been seriously damaged.

The Mausoleum of Emperor Wen (Baling)

Baling, located west of Xi'an, was dedicated to Emperor Wen (r. 180–157 B.C.). There was no need to build the grave mound because Baling was built on a mountain,[13] therefore, no grave mound is evident on the ground. To the southwest of Baling is the tomb of the Empress Dowager Bo (d. 155 B.C.), the mother of Emperor Wen, and to the northeast of the Du is the tomb of Empress Dou (d. 135 B.C.). In 1966 archaeologists surveyed the tomb of Empress Dowager Dou, and excavated

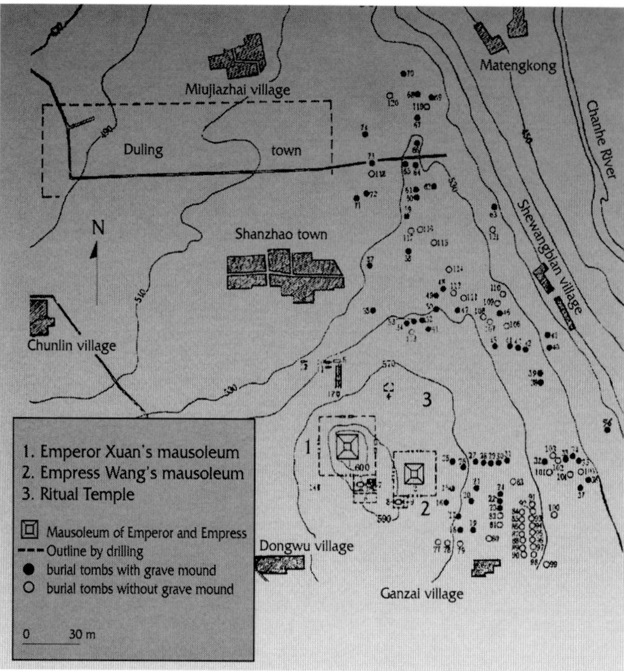

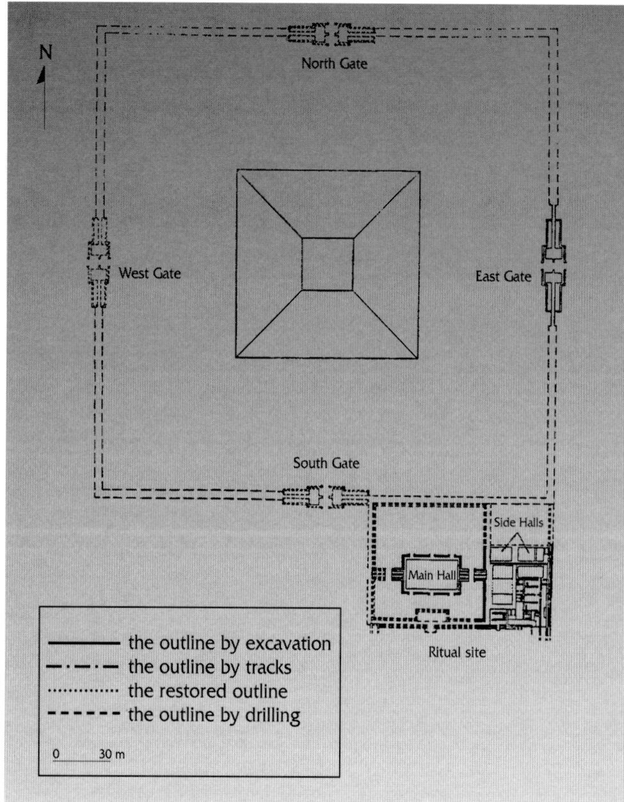

Fig. 1.12. Plan of Emperor Xuan's mausoleum.

forty-seven pits, which yielded female pottery figures with painted designs (cat. nos. 30–32), ceramic pots, and ceramic domestic livestock. Buried alive were animals and fowls such as horses, sheep, pigs, dogs, chickens, and cranes. These pits and their contents show the continuity of animal sacrifice practiced since the Shang dynasty, with the exception that, in Han tombs, pottery figures instead of living animals were preserved.

The Mausoleums of Emperor Hui and Emperor Wu (Anling and Maoling)

In addition to the mausoleum of the Empress Dou, archaeologists surveyed other mausoleums and excavated some accompanying tombs, as well as attendants' tombs. These included a large-scale tomb excavated in 1965 at Yangjiawan and a burial pit of the tomb of Emperor Hui (r. 195–188 B.C.), Anling, from which pottery figures have been recovered. Meanwhile, a large number of legacies were found to have been destroyed. The mausoleum of Emperor Wu, Maoling, exemplifies this tragedy. According to the historical literature, during the fifty-four year reign of Emperor Wu, fifty-three years were spent building his mausoleum. The national law of the Western Han allowed one-third of tributes and taxes to be used for the construction of emperors' mausoleums. The mausoleum of Emperor Wu was the largest Western Han mausoleum, and it housed numerous types of treasures. According to ancient literature, during the peasant uprising in the late Western Han, tens of thousands of soldiers entered the mausoleum, looting the funerary objects for days. However, as it is recorded, "its burial articles could not be reduced by half."[14] How many artifacts were originally stored in the mausoleum is still a mystery.

The Mausoleum of Emperor Jing (Yangling)

In 1990 during the construction of a highway between Xi'an and the Xianyang Airport, a group of tomb sites was discovered near the mausoleum of Emperor Jing. The excavation, undertaken by the Shaanxi Provincial Institute of Archaeology, revealed an area of 125,000 square meters containing twenty-four pits, built as accompanying tombs for Emperor Jing. The pits were two meters deep, roofed with wooden timbers and mats, and then covered with dirt. Hundreds of pottery figures were unearthed from the pits, some painted in color, others carrying swords or production tools, all cast in iron. The unearthed figures also included some nude figures, originally clothed with fabric, which has since deteriorated (cat. nos. 34 and 35). One of the notable discoveries was a group of animal figurines, some painted in bright colors (cat. no. 43). Considering the location and contents of these tombs, archaeologists believe that they are accompanying tombs of the mausoleum of Emperor Jing.

Conclusion

The excavations of Qin and Han archaeological sites are continuing projects, which require long-term scientific planning. Many exposed and investigated sites in the Xi'an area have not been excavated. For instance, none of the Qin tomb sites found at the east mausoleums in Zhiyang have been excavated. In addition, socio-cultural implications of excavat-

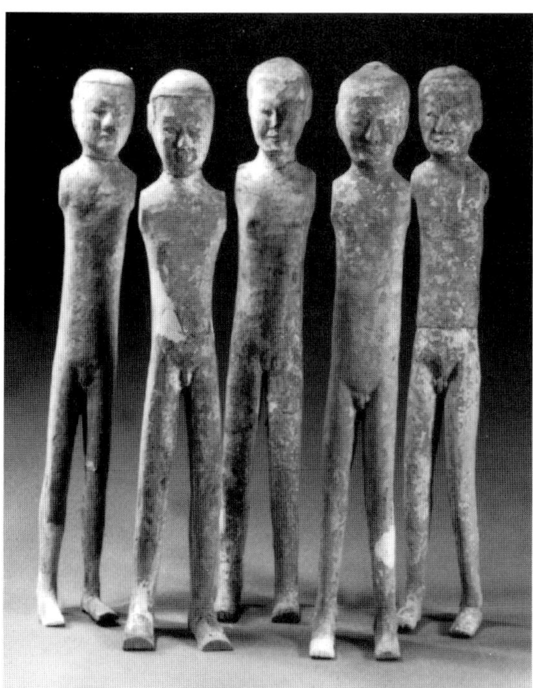

Fig. 1.13. Pottery figures excavated from Emperor Xuan's mausoleum. Western Han, 49 B.C.

ed materials need further investigation. For instance, the artifacts investigated in the Qin palaces at Xianyang need to be studied for a comprehensive understanding of their cultural setting. Recently the topics related to ceremonial structures have drawn a great deal of attention from archaeologists and scholars. The richness of the sites of Qin-Han cities, tombs, and their contents in the Xi'an area could provide valuable archaeological data. The ritual sites, which have been revealed at the Han mausoleums in Xianyang, will give impetus to new archaeological excavation and research.

The task of archaeologists is to collect contextual data through organized excavations and then to analyze and interpret this collected data. The goal of archaeological research is to interpret archaeological finds in order to discern political, economic, and cultural patterns of the society, as represented by the material artifacts. Through excavation and interpretation we can gain insights into various aspects of the Qin and Han societies and shed new light on Qin and Han material and cultural history.

Legacy and Innovation

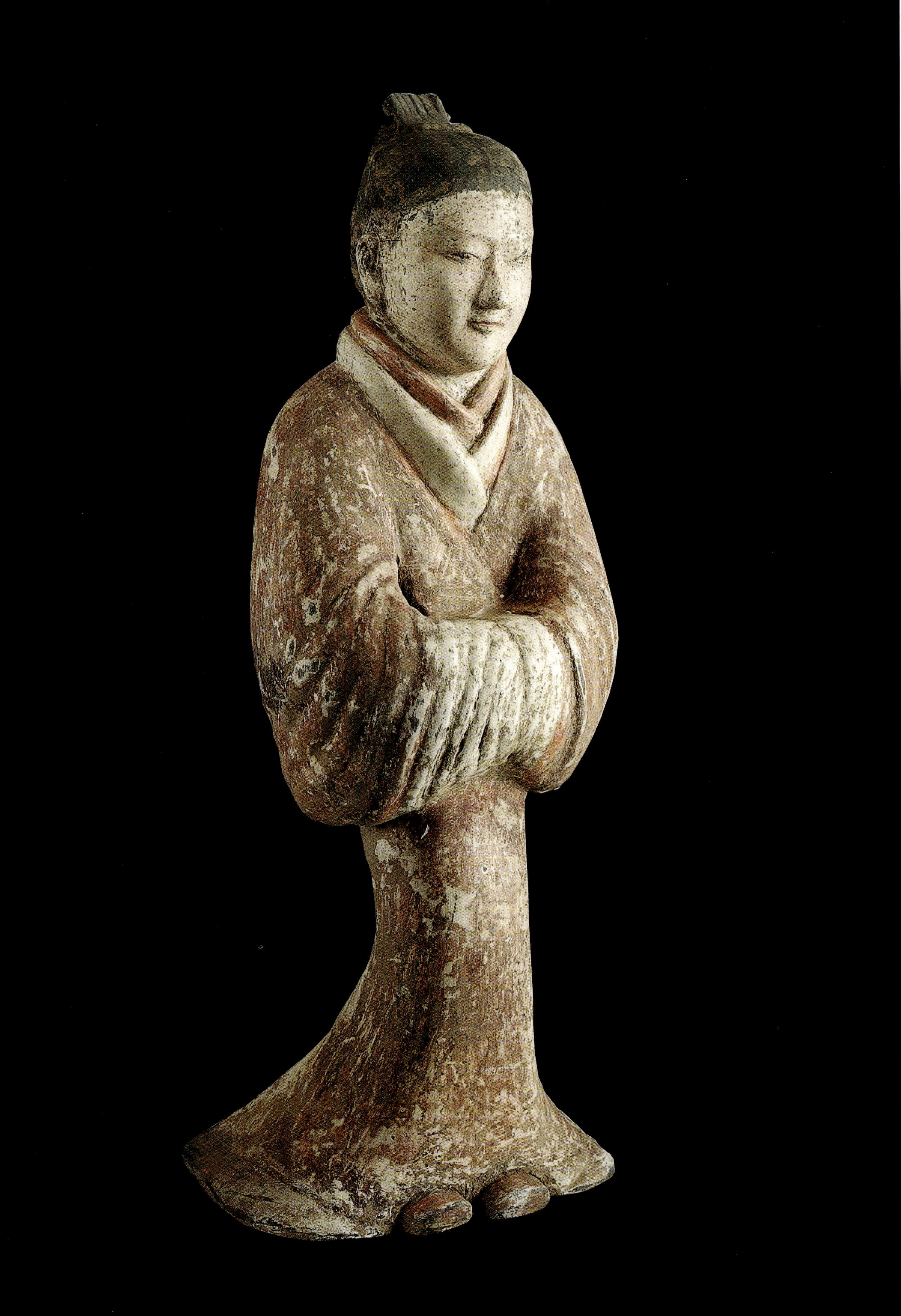

Legacy and Innovation: Western Han Dynasty and Wang Mang Interregnum Sculpture from Shaanxi Province

Susan N. Erickson
University of Michigan-Dearborn

The tombs of the emperors of the Western Han dynasty located in the vicinity of Chang'an are obvious sites for archaeological excavations; however, none of the tombs have been opened. Most of the imperial tombs are north of Chang'an and of the Wei River: Changling, Anling, Yangling, Maoling and Pingling (fig. 2.1). The tombs of emperors Wen and Xuan, that is Baling and Duling, are situated southeast of the capital. All of these tombs are marked by earthen tumuli like that of the first Qin emperor, with the exception of the tomb of Emperor Wen, which was dug into the side of a mountain, apparently in order to cut costs. Han dynasty texts supply no textual documentation for the interiors of the emperors' tombs or for specific information about burial goods, but lesser tombs and satellite pits that were part of these mausolums complexes have yielded art works that provide some evidence concerning art associated with the impe-

ial palaces, as is evident from inscriptions or from the superb designs of the objects; for example, see the mountain-lidded censer and the gilded bronze horse (cat. nos. 45 and 46, fig. 2.2). Western Han dynasty mausolums also were surrounded by large pits containing earthenware figurines like those holding the terracotta warriors discovered in the vicinity of the tumulus of the first emperor of Qin at Lintong. The figurines excavated from pits in the environs of Yangling Mausoleum

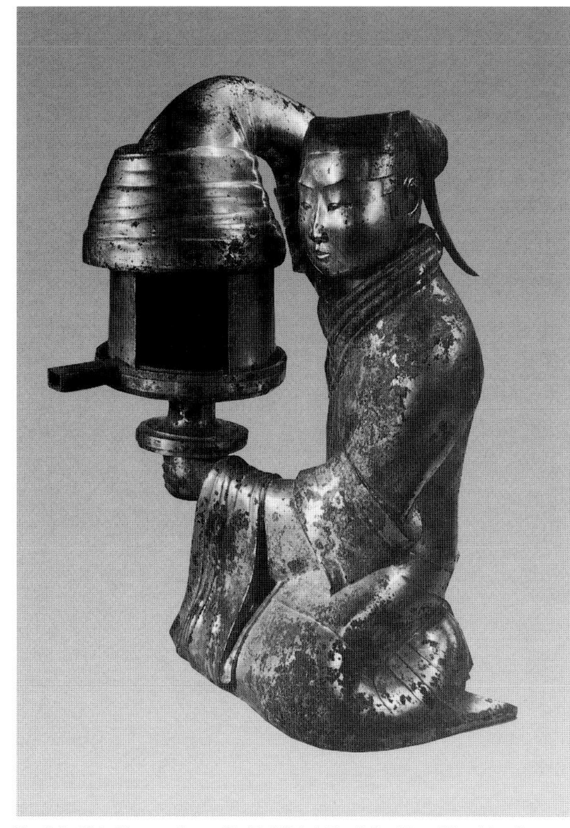

Fig. 2.2. Gilded bronze lamp (H. 18 7/8 in.), Tomb 2 of Dou Wan, Mancheng, Hebei Province. After *Zhongguo wenwu jinghua* (Beijing: Wenwu Chubanshe, 1992), pl. 114.

Western Han Dynasty Emperors and Their Mausoleums

Dynastic Name	Personal Name	Tomb	Reign
Gaodi or Gaozu	Liu Bang	Changling	202–195 B.C.
Huidi	Liu Ying	Anling	195–188
Wendi	Liu Heng	Baling	180–157
Jingdi	Liu Qi	Yangling	157–141
Wudi	Liu Che	Maoling	141–87
Zhaodi	Liu Fuling	Pingling	87–74
Xuandi	Liu Bingyi	Duling	74–49
Yuandi	Liu Shi	Weiling	49–33
Chengdi	Liu Ao	Yanling	33–7
Aidi	Liu Xin	Yiling	7–1
Pingdi	Liu Jizi	Kangling	1 B.C.–A.D. 6

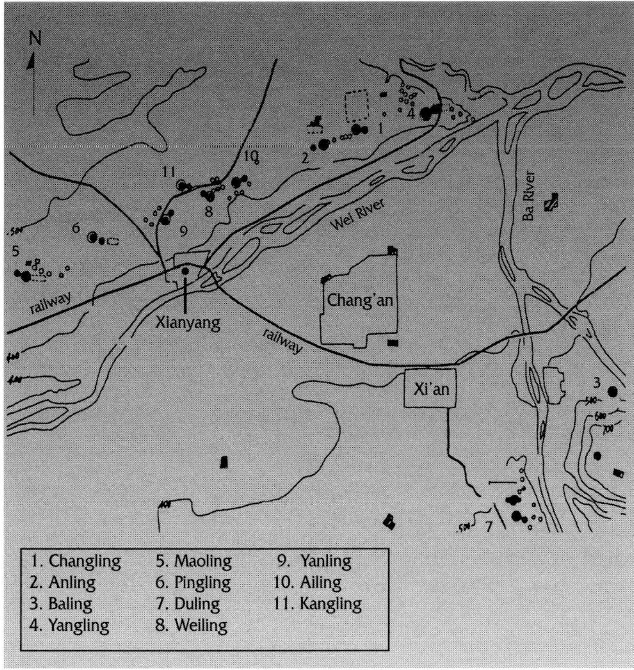

Fig. 2.1. Locations of Western Han Imperial Tombs, Chang'an, Xi'an, and Xianyang. After *Kaogu yu wenwu* 3 (1989), 28–35.

are illustrative of imperial burial practices during the reign of Emperor Jing (r. 156–141 B.C.) (cat. nos. 33–35).

Salvage archaeology in the areas of the mausoleums has provided remarkable finds by which a glimmer of the splendor of Western Han dynasty art can be gauged even though the actual contents of the emperors' tombs is not yet known. It is admittedly only a faint vision, but on the other hand, many excavations have caused scholars to reassess the artistic possibilities of this era. In general, sculpture of the Western Han dynasty and the Wang Mang Interregnum can be considered within the broad categories of palatial objects, tomb wares, outdoor sculpture, miniatures, and architectural reliefs.

Vestiges of the Imperial Style of Sculpture in Other Parts of the Empire

Outside of Shaanxi Province, tombs of the princes of the Liu family that have been scientifically excavated offer another kind of evidence for what might be considered the imperial style. One of the most famous tombs is that of Liu Sheng, the half-brother of Emperor Wu, also known as Prince Jing (Jing Wang) of Zhongshan. Liu Sheng and his consort, Dou Wan, were buried in rock-cut tombs at Mancheng, Hebei Province. These tombs were excavated in 1968; the burials had remained undisturbed since they were sealed in ca. 112 B.C. Objects made of earthenware, stone, and metal survived in remarkable condition, but the more perishable materials such as textiles, wood, and lacquers are only known through the impressions left in the soil or the remains of metal fittings that once were part of the vessels. Nevertheless, the luxurious nature of these tombs is indicated by the fact that both of the deceased were buried in suits made of flat pieces of jade wired together at the corners with gold and silver threads.

Exquisite objects made of jade and bronze were found in the tombs, but obviously they were cast to be used in the palace, and they reflect princely or perhaps imperial taste. For example, a gilded bronze lamp in the form of a seated attendant was found in the tomb of Dou Wan (fig. 2.3). It bears an inscription that mentions the Changxin palace in Chang'an and indicates that the lamp was used first by Empress Dou (d. 135 B.C.) and later was transferred to the household of Princess Yangxin, eldest sister of Emperor Wu. Finally, this heirloom object presumably was given to Dou Wan, whose husband was the half-brother of the emperor. Stylistically, the rendering of the bronze figure is comparable to the figures from Langjiagou and Yangling seen in this exhibition (cat. nos. 28–35). The clothing of the bronze youth has been suggested through shallow modeling at the neckline or where the cloth falls into folds, but the structure of the body is not shown. The focus is on the face, which reveals the serious but attentive disposition of this young servant. In Liu Sheng's tomb, there was a mountain-lidded censer (*boshanlu*) that displays a consummate level of

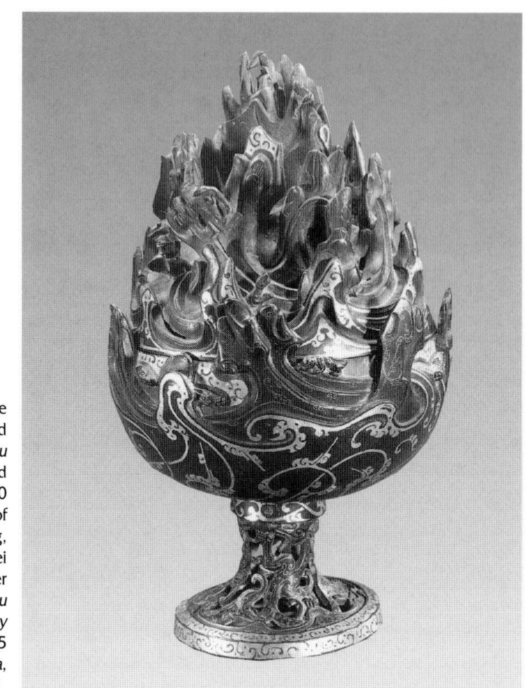

Fig. 2.3. Bronze mountain-lidded censer-*boshanlu* with inlaid gold and silver (H. 10 1/4 in.), Tomb 1 of Liu Sheng, Mancheng, Hebei Province. After *Zhongguo meishu quanji: gongy meishu bian #5 qingtong qi, xia*, pl. 201.

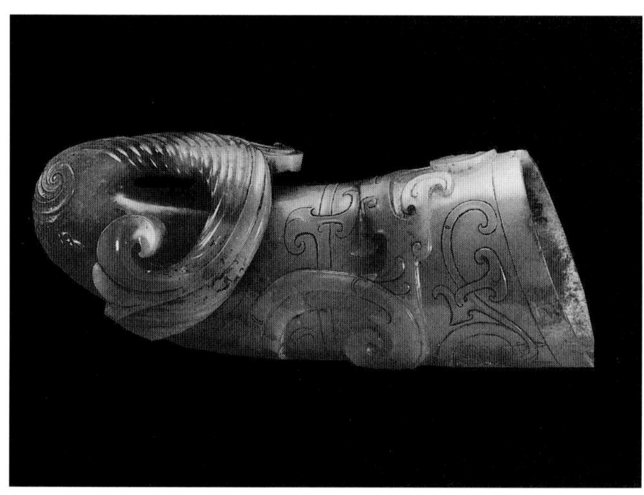

Fig. 2.4. Jade rhyton (H. 7 1/4 in.), Tomb of the Prince of Nanyue, Guangzhou, Guangdong Province. After *Nanyue wang mu yuqi* (Guangzhou and Hong Kong: The Museum of the Western Han Tomb of the Nanyue King; The Art Gallery, The Chinese University of Hong Kong; Kau Chi Society of Chinese Art; and the Woods Publishing Company, 1991), pl. 102.

metalworking equivalent to that of the incense burner in this exhibition that also was used by Princess Yangxin (cat. no. 46, fig. 2.4). The use of bronze with the addition of gilding or inlaid gold and silver and the unique and complex designs of these censers signal the taste of the imperial family for opulent goods. Both are exceptional examples of the Western Han dynasty practice of disguising functional vessels, in this case incense burners, as three-dimensional sculpture.

A second site that has contributed to understanding Western Han dynasty imperial art is the unplundered tomb of the ruler of Nanyue, which was excavated in 1983 in Guangzhou, Guangdong Province. It is the tomb of Zhao Mo (d. 122 B.C.), who was the Prince of Nanyue and called himself "Emperor Wendi." Like Liu Sheng and Dou Wan, he was buried in a suit made of pieces of jade. Attesting to the superior jade-carving techniques of this era, spectacular jades like a

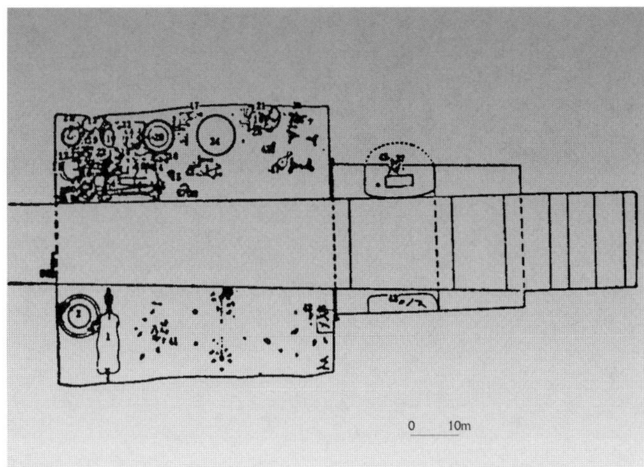

Fig. 2.5. Plan of pit 1, located south of Maoling, the Mausoleum of Emperor Wu, Shaanxi Province. After *Wenwu* 9 (1982), 1–17, fig. 6.

rhyton of western typology were found with his corpse as well as those of his concubines who also were placed in the tomb (fig. 2.5).

"Spirit objects—*Mingqi*:" Sculpture Made for Burial

Most of the items found in the subsidiary pits and tombs near imperial mausoleums are not works of art like those mentioned above, which were meant to be seen and used in the palaces of the emperors, rather they are of an entirely different nature. They are identified as *mingqi* or "spirit objects," which are surrogates for real things. *Mingqi* were made especially for placement within the tomb, and they include figurines and models of animals, as well as miniature buildings such as the painted granary from Yangjiawan (cat. nos. 24–27, fig. 5.1). Some royal tombs of the Western Han dynasty, like those of Liu Sheng and Dou Wan, were even designed to replicate a palace and were filled with *mingqi*, but also with some real goods to be used by the soul or the part of the soul that lived on in the tomb, or perhaps to accompany the deceased to the afterlife.

All of the earthenware figurines and animals in this exhibition are *mingqi*. They were never meant to be used by the living, and therefore it is expected that they were produced with less interest in creating a unique, exquisitely rendered, or expensively fabricated object. Yet at the same time, *mingqi* placed in these secondary tombs and pits provide significant information concerning the replication of the world of the Han since the included objects reflected the interests of the living. For instance, the great number of figures of cavalry soldiers from Yangjiawan mirrors the contemporary development of intense battles on horseback with the non-Chinese peoples who resisted Han expansion. In addition, these images are the best, extant evidence for considering changes in the Han approach to the human figure. The smiling but masklike faces of the warriors of Yangjiawan, which date to the early Western

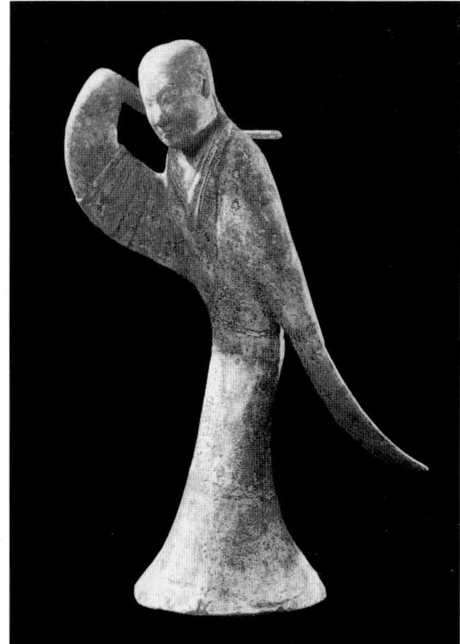

Fig. 2.6. Earthenware sleeve dancer (H. 19 5/16 in.), Baijiakou, Shaanxi Province. After *Zhongguo meishu quanji: diaosu bian #2 Qin Han diaosu* (Beijing: Renmin Meishu Chubanshe, 1985), pl. 61.

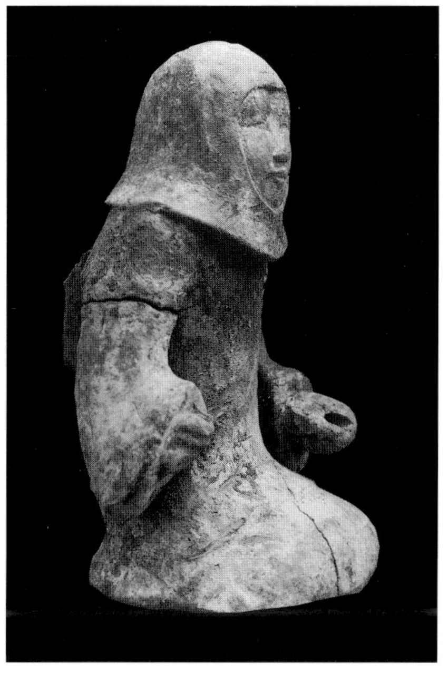

Fig. 2.7. Earthenware soldier (H. 9 7/8 in.), Shiziwan, Jiangsu Province. After *Zhongguo meishu quanji: diaosu bian #2 Qin Han diaosu*, pl. 57.

Han period, yield to the stoic but compelling visages of the figurines associated with the reigns of emperors Wen and Jing (180–144 B.C.) (cat. nos. 24–27, 28–29). In rendering the body, there is a shift from a sole focus on costumes and battle gear to a full depiction of the body of the surrogate, with the addition of cloth garments or armor made of pieces of wood as exemplified at the Yangling find (cat. nos. 33–35).

The figurines and animals are represented in a manner that increasingly depends on bringing particular realistic details to the earthenware surrogates: sometimes it is through an energized pose like that of the famed sleeve dancers or through the attempt to bring a sense of animation to the face (fig. 2.6). However, artisans never aimed for portraitlike faces or carefully observed anatomy. The figurines excavated from pits near Yangling reveal an interest in providing minimal naturalistic details but definitely do not suggest that an exact imitation of the real was necessary. Their faces are quite sensitively

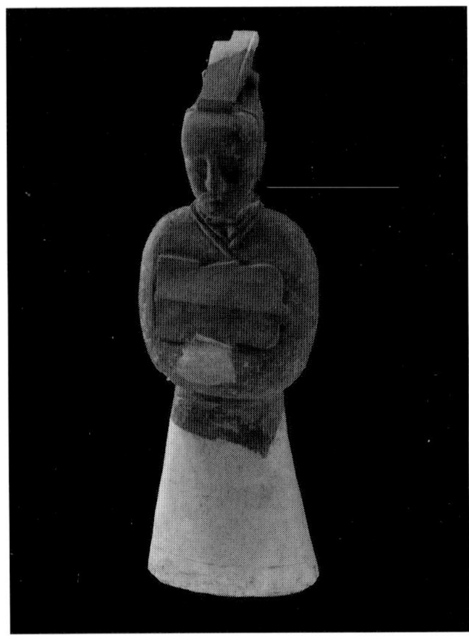

Fig. 2.8. Earthenware guard (H. of soldiers: 28 5/16 to 32 11/16 in.), Chang'an, Shaanxi Province. Photo Courtesy Shaanxi Museums and Archaeological Data Bureau.

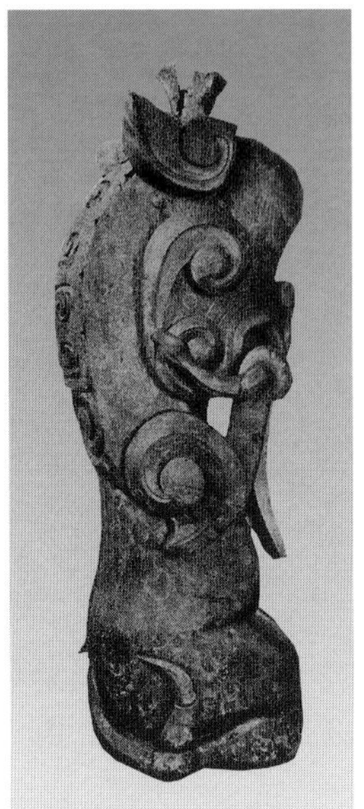

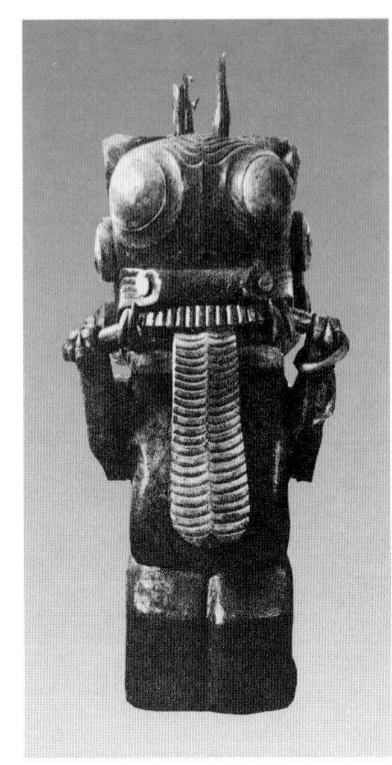

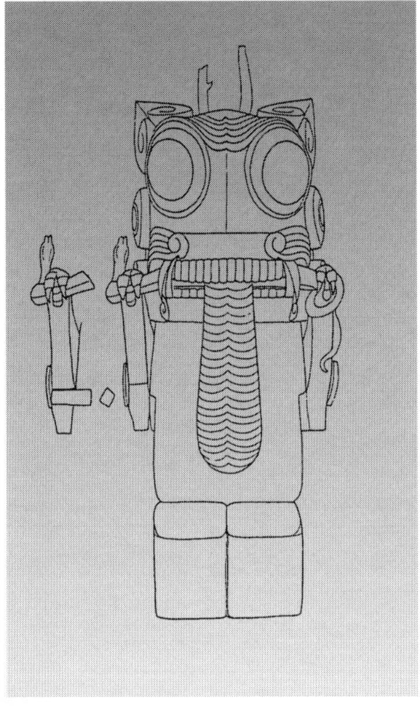

Fig. 2.9. Wood tomb guardian (H. 50 3/8 in.), Tomb 1, Xinyang, Henan Province. After *Xinyang Chu mu* (Beijing: Wenwu Chubanshe, 1986), fig. 41, pls. 58–59.

modeled, but their bodies are like posts. The skeletal structure, the musculature, the veins of the circulatory system and the texture of skin are not described in these depictions; however, the genitalia are rendered even though the figures were covered with clothing and sometimes armor. It seems to have been important to provide only enough information to make clear the essential nature of the person (gender or status, for example) or for objects to be conveyed from this world to the afterlife. The interest in representing the genitalia of the Yangling figurines is seen only during a limited period of time and perhaps is linked to the appearance of bronze and silver phalluses in other Western Han period tombs.

The range of earthenware figures in the exhibition suggests that surrogates like these must have been commonplace throughout China during the Qin and Han dynasties, but that would be a false assumption. The vast numbers of figurines placed in the vicinity of the imperial burial are not matched in any other site in China at this time with the exception of two locations near Xuzhou, Jiangsu Province. At Shizishan, a terracotta army of over two thousand consisting of infantry, guards, and horses was found in pits believed to date to the reign of Emperor Jing or Wu (141–87 B.C.) and associated with the burial of a local Chu prince (fig. 2.7). The commander of the army stands 21 1/4 inches in height, the infantry 18 1/2 to 19 1/8 inches, and the kneeling foot soldiers 10 to 10 5/8 inches. A second site ten kilometers from Xuzhou at Beidongshan, also believed to be the tomb of a Chu prince of the Liu family dating between 175 and 128 B.C., yielded 422 painted earthenware figures. These images represent attendants, guards, musicians, and dancers, and they range in size from about 19 5/8 to 21 5/8 inches in height. No military figures were excavated here. The structure of this tomb imitated a palace, so servant figures were appropriate in this context. Other than these isolated examples from the vicinity of Xuzhou (Pei County), the birthplace of Liu Bang, founder of the Han dynasty, which was given special status during the early Han dynasty, the earthenware armies found in the vicinity of Xi'an are, thus far, associated with imperial funerary sites.

Traditions of Tomb Figurines

It is clear that the emperors of the Western Han dynasty followed in the footsteps of the first emperor of Qin in commissioning multitudes of figurines for placement in satellite pits near their tombs. Although the tomb of the first Qin emperor is described by Sima Qian in his history of the Qin dynasty in the *Shi ji* (Records of Grand Historian), the army of thousands of soldiers placed in pits to the side of the mausoleum is not mentioned. Tales of the underground army must have circulated, and the Han emperors followed the practice. The important factor is the great disparity in size between Qin and Han dynasty figures. However, several comparatively large, early Han earthenware figures have been unearthed in the vicinity of Chang'an that may serve as a link

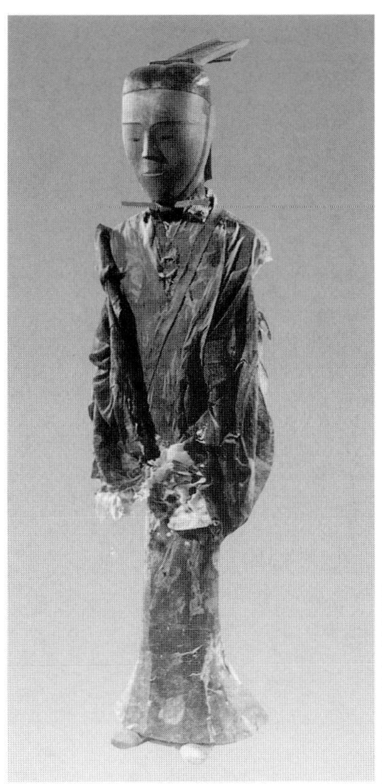

Fig. 2.10. Wood figurine (H. 33 1/4 in.), Tomb 1 of Lady Dai, Mawangdui, Hunan Province. After *Changsha Mawangdui yi hao Han mu* (Beijing: Wenwu Chubanshe, 1973),

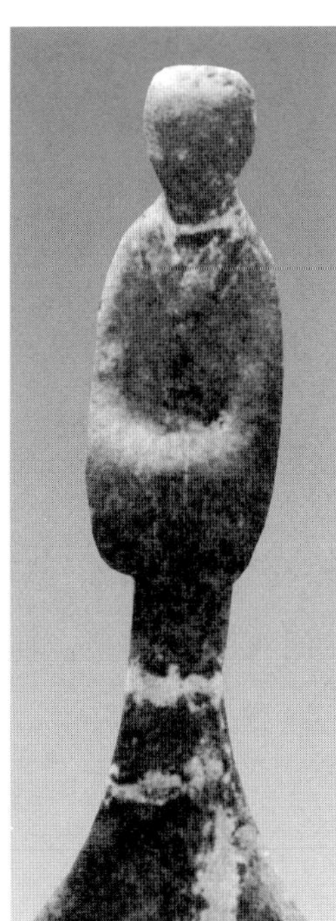

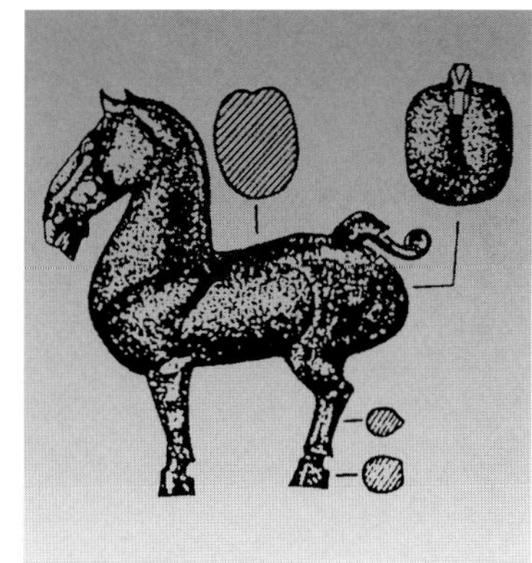

Fig. 2.11. Lacquered wood horse (H. 28 5/16 in.) and earthenware figurine (H. 15 in.), Tomb 2, Shuangbaoshan, Sichuan Province. After *Wenwu* 10 (1996), 13–29, figs. 18.2, 9.

between the life-size Qin warriors and the much more diminutive figurines typical of the Western Han dynasty.

In 1985, at the northwestern corner of the old Han capital, fragments of several figures were found, and when restored, five figures representing guards were assembled (fig. 2.8). They stand between 28 5/16 and 32 11/16 inches in height. They wear hats and floor-length gowns that completely hide their feet. Four of the five figures have hands held together, concealed by long sleeves. They also hold shields against their chests, peculiarly placed lengthwise on their arms and across their bodies. The fifth guard is the tallest; his hands are positioned one above the other as if he once grasped a vertical shaft. Two of the figures have inscriptions on their hats, one of which has been interpreted as the name of the artisan who made the image. The type of hat, the *chang guan*, and the presence of inscriptions relate these figures to some of the warriors unearthed from pits near the Qin imperial mausoleum. Authors of the excavation report have dated these tall guards to the early Western Han period, and indeed they do seem to represent a scaling down of the labor and materials needed to produce a figure that would have been desirable during the frugal years of the early Han. They also display considerably less interest in the exquisite surface modeling that was characteristic of the Qin warriors. These figures move closer to the cavalry of Yangjiawan, which relies on painted details in lieu of extensive surface modeling to render clothing and armor.

Making surrogates for burial was not an innovation of the Qin, but is most closely associated with tomb preparations in the former Warring States period state of Chu. At several well-documented Chu sites, tombs typically have two to as many

as twelve figures which are generally made of wood with clothing painted on. In a few instances, the clothing is actually made of fabric. The figures range in size from 8 4/5 inches to 44 1/8 inches. Their faces contrast markedly with both the Qin and the Han earthenware examples: those from Chu, exemplified by one from Baoshan, have masklike faces lacking any attempt to create naturalistic detail (see cat. nos. 33–43, fig. 5.6). The escalation of size and quantity and the more naturalistic rendering of the figures, seem to be a Qin innovation, and the Han simply continued to produce them in the same vast numbers.

One type of burial sculpture from Chu-state tombs of the

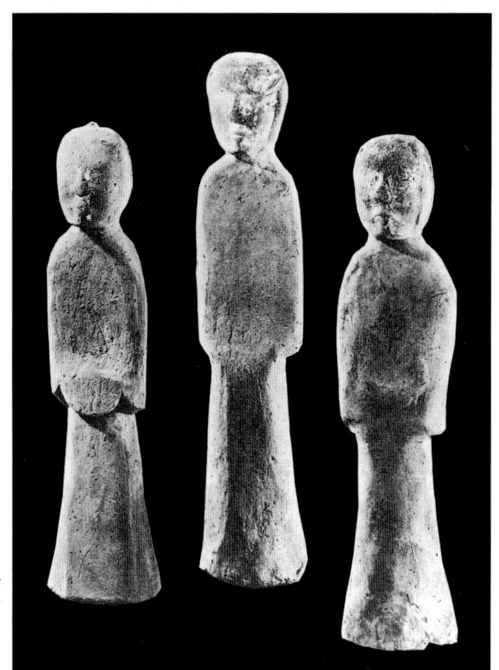

Fig. 2.12. Earthenware figurines (H. 15 to 15 3/4 in.), Tomb 1, Dabaotai, Hebei Province. After *Beijing Dabaotai Han mu* (Beijing: Wenwu Chubanshe, 1989), pl. 62.

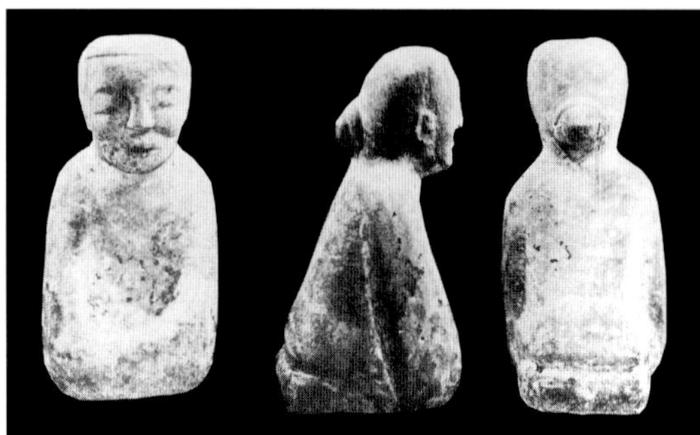

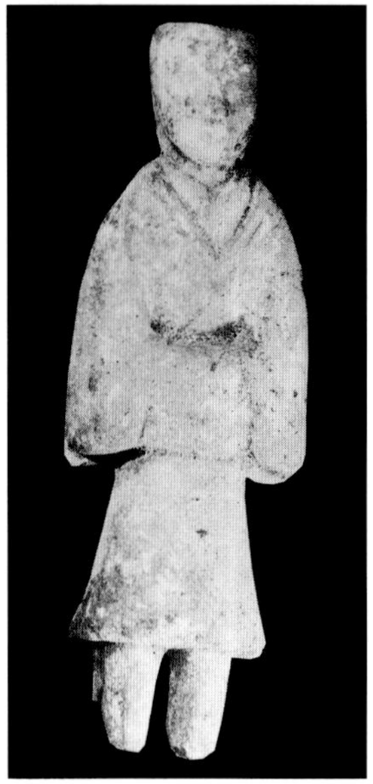

Fig. 2.13. Earthenware and stone figurines (H. 16 5/16 and 13 3/8 in.), Tomb 1 of Liu Sheng, Mancheng, Hebei Province. After *Mancheng Han mu fajue baogao* (Beijing: Wenwu Chubanshe, 1980), pls. 146.2, 148.1.

pre-dynastic Qin period that was not perpetuated in the Han era is the large-scale, wood guardian. Sometimes they are in the form of birds standing on the backs of tigers, sometimes they are composite creatures with antlers, extended tongues, and large bulging eyes (fig. 2.9). These creatures range in height from 22 1/4 to 50 3/8 inches. Their apotropaic and protective functions seem to be fulfilled in the Western Han context by the hybrid beasts of the *pushou* mask ring-holder (cat. no. 48) and in the creatures of the cardinal directions on roof tiles of ritual buildings or on bricks from tomb walls (cat. nos. 49, 56–59). There may be some conceptual connection, however, between the tall, protective/apotropaic guardians and the large stone creatures on the outside of the tomb of Huo Qubing (cat. no. 54).

Even though the tomb guardians ceased to be made, other types of wood figurines continued to be sculpted in the former state of Chu and nearby areas during the Western Han period. The tomb of Lady Dai (d. 168 B.C.) at Mawangdui in Hunan Province included figures with actual clothing but also images with clothing painted on the surface (fig. 2.10). Several tombs in Sichuan Province located in-between the Chu sites in Hunan and Hubei and the site of the Han capital in Shaanxi also included attendants, men mounted on horses, and farm animals made of wood. Tomb 2 at Shuangbaoshan in Sichuan, which dates to the reign of Emperor Wu, held 118 wood figurines and 100 lacquered wood horses, but three earthenware

standing attendants of about 15 inches in height also were found, suggesting the dual influence of the Chu and of the Han Chang'an traditions (fig. 2.11).

The holdings of figurines in princely tombs dated to the Western Han dynasty and located outside of Shaanxi Province present a different picture. Most of the figures are attendants, and their representation is markedly less exacting than those from the vicinity of the imperial tombs. At Tomb 1 at Dabaotai, near Beijing, probably the burial of Liu Jian of Guangyang (d. 45 B.C.), 240 clay figures, ranging in height from 15 to 15 3/4 inches for standing attendants, were excavated (fig. 2.12). They are rendered in a very simple style with a minimal suggestion of clothing. There is a slight indication of arms folded in front of the body, but the figures are very close to being just planks with facial features. The faces are flat disks with very subtle modeling to suggest the nose, eyes, and mouth, to which a few painted details have been added. Tomb 1 at Mancheng, the tomb of Liu Sheng, included fewer figures: five of stone and eighteen earthenware (fig. 2.13). The clay images stand about 16 inches in height and were all found in the central chamber, interpreted as the banqueting hall. They are far from remarkable in their depiction. The stone figures are all represented in a kneeling position, and they range in height from 13 3/8 to 18 1/2 inches. One was found in the central chamber, three in the passageway to the back chamber, and one in the back chamber where the deceased was placed. They are quite like the Dabaotai figures in their simple, closed volumes and minimum of detail. Considering the style and the level of skill shown in the figurines, it seems likely that these princes did not have access to workshops like those of the emperor. Nevertheless, the spare style of the stone figures is comparable to the outdoor sculptures from the tomb of Huo Qubing, which show little modification of the original stone (cat. no. 54).

Stone Sculptures from Open-air Sites

The large sculptures found on the exterior of the tumulus of General Huo Qubing (d. 116 B.C.), one of the tombs associated with Maoling, the mausoleum of Emperor Wu, seem to be linked to the horses of the Qin dynasty army because of their larger size, but they differ in being made of stone and in their placement above ground. These stone creatures include three horses, an elephant, a tiger, an ox, a boar, a toad, a frog, two fish, and also a fantastic beast with a small animal in its mouth and a man with a bear. It is difficult to explain the group as part of a unified iconographic program. Whether they are images of conquest (one horse is trampling a man) or simply representative members of the animal kingdom populating the mountain-shaped tumulus of General Huo, their function is unresolved. They are not mentioned in any contemporary Han texts, but their style is in keeping with other

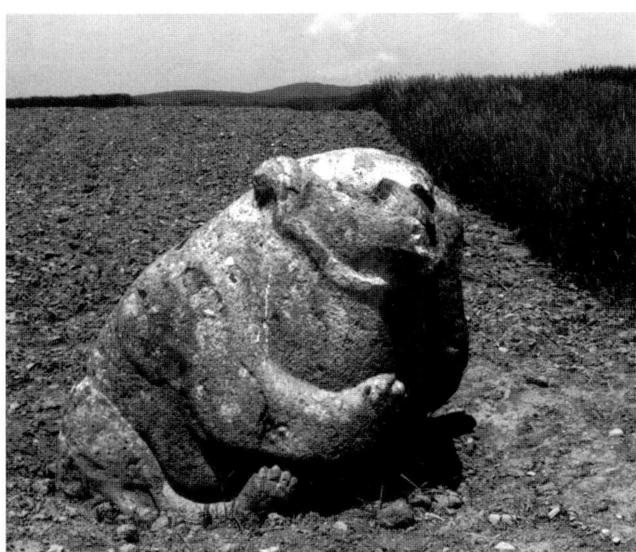

Fig. 2.14. Stone bear (H. 29 1/4 in.), Sweet Springs Mountain, Shaanxi Province. Photo Courtesy Zhang Tong.

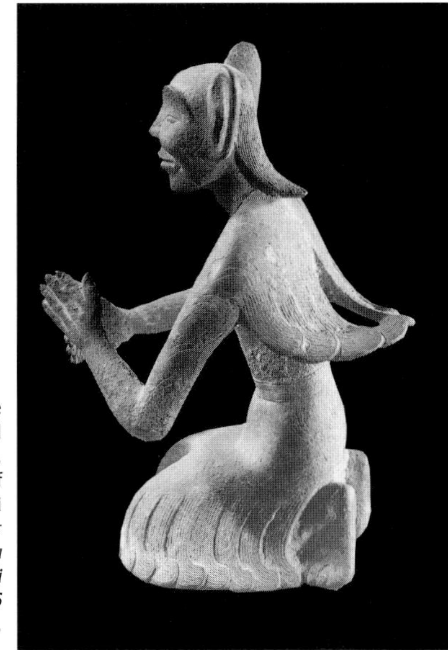

Fig. 2.15. Bronze figure of immortal (H. 6 1/16 in.), North suburbs of Xi'an, Shaanxi Province. After *Zhongguo meishu quanji: gongyi meishu bian #5 qingtong qi, xia*, pl. 212.

examples of Han dynasty art. Several other large-scale sculptures have come to light that may suggest the impetus behind the innovation of monumental stone sculpture placed at open-air sites.

A large, reclining bear was found at the foot of Sweet Springs (Ganquan) Mountain where the Sweet Springs Garden was situated north of Chang'an (fig. 2.14). Originally the location of a Qin dynasty palace, Emperor Wu continued to develop the site with the construction of new residences, and he used it as a location for sacrificial purposes, especially the sacrifice to the Supreme Deity (Taiyi). He erected buildings such as the Sky Piercing Tower (Tongtian tai) where he hoped to meet an immortal like the bronze image of one unearthed in the vicinity of Chang'an (fig. 2.15). Lodges at the site were called Increased Longevity (Yishou) and Extended Longevity (Yanshou). The site was described by Yang Xiong (53 B.C.–A.D. 18) in his composition entitled "Sweet Springs Rhapsody" (Ganquan fu). The bear that was found here is 49 1/4 inches in height and 115 1/4 inches in circumference. It crouches and uses one paw to scratch its ear. The closed pose, the carving technique, and the sense of monumentality are comparable to the sculpture of a tiger from General Huo's tomb. As for the meaning associated with the bear during the Western Han dynasty, one point of reference is Yu the Great, the founder of the Xia dynasty and controller of devastating floodwaters, who was transformed into a bear. The shape-shifting ability of Yu and his movement referred to as the Step of Yu (Yu bu), are related to ritualistic motions like the "bear ramble" (*xiong jing*) illustrated and labeled in a manuscript (*Daoyin tu*) with pictures of people performing calisthenics from Tomb 3 at Mawangdui. In addition, in the *Zhuang zi*, the "bear ramble" is one of the *daoyin* gymnastic exercises used by those seeking to preserve the vitality of the body, which can result in longevity:

To pant, to puff, to hail, to sip, to spit out the old
breath and draw in the new, practicing bear-
hangings (*xiong jing*) and bird-stretchings,
longevity his only concern—such is the life
favored by the scholar who practices gymnastics
(d*aoyin*), the man who nourishes his body, who
hopes to live to be as old as Pengzu, for more
than eight hundred years.

This interpretation of the bear corresponds with the motivation behind many of the construction projects of Emperor Wu at Sweet Springs Mountain—the extension of life or the avoidance of death altogether.

Another large stone carving was found in the vicinity of the capital at Grand Fluid Pond (Taiye chi) (fig. 2.16). In 1973 a fish-shaped sculpture approximately five meters long was discovered north of the pond. It is extremely generalized in form with almost no detail. Grand Fluid Pond was a man-made body of water north of the Jianzhang Palace of Emperor Wu. Within the pond, there were four islands which were meant to replicate the famous isles of the immortals: Yingzhou, Penglai, Huliang, and Fangzhang, which were said to appear in the Bohai gulf. Emperor Wu and also the first Qin Emperor sent expeditions to the gulf in the east in search of these islands, because if located, they might enable these

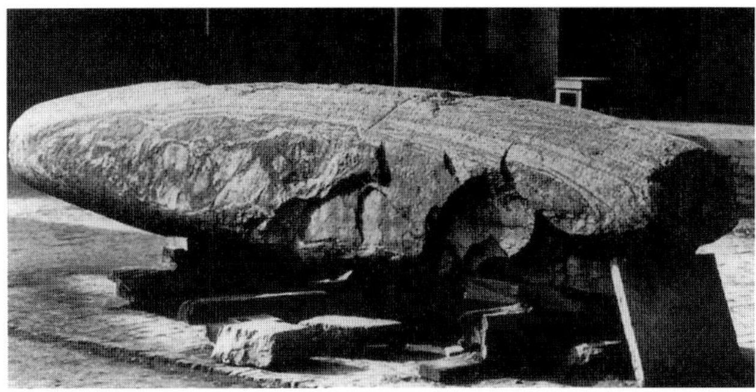

Fig. 2.16. Stone fish (L. 16 ft. 4 7/8 in.), Grand Fluid Pond, Shaanxi Province. After Ann Paludan, *The Chinese Spirit Road: The Classical Tradition of Stone Tomb Statuary* (New Haven: Yale University Press, 1991), fig. 7.

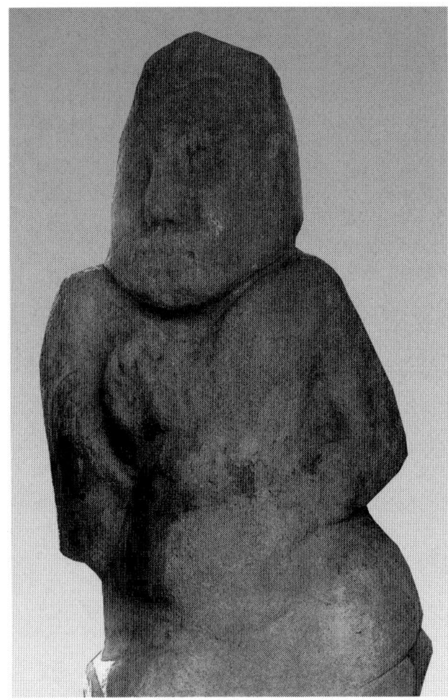

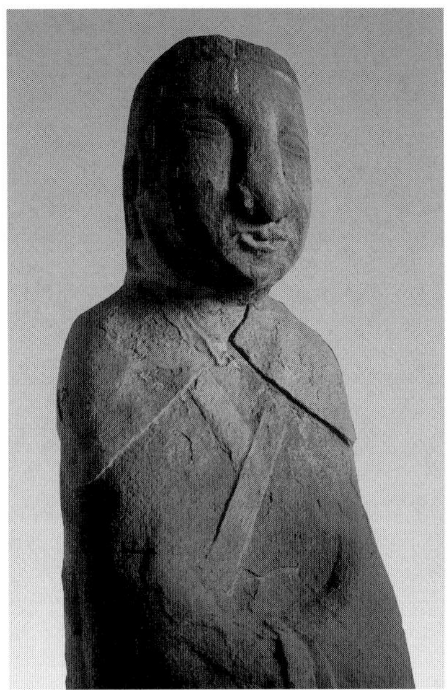

Fig. 2.17. Stone figures of Oxherd and Weaving Maid (H. 6 ft. 2 6/8 and 7 ft. 6 1/2 inches), Shaanxi Province. Photo Courtesy Wang Baoping.

> "And look down on the Kunming Pond. On the
> left is the Oxherd, on the right the Weaving Maid."

These lines refer to the fact that at each end of the Milky Way there are two, first magnitude stars, Vega and Altair, which since the Zhou dynasty had been personified as the Oxherd (*Niu lang*) and the Weaver Maid (*Zhi nü*). An image of the Oxherd was placed on the east side of Kunming Pond and the Weaving Maid on the west side, and the rough sculptures in figure 2.17 are believed to be those famed works. They are carved much like the small tomb figures from Mancheng, except that they are considerably taller, standing 74 3/4 and 90 1/2 inches in height.

Professor Wu Hung has suggested that the rather sudden interest in monumental stone sculpture, as exemplified by the images from the tumulus of General Huo, may have resulted from contact with the west because of the many military expeditions during the Western Han dynasty. Professor Wu proposes that ". . . these were frozen in stone, an 'eternal' material belonging to the 'western' world of immortality and death." This statement seems to refer to one of the most important deities, the Queen Mother of the West (Xiwangmu), who was believed to live in the west and was celebrated as the keeper of the elixir of immortality. The Queen Mother of the West became increasingly popular as a subject in tomb reliefs during the Eastern Han dynasty, as exemplified in the relief from Yulin in northern Shaanxi Province in this exhibition (cat. no. 63). At the very least, the three-dimensional monumental stone sculptures are an important innovation during the Western Han period, and they seem to have initially proliferated in the places of the living rather than the dead. In addition, all of the places mentioned above were sacred sites and were the projects of Emperor Wu, who was one of the most avid seekers of immortality by various means. Because these relatively large sculptures were located in the open air and exposed to the elements, it was necessary that they be made of a durable "eternal" material like stone. Moreover, their larger, more realistic size allowed them to function very effectively in lieu of real creatures in the open terrain on a perpetual basis.

rulers to achieve immortality. Just as surrogate tomb figures could stand in for real attendants in the funerary context, it seems that the construction of these isles in the sea might be "real" enough to facilitate the quest for immortality. To complete the aquatic scene, stone creatures were set by the edge of the pond, and perhaps this stone fish is one of them.

A second, man-made lake in the vicinity of the capital also was apparently the locale of large stone sculptures. Kunming Pond was excavated southwest of the capital, inside the famed Shanglin Park during the reign of Wudi. Two stone figures have been associated with ancient literary descriptions of the site (fig. 2.17). Kunming Pond was viewed as a miniature version of the Milky Way and thus a re-creation of part of the cosmos in the park of the emperor. In the "Western Capital Rhapsody" (Xidu fu) by Ban Gu (A.D. 32–92), the scene is briefly described:

Sculpture in Miniature

On the opposite side of the spectrum, Han sculptors also produced miniatures in a variety of materials: jade chimeras (*bixie*), stone weights shaped like fantastic animals, a bronze mouse, and even a gilded bronze silkworm (cat. nos. 47, 50, 51, 53, fig. 2.18). The subjects of these hand-held sculptures were based on creatures of the natural and the supranatural worlds also depicted in literature of the period. Like the larger earthenware animals that were used as *mingqi*, the bodies of the small creatures still maintain a simple form with little interest in support structures like muscle or bone. There is,

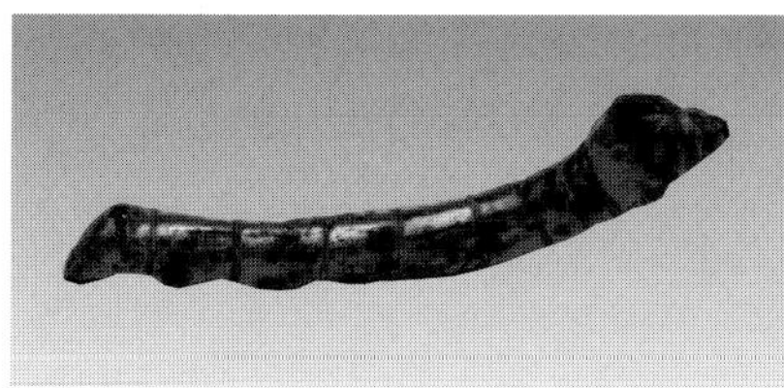

Fig. 2.18. Gilded bronze silkworm L. 2 3/16 in.), Shiquan County, Shaanxi Province. Photo Courtesy Shaanxi Museums and Archaeological Data Bureau.

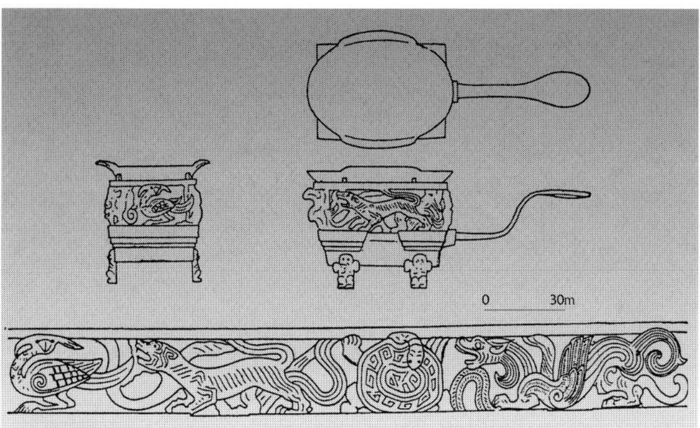

Fig. 2.19. Line drawing of bronze brazier (H. 4 1/16 in.), tomb at Maquan, Xianyang, Shaanxi Province. After *Kaogu* 2 (1979), 125–35, figs. 5.7, 6.

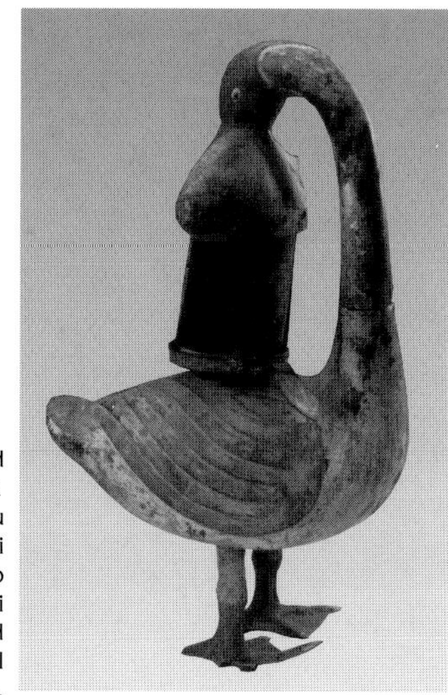

Fig. 2.20. Painted bronze goose (H. 21 1/4 in.), Shenmu County, Shaanxi Province. Photo Courtesy Shaanxi Museums and Archaeological Data Bureau.

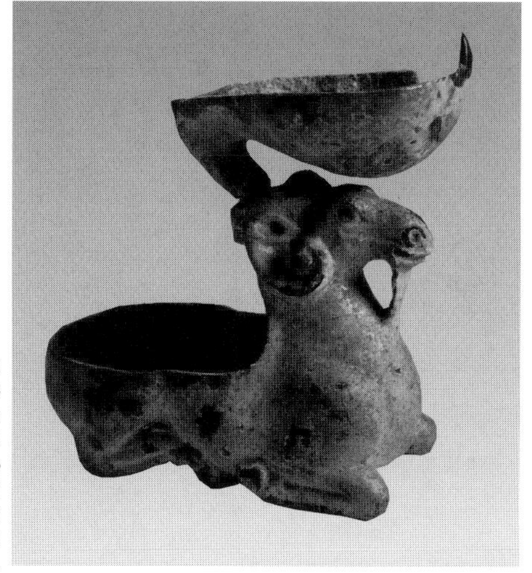

Fig. 2.21. Gilded bronze ram (H. 5 1/2 in.), Tongquan County, Shaanxi Province. Photo Courtesy Shaanxi Museums and Archaeological Data Bureau.

however, an attempt to animate them through attention to pose and/or facial expressions. Sometimes details like fur are added to the surface description, but these are just as likely to be geometric decor. Combining abstract designs with features of optical reality is a hallmark of the Western Han dynasty style. For example, similar "cloud" patterns adorn the surfaces of a model of a granary and the boots worn by the earthenware general (cat. nos. 24–27, figs. 5.1–2). It also is important to note that this decoration is related to designs on the sides of the Qin dynasty bronze chariot seen in replica in the exhibition.

Sculpted miniatures were apparently very attractive to Han people, and these finely carved images sometimes were included in the burial for eternal enjoyment. Small images of animals or humans also were used as legs for utilitarian objects, like those on a bronze brazier which also has the creatures of the cardinal directions represented on its sides (fig. 2.19). The melding of sculpture and functional vessels already has been mentioned above, but many other examples can be cited, like lamps in the form of a goose excavated in 1985 at Shenmu County or a kneeling ram excavated in 1987 at Tongchuan City (figs. 2.20–21).

Architectural Sculpture

The last kinds of sculpture from the Western Han period are clay eave tiles and hollow bricks that have molded decorative patterns on their surfaces. Favored iconographic programs for these architectural elements include auspicious motifs like the phoenix (*Fenghuang*) or the four creatures which symbolize the cardinal directions: the Green Dragon of the east (*Cang or Qing long*); the White Tiger of the west (*Bai hu*); the Vermilion Bird of the south (*Zhu que*); and the Black

Warrior of the north (*Xuan wu*; the serpent and tortoise) (cat. nos. 55–59). Both the tiles and the bricks have their roots in earlier Qin practice, but the hollow bricks from the interior wall of a tomb at Taerpo forecast the much more extensive programs on the walls of tombs and shrines popular during the Eastern Han dynasty throughout China (cat. no. 55). Compared to the decorative schemes in these tombs dating to the later Han, the compositional approach at Taerpo is more simple since the bricks serve as surfaces for independent designs without a unified arrangement. At the same time, the function and placement of these tiles are related to wall-painting programs in Western Han tombs. Rare examples of wall painting in Shaanxi Province have been unearthed from a tomb in Qianyang County dated to the late Western Han or Xin period and excavated in 1972 and another tomb near Jiaotong University in Xi'an dated to the late Western Han and excavated in 1987. At Qianyang, the paintings were located on the east and west side walls (fig. 2.22). On the east wall, the sun with a bird in the center of the orb, stars, and a portion of the Green Dragon still remain. On the west wall, the moon, stars, and the rear half of the White Tiger can be discerned. The tomb at Jiaotong University has more painting preserved on the side walls and the ceiling, but the program

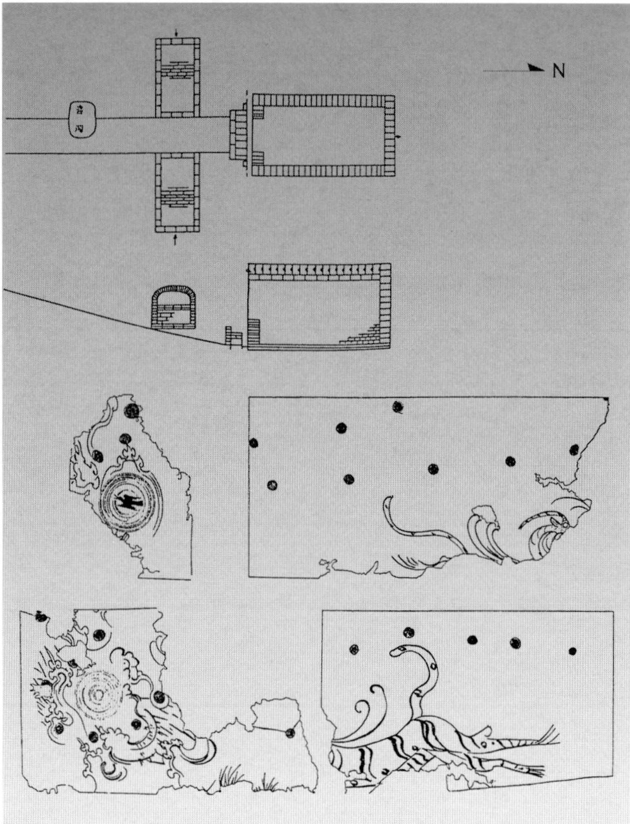

Fig. 2.22. Line drawing of wall painting, tomb located at Qianyang County, Shaanxi Province. After *Kaogu yu wenwu* 4 (1990), 57–63, figs. 5-8.

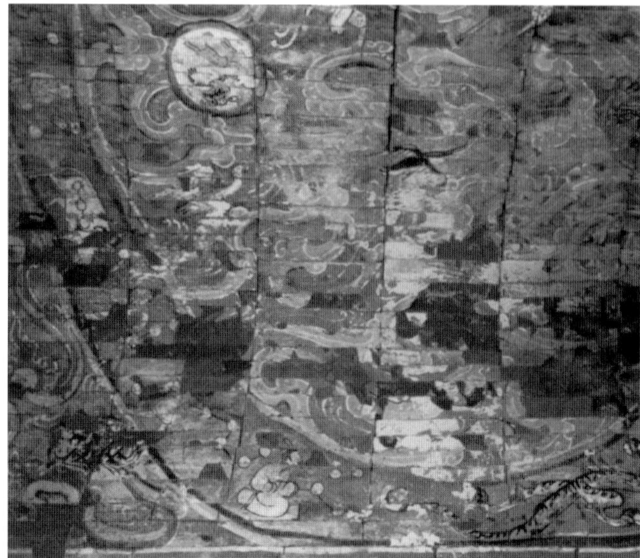

Fig. 2.23. Wall painting, tomb located at Jiaotong University, Xi'an, Shaanxi Province. After *Zhongguo meishu quanji: huihua bian #12 mushi bihua* (Beijing, Wenwu Chubanshe, 1989), pl. 9.

is virtually the same even if more elaborate (fig. 2.23). The twenty-eight constellations are depicted on the ceiling along with the sun, the moon, and the creatures of the cardinal directions. According to Sima Qian, the tomb of the First Qin Emperor had the heavens painted on the ceiling of the chamber, and apparently this feature has been transferred to these small tombs. It also is probable that even more elaborate versions of this theme were painted in the interiors of the tomb chambers of Han mausolums. Although imperial architecture featured wall painting, nothing remains of these compositions, not even to the extent of the fragments of painting extant from one of the Qin palaces at Xianyang. In addition, painted lacquerwares used at other sites in China to study the development of painting have not been preserved to the same degree in Shaanxi Province; only bronze fittings of what once were lacquered vessels commonly remain in tombs. Therefore, the few sites which have paint preserved on the walls of the tomb chambers are extremely valuable.

Conclusion

The fall of the Qin dynasty was still a vivid memory for early Han rulers, and the Qin model of imperial burial was followed, but with some modifications to suit new needs. Further excavation of imperial sites likely will reveal more correspondences between the Qin and Han dynasties. For instance, recently the bones of at least ten different animals (pigs, goats, dogs, chickens, fish, turtles, and crane-like birds) that had been placed in an underground barn were unearthed in the vicinity of the tumulus of the first Qin emperor. This menagerie is very close to the selection of earthenware creatures which were produced for the burials of the early Han rulers, as seen at the pits at the Yangling mausoleum.

Connections to prior traditions like those of Chu and Qin are clear, but it is also apparent that the Han were not content to simply imitate the past. They turned away from the individually carved tomb figures of wood prevalent in Chu tombs, and instead preferred the earthenware figurines that the Qin had already proved could be produced in quantity through the use of molds. The smaller scale of Han figurines is most likely due to the conservative trends of tomb preparation in the opening years of the dynasty or perhaps to the purposeful differentiation from those made by prior rulers. The variety of type seen in Han figurines, as distinguished from the warriors characteristic of the Qin, reveals the growing importance given to tomb surrogates, or *mingqi*, during the Han dynasty. Other significant developments include the diversity of type meant for use by the living, including hand-held miniatures and also large sculptures that served as petrified creatures, forever part of the realm of Emperor Wu. The naturalistic features of these subjects, a characteristic of Han art noted by many scholars, are complemented by references to the fantastic or by decor such as cloud designs that might be seen as symbolizing the place where immortals existed and that was just as in tune with the Han perspective as any "realistic" trait. In Han dynasty China, sculpture was important in the context of the living and of the dead, and the images in this exhibition establish its significance before the next great age of sculpture in China, which was influenced by the introduction of Buddhism.

Classification of Han Pictorial Stone Carvings from Northern Shaanxi

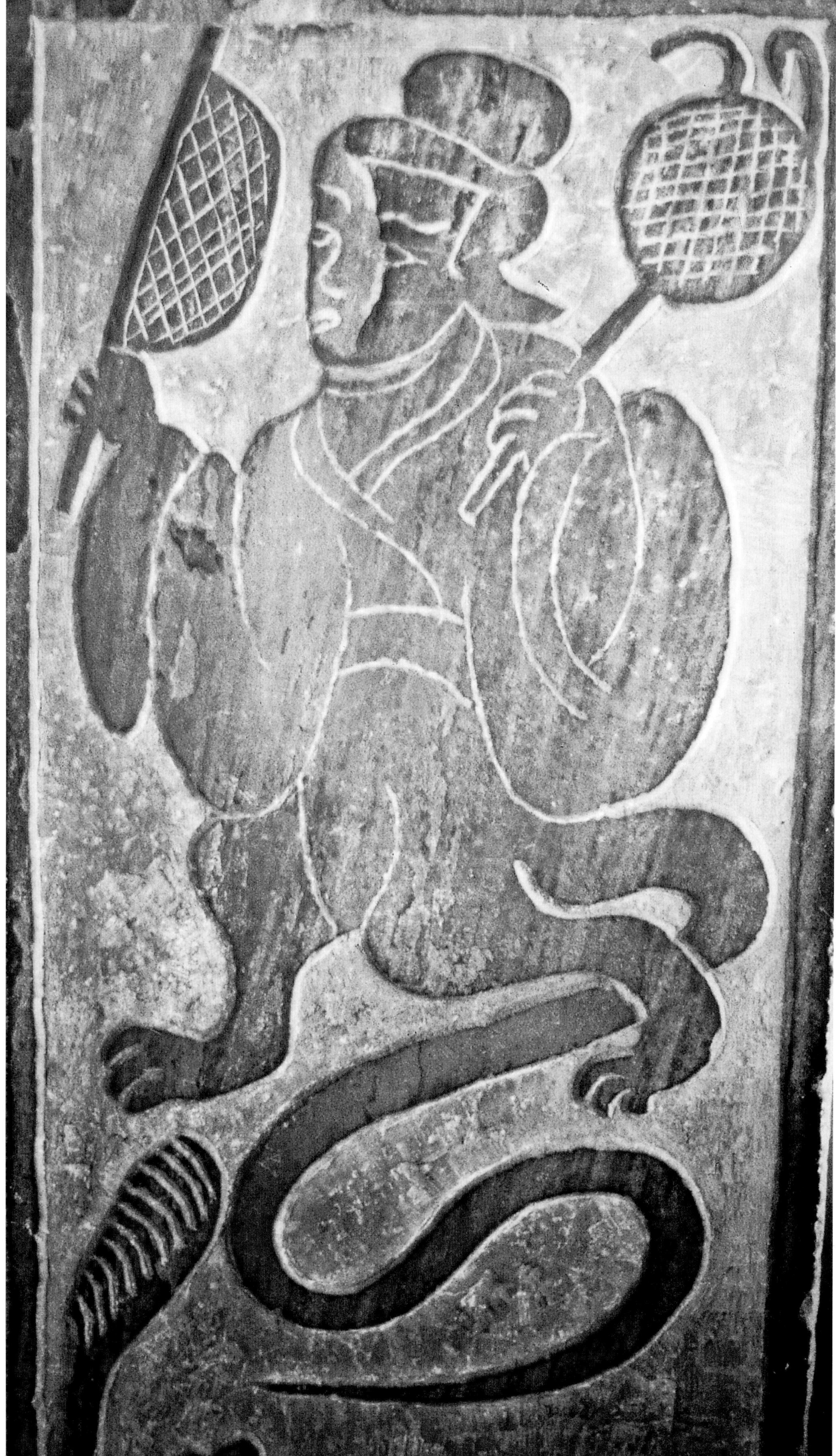

Classification of Han Pictorial Stone Carvings from Northern Shaanxi

Li Jian
The Dayton Art Institute

Since the 1950s, Shaanxi stone carvings have been found from tombs along the Wuding River at Suide, Mizhi Yulin, Hengshan, and Shenmu, all in northern Shaanxi Province (fig. 3.1). These carvings number more than seven hundred to date. These pieces, made as components of the tomb entrance, walls, and ceilings, are carved with human figures and religious scenes in low relief and reflect not only aesthetic values, but also social and cultural aspects of the Han dynasty.

Two thousand years ago, what today is northern Shaanxi was covered with ranches and forests. It was an important frontier that linked China with a few northwest nomadic peoples, including the Xiongnu and Qiang. This region was prosperous during the early Eastern Han dynasty because of its strategic location and cultural, and economic diversity, which included grazing, hunting and trading activities. Under this stimulus, funeral practices grew increasingly prevalent, especially among wealthy landowners and military and civil officers. A tomb precinct functioned as a ritual site where ceremonial services were performed in memory of the virtues of the tomb occupant and in honor of wise rulers. At the same time, the scale of the tomb and its decoration became expressions of filial piety, a Confucian doctrine that influenced all aspects of life during the Han period. It was ingrained in the fabric of this society that people would strain family resources to build a proper tomb for the deceased. Stone-built tombs decorated with human and religious subjects reflected this social and ideological phenomenon.

The regional pictorial art has been insufficiently studied. This is due in part to its supposed inferiority in themes and techniques to the work of other carving centers. For example, Shaanxi carvings have been considered less distinguished than carvings of Sichuan Province, which are characterized by vivid representations of daily life, and less profound than Shandong carvings known for their solemn subjects of Confucian ideology and iconography. A variety of stylistic and iconographic changes in Shaanxi stone carvings can be identified by examining tomb constructions and their carvings. This process in turn provides insight into social, cultural, and ideological values that may have influenced the stylistic and iconographic

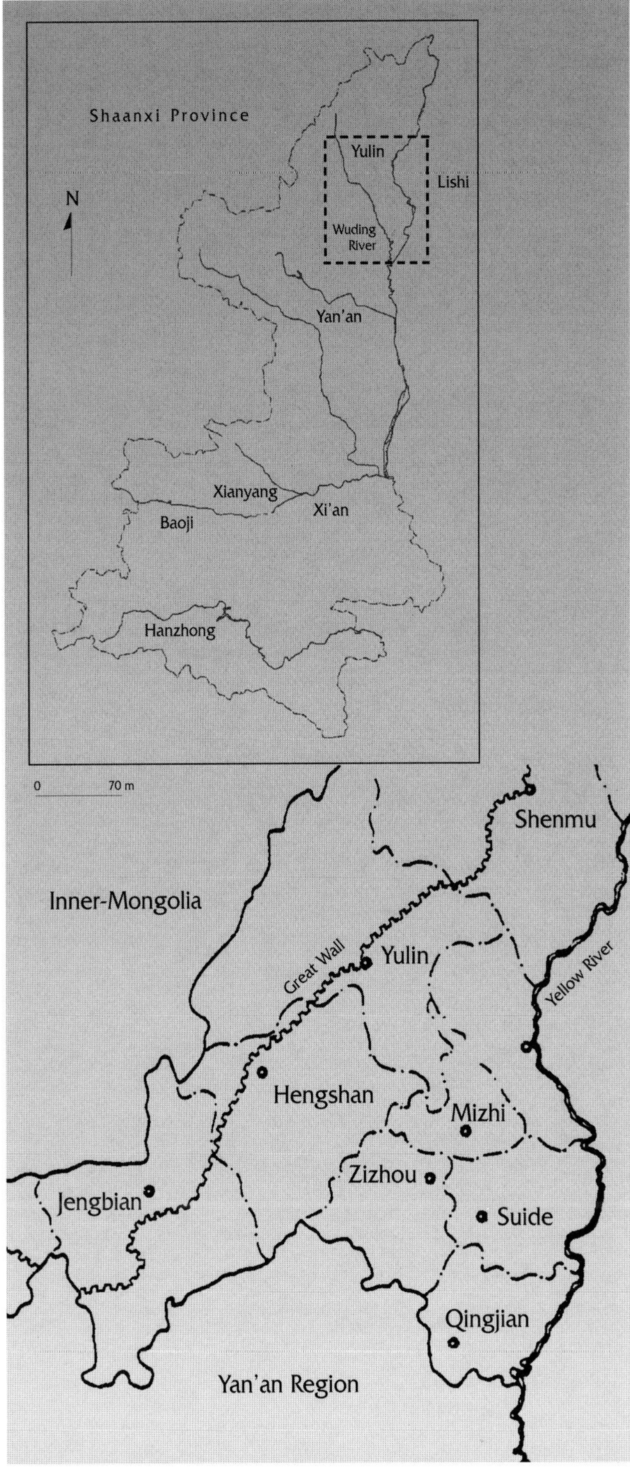

Fig. 3.1. Major sites of Han stone carvings in northern Shaanxi. Based on Li Lin et al., *Shanbei Handai huaxiangshi*, 1995.

changes in Shaanxi carvings.

Discovery and Publication on Stone Carvings of Northern Shaanxi

The discovery of Shaanxi carvings began only recently. The earliest finds were made most likely in the late 1920s, as recorded in two rubbings now in the collection of Beijing University. A significant discovery was made in 1953 when a group of twenty-six reliefs was unearthed in Suide from the tomb of Wang Deyuan, dated to A.D. 100. By 1957 more than 150 stone slabs had been found in Suide and Mizhi, all now in the collection of the Xian Stele Museum. The results of these discoveries were published by the Shaanxi Provincial Museum in 1958.[1] Despite the lack of excavation data, the discoveries of the 1950s are significant for indicating that northern Shaanxi, along with Shandong, Henan and Sichuan provinces, was one of the four Han stone carving centers.

The first article in English that introduced Shaanxi carving was published by Hsio-Yen Shih in 1960. By examining selected examples from the 1950s' discovery, Shih identified images and themes and indicated possible artistic influence from other regions.[2] In 1971, Kate Finsterbusch illustrated with data more than 120 Han stone slabs unearthed from Shaanxi prior to 1964, along with stone reliefs discovered from other stone carving centers.[3]

Unlike Shandong and Nanyang carvings, which have textual references as early as the Eastern Jin and the Northern Wei dynasties,[4] no historical texts on Shaanxi carvings have been discovered. Since the 1970s, newly unearthed carvings have been reported in Chinese periodicals, providing more information on tomb plans and structures, construction materials, and accompanying objects. This archaeological data is valuable for cataloguing, dating, and studying not only these objects, but earlier finds as well. In 1995 an illustrated catalogue of Shaanxi stone carving was published by a group of local scholars Li Lin, Kang Lanying, and Zhao Liguang.[5] The authors document Shaanxi pictorial carvings through illustrations accompanied by data and descriptive information on imagery. Presently this catalogue is the most comprehensively illustrated reference for the study of Shaanxi carving.

The current study of Shaanxi carving focuses primarily on illustrating finds, interpreting themes, and identifying carving techniques. Stylistic classification of Shaanxi carving has been largely ignored. Besides the supposed inferiority of reliefs from this region, another barrier to the classification has been the lack of complete archaeological data. Most finds surface accidentally as a result of irrigation projects or road or building construction, where the original tomb structures have not been preserved and the burial objects have been dispersed.

In 1989, Xin Lixiang of the Historical Museum in Beijing classified Shaanxi stone carvings for the first time. In Xin's classification, Shaanxi carving is divided into three categories: slabs incised with simple designs, all the carvings found in Shaanxi since the 1950s, and the carvings found in today's Lishi, east of Suide in a neighboring province.[6] This classification provides a primary guide to the categorizing of Shaanxi and Lishi carvings. The second category, however, comprising more than 95 percent of the total finds from Shaanxi and embodying a variety of themes and designs, needs further classification.

Classification of Shaanxi Stone Carvings

A Han tomb consisted of two main sections: the aboveground structure and the underground structure. The structure aboveground originally included a ceremonial shrine and a burial mount enclosed by a wall; unfortunately, few of these survive in Shaanxi today. The underground structure usually consisted of a sloping passage constructed of stone slabs, leading to one or more tomb chambers. A single chamber was formed in the shape of the character *tu* and a double chamber in the shape of *ri* (fig. 3.14a). A multiple-chambered tomb was created by adding one or two side annexes to a double chamber, forming the character *shi* (figs. 3.15a, 3.17a). The chamber usually had a vaulted or tapered ceiling or, less often, a flat ceiling. All were built of blocks and slabs of stone, which were also used for paving the floor. Images appear on the slabs of entrances, walls and ceilings are normally found in the front chamber. These stone carvings illustrate a broad array of imagery and techniques, from which the following four styles should be distinguished.

Style I

This category of carvings is represented by only a few examples, mostly door panels. On only a few surviving examples, images of mythological masks (*pushou*), phoenixes, and tigers are composed asymmetrically and rendered in a simple, bold manner. The contours that define the images have been hollowed out, leaving a large area of the stone surface untouched (fig. 3.2). Although no dated samples have been found, this economical and labor-saving carving method combined with iconic characters are indicative of this early stage of stone carving. In comparison with later objects this group of carvings could be dated to the late Western Han or the early Eastern Han period.

Style I is represented by a door panel (fig. 3.2) unearthed at Hejiawan in Suide in 1957. In the center of the panel is a *pushou* placed below a phoenix and flanked on one side by a dragon. The phoenix is depicted in an unbalanced posture, standing on one foot, a pose quite different from that of the well-balanced phoenixes carved in the succeeding period. Furthermore, the asymmetrical position of the dragon differs from the vertical presentation of the phoenix-*pushou*-dragon scheme found in most Shaanxi carvings. The *pushou* has a small head and holds in its mouth a large ring, in a manner similar to the *pushou* in bronze, jade, and pottery of the Western Han period (cat. nos. 48, 49). This similarity suggests that, during the late Western Han or the early Eastern Han period, the use of the imagery of *pushou* was extended to the new medium of stone and was applied with other mythological creatures in a new scheme.

None of the carvings in Style I are supported by scientific excavations or archaeological surveys. Most of the samples

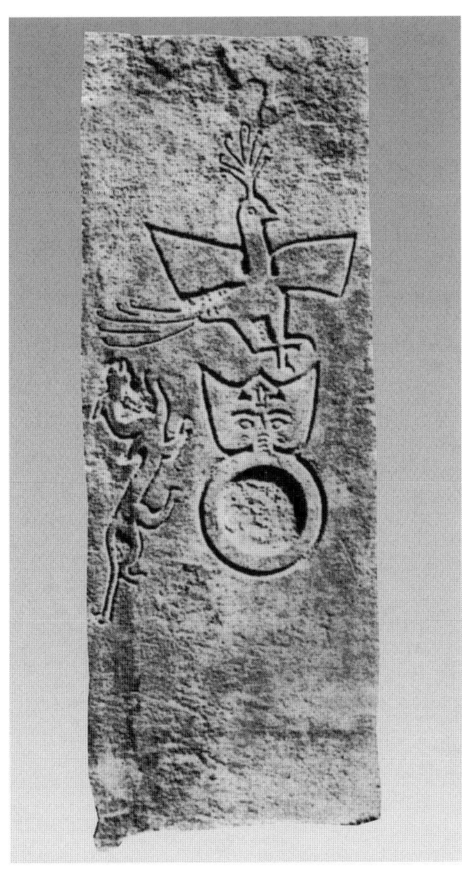

Fig. 3.2. Phoenix, beast mask, and dragon on door panel. Style I. Late Western Han to Early Eastern Han. Found in 1957 at Hejiawan, Suide. After Shaanxi Provincial Museum, *Shanbei Donghan huaxiang shike xuanji*, 1958, fig. 119.

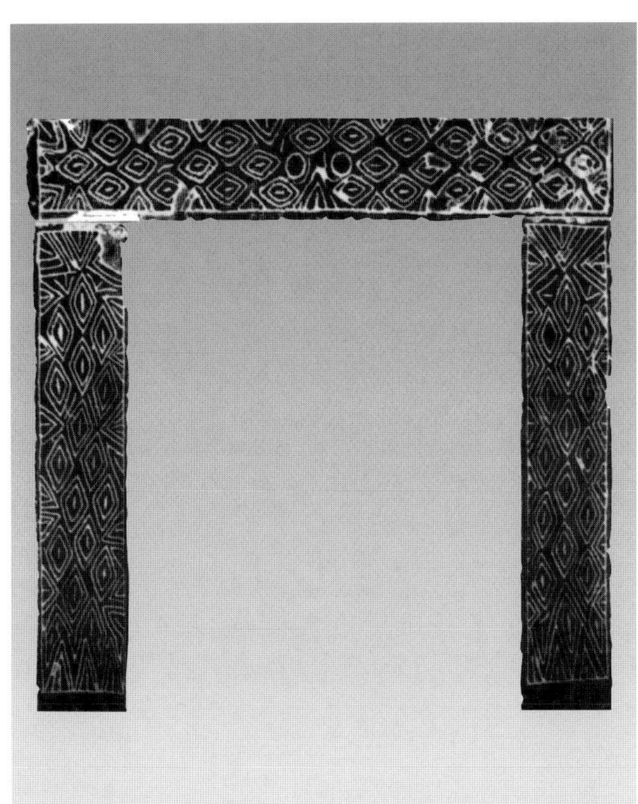

Fig. 3.3. Rubbing of entrance ensemble with geometric patterns. Style II. Early Western Han. Found in 1956 at Yuanzigou, Suide. After Li Lin et al., *Shanbei*, figs. 221–23.

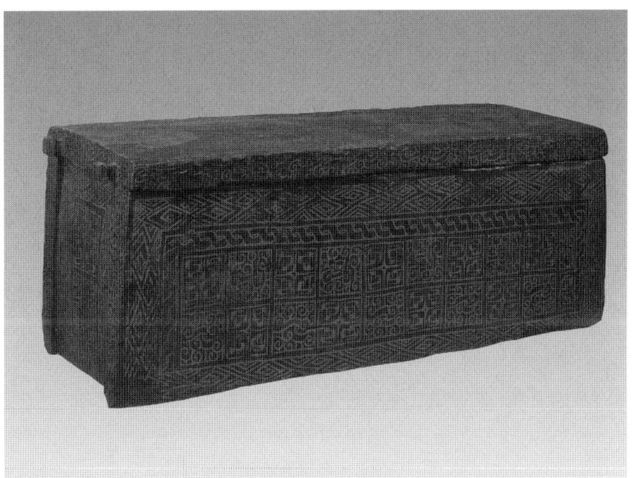

Fig. 3.4. Lacquered coffin with painted design. Warring States period, about 433 B.C. Excavated in 1978 at the tomb of Marquis Yi of Zeng, Sui, Hubei Province. L. 191 cm.; W. 70 cm.; H. 72 cm. Photo courtesy Hubei Provincial Museum.

were collected without knowledge of provenance and without associated tomb mounts, structures, or accompanying objects. In some cases the carvings themselves are lost; only their ink rubbings remain. Since only a few examples survive, usually as a single fragment, it is impossible to envision the entire image and its complete pictorial scheme.

Style II

The examples in Style II are characterized by geometric designs such as diamonds, triangles, waves, and woven patterns. Animal images such as birds and fish appear on a small scale, and human figures and inscriptions emerge. This variety of motifs is consolidated, in contrast to the earlier tradition: images are no longer presented separately but as compositional elements within a constructed whole. Also new is that a great number of slabs has been found from a single site. For instance, five slabs forming a post and lintel door module were recovered, forming a complete entrance. On these pieces, images are carved in low relief, and geometric designs are engraved on a diagonal. Similar to the earlier examples of Style I, carvings have been found accidentally without any excavation data, and little is known about their related tombs.

One of the new innovations in this phase is the application of architectural decor. The tomb entrance shown in figure 3.3 consists of two rectangular posts and a lintel found in Suide in 1956. This set of entrance pieces is carved entirely with linear, geometric designs, probably derived from the pattern of building materials in an actual entrance. This corresponds to geometric patterns that were frequently used in ancient Chinese architectural designs. The absence of other decorative motifs gives this ensemble a pure simplicity. An identical decor is evident on a painted coffin (fig. 3.4) from the tomb of Marquis Yi of Zeng, dating to the fifth century B.C. On this coffin, a geometric pattern almost identical to the design on the stone carving from Suide is painted in the border of each side and end panel. The square or rectangular designs in the center of each of these panels may indicate windows or doors. This further suggests that the geometric design in the borders of the coffin might have been derived from architectural decor,

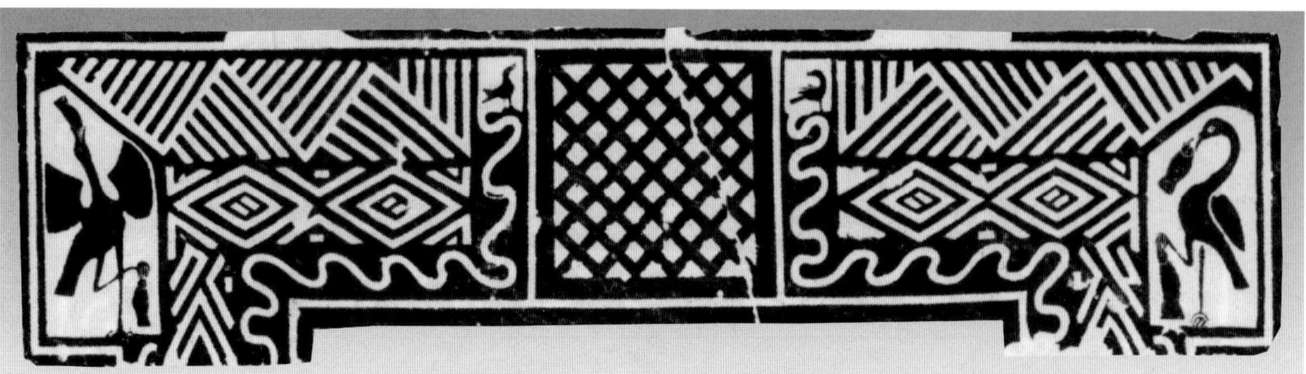

Fig. 3.7. Rubbing of window lattice pattern on lintel. Style II. Early Eastern Han. Found in 1976 at Liujiawan, Suide. After Li Lin et al., *Shanbei*, fig. 335.

applied to burial objects as well as structures of the type illustrated by figure 3.3.

Figure 3.5 illustrates a carved-stone entrance ensemble imitating a wooden structure. Decorated with a woven pattern on the piers, this entrance portal, found in Sishipu, Suide in 1983, is fashioned with double door panels. Each panel is carved with a framework in the manner of an actual wooden door panel. A similar door opened into a granary unearthed from a tomb at Laodaosi, Shaanxi, in 1978 (fig. 3.6, cat. no. 73). At the lower level of the granary was a door panel recessed within a door frame. A removable crossbar in the mid-section of the door could be fixed into the frame as a lock. Coins cast with the characters *wu zhu*, typical of coinage circulated during the mid-Eastern Han dynasty, were found with the granary.[7] From the discovery of these coins, it may be inferred that the stone entrance dates to the same period.

A lintel decorated with a window lattice pattern in the central section is illustrated in figure 3.7. This design resembles the window lattice molded on a ceramic tower excavated from the same tomb at Laodaosi (fig. 3.8). This resemblance further suggests that the ornament on Han stone tomb chambers in Shaanxi imitates the designs on actual timber structures of the Eastern Han dynasty.

Human figures are also represented at this early stage. An isolated pier, unearthed in 1953 at Hejiawan, Suide, shows a standing guard attired in a long gown, holding a spear (ge) (fig. 3.9). The contour of the guard's silhouette and his facial features are defined by incised lines. Above the figure and on the left are continuous geometric patterns. On the other side of the pier is an abstract design, identified by experts as the character *xian*, which literally means "immortality."[8] A similar guardian was found in 1961 in Yongcheng, Henan (fig. 3.10). The examples are almost identical to each other in terms of the image and the incised method of carving. The tomb from Henan has been dated to the early Eastern Han dynasty.[9]

Style III

In contrast to the earlier traditions, the carvings of this style consist of groups of slabs used to construct not only entrances,

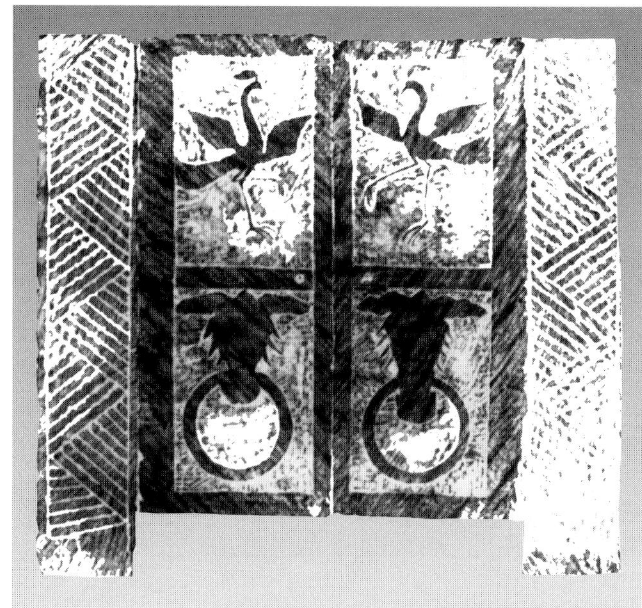

Fig. 3.5. Rubbing of lumber frame ornament on carved stone door panels. Style II. Early Eastern Han. Found in 1983 at Sishipu, Suide. After Li Lin et al., *Shanbei*, figs. 420–24.

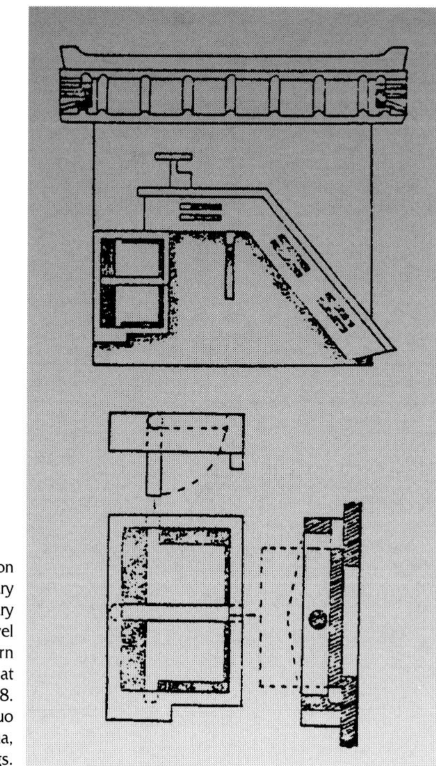

Fig. 3.6. Elevation of pottery granary (above); granary door at lower level (below). Eastern Han. Excavated at Laodaosi in 1978. Based on Guo Qinghua, "Shanxi," figs. 11–12.

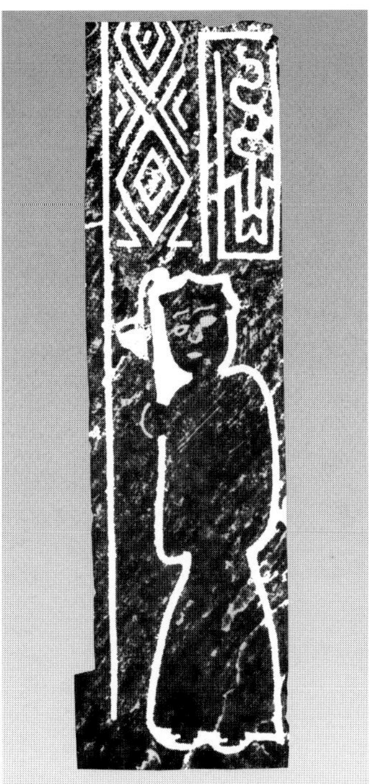

Fig. 3.9. Rubbing of guardian and inscription. Style II. Early Eastern Han. Found in 1953 at Hejiawan, Suide. After Li Lin et al., *Shanbei*, fig. 553.

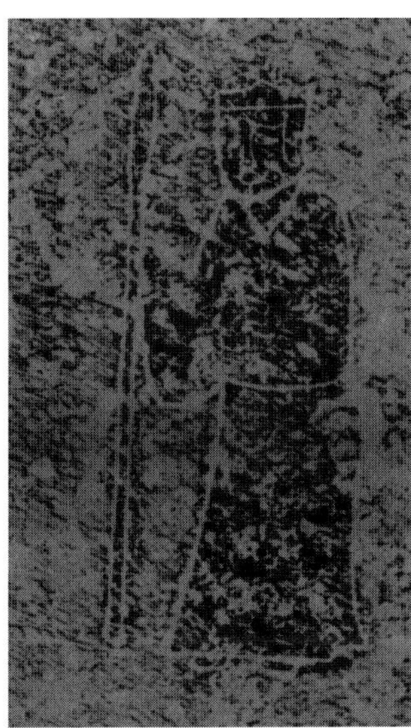

Fig. 3.10. Rubbing of guardian. Early Eastern Han. Excavated in 1961 from Tomb no. 2 at Yongcheng, Henan Province. After Yan Genqi et al., *Shangqu*, 47.

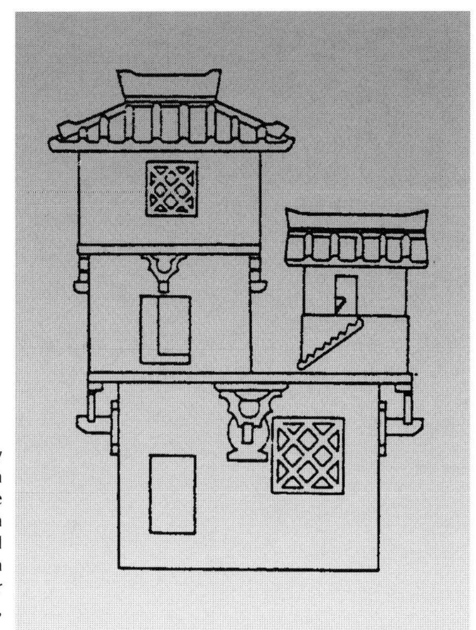

Fig. 3.8. Pottery watchtower with window lattice pattern. Eastern Han. Excavated at Laodaosi in 1978. After Guo Qinghua, "Shanxi," fig. 8.3.

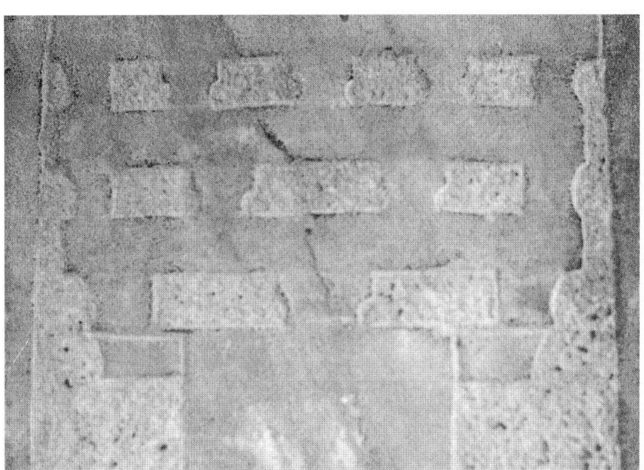

Fig. 3.11. Column with arches. Style III. Mid-Eastern Han. Painted stone relief unearthed at Mizhi.

but also the walls of chambers. Images are rendered in low relief, occasionally with details incised or painted in ink. Color is applied to highlight cosmic or mythological images and architectural designs (fig. 3.11). Data on excavation sites, tomb structures and locations of reliefs become available with this style. Significant finds include inscribed slabs that often bear dates indicating when the reliefs were created.

In Style III, a broad range of imagery begins to be composed in a formulaic system. In the post and lintel door scheme the door panel is usually decorated vertically with a phoenix, a *pushou* and a unicorn or tiger. The rectangular post is divided into multiple registers carved with mythological and ritual scenes. The popular iconography includes the Queen Mother of the West, the King Father of the East, immortals, guardians, Fuxi and Nuwa (fig. 3.12), human figures and activities (fig. 3.13), domestic animals, mythological beasts, foliate

motifs, ceremonial objects, and architectural structures. The lintel usually provides a continuous space carved with processional and ceremonial scenes, hunting activities, or historical events. Other examples are divided into vertical or horizontal segments with the outside border filled with foliate designs entwined with mythological figures and animals. This style encompasses approximately 80 percent of the reliefs discovered in Shaanxi and marks the most presentable category compared to the earlier styles.

One of the dated tombs is that of Niu Wenming, excavated along the western shore of Wuding River at Guanzhuang in Mizhi in the spring of 1971. Also called Tomb no. 4, this tomb consists of two square chambers with a total area of eighteen square meters, forming the character *ri* (fig. 3.14a). Twenty-one reliefs were used for constructing the entrances, the ceilings, and the walls. The most significant discovery is a slab that bears an inscription indicating the burial date of A.D. 107[10] (fig. 3.14b). Characterized by a balanced and controlled form and strokes, this inscription, consisting of twenty-one characters

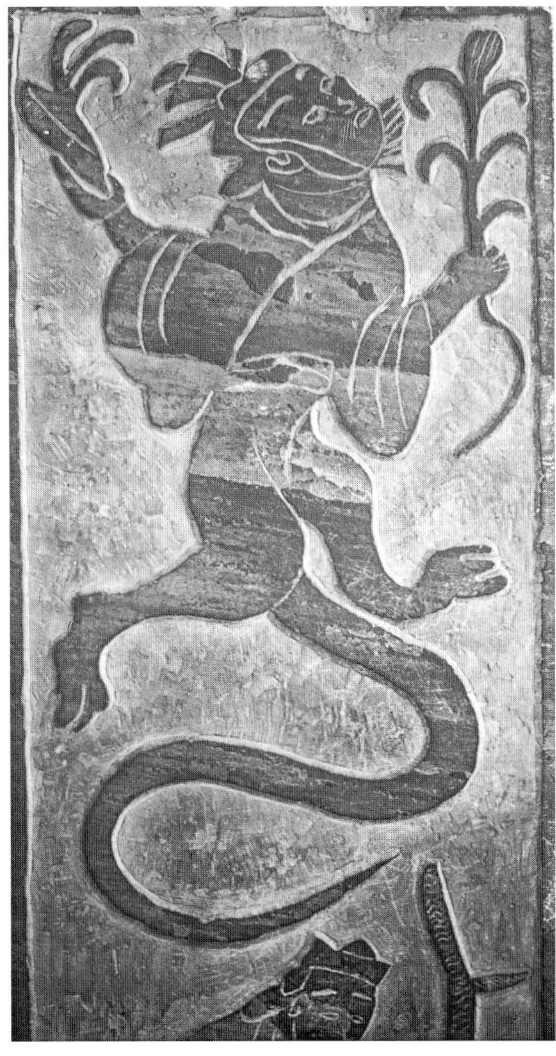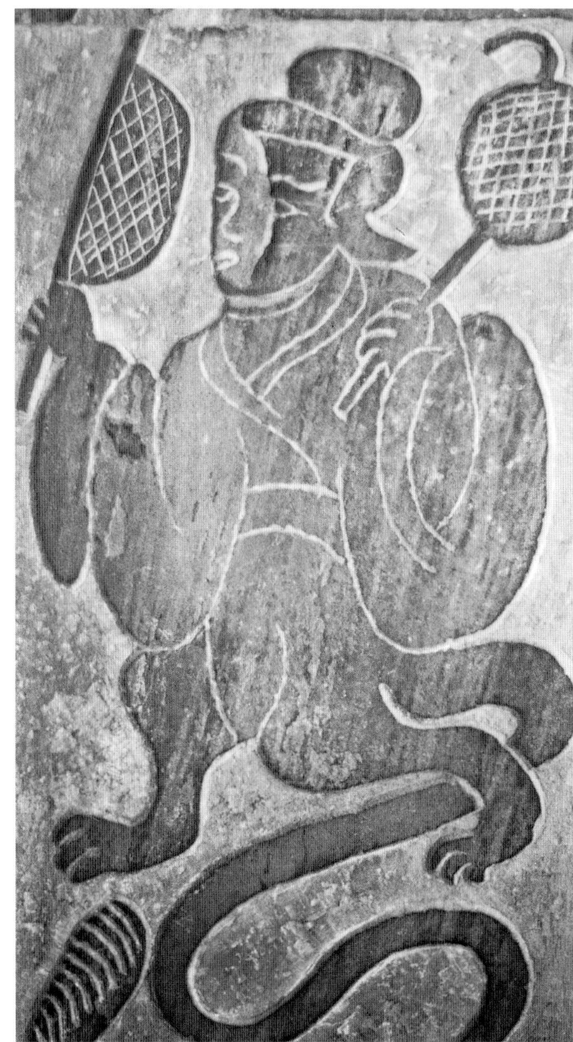

Fig. 3.12. Fuxi and Nuwa. Style III. Mid-Eastern Han. Stone relief unearthed at Mizhi.

written in styles of both seal (*zhuan*) and clerical (*li*) scripts, marks the transitional period of calligraphic style during the early second century A.D. The line variation of the *li* calligraphic style is first seen in the pictorial art during this phase.

The entrance in figure 3.14c represents the standard post and lintel door module. The lintel relief depicts a processional scene with chariots and guards on horseback. Two large circles carved at the ends of the lintel represent the sun and the moon. The left post depicts the King Father seated on a high-stemmed platform and with a winged immortal; below the platform is a deer. The right post shows the Queen Mother enthroned in company with a winged immortal and an elixir rabbit. Standing guardians with a broom and a spear (*ji*) are posed in the lower registers. On each door panel are mythological images of a phoenix, a *pushou*, and a unicorn, with details painted in ink. In the front chamber, the ceiling tapers above the walls to form a square slab carved in low relief with a large circle painted in red, indicating the sun (fig. 3.14d). The ceiling of the rear chamber is rendered in a similar manner but painted in black, indicating the moon.

Another distinguishing aspect of these reliefs is the connection between scenes displayed in separate registers. A rectangular post from the front chamber (fig. 3.14e) shows two figures, one standing and the other kneeling, overlapping the border of the register to communicate with two figures depicted in another register on the right. Likewise, the plowing scene at the bottom of the same rectangular slab is forecast by the harvest scene illustrated above. This type of association between scenes is rarely visible in the earlier styles.

The climax achieved in Style III is the appearance of the chamber fully decorated with grand scenes. A tomb found at Guanzhuang Village in the autumn of 1980 exemplifies this high point. Constructed of stone bricks and slabs, the tomb consists of a front and rear chamber, as well as a side chamber (fig. 3.15a). The entrance and all the walls of the front chamber are decorated with sixteen reliefs. The two covering the west wall of the front chamber (fig. 3.15b) are magnificent in scale and are said to be the largest set of Han reliefs discovered from Shaanxi.[11] This series of reliefs seems to depict in sequence a variety of activities and events at the tomb site during a ceremonial service. Scenes are staged on the grand architectural background with columns upholding laminated arches and wavy draperies. The stylized ribbons penetrating discs (*bi*) indicate the luxurious exterior and interior designs used in the Han period.

The relief presents in two bands an impressive procession

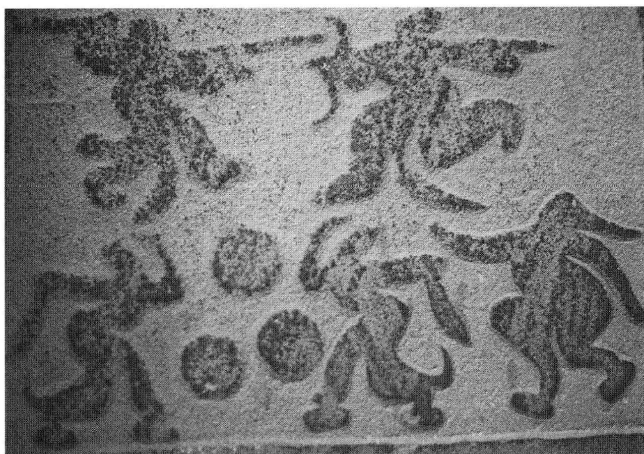

Fig. 3.13. Performers. Style III. Mid-Eastern Han. Stone relief unearthed at Mizhi.

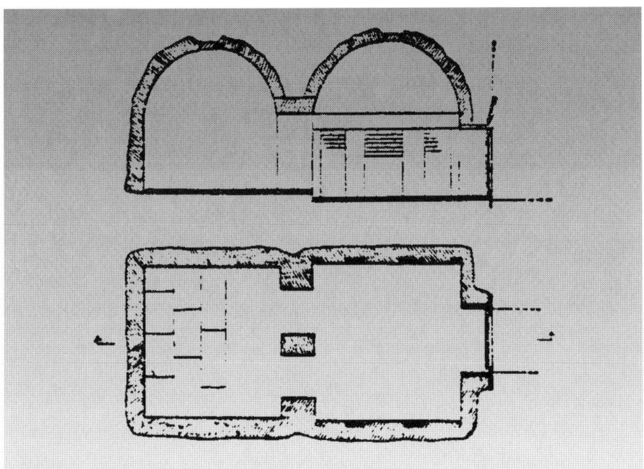

Fig. 3.14a. Elevation and floor plan of the tomb of Niu Wenming (Tomb no. 4), excavated in 1971 at Guanzhuang, Mizhi. After Shaanxi Provincial Museum, *Wenwu* 3 [1972], figs. 3–4, 10, 13.

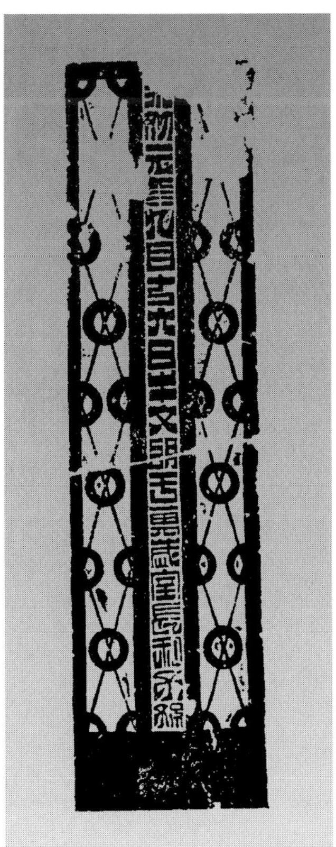

Fig. 3.14b. Rubbing of rectangular slab with dated inscription. Style III. Mid-Eastern Han, A.D. 107. Excavated from the tomb of Niu Wenming.

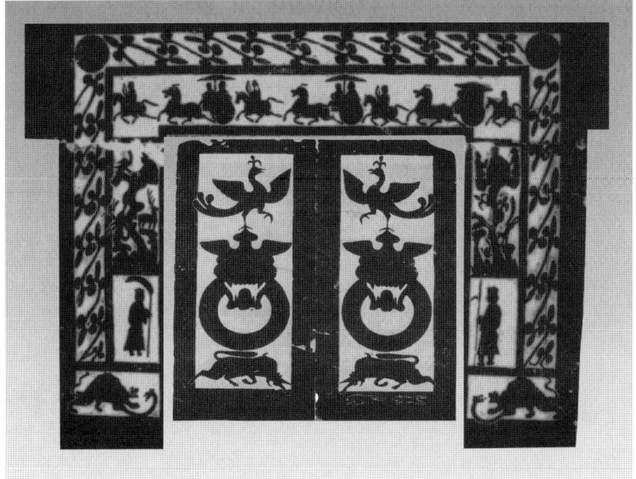

Fig. 3.14c. Rubbing of entrance of the tomb of Niu Wenming. After Li Lin et al., *Shanbei*, figs. 57–61.

of chariots and riders, greeted by three figures at the upper left corner. The ritual scene is displayed in the central section under a double-roofed ceremonial pavilion flanked by a tower (*que*) on each side. Its spiritual meaning is implied by an immortal and a mythological animal mounted on the roof. Depicted on each side of the pavilion are performances of acrobats, archers, and dancers. On the bottom band is a hunting scene showing archers on horses chasing fleeing animals. Its humanistic and spiritual themes, well-balanced forms, and the competent carving mark it as one of the most remarkable reliefs from the Shaanxi area.

Style IV

In this category of stone carvings the number of registers is usually reduced to a minimum to emphasize the overall composition rather than separate registers. The theme focuses on the immortal world and its legendary figures. The images and motifs, either real or imaginary, are highly intertwined and convey a strong sense of dynamic movement. Foliate and animal patterns are richly ornamented, serving as a background for the primary images. These stylized designs tend to revive the elaborate and luxurious compositions seen in objects from aristocratic tombs dating to the Western Han dynasty or even as early as the Warring States period. Architectural structures are delineated with diagonal lines to achieve a three-dimensional perspective. The carving is intricate and represents the most elaborate technique of Han craftsmen.

This style probably derived from a prototype, with designs reminiscent of the flowing and bold lines of painting and calligraphy. This prototype is exemplified by a few reliefs excavated in 1984 from Tomb no. 11 at Huangjiata, Suide. Paved with stone slabs, this single-chambered tomb has an entrance consisting of five reliefs, decorated with highly stylized clouds intertwined with ornamented beasts. On the post (fig. 3.16) the images run vertically from top to bottom. They include a

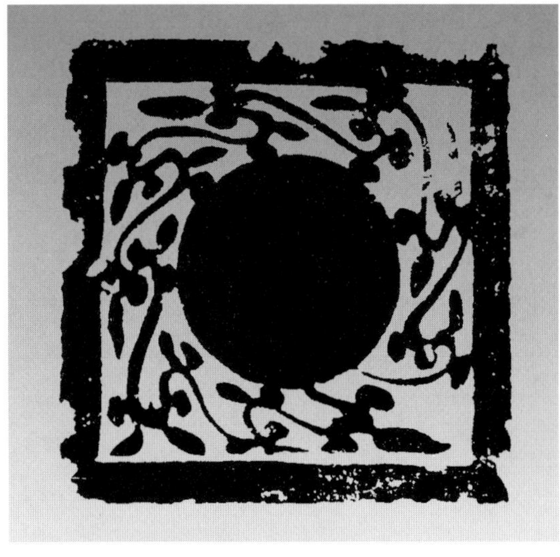

Fig. 3.14d. Rubbing of ceiling slab with design of the sun from the tomb of Niu Wenming.

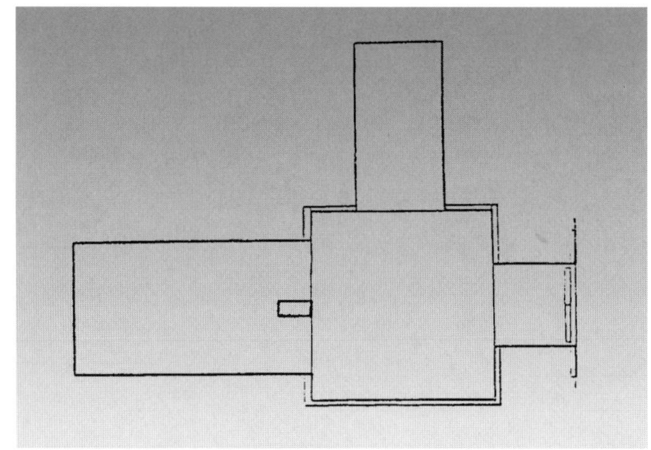

Fig. 3.15a. Floor plan of multi-chambered Han tomb excavated in 1980 at Guanzhuang, Mizhi. After Wu Lan, *Kaogu* 11 [1987], fig. 1.

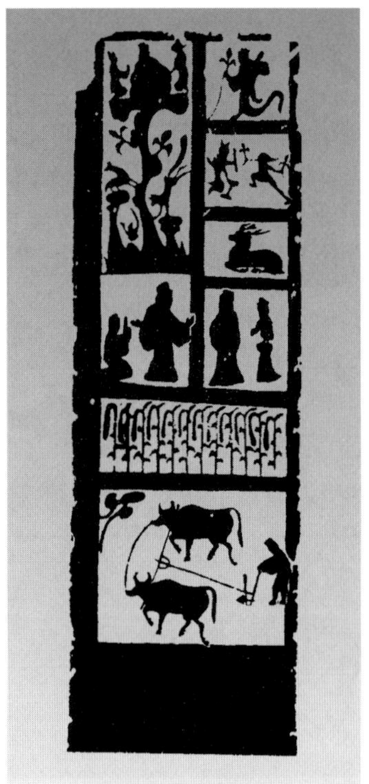

Fig. 3.14e. Rubbing of human and spiritual scenes in divided registers from the tomb of Niu Wenming.

growling leopard, a large bear, a warrior shooting a bow, a truncated figure with an arm stretched forward, a mouse-like creature, and a unicorn. Without additional bands of decorative motifs, the reliefs, rendered with flowing lines of alternating thicknesses, convey a strong expression of continuity, movement, and unified harmony.

No examples in this style are more compelling than a group of twenty-five reliefs excavated in 1975 from Tomb no. 1 at Yanjiacha in Suide. The floor plan and the stone carving suggest that the tomb may have been built for an aristocrat. With a cross-shaped floor plan, the tomb consists of a front chamber, a rear chamber, and two side chambers (fig. 3.17a). The entrance faces west, yet its sloping passageway that lead to the ground is unclear. Both chambers are paved with stone slabs and the wall is constructed with stone bricks. The ceiling of the front chamber is tapered with a square slab, carved with

a large circle painted in red with arrow designs, indicating the shining sun. The moon is painted in white above the lintel on the east wall of the front chamber. The only burial object surviving from this tomb is a stone stove, hollowed with three holes for cooking and carved on the surface with cooking utensils in low relief.[12]

The most celebrated scene from the Yanjiacha site is that of the immortal realm, displayed on the three-piece entrance (fig. 3.17b). Set on the east wall of the front chamber, this entrance depicts on its lintel the scene of ascending to immortality. From left to right, the scenes depict the God of Rivers (Hebo) riding a carriage drawn by fish, the God of Thunder (Leigong) riding a carriage pulled by lions and loaded with his drum, followed by another vehicle drawn by deer that carries a winged immortal with an evergreen tree. Flanking the tree are the immortals mounted on cranes. The final image is of a carriage pulled by three dragons, perhaps originally bearing the image of the tomb occupant. Unfortunately, this portion is damaged.

The left post is vertically divided into three sections. The middle section depicts the Queen Mother of the West, portrayed frontally on a platform set on a support and surrounded by cloud motifs. On the opposite side is the peak of Kunlun, the magic mountain of the immortal realm, flanked by two immortals.[13] A dragon is posed vertically below. In the outside border of each post, dragons are stylized in diagonal forms and are intertwined with divine birds.

The entranceway on the west wall of the front chamber depicts a hunting scene represented from a bird's-eye view (fig. 3.17c). From left to right, the scene depicts hunters mounted on horses, chasing fleeing animals in a landscape rendered by a row of hills and trees at the lower left end (fig. 3.17d). It is noteworthy that a similar row of hills is repeated on the upper section to define an enclosed space. This conception of a landscape is rarely seen in the earlier tradition. Following the hunters are processional chariots in company with guards on horseback, dashing away from a courtyard

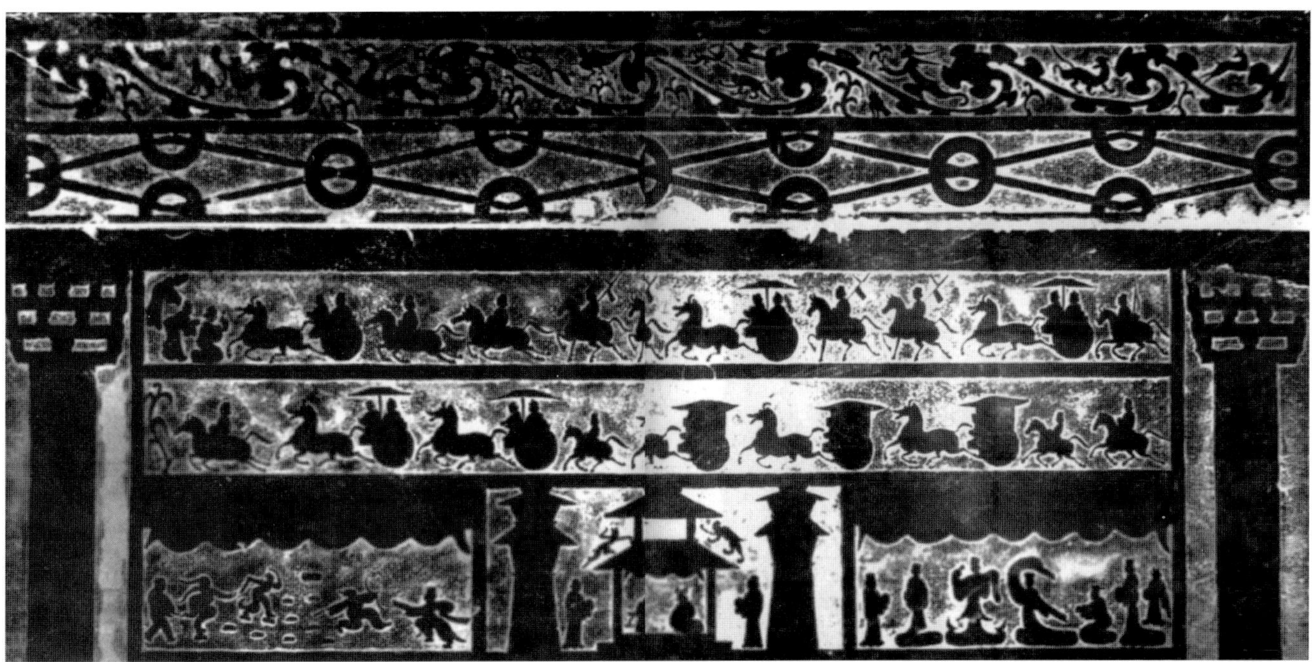

Fig. 3.15b. Rubbing of reliefs on west wall of front chamber of the tomb excavated at Guanzhuang. Style III. Mid-Eastern Han. After Li Lin et al., *Shanbei*, figs. 93–94.

complex depicted at the right end. This complex (fig. 3.17e) consists of a series of courtyards divided by hallways and walls. In the large courtyard is a covered platform, enclosed by railings. The serenity of the courtyard contrasts dramatically with the hunting scene represented on the left.

More inventive designs are apparent in this category. On a rectangular post excavated at Guanzhuang, Mizhi, in 1981 (fig. 3.18), the figures of various animals, such as deer, buffalo, and phoenixes, are depicted against the intricate background of clouds and foliage, interspersed with flowing lines and tiny dots. Another novel design is a beast mask in the upper section; a similar motif is not in evidence in the previous styles.

Key Issues in the Classification of Shaanxi Stone Carvings

References useful for classifying Han tomb slabs from Shaanxi could come from additional sources, such as associated tomb structures and burial objects. Unfortunately, few Han structures above ground exist in Shaanxi today. Burial objects are equally deficient, since most of the tombs found in Shaanxi had been plundered and the burial objects removed long before reliefs were unearthed. A classification based on iconography, pictorial compositions, carving techniques, and comparative methods still leave some questions unanswered.

Style I can be classified with certainty. Although no dated evidence has been found, examples from this style are characterized by incised designs, simple pictorial composition, and crude carving skills. All these combined with the absence of reliefs and designs invented in later styles point to an incipient stage of stone carving. In Style II, geometric and architectural designs are blended with archaic features inherited from Style I

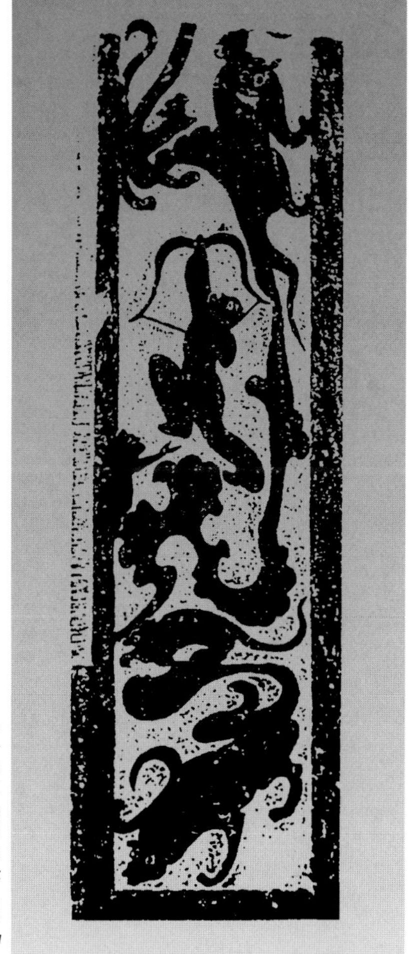

Fig. 3.16. Rubbing of spiritual and human figures. Style IV. Late Eastern Han. Excavated in 1984 from Tomb no. 11 at Huangjiata, Suide. After Dai Yingxin, *Kaogu* 5–6 [1988], fig. 7.1.

and standard factors from the later period. This combination suggests a transitional period, occurring between the primitive style and the standard one. In this transitional stage the engraving is evenly executed; geometric patterns are

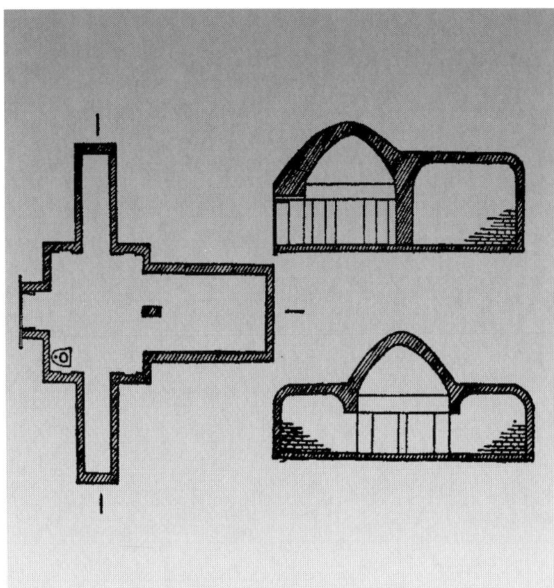

Fig. 3.17a. Floor plan and elevations of multi-chambered tomb (Tomb no. 1) excavated in 1975 at Yanjiacha, Suide. After Dai Yingxin, *Kaogu* 3 [1983], fig. 1.

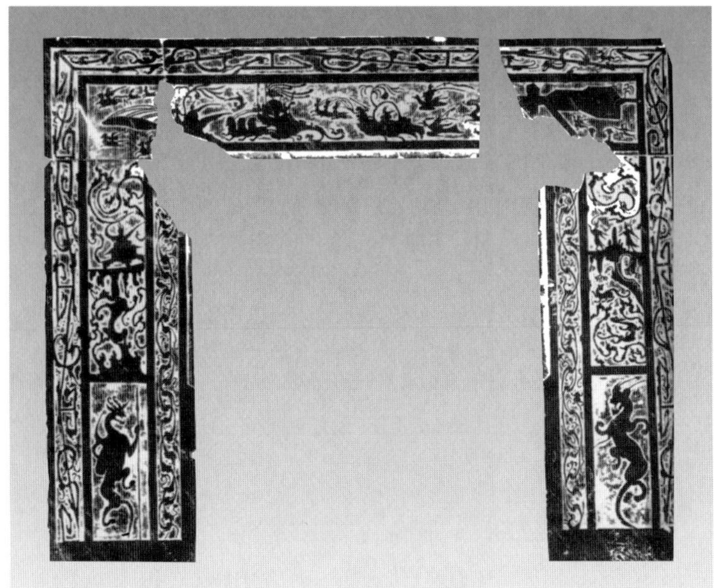

Fig. 3.17b. Rubbing of entrance on east wall of front chamber of Tomb no. 1 at Yanjiacha, Suide. Style IV. Late Eastern Han. After Li Lin et al., *Shanbei*, figs. 260–62.

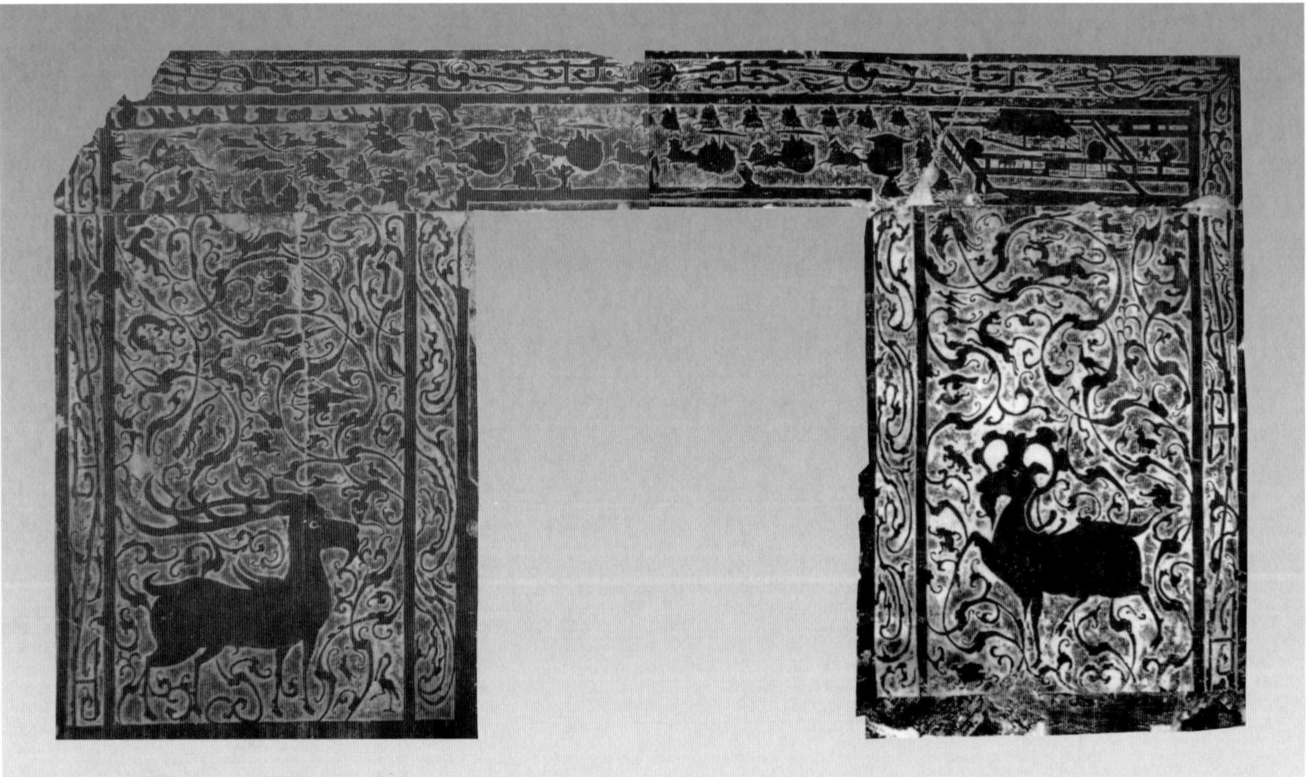

Fig. 3.17c. Rubbing of reliefs on west wall of front chamber of Tomb no. 1 excavated in 1975 at Yanjiacha, Suide. Style IV. Late Eastern Han. After Li Lin et al., *Shanbei*, figs. 246–48.

engraved at a diagonal to an even depth, demonstrating an advanced carving technique.

Compared to earlier examples, the reliefs of Style III present promising evidence supported by inscriptions and dated examples. Significant tombs include the tombs of Wang Deyuan (dated to A.D. 100), Yang Mengyuan (A.D. 96), and Wang Shengxu (A.D. 104), and the tomb of Niu Wenming (A.D. 107).[14] Of eleven dated examples, only six, including fragments, are accompanied by reliefs with pictorial images. Within the one-hundred-fifty-year history of Shaanxi carving, the dated reliefs have only a short span, A.D. 90–107.

Controversial issues have resulted from Style IV. First, its distinct motifs, such as highly stylized clouds and animals, do not have much connection to the earlier finds. Second, these luxurious motifs, executed in a highly stylized fashion, have no parallel in other provinces such as Shandong, Sichuan, or Henan. Without dated references, questions arise: where did this style originate, and where does it fit? One answer to the first is that this luxurious style might have coexisted alongside Style III around A.D. 100. The cloud and animal designs recall the designs seen in Han pottery, lacquer, and textiles. A pottery plate painted with cloud and dragon designs was

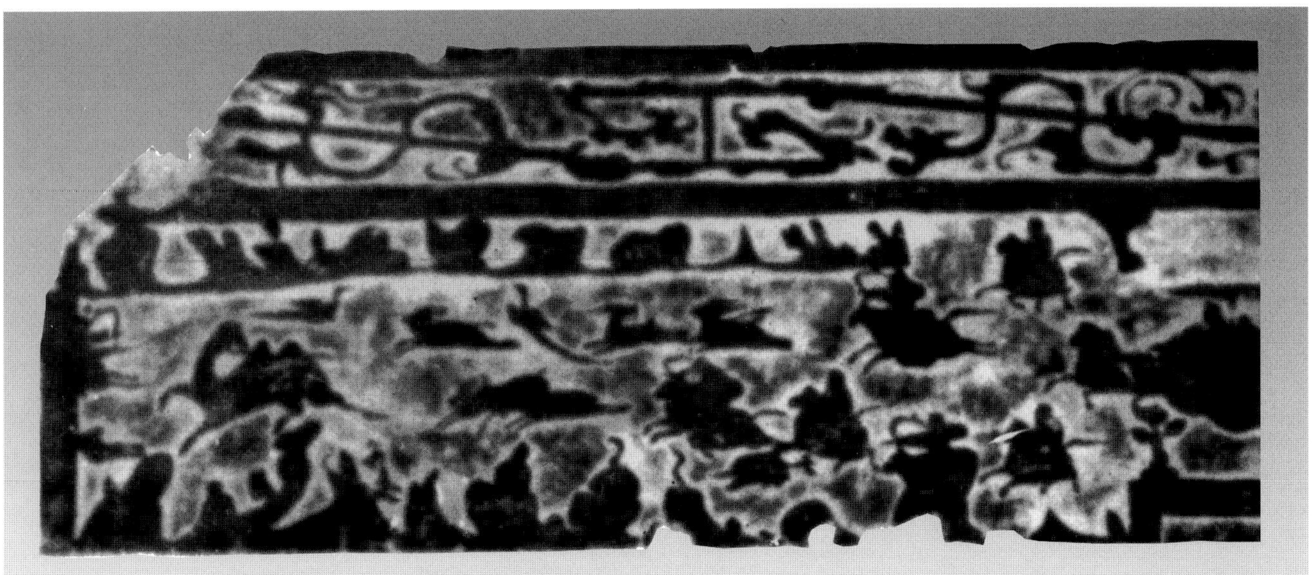

Fig. 3.17d. Hunting scene (detail of fig. 3.17c).

unearthed in 1956 from Tomb no. 1 at Kuaihualing, Suide (fig. 3.19). From the same tomb, four reliefs linked to Style III have been recovered. Notably, the flowing lines of clouds and dragons on the plate are very similar to the design on Shaanxi carvings. This similarity suggests a cross-media influence. As a tradition developed, artisans may have become more confident in handling stone and might have looked to other materials such as pottery, lacquer, bronze, inlaid metal, painting, and textiles for inspiration and to show their talents were equally competent.

In a normal stylistic progression, contemporary motifs are partially visible in the preceding period. However, few distinguished designs in Style IV are foreshadowed in Style III, and these designs have advanced too dramatically to have a trace of association with earlier styles. For instance, human figures and activities, frequently depicted in Style III, are now reduced to the minimum in Style IV. Instead, what becomes dominant instead are mythological scenes, represented against a background decorated with richly ornamented motifs. Old images of deer, ox, or goats are now transformed into a new style—portrayed in large scale with wings, and standing with dignity in a prominent location in the pictorial scheme (fig. 3.17c).

We know little about the date of this luxurious style and its connection to the discoveries from other regions. However, this style may be traced back to the Western Han period, as represented by richly ornamented lacquer, bronze, and harnesses favored by the court and aristocrats. Despite rejection by Confucian scholars, who instead promoted a frugal style, this aristocratic fashion still remained in the circle of noblemen and merchants in Henan Province during the Eastern Han period.[15] However, at what date the style was introduced to Shaanxi from the southeast and employed in stone carving is still a mystery.

It is notable that Shaanxi carving developed a unique aesthetic trend in Style IV, characterized by richly stylized clouds

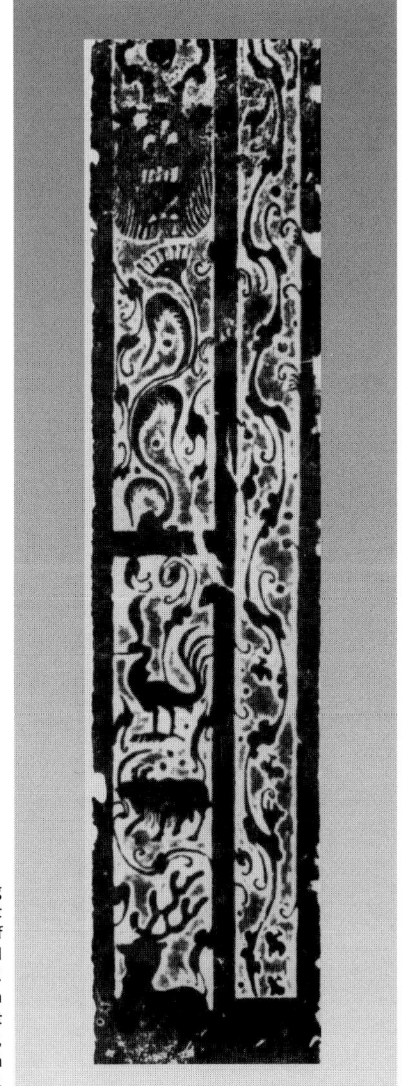

Fig. 3.18. Rubbing of rectangular post with design of foliage and animals. Style IV. Late Eastern Han. Found at Guanzhuang, Mizhi. After Li Lin et al., *Shanbei*, fig. 159.

and animal motifs (figs. 3.17b-c) and refined foliate motifs (fig. 3.18), derived most likely from the grassland and ranches in the region. Similar designs are seen in two further examples, both dated to the Eastern Han period. A bronze mirror (fig.

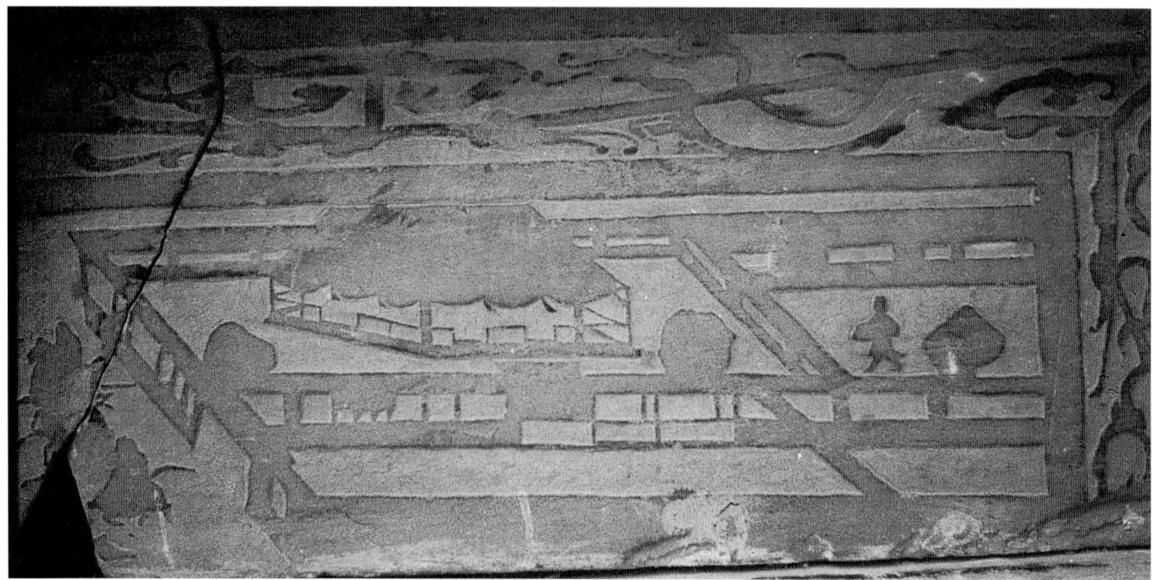

Fig. 3.17e. Courtyard scene (detail of fig. 3.17c).

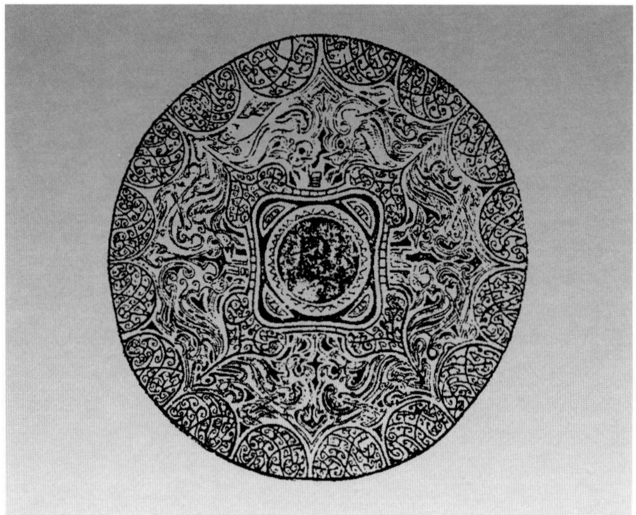

Fig. 3.20. Iron mirror with inlaid designs of foliage and animals. Eastern Han dynasty. Excavated in 1969 at Wuwei, Gansu. After Sun Ji, *Handai wuzhi wenhua ziliao tushuo*, 1991, fig. 69–4.

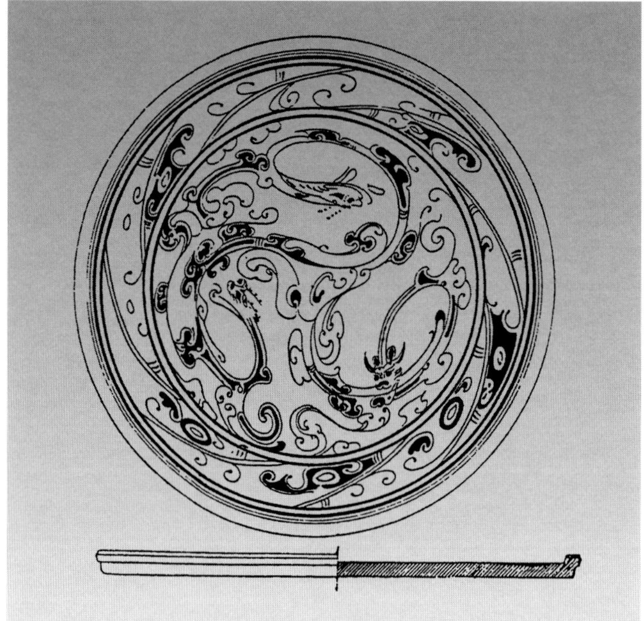

Fig. 3.19. Painted pottery plate with designs of clouds and dragons. Diam. 37 cm. Mid Eastern Han. Excavated at Kuaihualing, Suide. After Shaanxi Provincial Museum, *Shanbei Donghan huaxiang shike xuanji*, 1958, fig. 11.

3.20) excavated in 1969 at Wuwei, Gansu, is elaborately decorated with foliate and animal motifs in a manner similar to the luxurious patterns seen in Shaanxi carving. Another novel image often appearing in Style IV is an animal mask with a long, flowing beard (fig. 3.18). A similar mask, woven into a brocade fragment (fig. 3.21), was found in Loulan, Xinjiang. The two articles were found either in the Shaanxi area or to the west of central China. Does this mean that this luxurious style is a revival of the tradition of the Chu from the Warring States period that spread westward? Or does it represent a style in some degree inspired by an outside influence?

Historically, the Qiang, a nomadic tribe living in the northwest of China, attacked the Han in A.D. 111. In the following year, Han China was forced to relocate its regional government from Shangjun at today's Yulin, to Baishui in central Shaanxi, forcing the local residents to move to the south. When the former residents returned to their homelands in A.D. 129, there was a short period of restoration. However, when the Qiang,

allied with the forces of the Xiongnu, attacked this area in A.D. 140, the Shaanxi area was occupied once again by the outsiders.[16] Could the funeral carvings have been revived in this luxurious style during the short period of A.D. 129–40, or did this occur at a later date?

An inscribed slab found alone at Guanzhuang, Mizhi in 1978 is a rare piece of evidence that records this revival. The slab bears an inscription of thirty-two characters, indicating that it was made for the tomb of Niu Jiping in the year of A.D. 139 (fig. 3.22).[17] This inscription, carved in the *li* style, differs significantly from earlier writings in the *zhuan* style. Its elegant strokes and balanced form prove that refined artistic activity still existed in the Shaanxi area around A.D. 140.

Shaanxi carving seems to have disappeared abruptly after that date. Nevertheless, its legacies are evident in the carvings

54

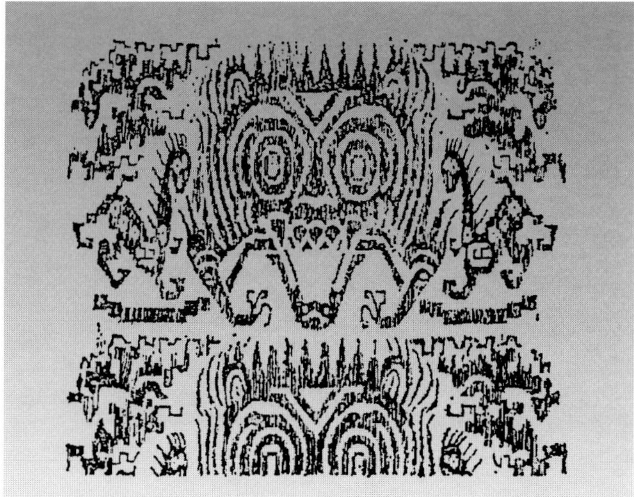

Fig. 3.21. Brocade with design of beast mask, Unearthed at Loulan, Xinjiang. Eastern Han dynasty. After Sun Ji, *Handai*, fig. 17–3.

found at Lishi, Shanxi, one hundred miles east of Suide, Shaanxi. The motifs on Lishi carvings capture the iconography seen in Style IV but in a naive manner, both in content and carving technique. An example unearthed in 1924 at Mamaozhuang, Lishi, is carved with an ascending scene, including images of the God of Rivers, carriages drawn by deer, tigers, and fish, in a manner similar to the scene in figure 3.17b. Another example shows a hunting scene with a landscape defined by rock motifs (fig. 3.23), similar to the landscape motifs in the hunting scene in figure 3.17d.[18] One of the most significant finds from Lishi is a dated pillar (fig. 3.24) with cloud and dragon designs in geometric patterns, similar to the designs seen in Style IV. This pillar is important because it bears on its opposite side the date of A.D. 150. This pillar could suggest two possibilities: first, that Style IV coexisted in the Suide and Lishi areas during A.D. 130–50; or second, the style emerged first in the Suide area sometime during the first half of the century and then influenced the Lishi reliefs in the following years. Future discoveries of dated slabs, groups of related carvings, or even fragments would help to solve these mysteries, and would certainly shed light on the further study of Shaanxi stone carvings.

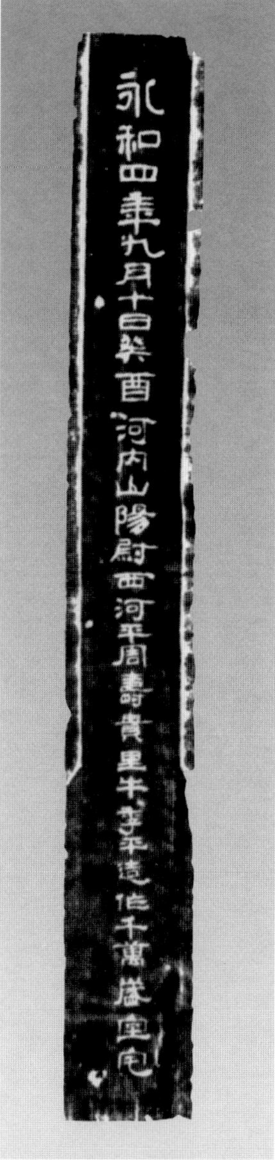

Fig. 3.22. Rubbing of stone pillar with dated inscription. Late Eastern Han, A.D. 139. Made for the tomb of Niu Jiping. Found in 1978 at Guanzhuang, Mizhi. After Li Lin et al., *Shanbei*, fig. 160.

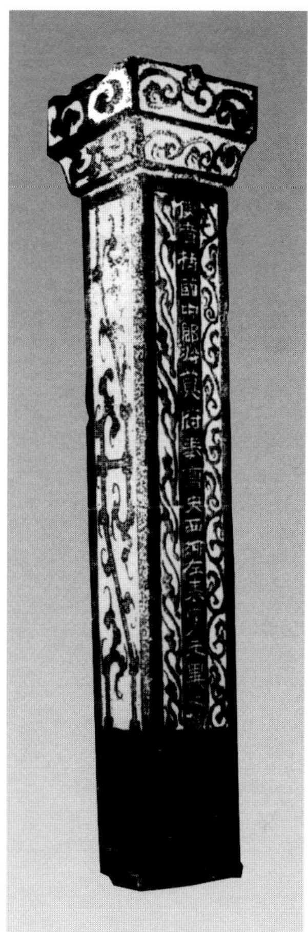

Fig. 3.24. Rubbing of pillar with dated inscription and designs of clouds and dragons. Eastern Han dynasty, A.D. 150. Found in 1924 in the tomb of Zuo Yuanyi at Mamaozhuang, Lishi. After Li Lin et al., *Shanbei*, fig. 673.

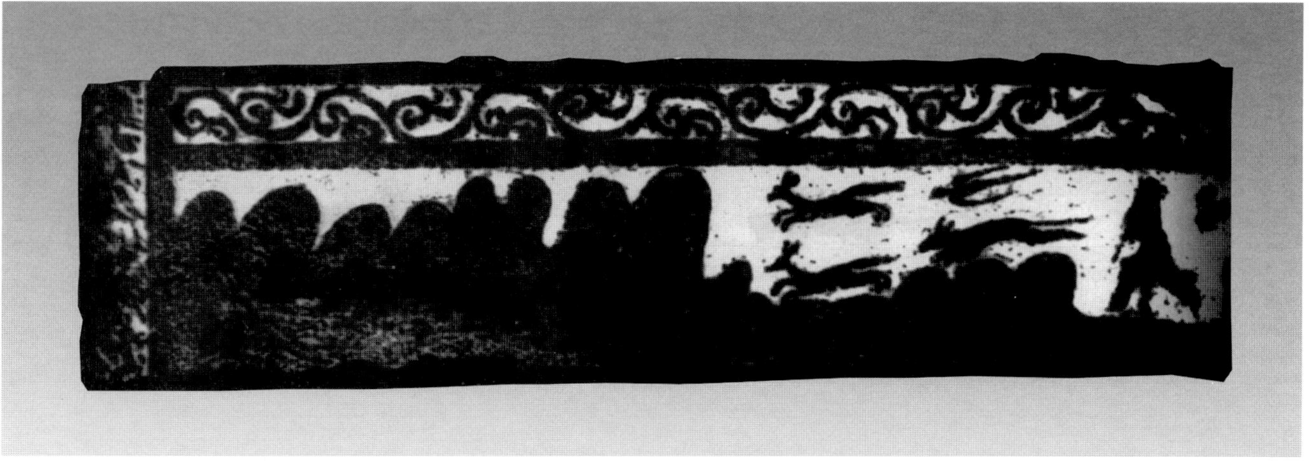

Fig. 3.23. Rubbing of hunting in the mountains. Late Eastern Han. Found at Mamaozhuang, Lishi. After Li Lin et al., *Shanbei*, fig. 664.

Catalogue Entries

Pre-Qin Period
(383–221 B.C.) and
Qin dynasty
(221–206 B.C.)

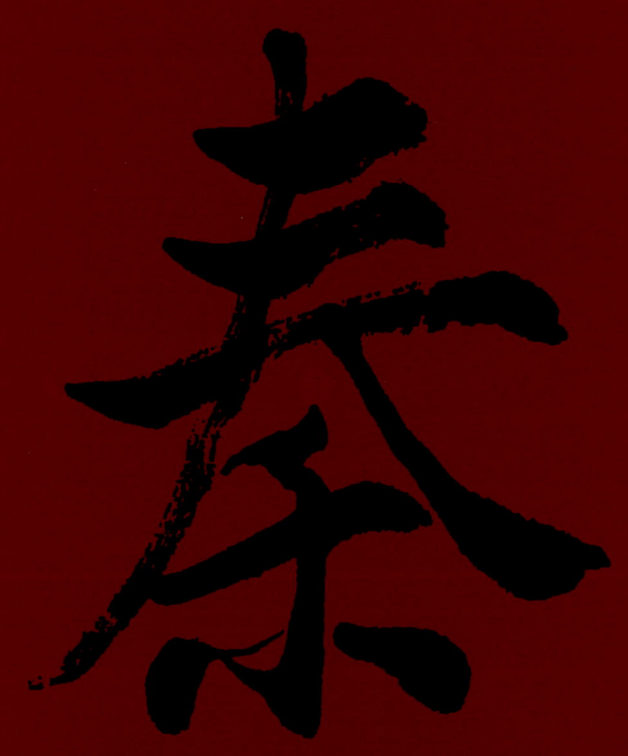

By the Eastern Zhou period, the imperial court was in decline, and the central regime lost control over the locally administered states. These states constantly battled over territory, property, and population. One of the states was the Qin, located in northwestern China. Although society experienced chaos caused by war, death, and political instability, it was also a time of cultural revival and ideological development. There was a strong desire to end the war and create peace among the common people. As the state that possessed the greatest economic and military power, the Qin state finally annexed the six states and unified China in 221 B.C. Qin Shihuang (259–210 B.C.) became the first emperor of China.

Under the government of Qin Shihuang, the country's economy, culture, and military brimmed with vigor. The emperor led a series of political, economic, and social reforms and promoted the evolution of the centrally controlled governing system. The country undertook large-scale projects, such as palaces and gardens, the tomb of the emperor, and the Great Wall, to indicate its economic prosperity and military strength. However, the Qin dynasty existed for only fifteen years. Cruel laws and conscripted labor caused great suffering among the people, and this social catastrophe led to the destruction of the Qin dynasty in 206 B.C.

I–3

In 1957, after a heavy wind swept across Nalingaotu village in Shenmu County, Shaanxi Province, the people of the village found gold and silver objects exposed in the sandy ground. This led to the discovery of a tomb with more than twenty objects, including gold and silver animals and ornaments. Due to the fine quality of these objects, scholars believe that the tomb occupant was a high-ranking official. Since excavated evidence is rare, this group of objects is noteworthy to help identify similar examples.

The Xiongnu, an ancient, nomadic people, lived on the vast Ordos plateau to the north of China during the Warring States period. The Xiongnu and the Chinese were sometimes at peace but also fought over territory and trading routes. The Great Wall, constructed as a military defense and running through present day Shenmu County, was built by the order of King Zhaoxiang (307–251 B.C.) of the Qin state during the third century B.C. This group of gold, silver and bronze objects represents the finest craftsmanship of artisans of the fourth to third century B.C.

Literature

Dai Yingxin and Sun Jiaxiang, "Shaanxi Shenmuxian chutu Xiongnu wenwu" (Xiongnu's cultural relics unearthed in Shenmu County, Shaanxi), *Wenwu*, no. 12 (1983): 23–30.

This gold figure is cast in the rounded form of a deer-like figure in openwork design. It has a huge hooked beak and extraordinary antlers outstretched in an arc to reveal abstract beast motifs. Decorated entirely with cloud patterns in low relief, the deer stands on a four-petal support; along its rim are twelve tiny holes. These distinguishing characteristics suggest that it would have been an ornament for a ceremonial headdress, perhaps used as a deity that predicted and directed the grazing, hunting, and prosperity of the Xiongnu people.

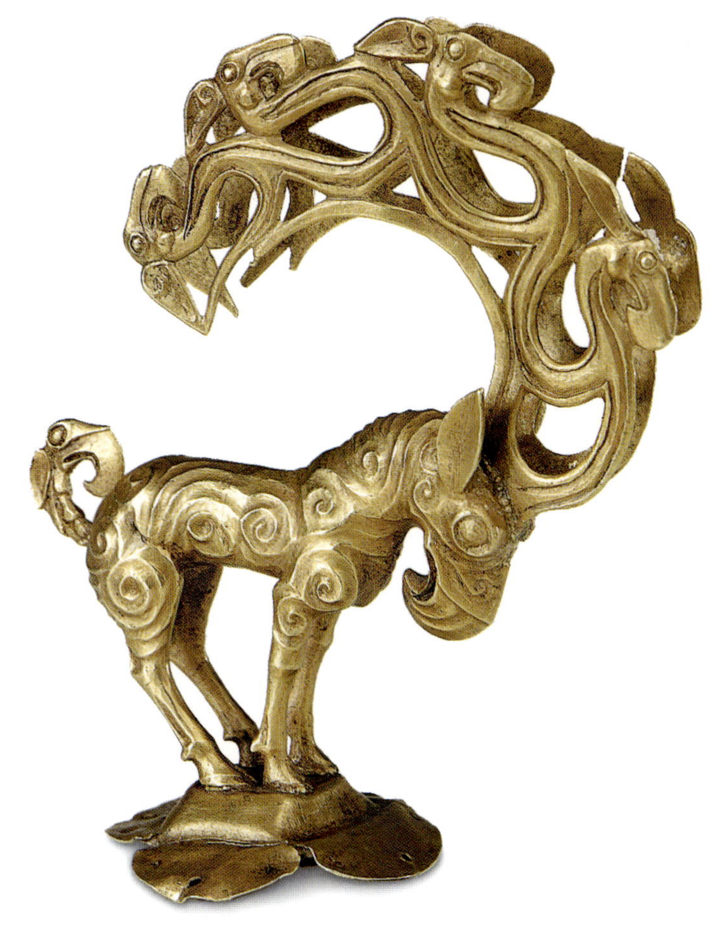

I MYTHICAL CREATURE
Warring States period, 4th–3rd century B.C.
Gold
H. 4 3/4 in. (12 cm.); L. 4 3/8 in. (11 cm.)
Unearthed in 1957 at Nalingaotu in Shenmu County
Shaanxi History Museum

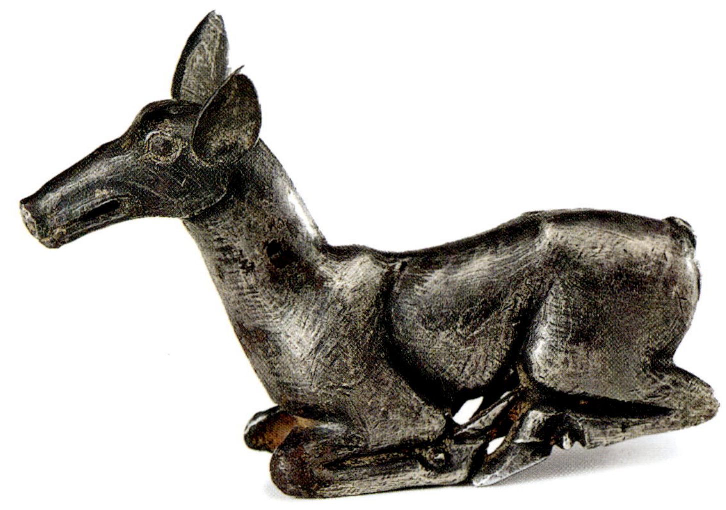

2 | DEER
Warring States period, 4th–3rd century B.C.
Silver
H. 2 3/4 in. (7 cm.); L. 3 4/8 in. (10 cm.)
Unearthed in 1957 at Nalingaotu in Shenmu County
Shaanxi History Museum

Among the objects found in Shenmu County are five silver deer, each cast in a rounded form and in a well-proportioned recumbent posture. The pose of this female deer is alert; its long, pointed ears stand erect and her hind legs lifted slightly, as if ready to jump up and run away.

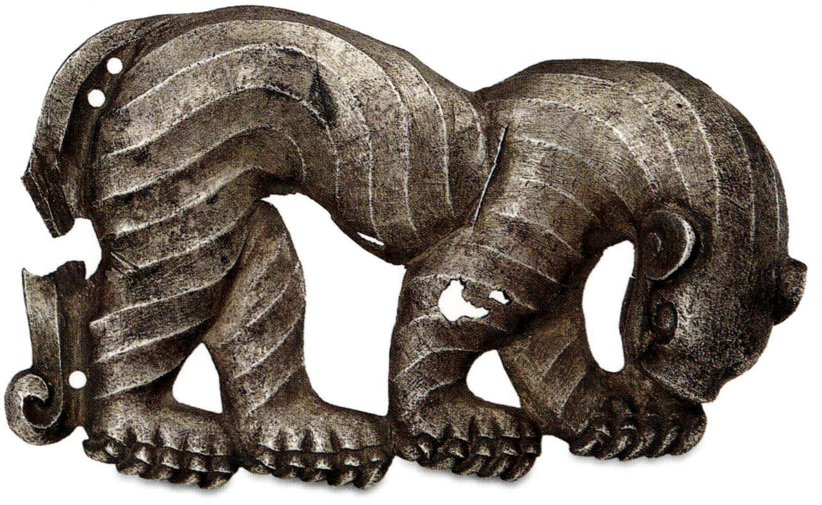

3 | TIGER

Warring States period, 4th–3rd century B.C.
Silver
H. 2 3/4 in. (7 cm.); L. 4 3/4 in. (12 cm.)
Unearthed in 1957 at Nalingaotu in Shenmu County
Shaanxi History Museum

This silver plaque shows a tiger in profile with lowered head, striding forward. The tiger's body is hollow, decorated with diagonal lines in low relief to indicate fur. Its limbs are heavy, and its curved claws are particularly sharp and strong.

A similar tiger, facing in the opposite direction, was found in the same tomb. These mirror images suggest that they were cast as a pair, one tiger playing with the other. It is amazing to see how the ancient Xiongnu were able to represent the most fierce beasts as lively animals in this witty manner.

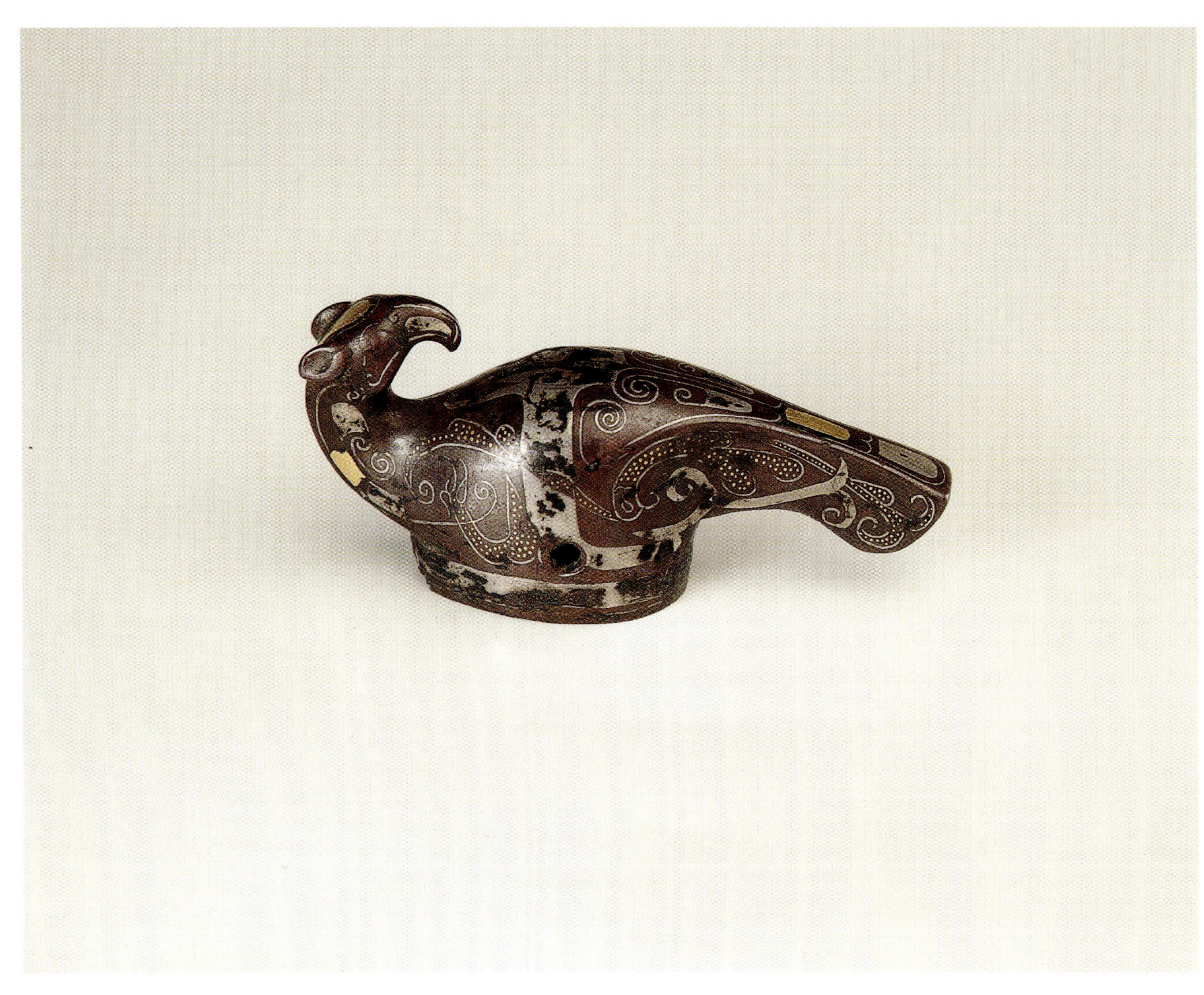

4 | STAFF HANDLE IN THE SHAPE OF A TURTLEDOVE
Warring States period, ca. 3rd century B.C.
Bronze with gold and silver inlay
H. 1 1/4 in. (3 cm.); L. 3 in. (7.8 cm.)
Excavated in Xi'an
Xi'an Institute of Cultural Relics and Archaeology

This bronze pommel is cast in the form of a turtledove, whose head turns back to its long, curved tail. It has large, rounded eyes and a sharply hooked beak indicating strength. Its surface is decorated with linear scrolls and stylized motifs inlaid in gold and silver. The base of the body is oval, with a hole on each side. This ornament was probably made to decorate the top of a cane.

From early literary accounts, we know that the turtledove had symbolic meaning in ancient China. The turtledove is described in an ancient text as a divine being that could not choke while eating. Because of this symbolic meaning, the Qin state would have be-stowed canes decorated with turtledove pommels on senior residents to wish them good health.

Literature

Wang Changqi, "Xi'an diqu faxian de Chunqiu Zhanguo Qin Han shiqi de qingtongqi" (Bronze objects found in the Xi'an area dating from the Spring and Autumn, Warring States to Qin and Han periods), *Kaogu yu wenwu*, no. 5 (1992): 1, 7.

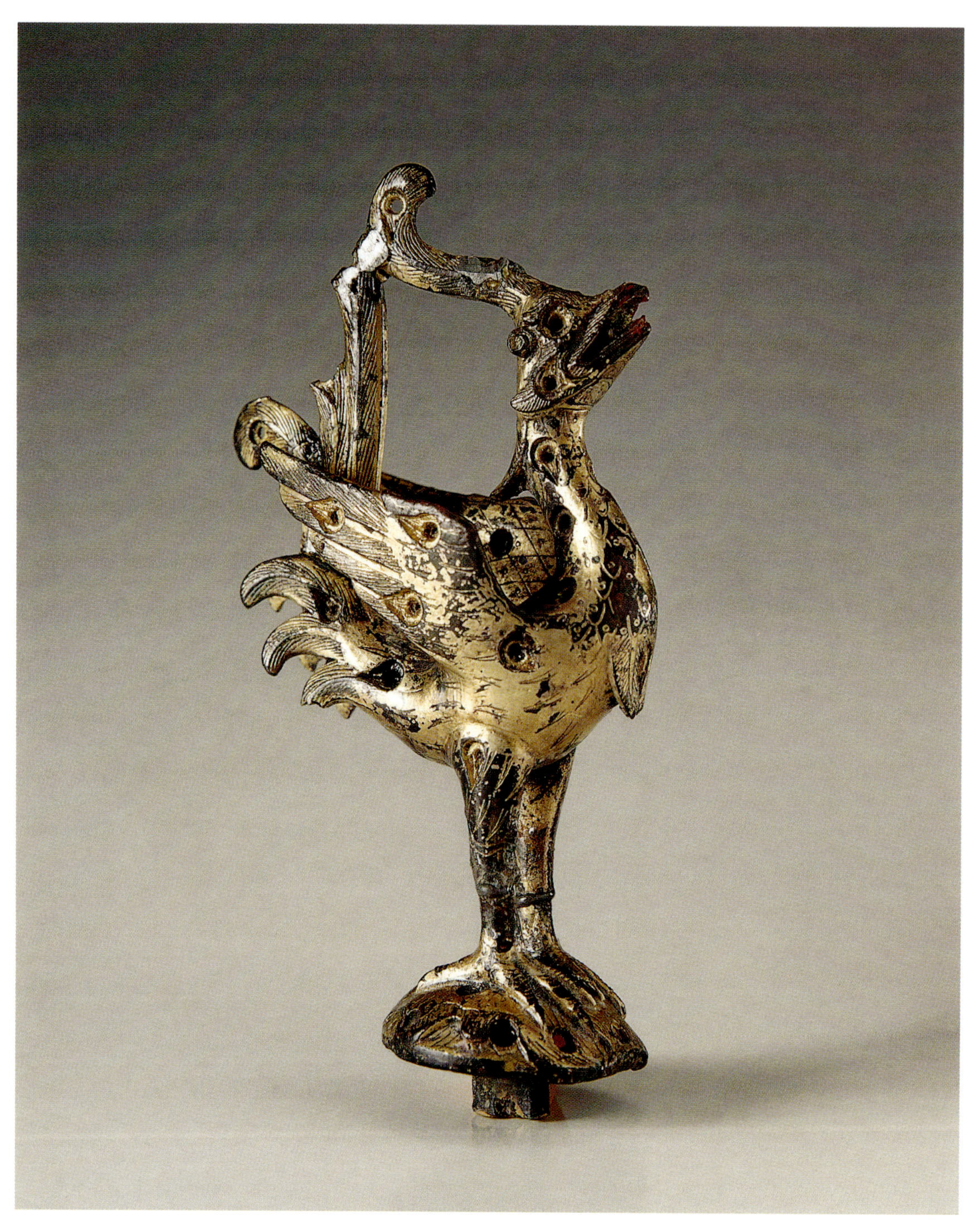

5 | PHOENIX (*feng*)
Qin dynasty (221–206 B.C.)
Gilded bronze
H. 4 1/8 in. (10.5 cm.)
Excavated in 1980 at Yueyucun, Lintong County
Lintong County Museum

Unearthed nearly one kilometer to the north of the Qin Shihuang mausoleum, this bronze bird stands in a graceful pose, head up, wings fully spread, and its lengthy comb flowing back to touch its tail. The surface of the bird is gilded and was originally inlaid with turquoise, which has been lost. The feathers are denoted by fine lines. The bird stands on a rounded support, pierced with tiny holes along the edge; there are similar holes also at the tips of the wings. With its elaborate shape and decoration, this bird might be an example of items from the Qin Shihuang mausoleum.

In ancient Chinese legend, the *feng* and *huang* are considered as a pair of noble, sacred birds. *Feng* indicates a male bird and *huang*, a female, and both symbolize beauty, fortune, and the love of a happy couple. These auspicious birds frequently have been cited in ancient Chinese literature. In the *Shi jing*, the first Chinese poetry anthology, completed in 600 B.C., it is recorded that "*feng* and *huang* are singing at the peak of the hill."

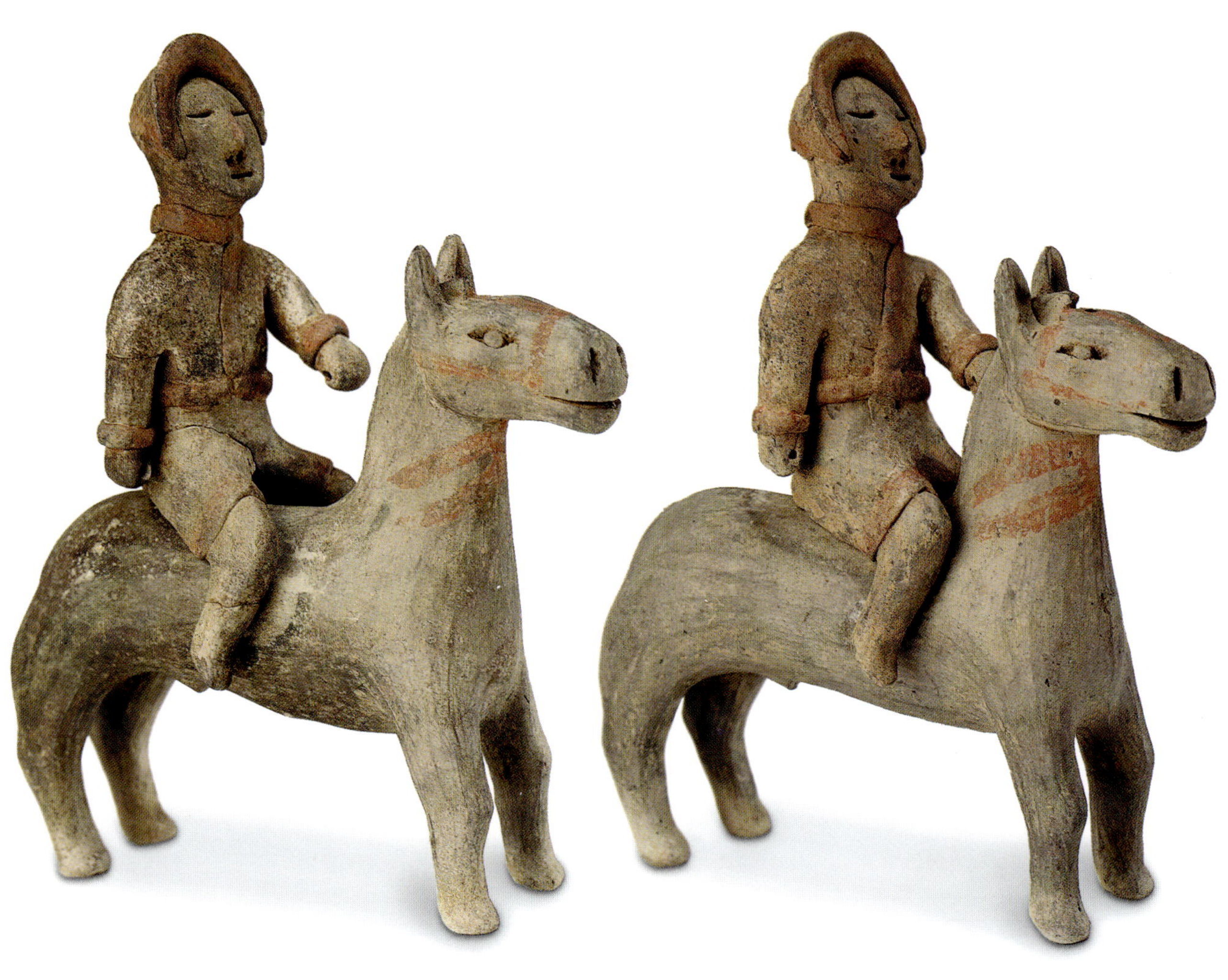

6 | PAIR OF CAVALRYMEN
Warring States period, ca. 3rd century B.C.
Earthenware with painted decoration
Left: H. 9 1/4 in. (23.5 cm.); L. 7 in. (18 cm.)
Right: H. 9 1/4 in. (23.5 cm.); L. 6 3/4 (17.5 cm.)
Unearthed in 1995 at Tomb no. 2, Steel Factory, Xianyang City
Xi'an Institute of Cultural Relics and Archaeology

In ancient times, northern China was covered with broad grasslands. As early as the Eastern Zhou period (771–256 B.C.), the nomadic people living in northwest China established military forces, particularly cavalry troops, that formed a considerable threat to the Chinese. In order to protect their territories, all the states in central China founded their own cavalries. From ancient literary records, we know that by the Spring and Autumn period (722–481 B.C.), the Qin had already built up their riding troops, and by the Warring States period (480–221 B.C.), this force had grown to be the most powerful one in central China.

Excavated in 1995 from a tomb of the Qin period in Xianyang, these two figures are known as the earliest pottery cavalrymen found in China. Molded by hand, each of the warriors is shown on the horseback, with his head up, revealing his disc-like, rounded face. Attired in military uniforms with a round skull cap with a wide brim, each rider has his left hand raised as if holding the reins, while the other hand hangs down as if grasping a horse whip. Their facial features, along with those of the horses, perhaps were carved with a bamboo stake. The horses have elongated bodies, and stand with their ears erect and alert, with holes pierced on their foreheads, perhaps for some sort of ornament. The unsophisticated craftsmanship gives them a primitive feeling.

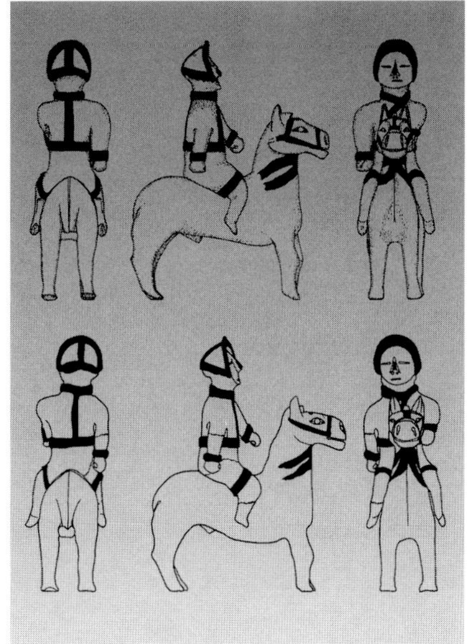

Fig. 4.1. Drawing of cavalrymen. Warring States period. After Xianyang Institute of Cultural Relics and Archaeology, fig. 9.

Literature

Xianyang Institute of Cultural Relics and Archaeology, "Xianyang Shiyou Gangguan Gangsheng Chang Qinmu qingli jianbao" (Brief report on the investigation of Qin tombs at Xianyang Petroleum Steel and Wires Plant), *Kaogu yu wenwu*, no. 5 (1996): 1–8.

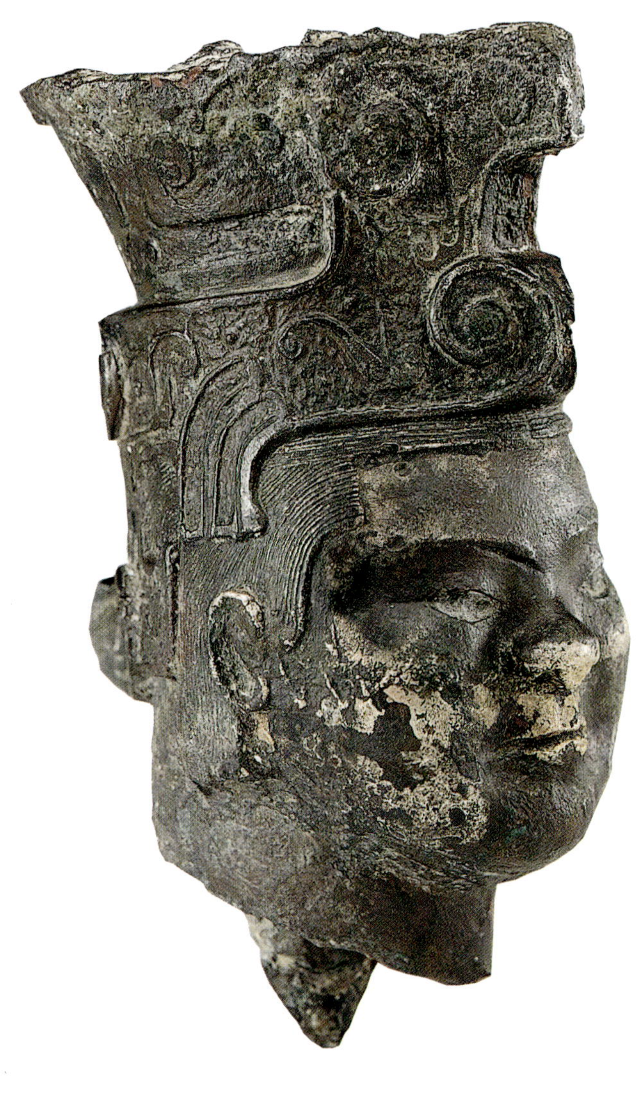

7 | HEAD OF WARRIOR
Qin dynasty (221–206 B.C.)
Bronze with traces of gilding
H. 4 3/8 in. (11 cm.); W. 3 in. (7.5 cm.)
Excavated in 1982 in Xianyang City
Xianyang Museum

This rare bronze head was excavated in 1982 at a workshop site, four kilometers west to the site of the Qin palace in Xianyang. This piece was part of a group of more than 320 bronze objects, including chariot harnesses, weapons, tools, and utensils of daily life. One of the most important finds was a bronze edict submitted by the First Emperor in 221 B.C., soon after the unification of the country. Because this dated edict was found with the head of a warrior, it allows us to date the head to the Qin dynasty.

This figure has a rounded face, wide-open eyes and a prominent nose. All facial details convey a sturdy essence. The hair is defined by parallel, flowing lines, and the head is crowned with an elaborate tall headdress, decorated with whirling scrolls and T-shaped motifs. Obviously, to cast this object required not only exquisite craftsmanship, but also highly developed casting technique.

Ancient texts reveal that after the Qin unified China, the government confiscated all bronze weapons throughout the country, melted them down, and cast the metal into twelve large bronze figures, each weighing about sixty tons, and placed them in front of the palace. Although none of these figures survive today, this bronze head exemplifies the outstanding casting technique and the artistic achievement of the Qin artisans.

Literature

Chen Guoying, "Qindu Xianyang kaogu gongzuo sanshi nian" (Thirty years of archaeology and research on the Qin capital Xianyang), *Kaogu yu wenwu*, nos. 5–6 (1988): 130–31.

The most celebrated archeological discovery of the Qin dynasty was the excavation of the pits of terracotta warriors and horses of the First Emperor of the Qin. Since 1976, archaeologists have unearthed an imposing underground army of pottery warriors, horses, and military chariots from three large-scale pits in the Qin Shihuang mausoleum, located at the foot of Lishan in Lintong County, Shaanxi Province. Pit no. 1 contained pottery infantrymen and military chariots; pit no. 2, contained pottery infantrymen, cavalrymen, and military chariots. A supreme command headquarters with chariots and security guards were found in pit no. 3. These life-sized pottery figures were originally painted in bright colors, which has since flaked off.

More than one hundred military chariots, six hundred pottery horses, seven thousand pottery warriors, and tens of thousands of bronze weapons were excavated from a total area of 20,000 square meters. When these figures were restored and placed in their original formation, it provided an imposing scene of the two-thousand-year-old burial army of the First Emperor of the Qin.

Literature

Archaeological Team of Qin Terracotta Figures, "Lintongxian qinyongkeng shijue diyihao jianbao" (Brief report no. 1 on the test excavation of the pit of Qin terracotta figures in Lintong County), *Wenwu*, no. 11 (1974): 1–18.

———, "Qinshihuangling dongce dierhao bingmayongkeng zuantan shijue jianbao" (Brief report on investigation and test excavation of terrcotta army in pit no. 2, east of the Qin Shihuang mausoleum), *Wenwu*, no. 5 (1978): 1–19.

———, Qinshihuangling dongce disanhao bingmayongkeng zuantan shijue jianbao" (Brief report on the investigation and test excavation of terrcotta army pit no. 3, east of the Qin Shihuang mausoleum), *Wenwu*, no. 12 (1979): 1–12.

Shaanxi Institute of Archaeology, *Qinshihuangling bingmayongkeng yihaokeng fajue baogao* (1974–1984) (Excavation report on pit no. 1 of terracotta army of the Qin Shihuang mausoleum [1974–1984]), Beijing: *Wenwu*, 1988.

Wang Xueli, *Qinyong zhuanti yanjiu* (Special studies on Qin terracotta figures), Xi'an: Sanqin Chubanshe, 1994.

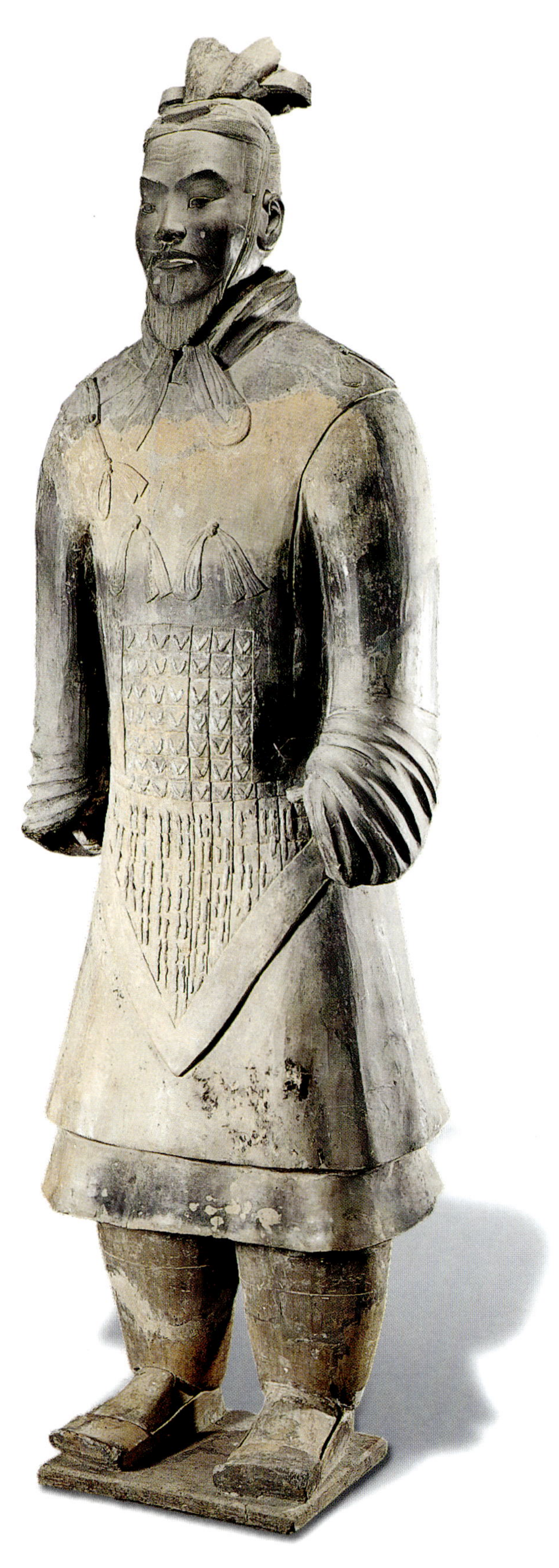

GENERAL
Qin dynasty (221–206 B.C.)
Terracotta
H. 77 1/4 in. (196 cm.)
Excavated in 1986 from pit no. 1 near the tomb of Qin Shihuang
Museum of the Qin Shihuang Terracotta Army

The pottery figures of generals are the highest ranking figures unearthed from the pits of terracotta warriors and horses at the Qin Shihuang mausoleum. Five out of the six generals discovered were standing on the commanding chariots, where a large bronze bell and a drum made of wood and leather were also found. In ancient China, troops were directed on the battlefield by bells and drums. Troops would advance when the drum was beaten and withdraw when the bell was rung. It was the general who controlled these instruments.

This pottery general stands lofty with magnificent height. He is dressed with a long, double-layer military uniform and an armor vest decorated with tassels. The military headdress that indicates his high position is in the form of a double-tailed bird, a symbol of bravery and skill on the battlefield. The expression of the general is solemn and stern, indicating his meditation upon military affairs.

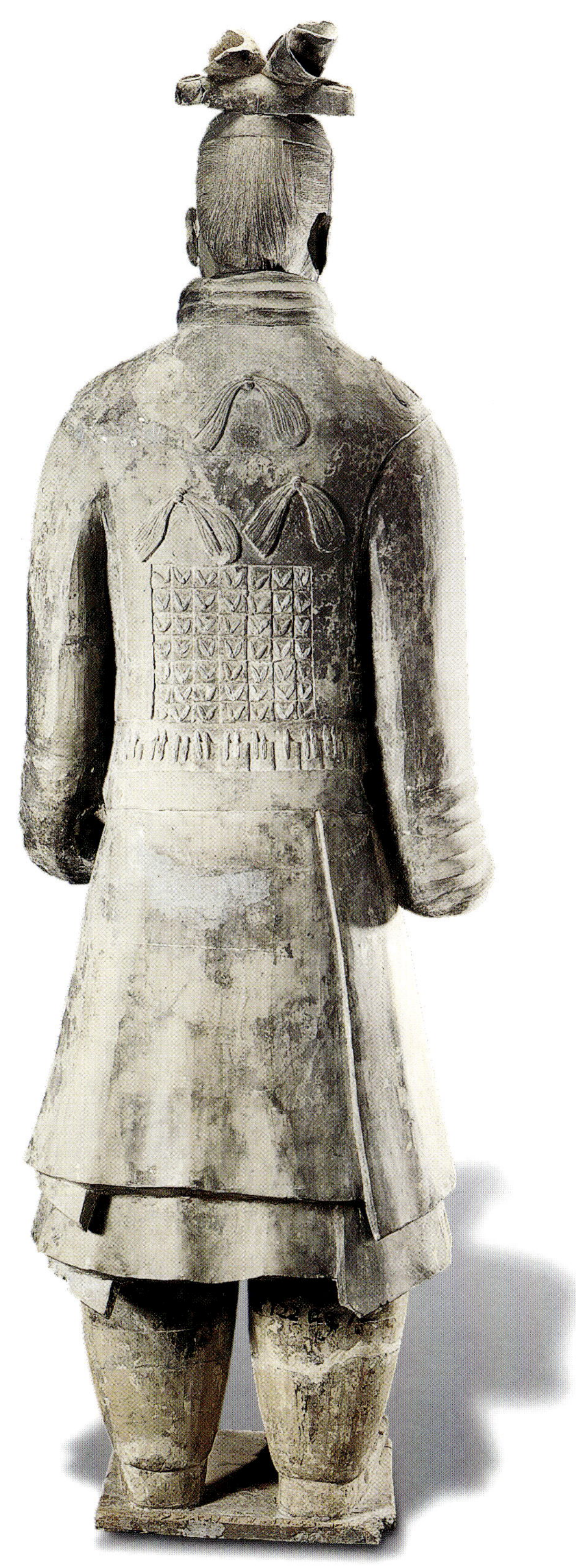

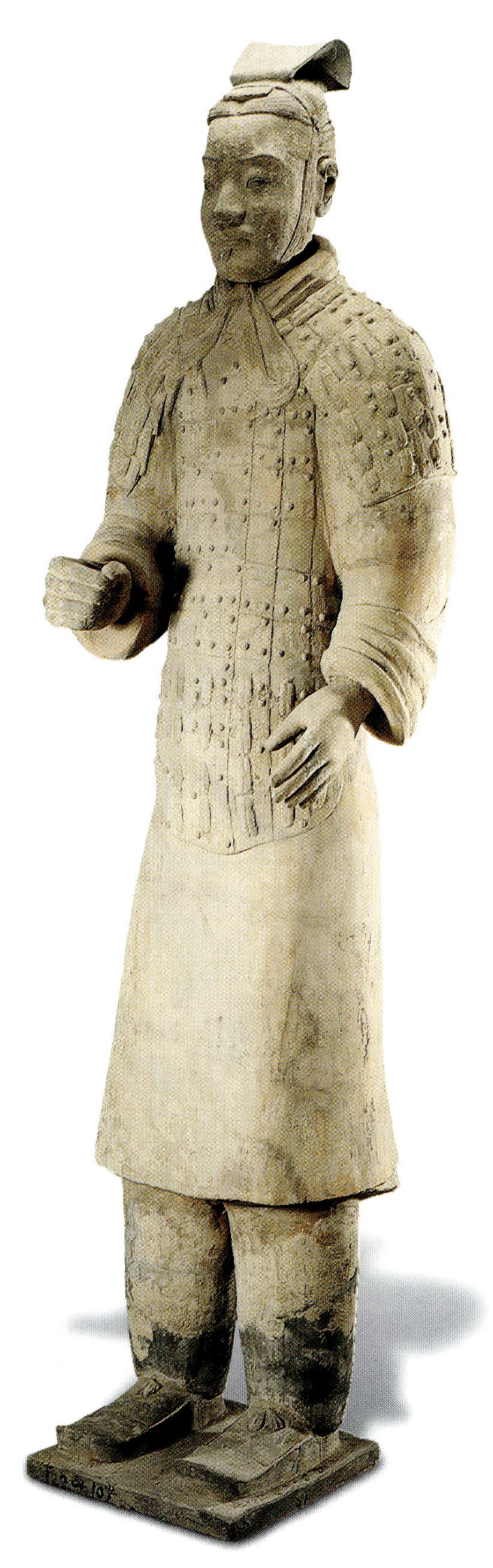

9 | MIDDLE-RANKING OFFICER
Qin dynasty (221–206 B.C.)
Terracotta
H. 74 3/4 in. (190 cm.)
Excavated in 1980 from pit no. 1 near the tomb of Qin Shihuang
Museum of the Qin Shihuang Terracotta Army

Of the pottery warriors unearthed at the Qin Shihuang mausoleum, the ranks of the army officers differ greatly. This figure represents an officer of middle rank wearing a long gown and armor, with his left hand posed as if holding a sword, and his right hand as if grasping a dagger-axe or spear.

The middle-ranking pottery officers unearthed from the Qin Shihuang mausoleum are attired in different styles of garments, some in Chinese, others in Central Asian type. Although these figures tend to show bravery, their facial expressions also reveal a variety of temperaments: competent, intelligent, pleasant, or laden with anxiety.

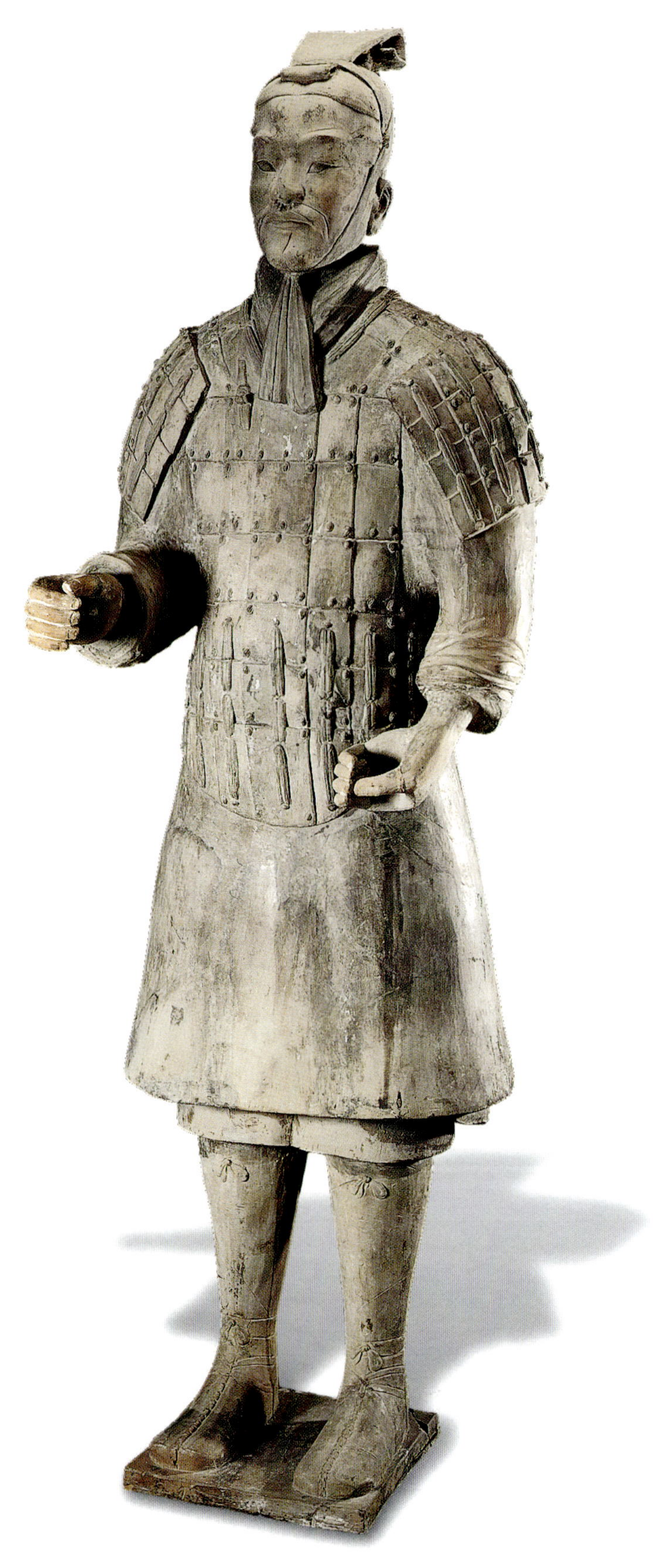

IO | LOWER-RANKING OFFICER
Qin dynasty (221–206 B.C.)
Terracotta
H. 75 1/4 in. (191 cm.)
Excavated in 1980 from pit no. 1 near the tomb of Qin Shihuang
Museum of the Qin Shihuang Terracotta Army

This figure represents one of the lower-rank officers unearthed at pit no. 1. These officers were found standing firmly and were depicted wearing military dress, armor, high headdresses, and holding weapons in their hands. Most of these officers were found in the front and the rear of the army formation.

The pottery army of the Qin Shiguang mausoleum is a valuable source of information on the military system of the Qin dynasty. The various headdresses, uniforms, and armor distinguish military ranks from one soldier to another. For instance, the headdress distinguishes officers from regular soldiers.

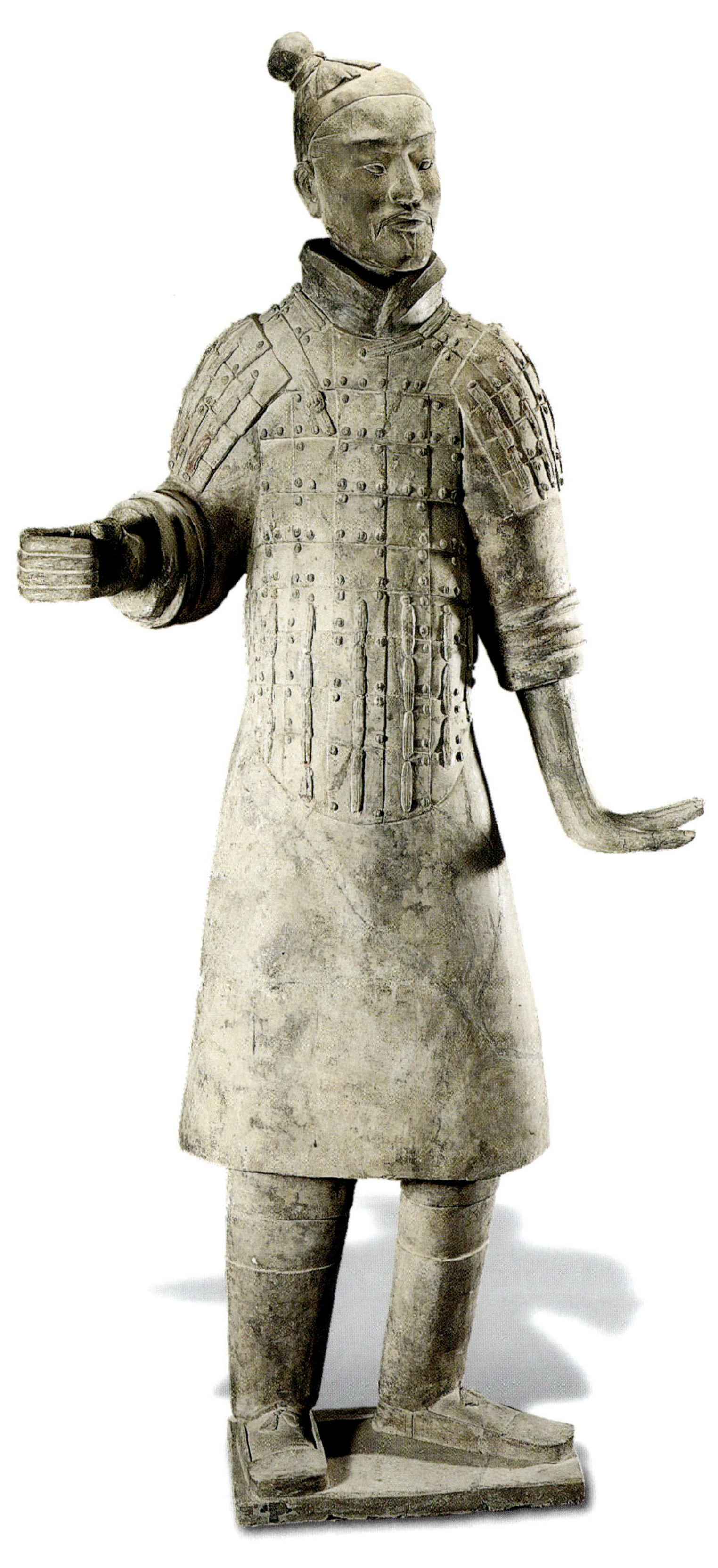

II-
I2

CHARIOT SOILDERS
H. 75 1/4 in. (191 cm.) H. 74 3/4 in. (190 cm.)
Qin dynasty (221–206 B.C.)
Terracotta
Excavated in 1977 from pit no. 2 near the tomb of Qin Shihuang
Museum of the Qin Shihuang Terracotta Army

Military chariots were manufactured in China as early as the Xia dynasty (ca. 2300–1600 B.C.) and Shang dynasty (1600–1050 B.C.). Early chariots often contained three soldiers: a driver in the middle and two charioteers, one on each side. From the pits of the terracotta army of Qin Shihuang, more than 130 wooden chariots, each manned by three pottery soldiers, were excavated.

Their unique hand positions indicate that these figures represent chariot soldiers, standing on either side of the chariot driver. Each figure is poised in a three-point balance. His one hand tends to hold a spear or an axe, the other probably rested on the railing of the chariot; his center of gravity is on his left or right foot. This natural posture, characteristic of a chariot soldier, differentiates these figures from other types of soldiers.

In ancient China, the national military force and economy was evaluated by the number of military chariots the state possessed. The *Shi ji* (Records of the grand historian) describes that the states of Qin, Zhao, and Chu all had more than one thousand military chariots, while the states of Yan and Wei had only about six hundred.

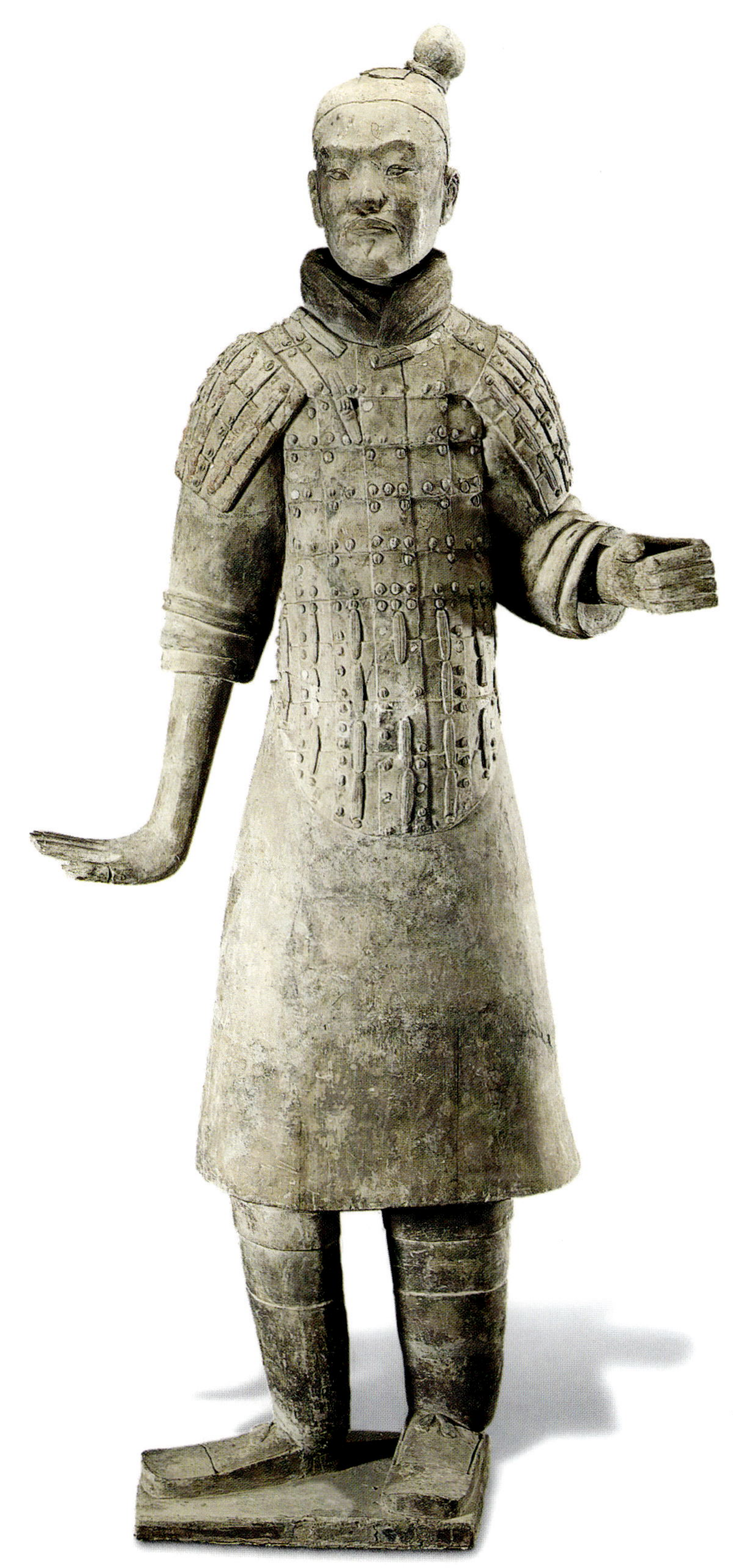

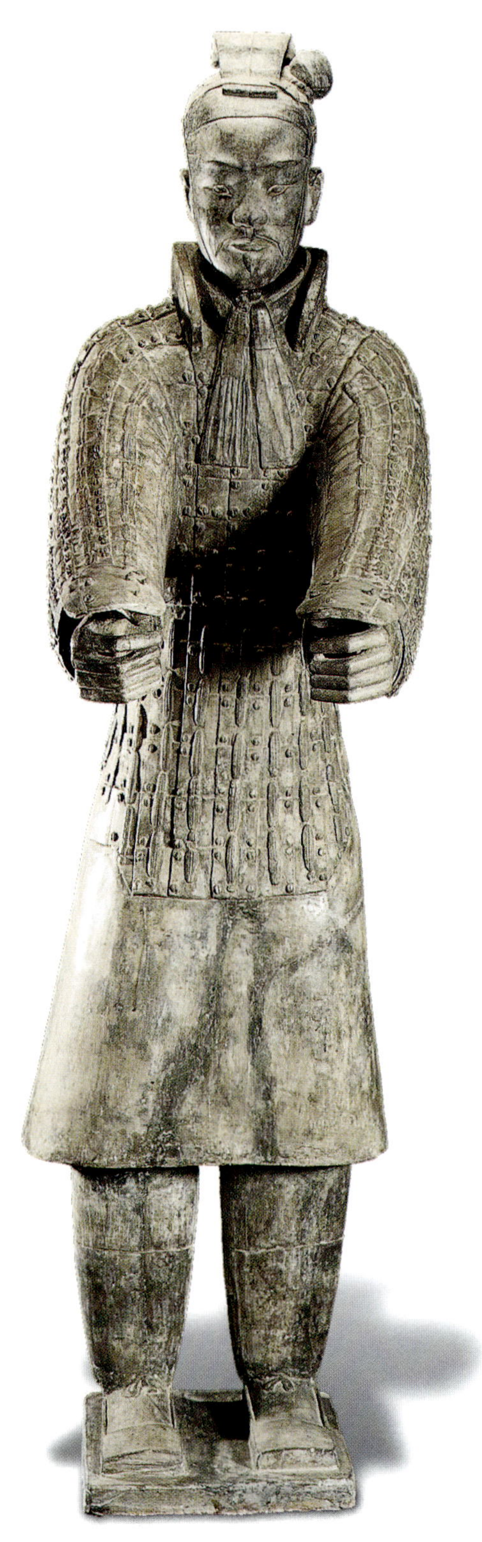

I3 | CHARIOTEER
Qin dynasty (221–206 B.C.)
Terracotta
H. 74 3/4 in. (190 cm.)
Excavated in 1977 from pit no. 2 near the tomb of Qin Shihuang
Shaanxi History Museum

In the Qin dynasty, the driver of a military chariot was highly honored and called *yushou*, which literally means "imperial charioteer." *Yushou* were found in all three pits of the terracotta army. Since a chariot driver could not defend himself when he was holding the reins, he needed a special uniform, including a long-sleeved armor to protect his arms and hands and a high collar to protect his neck.

Usually a figure with a high headdress can be identified as an officer, but all the chariot drivers excavated wear this type of headdress, while the two soldiers on either side do not. This suggests that the charioteer served as the head of riding and was responsible for commanding the chariot.

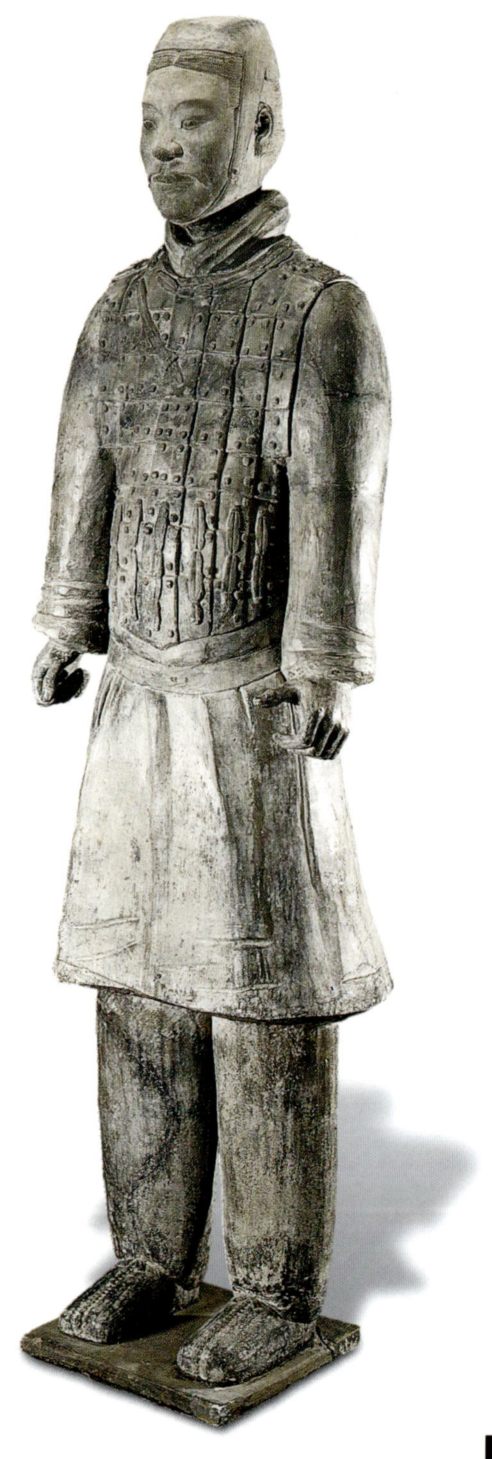

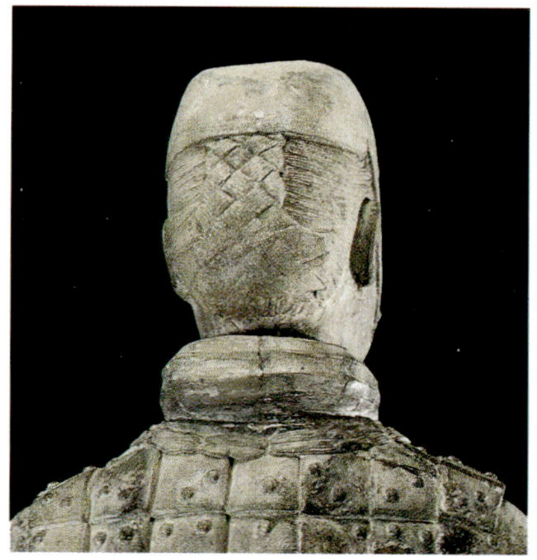

14-15 CAVALRYMAN AND HORSE

Qin dynasty (221–206 B.C.)

Terracotta

Cavalryman: H. 72 1/4 in. (184 cm.)

Horse: H. 68 1/2 in. (174 cm.); L. 83 7/8 in. (213 cm.)

Excavated in 1977 from pit no. 2 near the tomb of Qin Shihuang

Museum of the Qin Shihuang Terracotta Army

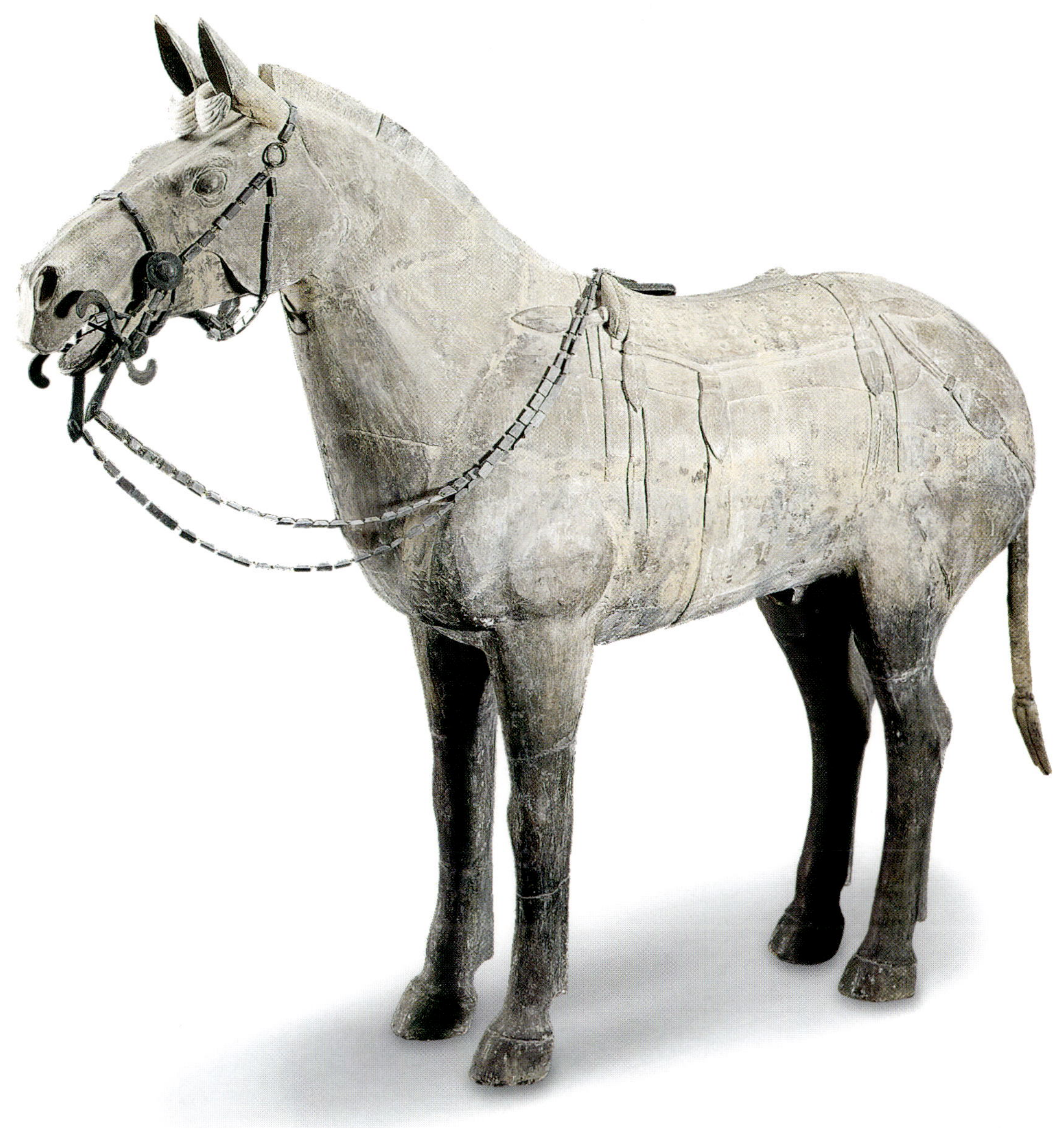

The cavalry was an important military force of the Qin dynasty. It was fast, nimble, and, especially in terms of defense, better able to adapt compared to the infantry and chariot forces. In pit no. 2, a total of 116 pottery cavalrymen were excavated. Compatible with fighting on horseback, these figures wear a skull cap, a short robe, tight long pants, short boots, an armor vest, and a leather belt.

This type of cavalryman tends to stand in front of his horse with one hand holding the reins, while the other grips a bow. His long, neatly groomed hair is parted in the center and the two tufts of his short beard show his dignity and strength.

The horse has a saddle that is decorated with nails, tassels, and belly bands. The head is executed in extremely fine detail, as seen in the tas-sels on its forehead, sharply erect ears, alert eyes, and the slightly opened mouth, all indicating the bravery and honesty of a military horse. The projecting bones on its head, abundant eyelashes, and wrinkles around its mouth were sensitively formed.

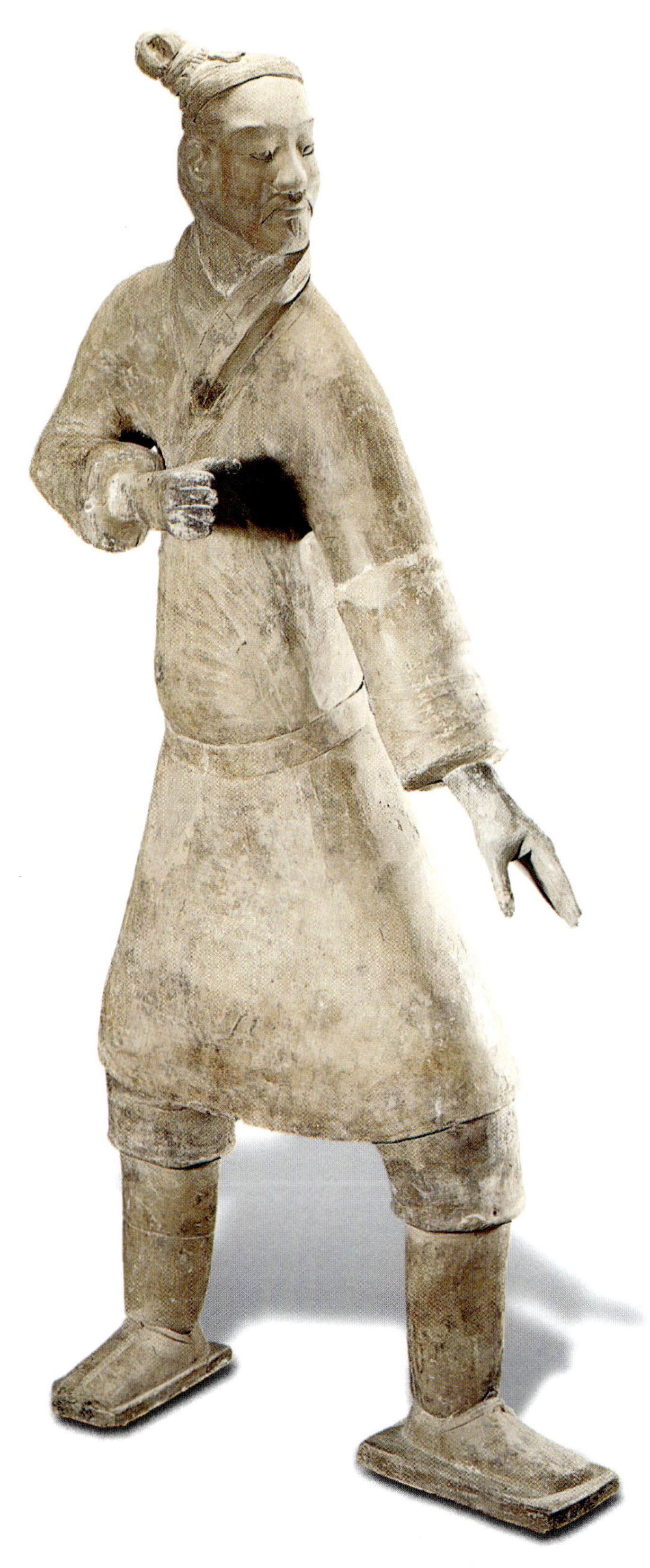

16 | STANDING ARCHER
Terracotta
Qin dynasty (221–206 B.C.)
H. 72 in. (183 cm.)
Excavated in 1980 from pit 2 near the tomb of Qin Shihuang
Museum of the Qin Shihuang Terracotta Army

The discovery of the burial army of the First Emperor demonstrates the use of archery in the Qin dynasty army. The pottery archers from pit no. 2 were found in a square battle formation with standing archers in the front row and kneeling archers in the rear. This figure depicts a tall and vigorous soldier, whose hand positions indicate that he is opening a bow with his left hand and holding an arrow in his right. Only a great sculptor would have been able to capture this dynamic and momentary pose.

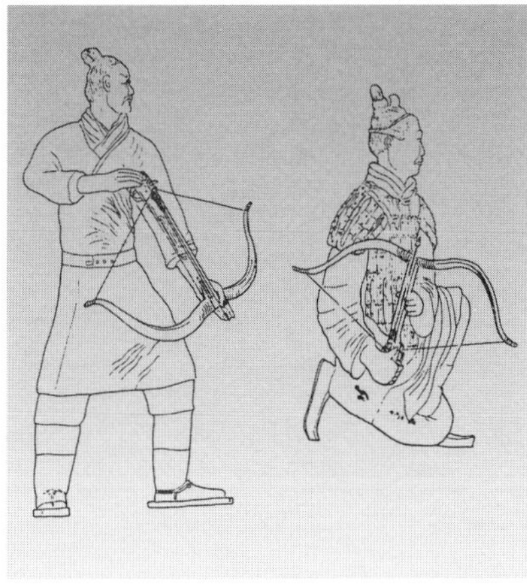

Fig. 4.2. Drawing of standing and kneeling archers with crossbows. After Wang Xueli, fig. I–10: 6, 7.

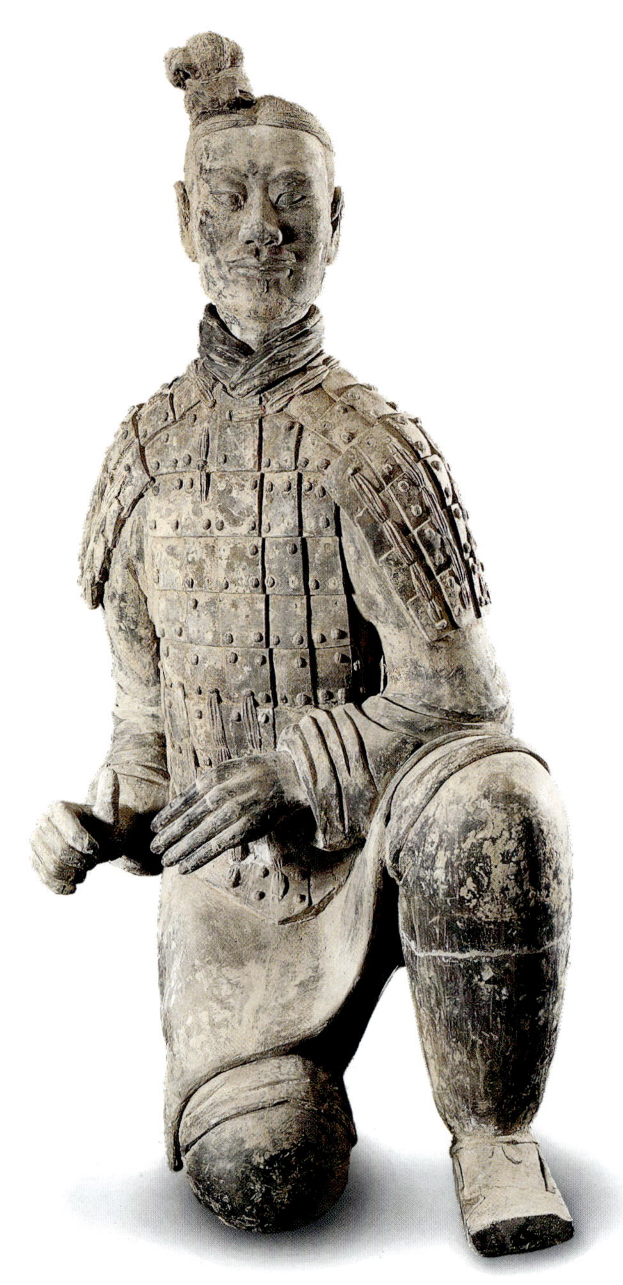

I7 | KNEELING ARCHER
Terracotta
Qin dynasty (221–206 B.C.)
H. 48 in. (122 cm.)
Excavated in 1977 from pit no. 2 near the tomb of Qin Shihuang
Museum of the Qin Shihuang Terracotta Army

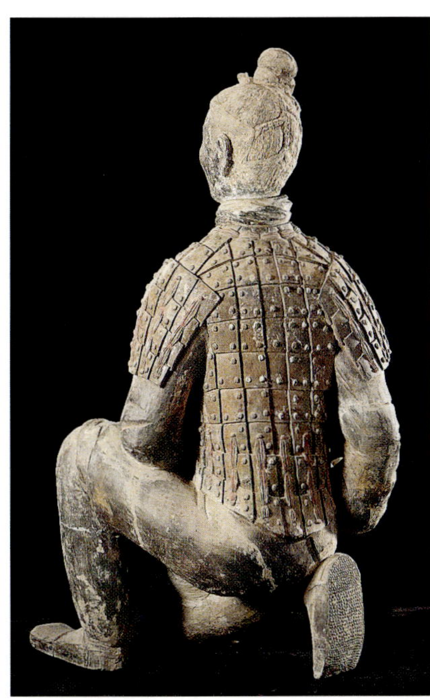

In ancient times, the maximum number of arrows that an archer could shoot at one time was three. To ensure a constant attack, archers were displayed in rows, one row firing arrows and the next preparing to shoot. This pottery soldier is posed with his hands to one the side of his body, as if he is loading an arrow onto a crossbow. His hair is pulled up and coiled into a bun, and his eyes stare ahead toward the target.

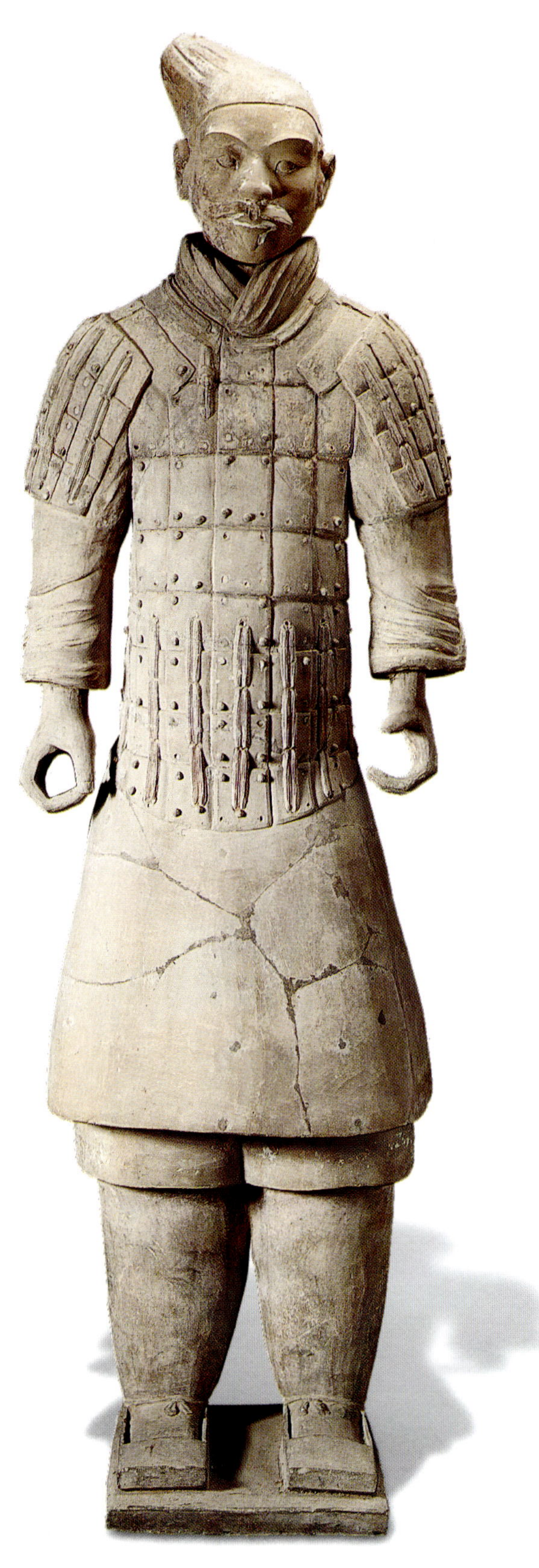

18 | WARRIOR WITH ARMOR
Terracotta
Qin dynasty (221–206 B.C.)
H. 73 5/8 in. (187 cm.)
Excavated from pit no. 1 near the tomb of Qin Shihuang
Museum of the Qin Shihuang Terracotta Army

This standing warrior is fully equipped with the Qin uniform of a long gown, armor, short pants, leg guards, and a headdress. From Qin pottery figures that have been excavated, we know that none of the soldiers wore a helmet with the armor; thus this is a characteristic uniform of the Qin army.

According to scholarly research, the physical characteristics of the pottery soldiers vary. These soldiers primarily resemble the people who presently live in central China, eastern Gansu, and Sichuan provinces.

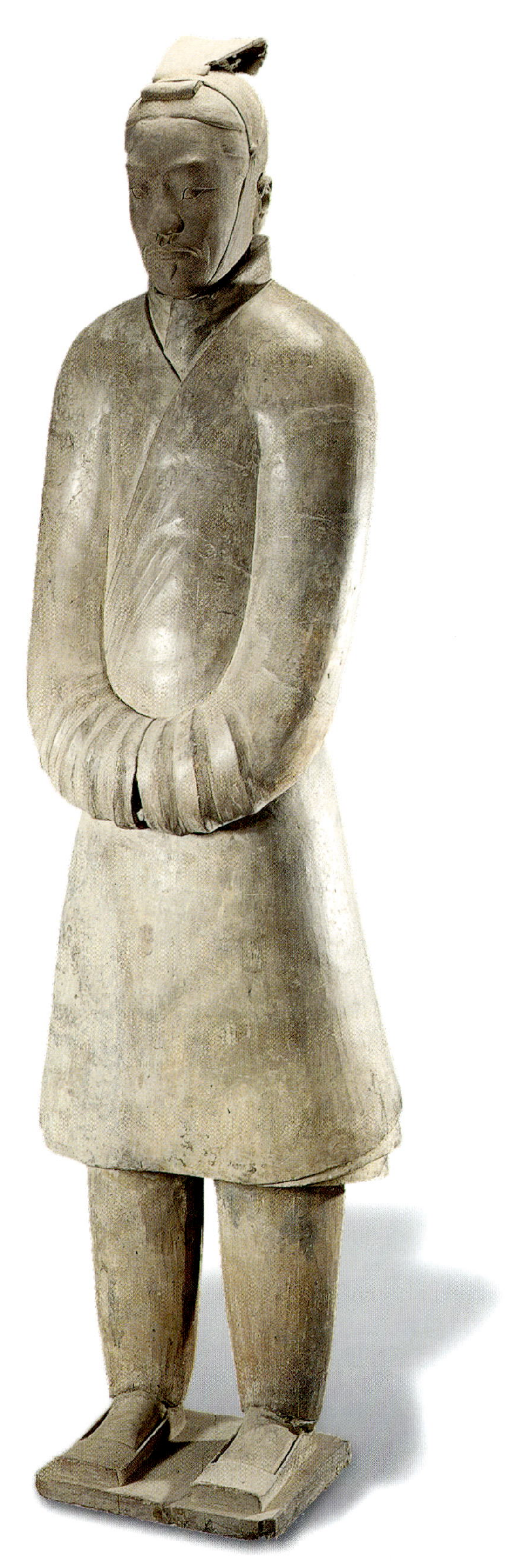

19 | STABLEMAN
Qin dynasty (221–206 B.C.)
Terracotta
H. 74 7/8 in. (190 cm.)
Excavated from the Qin Shihuang mausoleum
Shaanxi Institute of Archaeology

In the pit containing the horse stable, archaeologists unearthed several pottery stablemen, buried in the same pit with pottery horses or nearby. This figure depicts a stableman with his hands tucked into his long sleeves. His peaceful and relaxed countenance contrasts strongly with the alert and brave expressions of the warrior figures.

Since horses were primarily used for military purposes, the Qin government emphasized the management of horses to ensure sufficient logistics for military need. As indicated in ancient texts, the Qin court set up special administrative units in each locality to manage horse-related affairs.

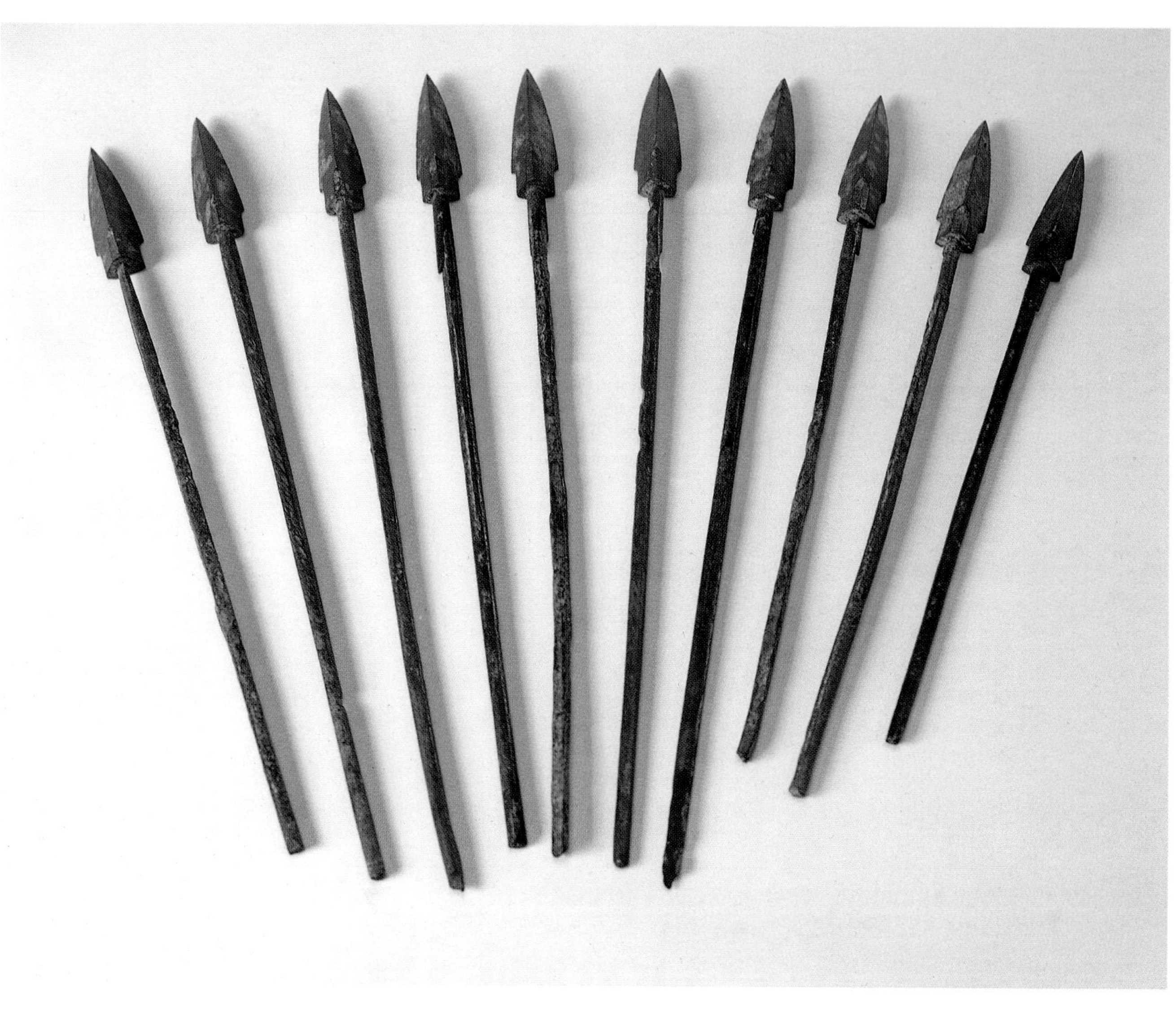

20 | TEN ARROWS (*zu*)
Qin dynasty (221–206 B.C.)
Bronze
L. 5 1/2–6 1/4 in. (14–16 cm.)
Unearthed from pit no. 1 near the tomb of Qin. Shihuang
Museum of the Qin Shihuang Terracotta Army

More than ten thousand genuine weapons, including seven thousand bronze arrows, were excavated with the pottery terracotta warriors and horses in pit no. 1. The arrowheads featured here exemplify this particular type of arrow used by the Qin soldiers. Each is constructed with two parts: a triangular head and a long arrow shaft. Some arrows are coated with chromium-oxide to prevent the metal from rusting.

The arrows were used for long-distance shooting. Neolithic arrows were made of stone, bone, and shell, and completed with the arrow shaft made of bamboo and wood. Not until the Xia dynasty, did the durable bronze arrows develop. Although bronze arrows were used extensively during the Shang and Zhou dynasties, earlier arrows made of other materials were still prevalent.

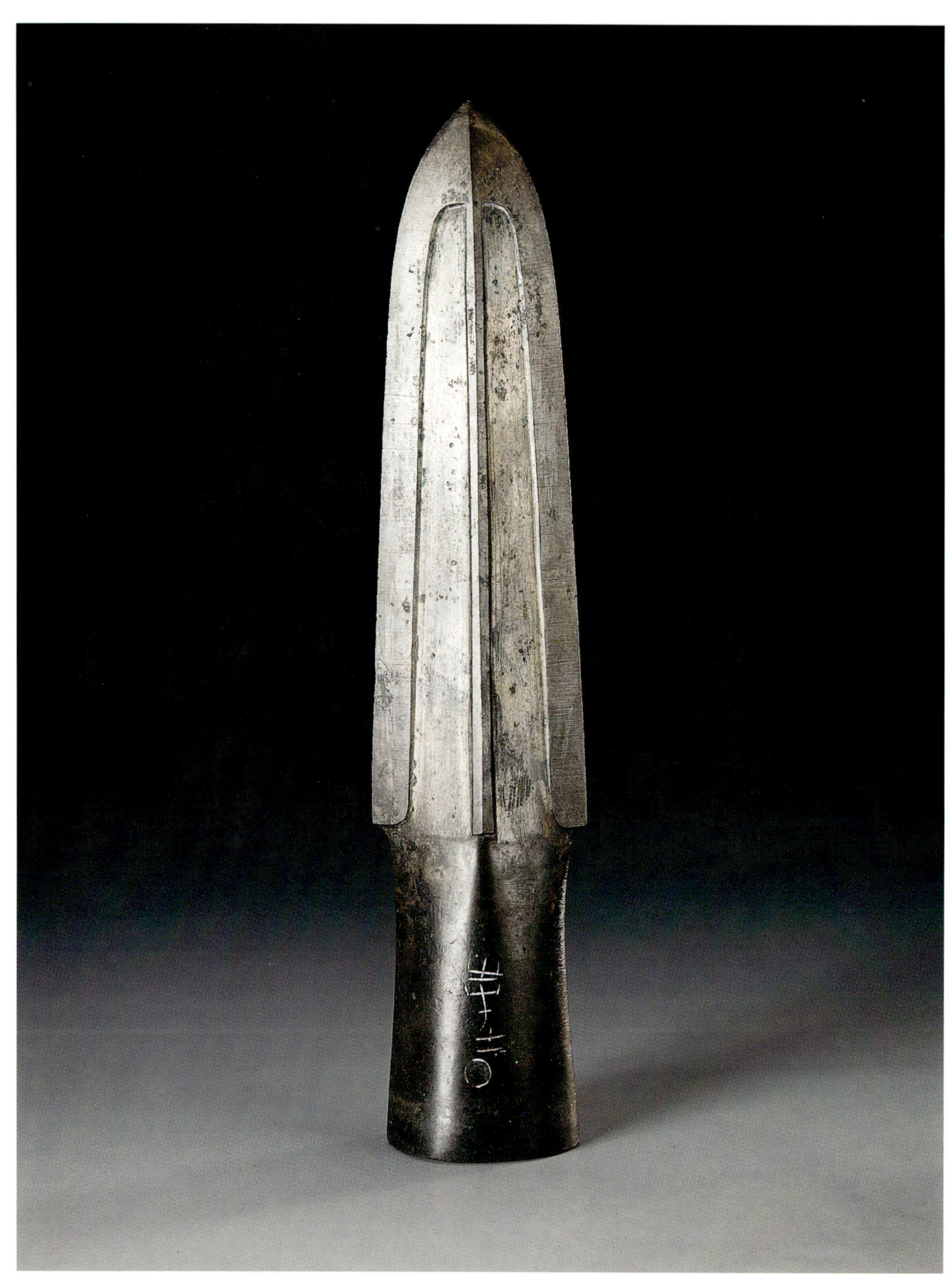

21 | SPEARHEAD (*mao*)
Qin dynasty (221–206 B.C.)
Bronze
L. 6 1/8 in. (15.7 cm.); W. 1 1/4 in. (3.2 cm.)
Unearthed in 1980 from pit no. 1 near the tomb of Qin Shihuang
Museum of the Qin Shihuang Terracotta Army

As one of the nine spearheads unearthed in pit no. 1, this spearhead is cast with double edges, which join at the tip to form a sharp point. Although the original wooden handle has decayed, the blade is as sharp as new. The characters *shi gong* are cast in the tubular tail of the spearhead. *Shi gong* is the name of a department of the Qin imperial court, mainly in charge of making weapons, chariot parts, and daily utensils for the imperial court. Of ten thousand weapons discovered from the three pits, only ten bronze weapons bear this inscription.

The spear, constructed with a spearhead and wooden shaft, was extensively used as an offensive weapon in ancient China. The history of the use of spears in China can be traced back to the Shang dynasty, as quantities of bronze spearheads have been unearthed from the Shang tombs in Anyang.

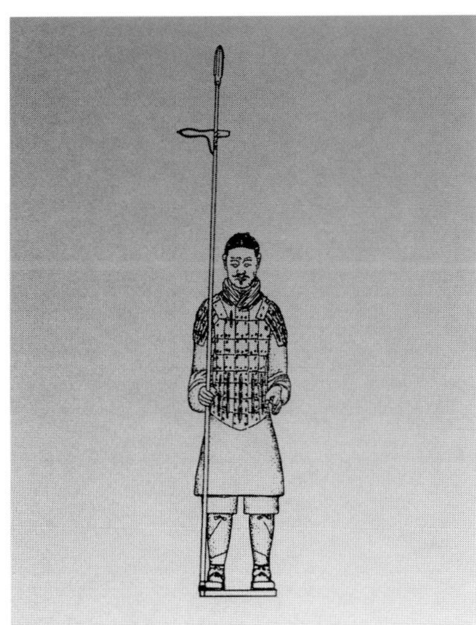

Fig. 4.3. Drawing of a soldier holding a spear. After Wang Xueli, fig. I–10:1.

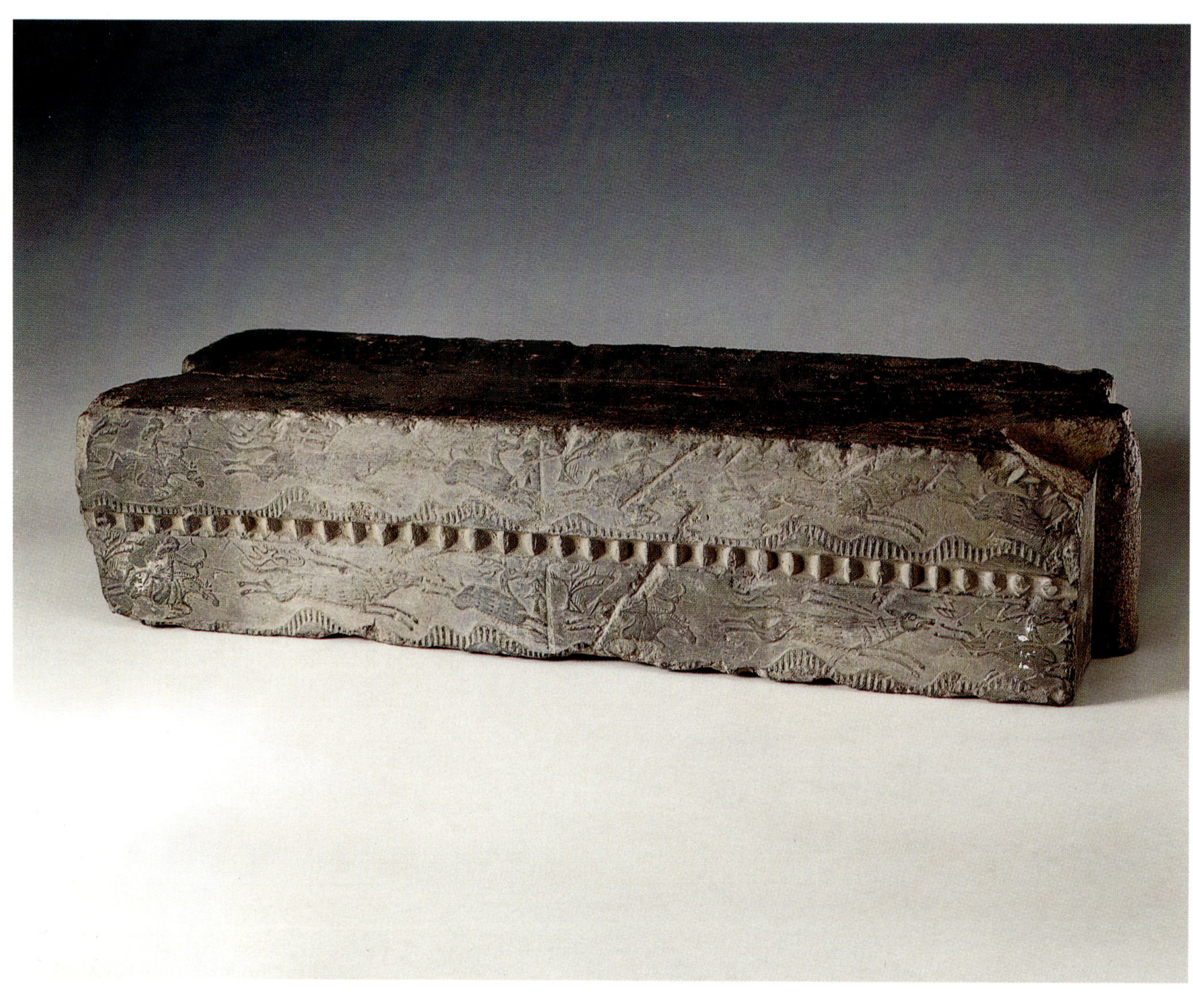

22 | BRICK WITH DESIGN OF HUNTING SCENE
Qin dynasty (221–206 B.C.)
Earthenware
H. 3 7/8 in. (9.8 cm.); L. 18 3/4 in. (47.5 cm.); W. 6 3/4 in. (17.2 cm.)
Unearthed in 1956 from Xi'an
Shaanxi History Museum

This brick depicts in a lively fashion an exciting hunting scene in two bands on the front. Each band depicts four wild beasts running at high speed in a hilly landscape, chased by two mounted warriors with bows and arrows. The sense of adventure and dynamic of the hunt is shown through the speed and rhythm of the images.

Molded with tenon and mortise, with one end raised and the other end sunk, this brick would join tightly with another brick. The high quality of this architectural segment shows that it was definitely used in the construction of one of the first-class palace buildings.

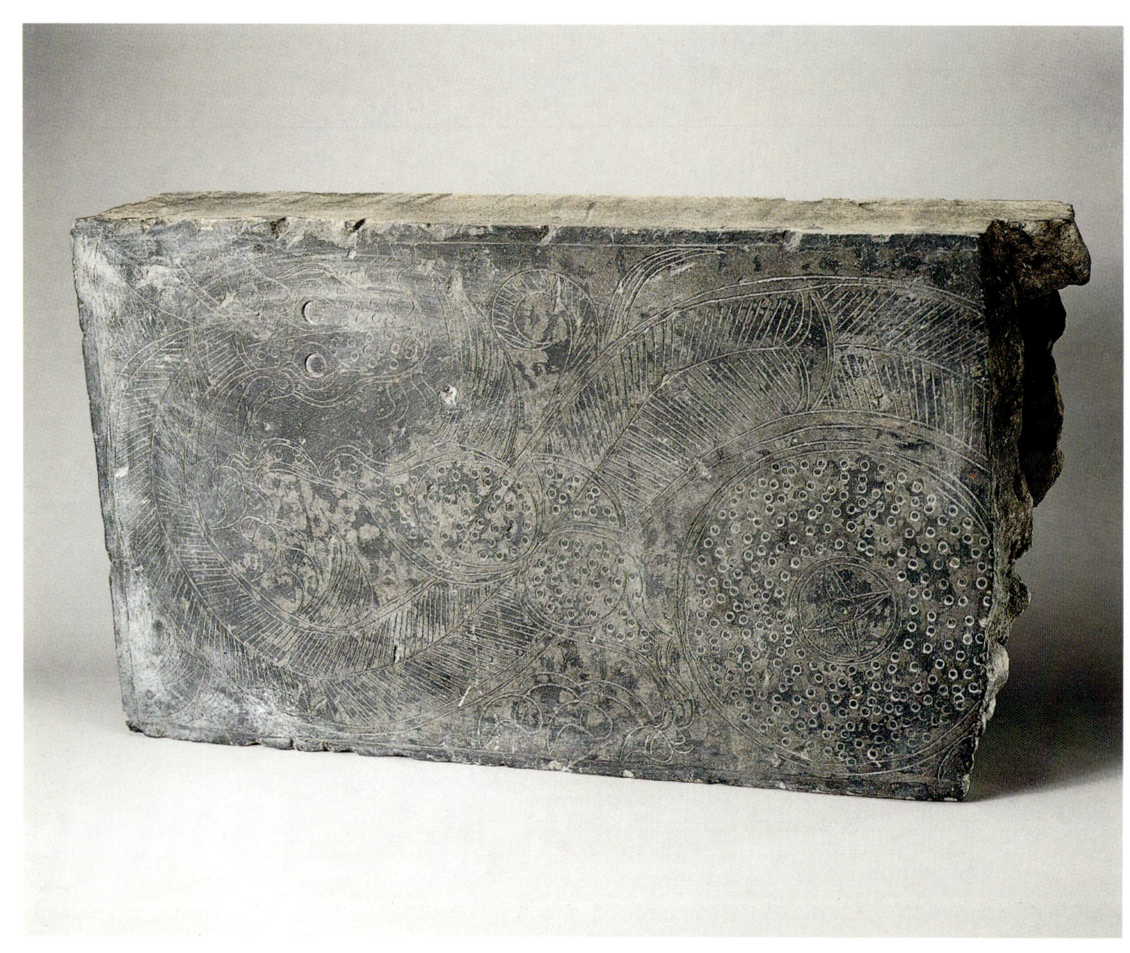

23 HOLLOW BRICK WITH DESIGNS OF DRAGON AND *BI* DISC
Qin dynasty (221–206 B.C.)
Earthenware
L. 28 3/8 in. (72 cm.); W. 15 3/8 in. (39 cm.); D. 6 3/4 in. (17 cm.)
Unearthed in 1974 from palace no. 1 at Xianyang palace, Xianyang City
Xianyang Museum

Xianyang was the capital city of the Qin dynasty after the unification of the country. It is recorded that many palaces on a large and splendid scale were spread across the eight hundred square kilometers of Xianyang City. Unfortunately, at the end of the Qin dynasty these palaces were burned in a fire that lasted for three months.

In the 1970s, archaeologists excavated a large-scale Qin palace complex, built between the later Warring States period and the Qin dynasty. This palace was decorated with colored frescoes on white walls and constructed of hollow bricks with molded designs. This brick, found in a segment of a stairway, was molded with incised designs of a twisted dragon among clouds, along with a *bi* disc decorated with a grain pattern in the center. A complete brick with an identical design was excavated in palace hall no. 2 and shows an image of a phoenix on the other side of the disc (fig. 4.4).

The dragon was an imaginary and mysterious being created by the ancient Chinese based on the characteristics of tigers, snakes, fish, and birds. It later became a symbol for the Chinese nation and also of the ancient emperors. Archaeological finds have proved that dragon worship has a six-thousand-year history in China. Dating to the Yangshao culture, the earliest dragon design inlaid with shells, was found in Puyang City in Henan Province.

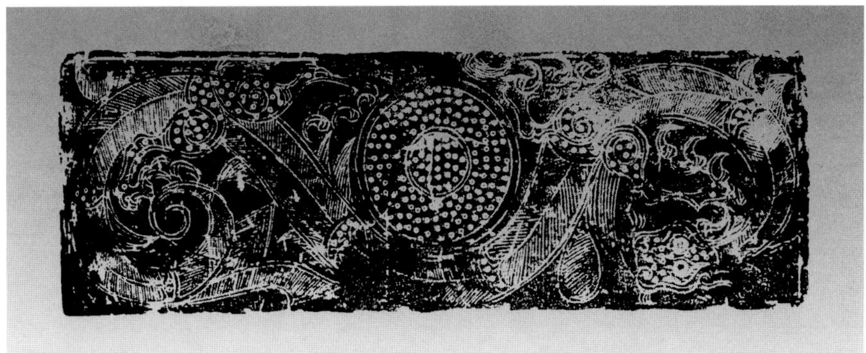

Fig. 4.4. Rubbing of brick with design of dragon, phoenix and disc. L. 46 in. (1.17 m.); W. 15 3/8 in. (39 cm.). Qin dynasty. Excavated from palace hall no. 2 in Xianyang. After Archaeological Station of the Qin Capital Xianyang, fig. 2.

Literature

Archaeological Station of the Qin Capital Xianyang, "Qindu Xianyang diyihao gongdian jianzhu yizhi jianbao" (Brief report on the remains of palace hall no. 1 in the Qin capital of Xianyang), *Wenwu*, no. 11 (1976): 12–24.

———, "Qin Xianyanggong Dierhao jianzhu yizhi fajue jianbao" (Brief report on the excavation of remains of palace hall no. 2 in the Qin Xianyang), *Kaogu yu wenwu*, no. 4 (1986): 13.

Western Han Dynasty (206 B.C.–A.D. 9) and Wang Mang Interregnum (A.D. 9–23)

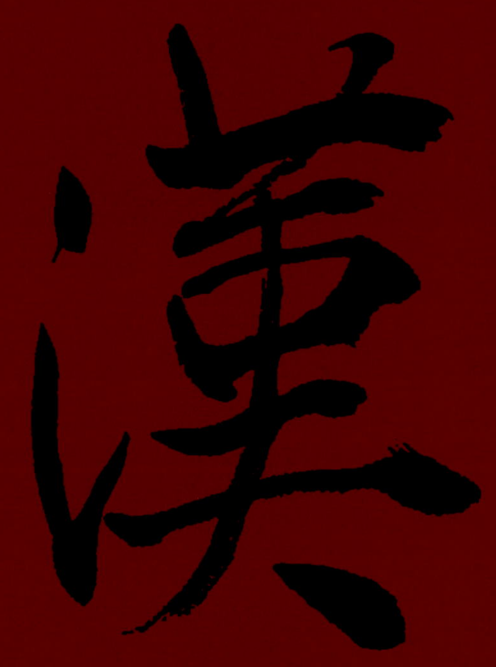

The Han dynasty was founded by Liu Bang, of peasant origins from Pei County (modern Xuzhou, Jiangsu Province), who would be known as Emperor Gao (Gaozu or Gaodi).[1] Previously Liu had ordered the Qin magistrate of Pei to be put to death, and he took the title of Lord of Pei (Pei Gong). Liu Bang later became the Prince of Han, the area located in the southwest part of Shaanxi from which the Han dynasty took its name. In 206 B.C. Liu crushed the Qin army in the Wei River valley, and in 202, he eliminated Xiang Yu, who was once his ally but became his rival. Liu proclaimed himself emperor and established his capital at Chang'an, southeast of the former capital of the Qin dynasty at Xianyang and northwest of modern Xi'an.[2] Although a new dynasty had been founded and those who had been oppressed by former rulers had to be pacified, many policies which were part of the Legalist statecraft advocated by the Qin were continued by the Han: organization of a strong military to facilitate a centralized government; transferals of population for political and economic reasons; and conscription labor for completion of public works projects. These Legalist ideas, together with "Han" Confucianism and Huang-Lao philosophy, which sometimes is considered a branch of Daoism, underlay the concept of imperial authority as part of the universal order during the Western Han dynasty.

In addition to maintaining order in the newly founded empire, the early Han emperors negotiated a balance of power with the peoples living at the borders of the empire. At the end of the Qin dynasty, the nomad tribes had formed a confederation led by the Xiongnu in the steppe zone. The early Han emperors first advocated a policy of appeasement (*he qin*), but during the reign of Emperor Wu (Wudi), this policy was abandoned and campaigns were launched against the Xiongnu from 127–119 B.C.

Wudi's desire to expand the influence of the Han empire in Asia was complemented by his personal quest to extend his life or to avoid death altogether. The intense pursuit of this goal was documented by the historian Sima Qian in his chronicle of the reign of Emperor Wu in *Shi ji*. Wu's expeditions to locate places where immortality was possible and his talent searches for *fangshi* magicians who could concoct the elixirs thought to confer immortality were supplemented by his elaborate construction projects at and around the capital. A striking example of Emperor Wu's belief in the possibility of the interpenetration of the spiritual world with the mundane world and the use of art to promote this interaction was recorded by Sima Qian:[3]

Shaoweng then said to the emperor [Wu], "I perceive that Your Majesty wishes to commune with the spirits. But unless your palaces and robes are patterned after the shapes of the spirits, they will not consent to come to you." He fashioned five chariots, symbolizing the five elements (*wu xing*) and painted with cloud designs, and on the days when each of the five elements was in ascendancy, he would mount the appropriate chariot and ride about, driving away evil demons. He also directed the emperor to build the Palace of Sweet Springs (Ganquan), in which was a terrace chamber painted with pictures of Heaven, Earth, the Great Unity (Taiyi), and all the other gods and spirits. Here Shaoweng set forth sacrificial vessels in an effort to summon the spirits of Heaven.

The power of the emperors of the Liu family waned after the reign of Wudi, and the close of the Western Han dynasty was marked by social and economic change. This opened the way for Wang Mang, who usurped the throne and ruled from A.D. 9–23. He established his capital at Chang'an and called his dynasty the Xin (New) dynasty, also known as the Wang Mang Interregnum.

<table>
<tr><td>

24-25

</td><td>

PAIR OF WARRIORS WITH SHIELDS
H. 19 3/8 in. (49 cm.)
H. 18 1/2 in. (47 cm.)

</td></tr>
<tr><td>

26-27

</td><td>

CAVALRY: HORSES AND RIDERS
H. 26 3/4 in. (68 cm.)
H. 22 3/4 in. (58 cm.)

</td></tr>
</table>

Western Han dynasty (206 B.C.–A.D. 9)
Earthenware with painted decoration
Excavated in 1965 from pits near two tombs at Yangjiawan, Xianyang City
Xianyang Museum

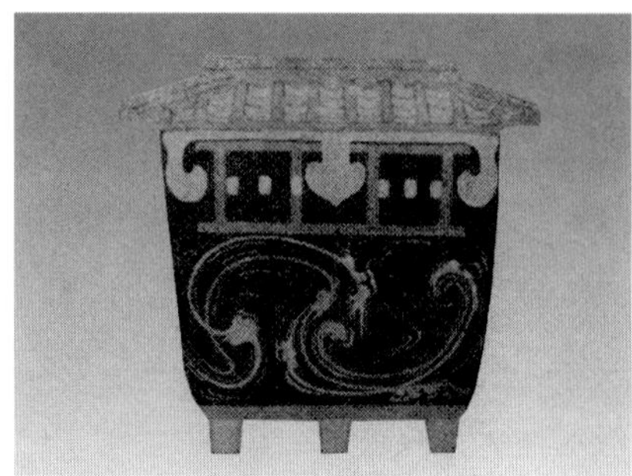

Fig. 5.1. Painted earthenware granary. After *Wenwu* 10 (1977), 10–21, fig. 5.

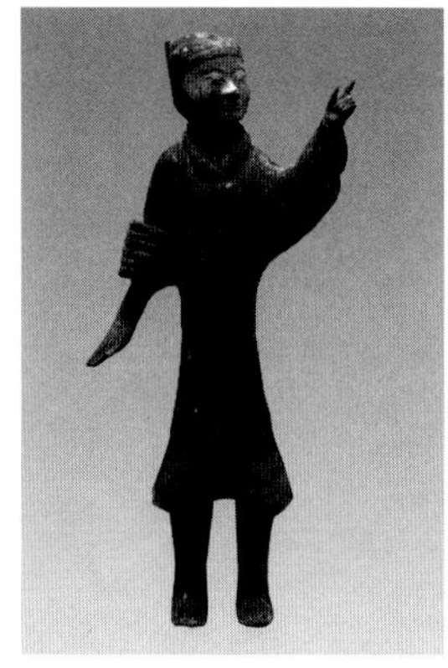

Fig 5.2. Painted earthenware commander of the army. Photo Courtesy Shaanxi Museums and Archaeological Data Bureau.

These figures were excavated from the satellite pits of two tombs (M4 and M5) at Yangjiawan in the northern outskirts of Xianyang City. The occupants of the tombs are believed to be Zhou Bo (d. 169 B.C.) and his adopted son, Zhou Yafu (d. 143), whose tombs are attached to Changling, the mausoleum of Emperor Gaozu (r. 206–195). The men had held positions in the military with the title of commander in chief and as prime ministers.

The figures in these pits are primarily military men, but musicians, dancers, and attendants were also found at the site. The group may have represented the funeral cortege appropriate for men who had served in the military and at court. The pits held cavalry (583 figures), infantry (about two thousand) and some chariot fittings. Artifacts of lacquer, ceramic, and iron were also found. The ceramic vessels are exquisitely painted with cloud designs which imitate lacquer decor (fig. 5.1).

The members of the infantry stand silently with their feet solidly planted, one arm held close to the side, which perhaps once grasped a weapon. The other arm is positioned in front of the torso, protecting the body with a shield. The heads are squarely set on the shoulders, and the eyes stare directly ahead. The figures range in size from 17 1/2 to 19 5/16 inches with the exception of a single figure, the commander, who stands taller than all other figures at a height of 22 inches. (fig. 5.2). In addition to being tallest, he also is differentiated by his more open pose, with his hand raised in a gesture of power and his more elaborate and carefully rendered armor and boots. The decor on his boots is like the cloud patterns on the ceramic vessels mentioned above.

The anatomy of the figures has been ignored, but the clothing has been depicted with enough detail so that the robe, belt, trousers, and stockings can be differentiated. The vivid use of color is also integral in distinguishing the elements of the warrior's wardrobe. One of the figures wears armor; he also has a quiver painted on his back. In general these figures have smooth surfaces, quite unlike the detailed surface modeling of the soldiers from the pits alongside the tomb of the first Emperor of Qin.

The horses of the cavalry stand at attention, but one lifts its head to whinny. The men are seated on the horses with their legs tensed, as if they could suddenly spur the beasts forward. Their faces, however, have frozen expressions, and their bodies have no anatomical detail. In fact, the technique of manufacture may have had an impact on the style. The legs and lower garments of the men have simply been molded onto the side of the horse. The head and torso of the soldiers were made separately and then placed on the back of each horse. This technique allowed less breakage of the fragile legs of the man, but any sense of the organic structure of the body is lost. The horse trappings are indicated only by painted details, and overall it is the addition of paint to the surface that makes the images convincing.

Literature

He Hannan, "Shaanxi sheng Xianyang shi Yangjiawan chutu da pi Xi Han caihui taoyong" (A large quantity of Western Han dynasty painted earthenware funerary sculptures excavated at Yangjiawan, Xianyang municipality, Shaanxi Province), *Wenwu* 3 (1966): 1–5.

"Xianyang Yangjiawan Han mu fajue jianbao" (Brief report on the excavation of the Han dynasty tomb at Yangjiawan, Xianyang), *Wenwu* 10 (1977): 10–21.

The Quest for Eternity: Chinese Ceramic Sculpture from the People's Republic of China. Los Angeles: Los Angeles County Museum, 1987, pls. 11–15.

Wong, Grace, ed. *Treasures from the Han.* Singapore: The Empress Place, Singapore, 1990, pp. 39–40.

Yang Bingli, "Qiantan Xianyang Yangjiawan Han bing ma yong yishu tezheng" (Brief discussion of the artistic features of the earthenware warriors and horses from Yangjiawan, Xianyang), *Wenbo* 2 (1993): 18–27.

Tomb Treasures from China: The Buried Art of Ancient Xi'an. San Francisco and Fort Worth: The Asian Art Museum of San Francisco and Kimbell Art Museum, 1994, pls. 11–15.

Yang Bingli, Shi Yukuo, and Liu Xiaohua, "Xianyang Yangjiawan Han mu bing yong fushi tantao" (Discussion of the military uniforms of the Han dynasty earthenware tomb figures at Yangjiawan, Xianyang), *Wenbo* 6 (1996): 38–45.

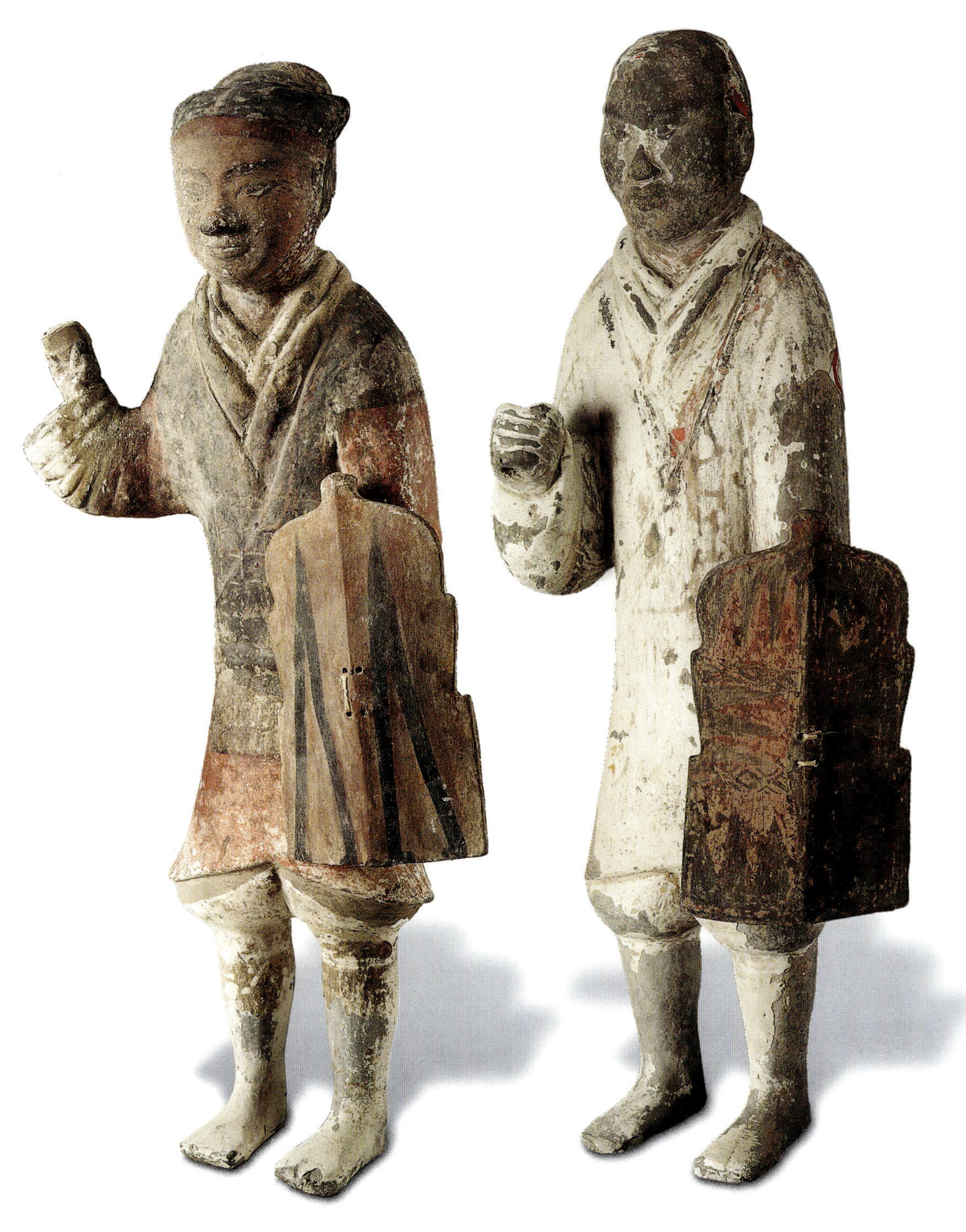

24-25 | PAIR OF WARRIORS WITH SHIELDS

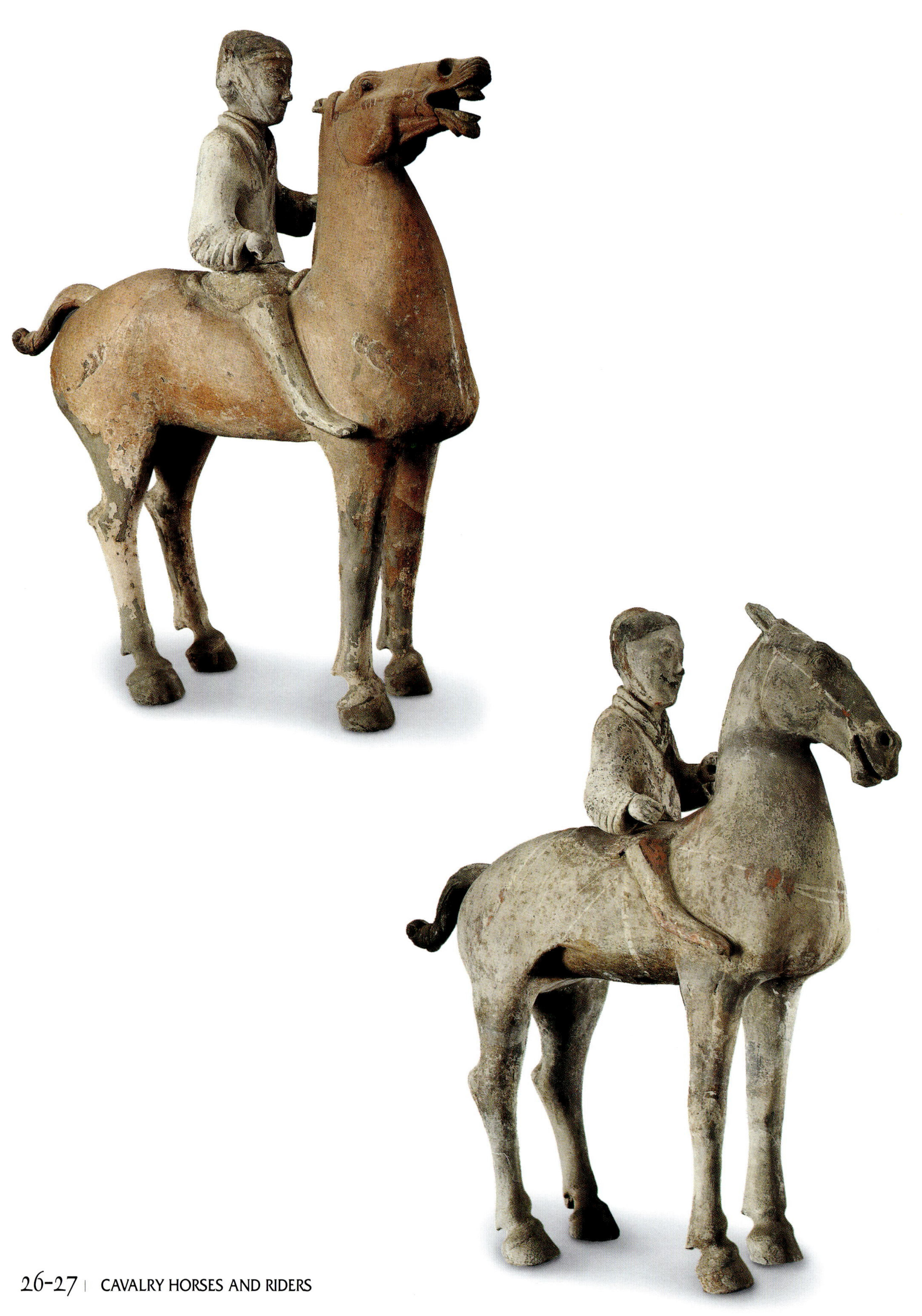

26-27 | CAVALRY HORSES AND RIDERS

In terms of pose, size, and the rendering of the drapery, these figures are very similar to figures unearthed at several other early Western Han dynasty sites, including Renjiapo and Lintong.[4] Their style is characteristic of the period of Emperor Wen (r. 180–157 B.C.). The bodies of the figurines are represented as tall, thin cylinders, and it would be difficult to distinguish the sex of the figure, if not for the coiffure. The figure on the right has her hands covered by the long sleeves of her gown, and her hair is parted in the center. The female on the left has her fists clenched and placed one on top of the other, because she once held a thin, upright object in front of her. Her hair is pulled back in a chignon. Little detail has been used in constructing the garments, only a slightly modeled neckline and incised lines to suggest folds in the fabric. The faces of these figures, however, have been given the most attention. They are not portraitlike faces; rather the sculptors have successfully humanized them by rendering them as if caught in a silent moment of thought. They do not have the broad smiles of the soldiers of Yangjiawan but cause the viewer to wonder about the interior lives of Han people.

Literature

Zhang Zibo and Wang Pizhong, "Han Anling de kancha ji qi peizang mu zhong de caihui taoyong" (Investigation of the Han dynasty mausoleum, Anling, and the painted ceramic figures in its satellite tombs), *Kaogu* 5 (1981): 422–23.

28 | STANDING WOMAN
| H. 20 1/2 in. (52 cm.)

29 | STANDING WOMAN
| H. 20 7/8 in. (53 cm.)

Western Han dynasty (206 B.C.–A.D. 9)
Earthenware
Unearthed at Langjiagou, Xianyang City
Shaanxi History Museum

30	KNEELING WOMAN H. 12 1/4 in. (31 cm.)
31	STANDING WOMAN H. 18 1/4 in. (46.5 cm.)
32	STANDING WOMAN H. 28 3/4 in. (73 cm.)

Western Han dynasty (206 B.C.–A.D. 9)
Polychromed earthenware
Excavated in 1966 at Renjiapo Village in the eastern suburb of Xi'an
Shaanxi History Museum

Twenty-nine seated and nine standing figures of women were found in thirty-seven pits excavated in the vicinity of the tomb of Empress Dou (d. 135 B.C.) at Baling, the mausoleum of Emperor Wen. Some of the pits featured ceramic caskets (*taoguan* or *waguan*) that held the figurines, as well as earthenware models of animals (fig. 5.3). Bones of horses and pigs also were found in some of the pits.

The standing figures range in size from 53–73 centimeters and the seated figures are 33–35 centimeters in height. The women are depicted in poses of attendance on a superior. Their narrow shoulders and slim waists suggest youthful types. Those who are kneeling sit with their legs folded under them and with their hands held together underneath the long sleeves of their gowns. The standing figures are in a closed position with their feet barely apart and with their arms in front of their bodies. They once held a vertical object in their hands. Their hair is severely drawn back, either tightly knotted at the nape of the neck or near the crown of the head, and the hair of the seated attendants hangs on their backs, loosely bound with a ribbon. The women wear simple clothing; sometimes both an outer and an inner robe are indicated. Some of the standing figures wear a long robe with trousers, and others simply wear a floor-length gown which leaves only the tips of their shoes exposed. The draping cloth at the neckline and also the folds of the sleeves are suggested by modeled ridges; however other details, such as belts, are indicated with simple incised lines. The bodies of the figures are not evident under the garments, but the faces of these women have been rendered with great attention to structure and to mood. Although they are passive in their appearance, the sculptor has evoked the calm, gentle demeanor of these young attendants.

Literature

Wang Xueli and Wu Zhenfeng, "Xi'an Renjiapo Han ling cong zang keng de fajue" (Excavation of the pits for funerary objects accompanying a Han mausoleum at Renjiapo, Xi'an), *Kaogu* 2 (1976): 75; 129–133; pls. 7–9.

The Quest for Eternity: Chinese Ceramic Sculptures from the People's Republic of China. Los Angeles: Los Angeles County Museum, 1987, pls. 11–15.

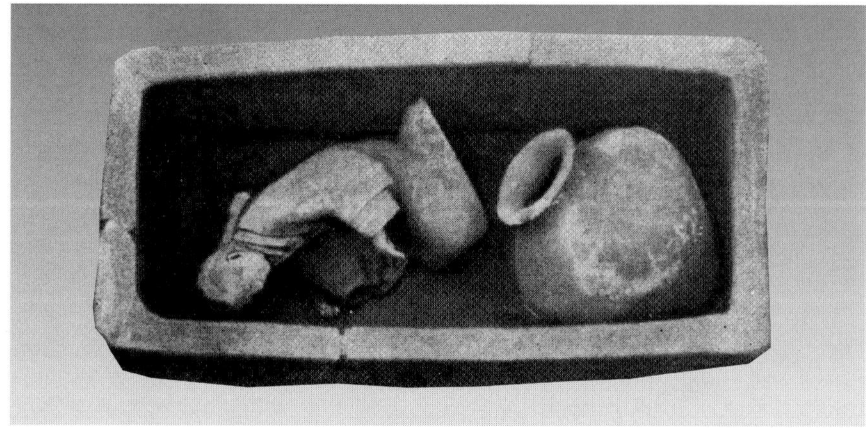

Fig. 5.3. Burial of figurine in ceramic coffin. After *Kaogu* 2 (1976): 129–33, pl. 7.3.

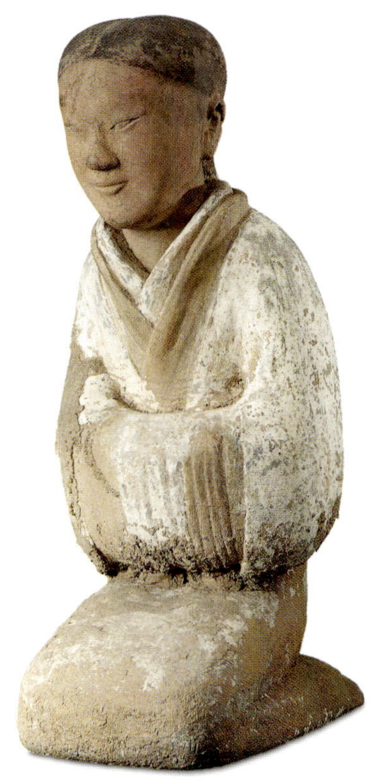

30 | KNEELING WOMAN

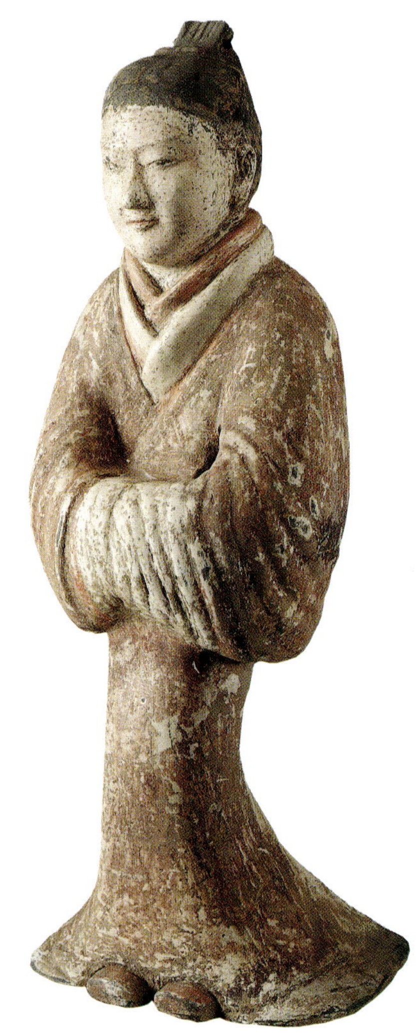

31 | STANDING WOMAN

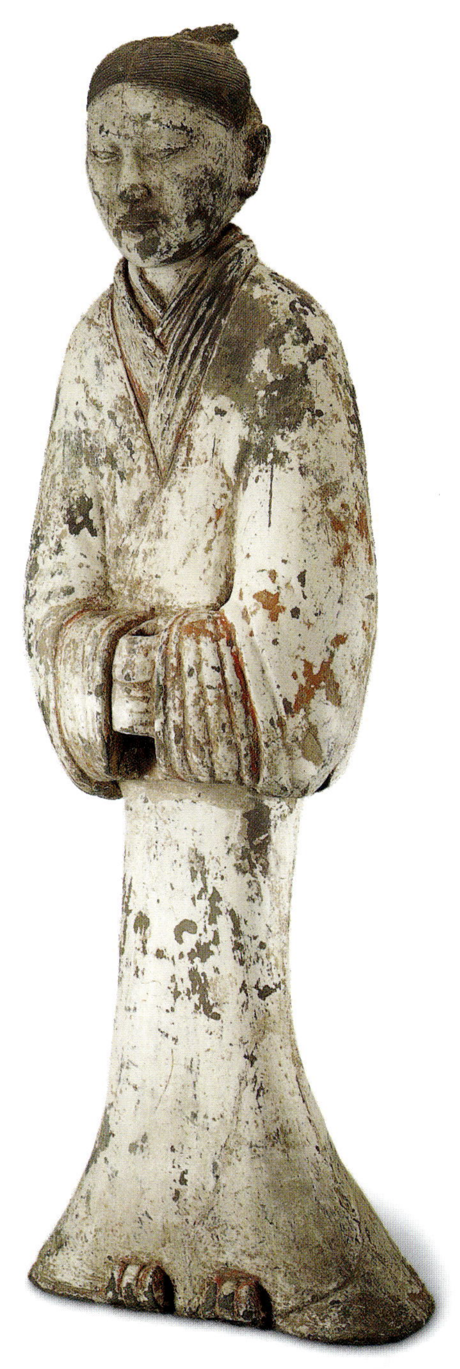

32 | STANDING WOMAN

33 | KNEELING CHARIOTEER
H. 13 in. (33 cm.)

34 | STANDING FEMALE FIGURE
H. 20 7/8 in. (53 cm.)

35 | STANDING MALE FIGURE
H. 23 5/8 in. (60 cm.)

36 | HEAD OF FEMALE
H. 3 1/8 in. (8 cm.)

37 | HORSE
H. 24 3/4 in. (63 cm.); L. 27 5/8 in. (70 cm.)

38 | OX
H. 15 1/2 in. (39.5 cm.); L. 27 5/8 (70 cm.)

39 | SHEEP
H. 14 3/8 in. (36.5 cm.); L, 16 7/8 (43 cm.)

40 | GOAT
L. 14 7/8 in. (37 cm.)

41 | SOW
L. 16 1/8 in. (41 cm.)

42 | PAIR OF DOGS
L. 11 7/8 in. (30 cm.)

43 | CHICKEN AND ROOSTER
H. 4 3/4 in. (12 cm.); H. 5 7/8 in. (15 cm.)

Western Han dynasty (206 B.C.–A.D. 9)
Earthenware
Excavated 1992–93 from pits near the Yangling Mausoleum of Emperor Jing and Empress Wang
Shaanxi Provincial Institute of Archaeology

South of the Yangling Mausoleum of Emperor Jing and his empress (d. 126 B.C.), twenty-four pits arranged in fourteen rows from east to west were excavated. The contents of these wood-lined pits is rich and diverse. Figurines of soldiers were found but also models representing attendants, guards, farmers, and animals. These additional figures were appropriate, since the pits held goods representing the granaries, kitchens, barns, arsenal, and treasury of the emperor. Actual stores of grain had been placed in the pits. Weights and measures, weapons, and tools, as well as money, were reproduced on a miniature scale in keeping with the size of the figurines.

The most arresting feature of the excavation was the number of nude figures. These figures were originally clothed as indicated by impressions of textiles found in the burial soil (fig. 5.4). Some had miniature bronze belt hooks five-eighth of an inch in length to fasten the garments. Soldiers from pit no. 20 once wore armor made of squares of wood, revealed by imprints in the soil and residual red and black color (fig. 5.5). The chariot driver is the sole example in this exhibition of a clothed figure from Yangling. He sits on his feet and his hands are positioned in front of him to hold the reins. The chariots included in the burial were made of wood. Cavalry figurines were not found at this site, but they have been unearthed from a tomb dating to the reign of Emperor Wu (before 118 B.C.) and located in the southeastern suburbs of Xi'an (fig. 5.6).[5] These soldiers, nude and without arms, are made in the same style as those from Yangling; however their legs have been bowed to fit around the horses' bodies.

Of course, rendering the nude bodies of these figures differentiates them from earlier figurines of the Han dynasty like those from Langjiagou (see cat. nos. 28–29). The use of the nude surrogate dressed in cloth garments was most likely a result of influence from people of the state of

Chu who practiced this burial custom. For instance the clothed figurines from Tomb no. 1 at Mawangdui, Hunan Province, are well known.[6] However, wood figures from a Warring States period tomb at Baoshan, Hubei Province, are more similar, since their legs and feet have been articulated and their arms were carved separately and then attached (fig. 5.7).[7] Although the figures from Yangling are now armless, they originally had wooden arms. The rendering of the genitalia of the Yangling examples also distinguishes them from figures from other sites and periods, even though their secondary sex features are given only enough attention to differentiate male and female. In a manner similar to figurines from other sites, the hair styles convey feminine or masculine fashions. In all cases the bodies have been given very little sense of bone structure or musculature. The feet look like scuba flippers with incised lines to indicate the divisions between toes, and the legs are like posts with only a slight narrowing of the leg at the ankle and just below the knee. The male torsos have modest modeling to create chest muscles, but the females do not have any indication of breasts. A small, circular depression in the center of the trunk represents the navel. At the shoulder there are holes to receive a protrusion presumably carved on the wooden arm in tenon and mortise fashion. Although the nudity of these figures first attracted attention to them, it is their faces that are far more interesting. These reveal an attempt to individualize the figures, from those with broad, square jaws like the figure in the exhibition, to others with round heads and smiling faces, and finally to the good-natured visage of an elderly woman. The skin is colored red, and the hair, eyebrows, mustache, and iris of the eye are indicated in black paint.

Some warriors were equipped with battle gear, including bronze cross bow mechanisms, bronze halberds (*ji*), iron spears (*mao*), iron swords (*jian*), and bronze arrow heads, all cast in miniature. Many soldiers once carried shields, but, being made of wood, they decomposed, leaving only impressions of their shape and structure in the burial earth (fig. 5.8). The outside of the shield was covered with black and red lacquer. Other objects in the pits included bronze horse trappings and iron agricultural tools. Miniature bronze banliang coins with a diameter of three-eighth of an inch also were included in the deposit. Banliang coins are round with a square hole in the center, and they were commonly used during the Western Han dynasty until the reign of Emperor Wu.

Although the excavation at Yangling represents the most extensive find of nude figurines, others have been found near several imperial tombs, including the tombs of emperors Gaozu (Changling), Xuan (Duling) and Wu tomb (Maoling).[8] Nude figures also have been unearthed at workshop and kiln sites, as well as at graves and in the ruins of the capital city.[9] Molds for making the nude figures have been found at a kiln site in the northwest corner of Han Chang'an (fig. 5.9).[10]

Polychromed earthenware animals were found in some of the pits at Yangling. The menagerie includes oxen, sheep, goats, hogs, horses, dogs, chickens, and roosters. The animals, with the exception of the fowl, have lost much of their original color. All of these creatures have been rendered with enough detail to be easily identified, but their creators had very little interest in the finer details of anatomy, just as in the human figures. Slight modeling and incised lines are used to create their facial features. The horses from Yangling and the horses created for the burial of the first Qin dynasty emperor (221–206 B.C.), demonstrate the continuity of the tradition of surrogate animals, but a comparison also reveals the differing approaches of the designers. The modeling of the head and legs of the Yangling horse is less subtle, and its body is nearly identical to the body of the sheep from the same site. The Han horse lacks the carefully groomed mane of the Qin horse. It is apparent however, that the designers wanted to capture salient details of some animals: the full belly of the sow, the tufted beard of the goat, and the raised tail and ears of the watchdog. All of the creatures stand completely at attention with their heads straight ahead, legs locked, and hooves, paws, or claws firmly planted on the ground. Some of the animals appear incomplete, since they originally had horns or tails made of wood that have disintegrated, leaving only circular holes where the appendages were once inserted. There seems to be some effort to suggest the different sexes of these creatures, in a manner similar to the gender distinctions that were important in the human figurines. It is interesting, however, that the sizes of the animals are not proportioned according to reality: the sheep are taller than the oxen. Unpainted earthenware animals like these have been found in the vicinity of the Anling mausoleum of Emperor Hui (r. 195–188 B.C.).[11]

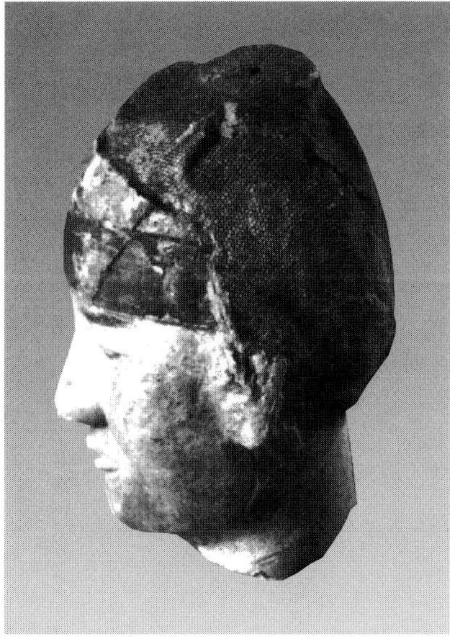

Fig. 5.4. Impressions of textiles worn by the soldiers remaining in the burial earth. Photo Courtesy Wang Baoping.

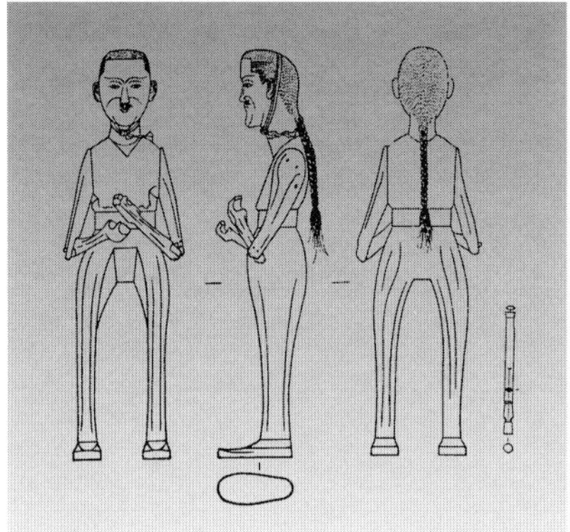

Fig. 5.5. Figurines and impressions of armor remaining in the burial earth. Photo Courtesy Wang Baoping.

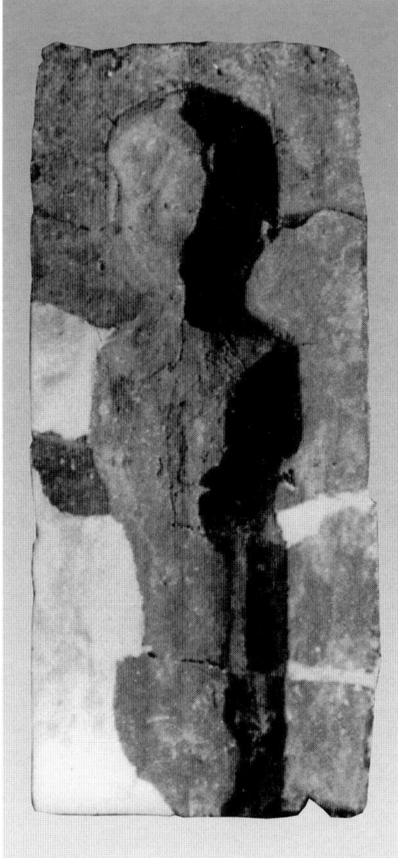

Fig. 5.9. Molds for making nude figurines. After *Kaogu xuebao* 1 (1994): 99–129, pl. 15.1.

Literature

"Xi Han Yangling lingyuan kaogu you zhongda faxian" (Major discovery of Western Han dynasty Yangling mausoleum archaeology), *Kaogu yu wenwu* 2 (1991): 1 and 96.

Wang Xueli et al., "Han Jingdi Yangling nanqu cong zangkeng fajue diyi hao jianbao" (Brief report no. 1 on the excavation of the attendant pits at the southern district of the Han dynasty mausoleum of Emperor Jing, Yangling), *Wenwu* 4 (1992): 1–13.

Mazzatenta, O. Louis, "A Chinese Emperor's Army for Eternity," *National Geographic* 182 (1992): 114–130.

Mou Yongkang, *The Coloured Figurines in Yangling Mausoleum of Han in China (Zhong guo Han Yangling cai tong)*, Xi'an: China Shaanxi Travel and Tourism Press, 1992.

Wang Xueli and Wang Baoping, "Han Jingdi Yangling nanqu cong zangkeng fajue dier hao jianbao" (Brief report no. 2 on the excavation of the attendant pits at the southern district of the Han dynasty mausoleum of Emperor Jing, Yangling), *Wenwu* 6 (1994): 4–23; 30.

Fig. 5.6. Wood figurine, Baoshan, Hubei Province. After *Baoshan Chu mu, shang*, fig. 170.

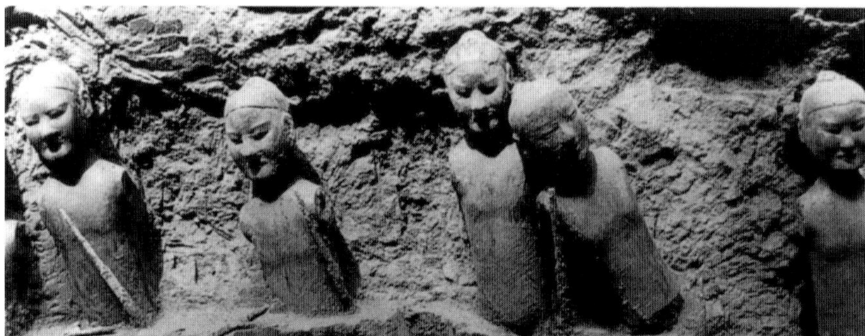

Fig. 5.7. Figurines and impressions of shields; H. 12 in.; W. 7 in. After *The Coloured Figurines in Yangling Mausoleum of Han in China*, p. 51.

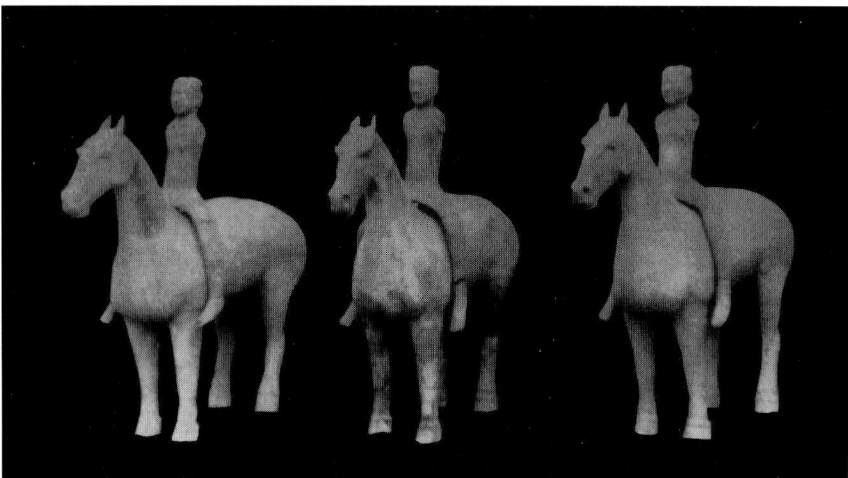

Fig. 5.8. Nude cavalry figure with horse, Xi'an. After *Kaogu yu wenwu* 4 (1990): 31–56, fig. 24.

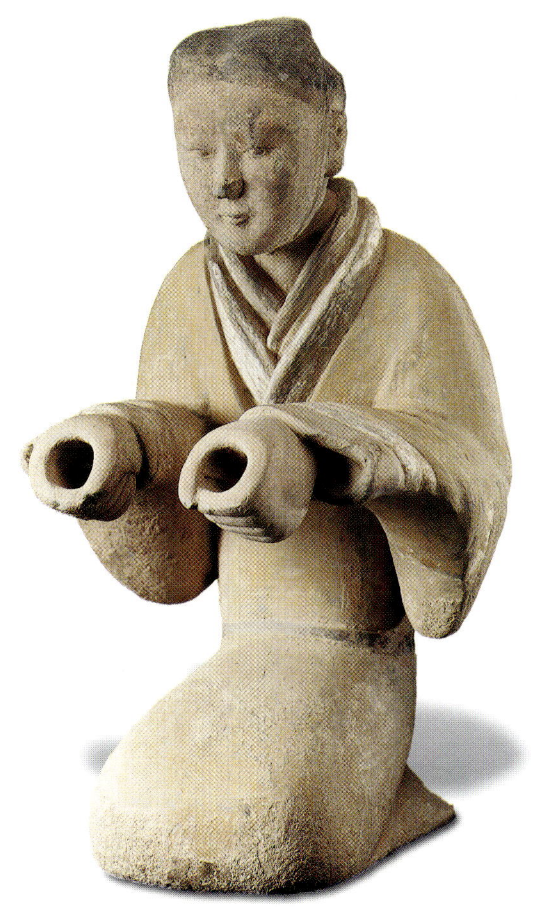

33 | KNEELING CHARIOTEER

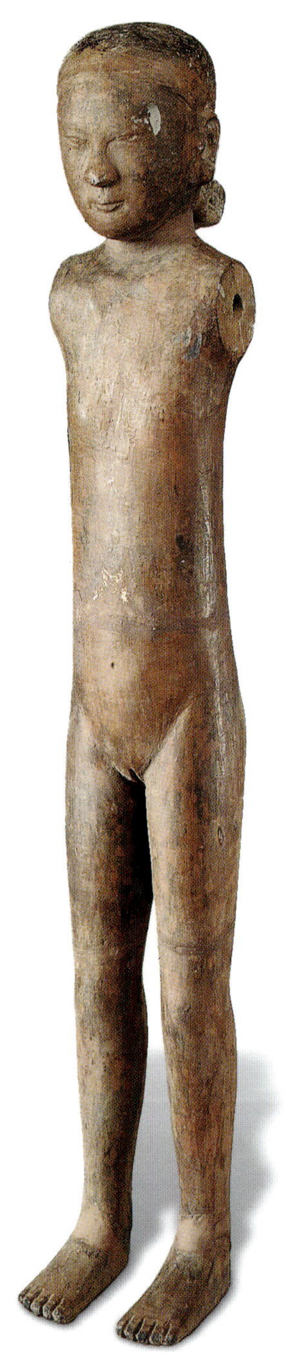

34 | STANDING FEMALE FIGURE

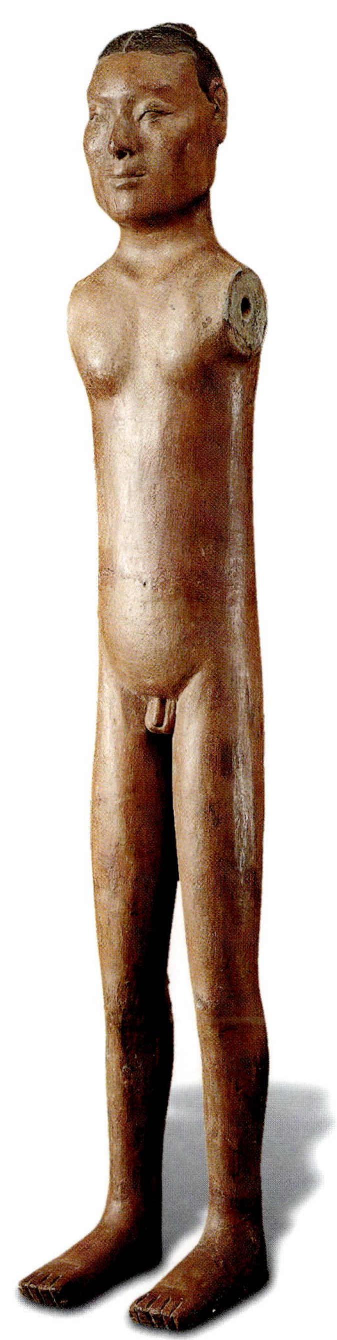

35 | STANDING MALE FIGURE

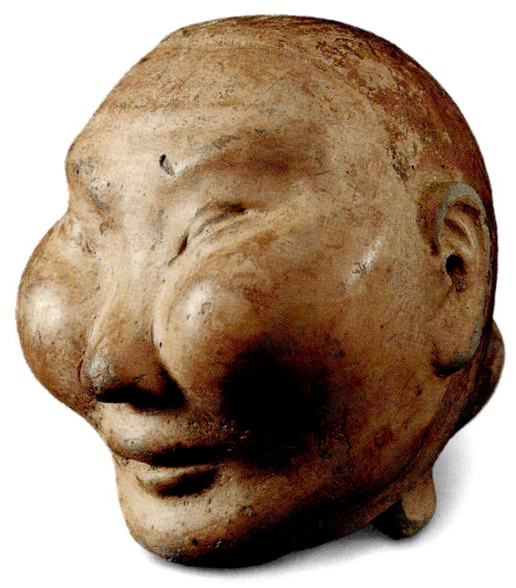

36 | HEAD OF FEMALE

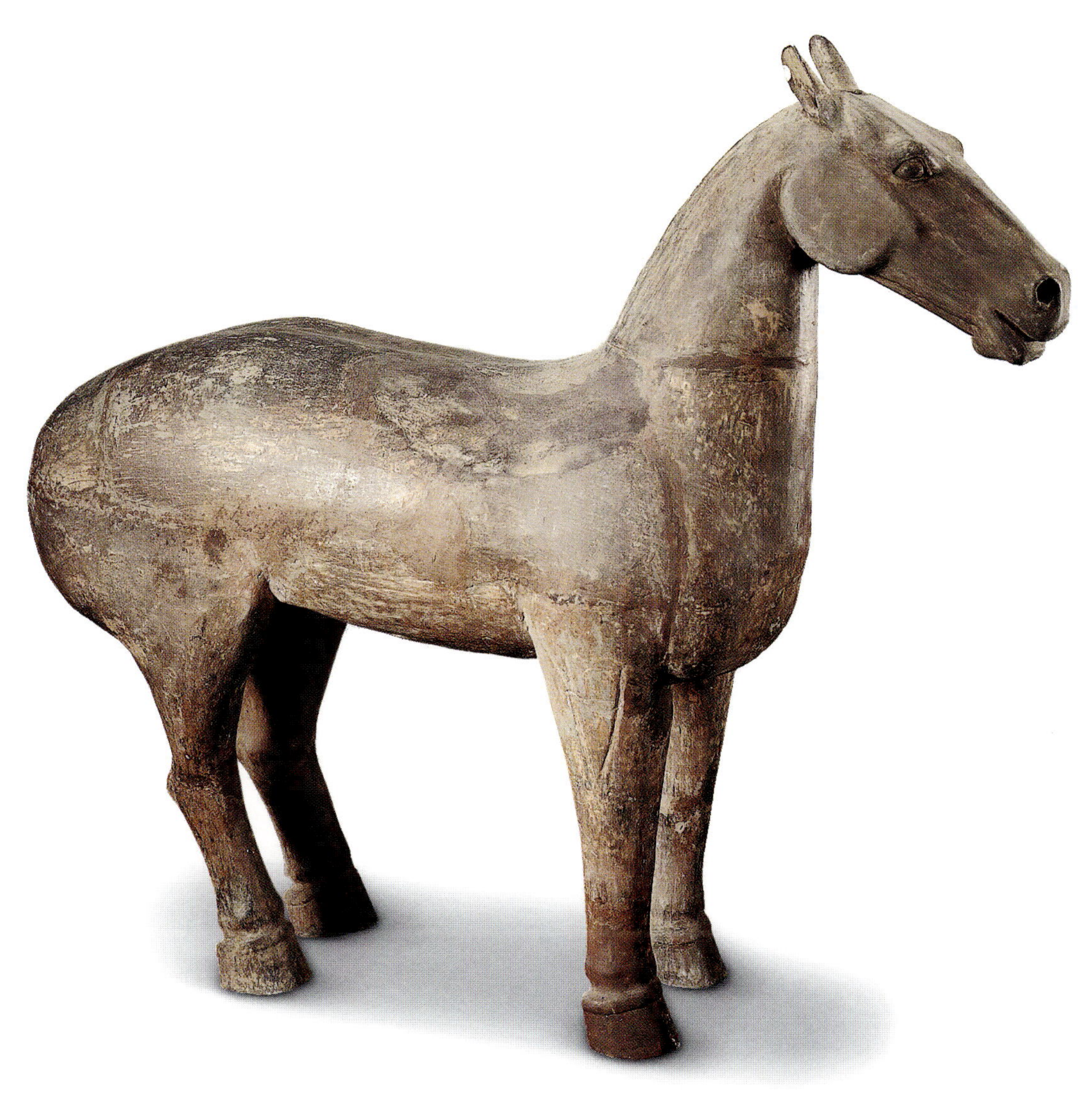

37 | HORSE

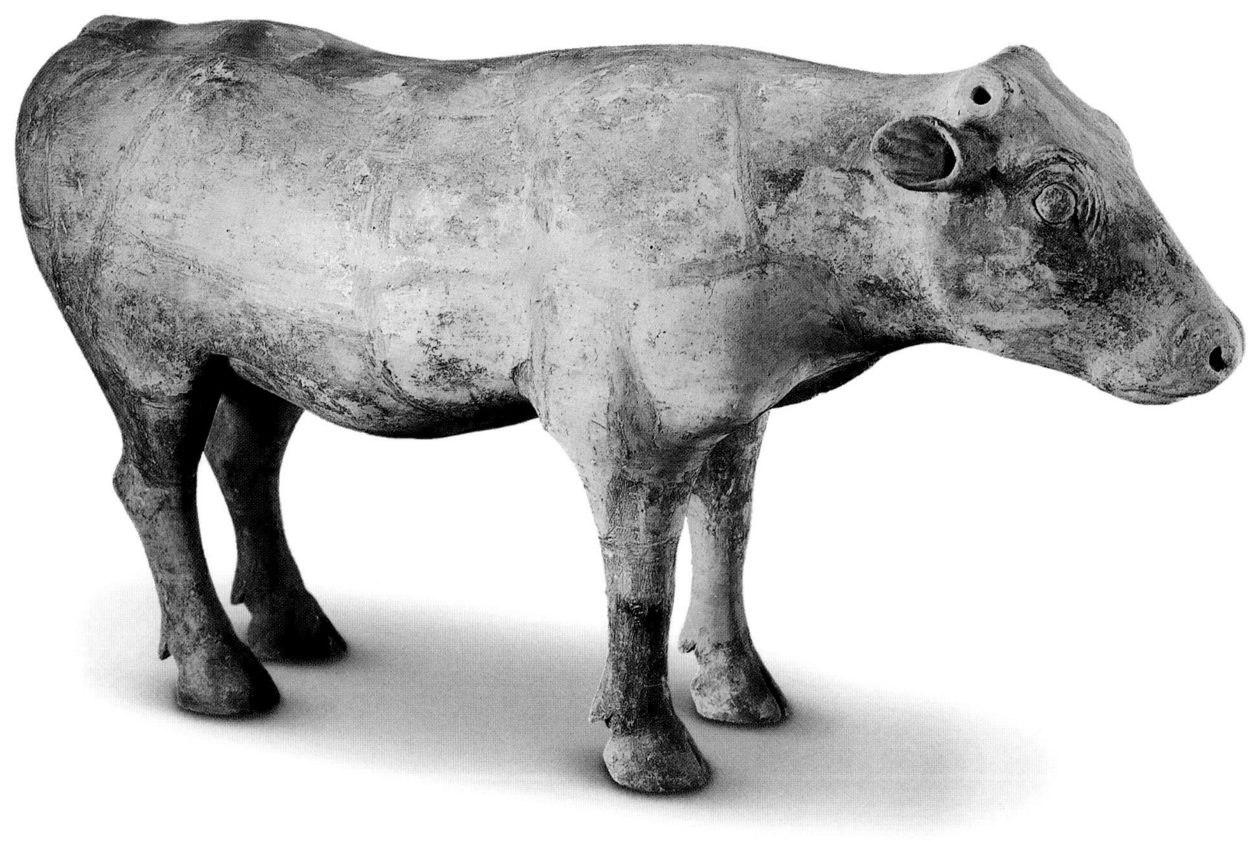

38 | OX

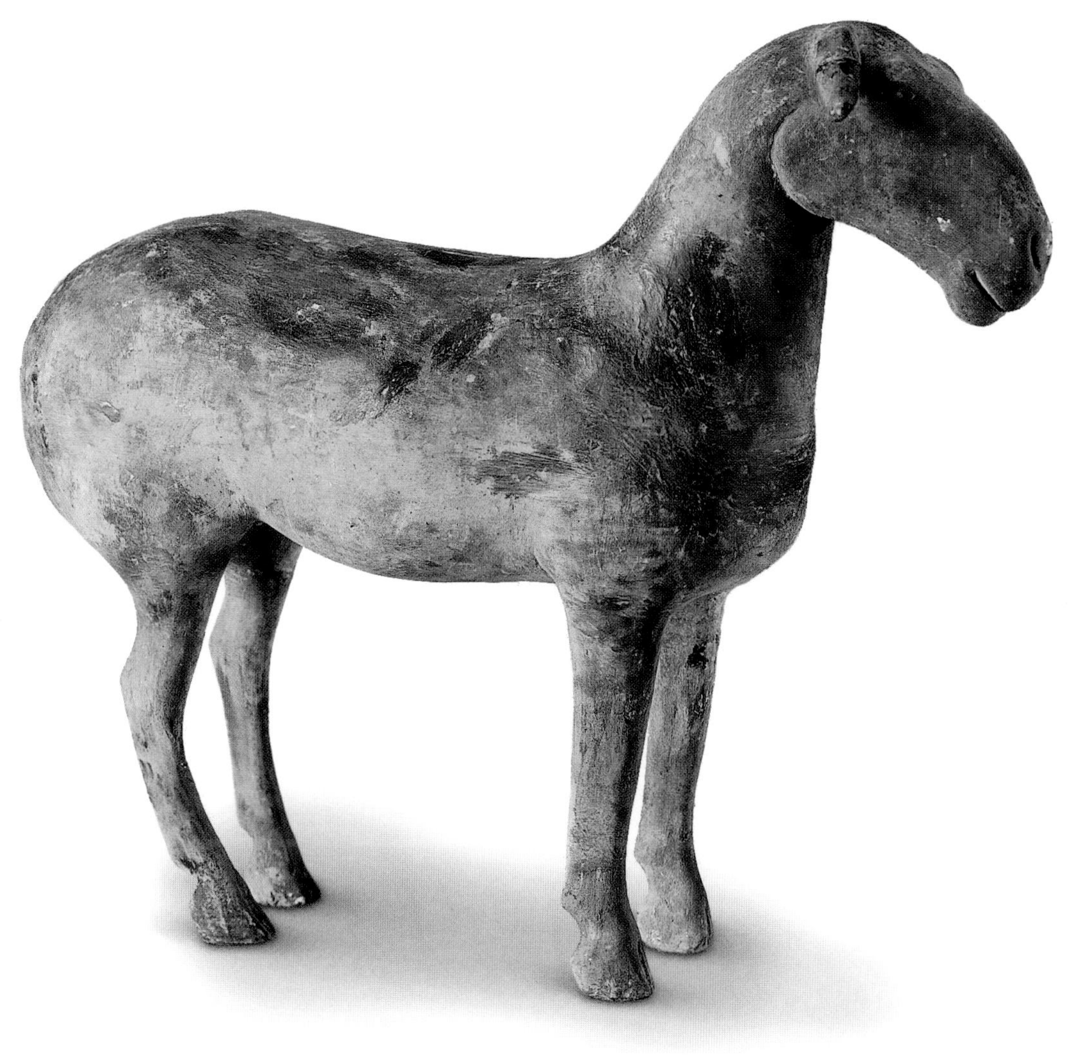

39 | SHEEP

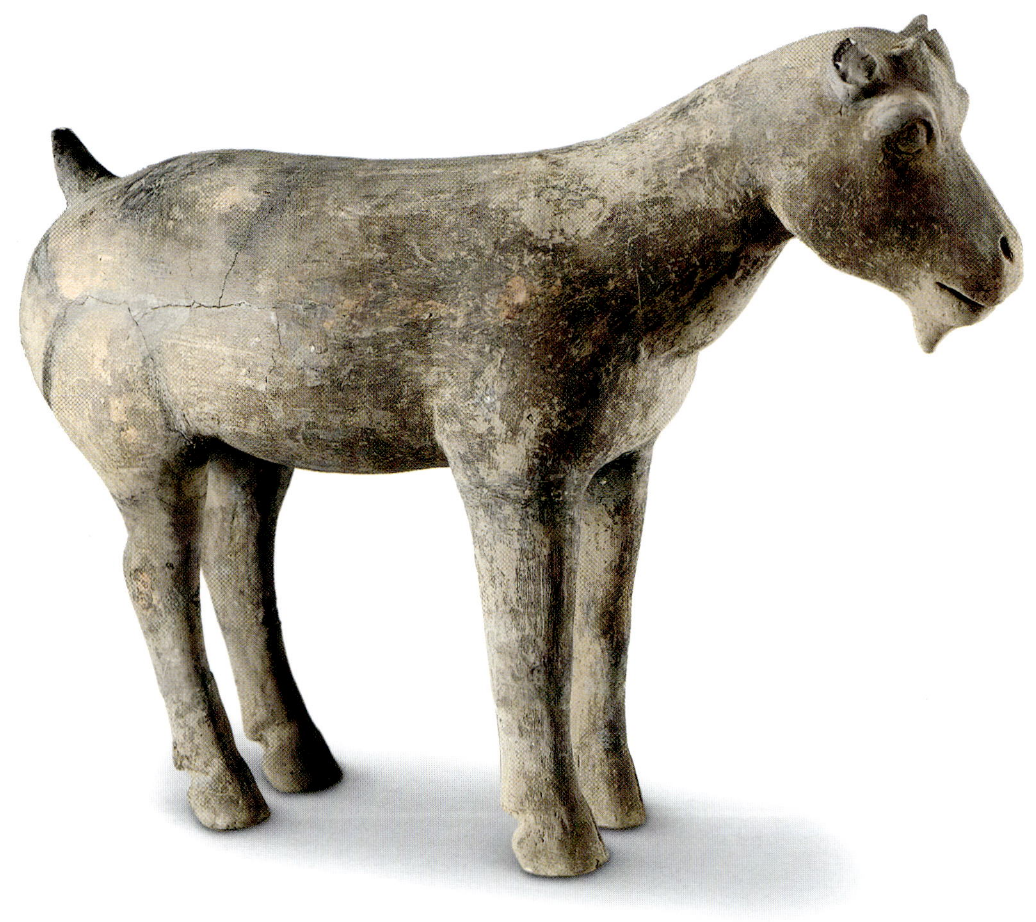

40 | GOAT

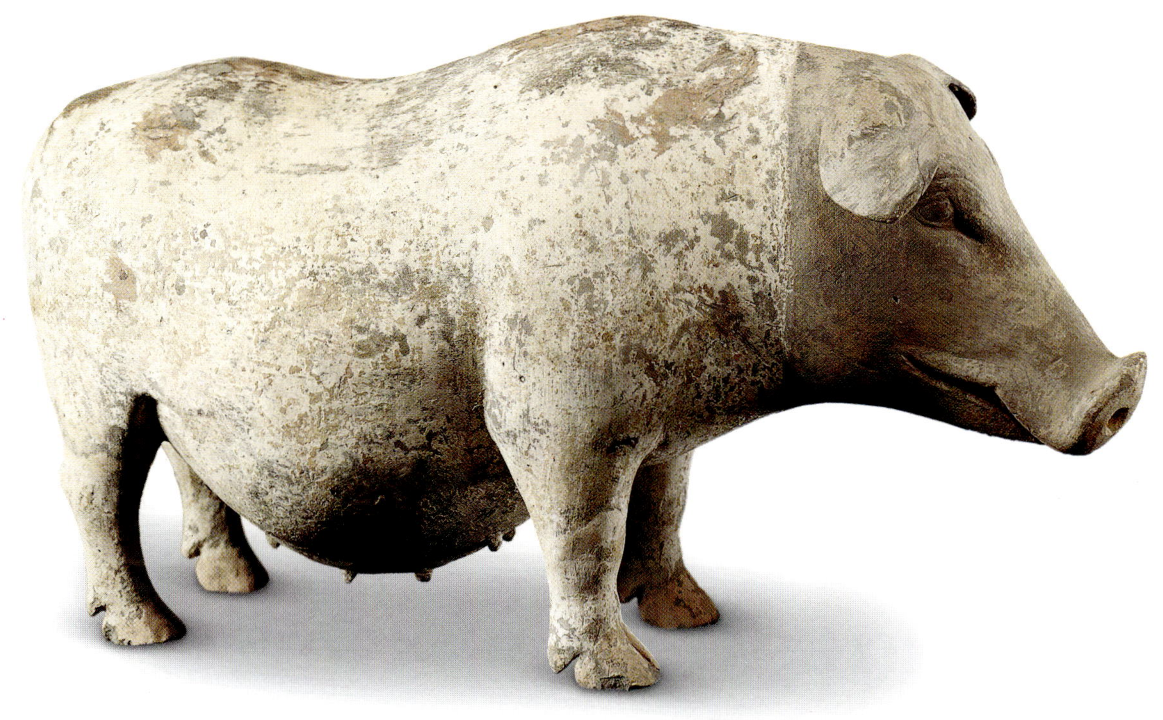

41 | SOW

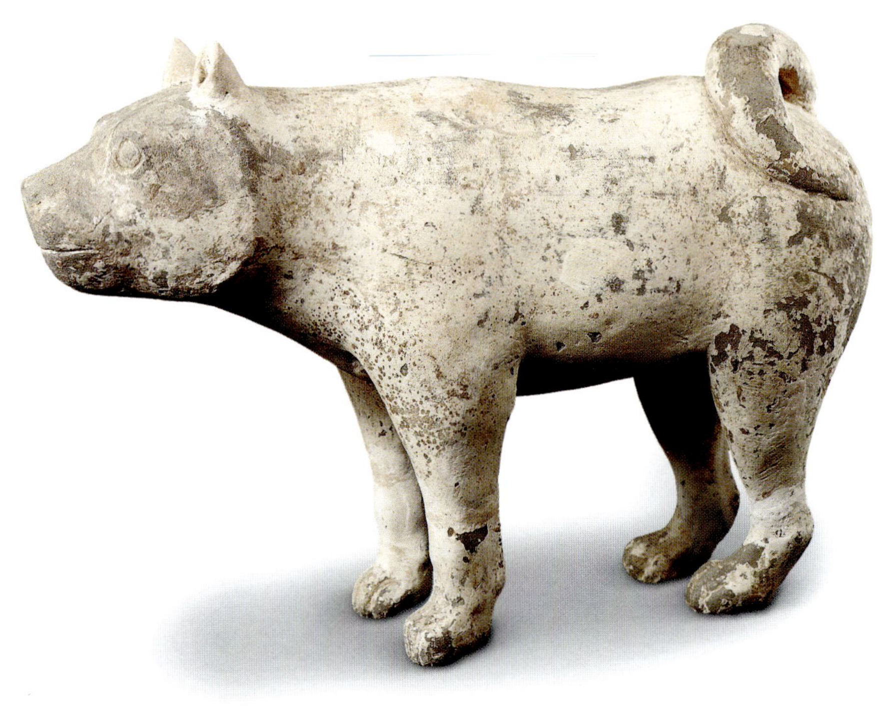

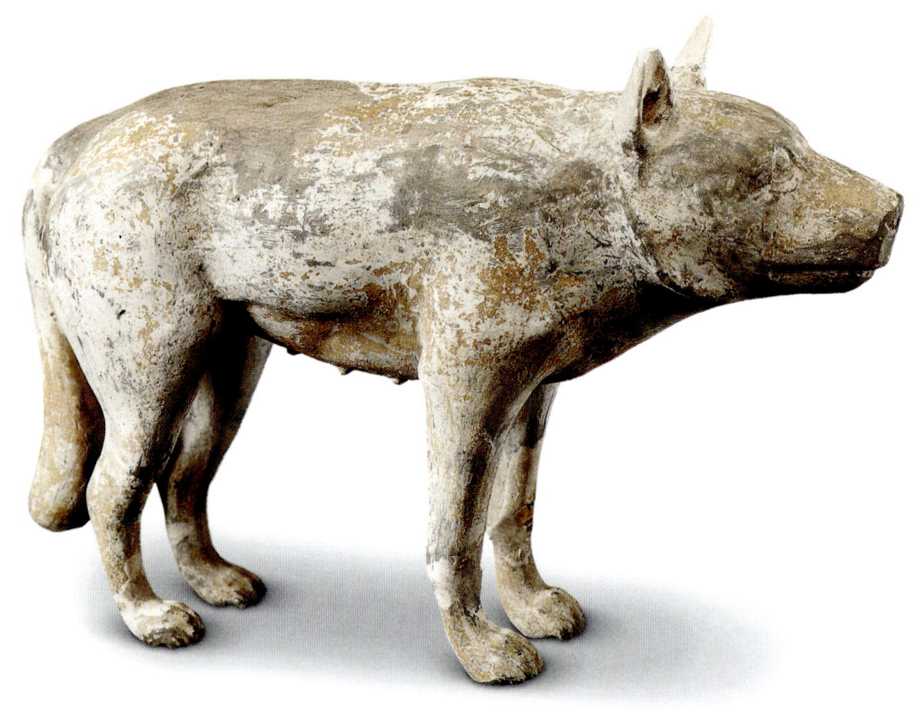

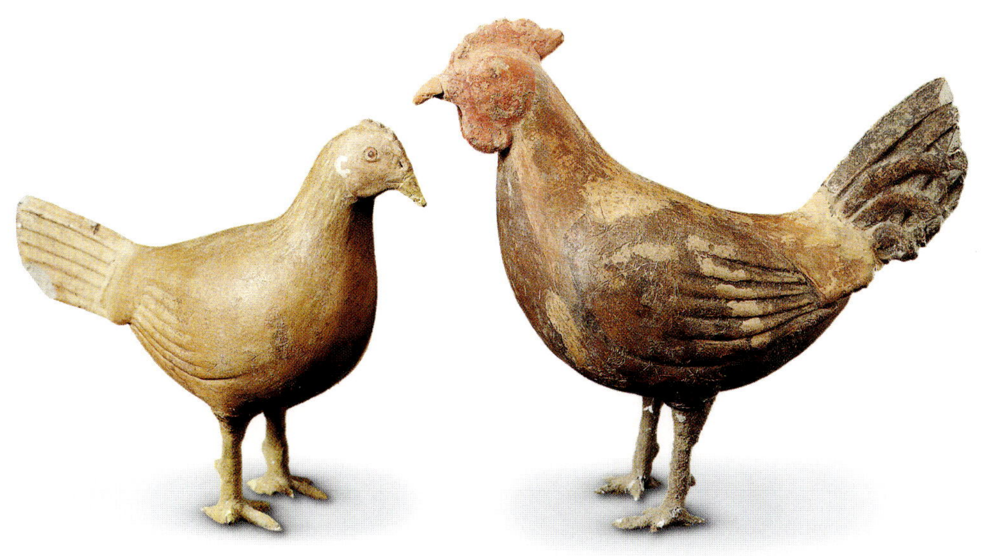

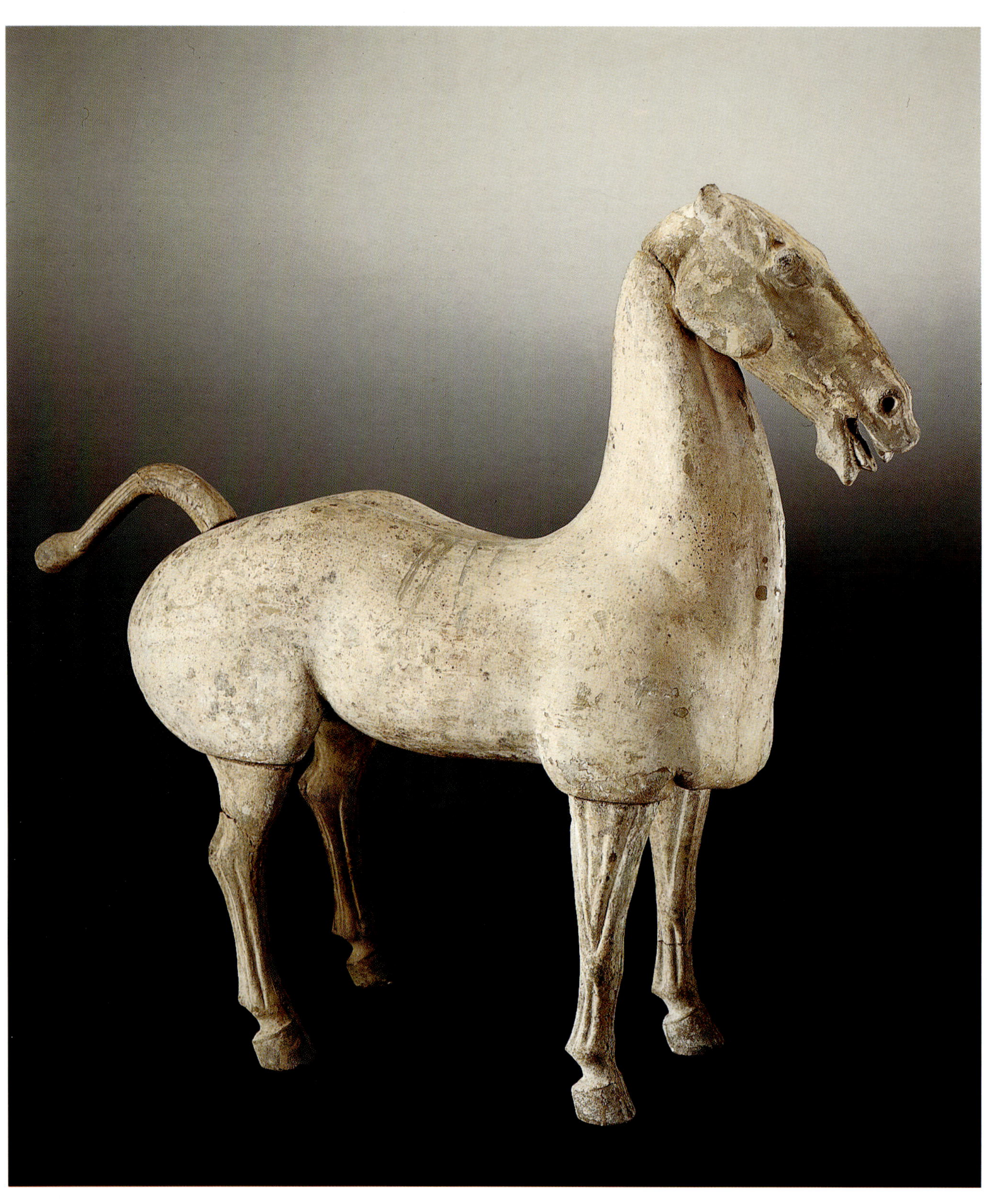

44 | HORSE
Western Han dynasty (206 B.C.–A.D. 9)
Earthenware with painted decoration
H. 23 1/4 in. (59 cm.); L. 25 5/8 (65 cm.)
Unearthed in 1984 at Zhuangtou Village, Xingping County
Maoling Museum

The construction of this earthenware horse was made by a distinctive assembly-line approach. The legs and tail were fired separately and then inserted into the body. The structure of the horse's body suggests a strong beast but not necessarily a fast runner, since its legs are quite short in proportion to its body. The musculature and skeletal structure of the legs have been suggested by modeling the surface, but the treatment appears stylized, especially the muscles of the forearm. The horse's body has been given little attention, and the deep arch of its back and the upright neck also contribute to the stylized appearance of this creature. The horse's trappings have been added as painted details. Horses of similar construction, accompanied by wood chariots which rotted in the ground, were unearthed from a burial near Changling, Emperor Gaozu's mausoleum.[12]

Literature

Tomb Treasures from China: The Buried Art of Ancient Xi'an. San Francisco and Fort Worth: Asian Art Museum of San Francisco and Kimbell Art Museum, 1994, pl. 21.

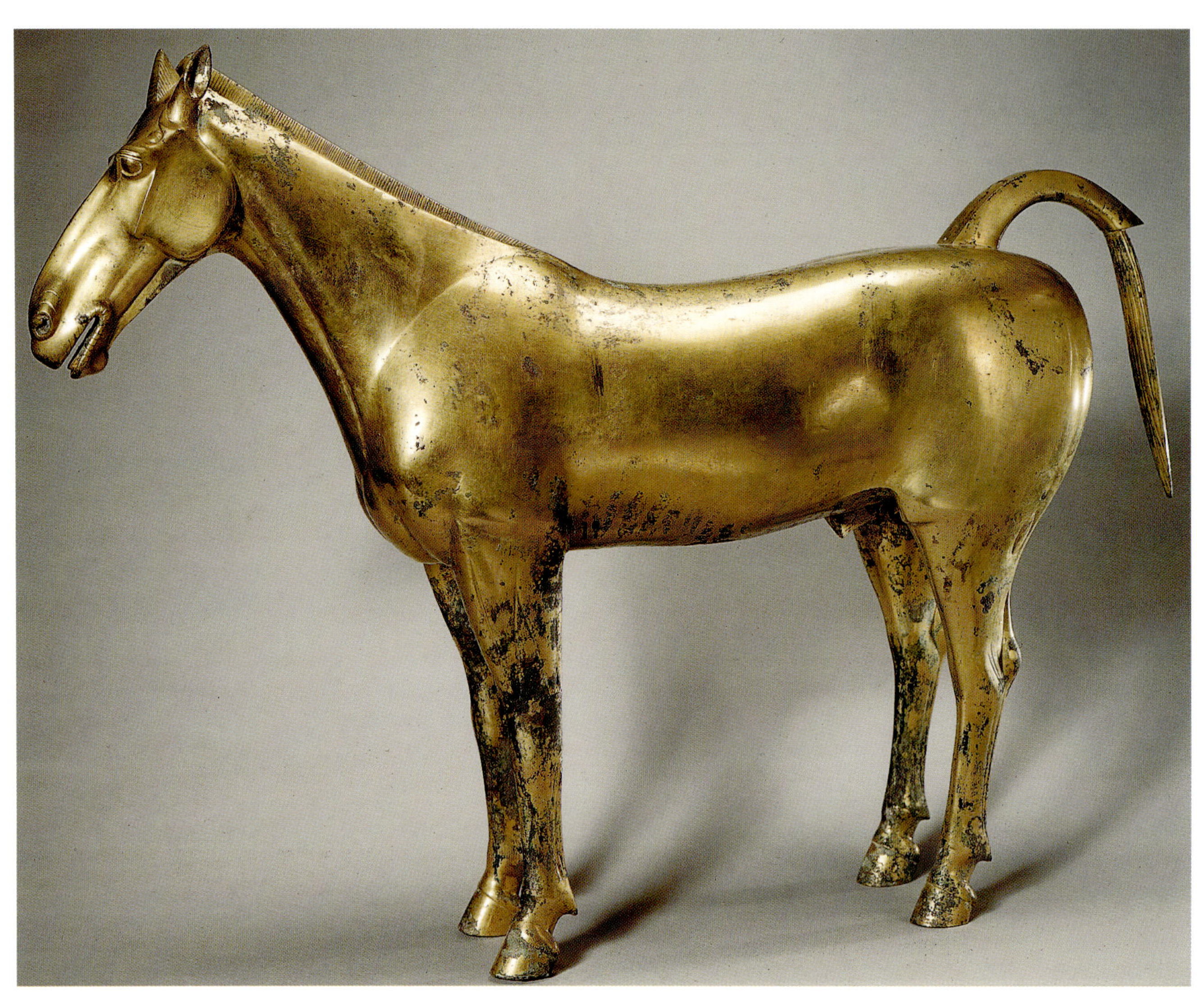

45 HORSE
Western Han dynasty (206 B.C.–A.D. 9)
Gilded bronze
H. 24 3/8 in. (62 cm.); L. 32 1/4 in. (82 cm.)
Unearthed in 1981 from burial pit near Tomb no. 1 on east side of Maoling
Maoling Museum

This gilded bronze horse was probably a treasured object in one of the palaces. It does not have an inscription but was found with inscribed artifacts that indicated that they were used by the imperial family, in particular Princess Yangxin, the elder sister of Emperor Wu. No other gilded bronze examples of a horse this size have thus far been excavated.

The horse stands at attention with all four legs firmly grounded. With eyes focused, ears erect, and mouth slightly open, it appears ready for action. The rendering of details of the horse's anatomy is sensitive and quite realistic. Muscles of the chest and shoulders are suggested through slight modeling. The structure of the legs is clearly indicated, but some of the details seem stylized because of the linear detail. Strands of hair in the mane and tail have been rendered with fine lines, and the forelock rises into a conical form quite unlike that of the Qin horses, whose manes have a tousled look. This horse has long, slender legs which would enable it to run swiftly, and its strong musculature would endow it with endurance—exactly the kind of horse treasured by the Han.

Horses, like silk goods, were valued commodities used in the tributary system to maintain border relations with non-Chinese peoples. The Han were particularly enamored of a breed of horses from the distant western region of Ferghana (Dayuan), who could run so fast that they were called *tian ma*, or heavenly horses.

Literature

"Shaanxi Maoling yi hao wuming zhong yi hao congzangkeng de fajue" (Excavation of burial pit no. 1 accompanying the tomb of unidentified occupant at Maoling, Shaanxi), *Wenwu* 9 (1982): 1–17.

Tomb Treasures from China: The Buried Art of Ancient Xi'an, San Franciso and Fort Worth: Asian Art Museum of San Francisco and Kimbell Art Museum, 1994, pl. 16.

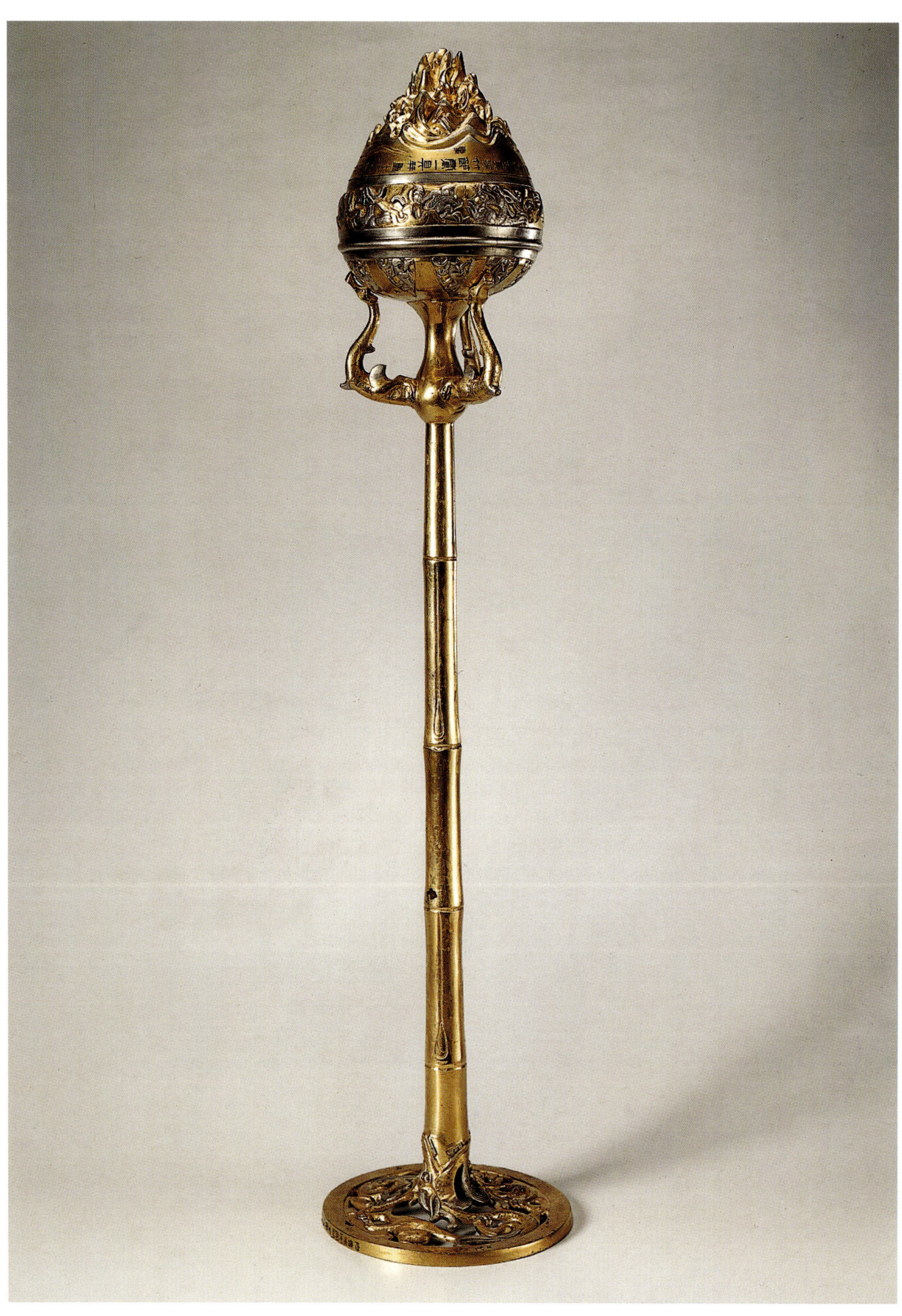

46 | MOUNTAIN-LIDDED INCENSE BURNER (*boshanlu*)

Western Han dynasty (206 B.C.–A.D. 9)
Bronze with gold and silver gilding
H. 22 3/4 in. (58 cm.); D. at base 3 1/2 in. (9 cm.)
Unearthed in 1981 from a funerary pit near Maoling, the mausoleum of
Emperor Wu
Shaanxi History Museum

This spectacular incense burner was made for one of the imperial palaces, the *Weiyang gong*, during the reign of Emperor Wu. The censer has two inscriptions that are nearly identical: one on the base of the lid and one on the edge of the foot. The inscription on the lid identifies the original location of the censer, its weight, the date it was made (137 B.C.), the date it was brought to the palace (136 B.C.), and its registration number (3):[13]

> Department of the Bedchamber in the Weiyang Palace belonging to the *neizhe*, an incense burner [with foot] in the shape of a bam boo section in gilt [bronze], weighing altogether 10 *jin* 12 *liang*, made the 4th year by the *neiguan*, entered [the palace] in the 10th month of the 5th year, no. 3.

It was found with inscribed objects belonging to Princess Yangxin, the elder sister of Emperor Wu.

Like many other bronze works produced during the Western Han dynasty, this vessel has a utilitarian function: incense burns in the bowl, and the smoke is released through hidden perforations in the lid. Nevertheless, it is conceived as a three-dimensional sculpture. The mountain peaks are irregularly formed, creating a rugged terrain. With the smoke escaping around the mountains, it would almost look like clouds surrounding lofty peaks.

This censer has a unique treatment of the stem. It is extremely elongated and segmented to suggest sections of bamboo. From a convex bulge near the top of the stem, the bodies of three winged dragons emerge, and their heads support the bowl of the censer where more dragons are rendered in low relief. The dragon motif is repeated at the base, where the stem is held in the teeth of a dragon, and its body forms a web between the center pole and the outer rim of the base.[14] Fine lines have been added to represent the dragon's scales. The beauty of the finely sculpted censer is enhanced with the use of gilding in mostly gold but some silver.

Although this object was enjoyed by the living, it may have had meaning for the dead. In fact, many Han tombs feature less expensive bronze or earthenware versions of the incense burner with mountain-shaped lid. The mountain motif was very important during the Western Han dynasty, especially during Emperor Wu's reign. Some mountains were considered sacred, and Wudi conducted sacrifices on particular mountains, hoping that he would be granted immortality (for instance the Feng and Shan sacrifices).[15] Since mountain peaks are close to the heavens, it was thought that spirits would gather there. Emperor Wu also sent expeditions to find mountainous islands in the sea where immortals dwelled. The mountain had specific associations during this period, and, coupled with the fantastic dragon, this kind of incense burner is a powerful image, conveying the desire to transend mortality.

Literature

"Shaanxi Maoling yi hao wuming zhong yi hao congzangkeng de fajue" (Excavation of burial pit no. 1 accompanying the tomb of unidentified occupant at Maoling, Shaanxi), *Wenwu* 9 (1982): 1–17.

Li Xueqin, "Some Problems Concerning Qin and Han Bronzes," *Early China* 11–12 (1985–87): 296–300.

Pirazzoli-t'Serstevens, Michéle, "Workshops, Patronage and Princely Collections during the Han Period," *Proceedings of the International Colloqium on Chinese Art History, Taipei. Antiquities*, pt. 2. Taipei: National Palace Museum, 1991, 415–30.

Erickson, Susan N, "*Boshanlu*—Mountain Censers of the Western Han Period: A Typological and Iconological Analysis," *Archives of Asian Art* 45 (1992): 6–28.

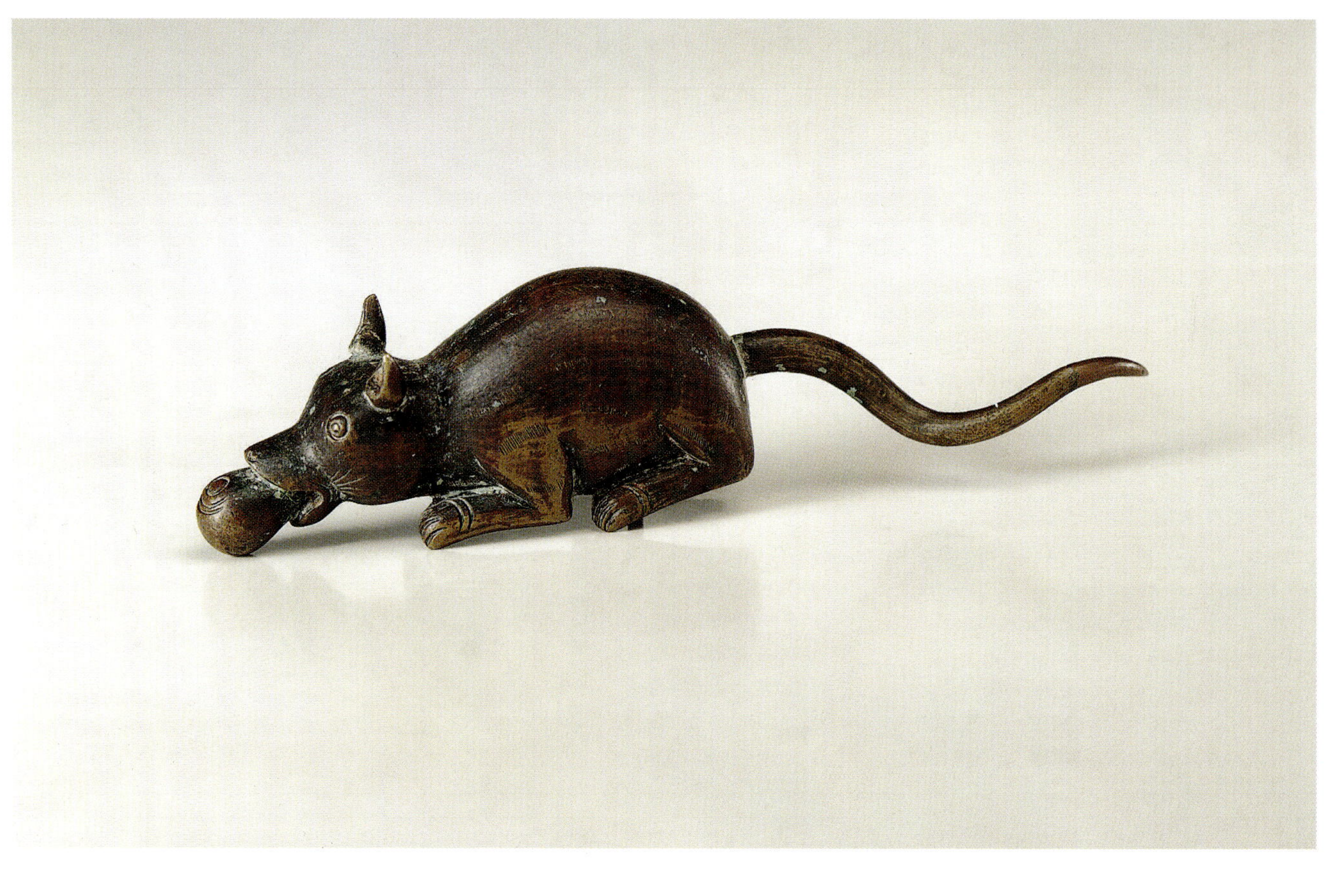

47 | MOUSE
Western Han dynasty (206 B.C.–A.D. 9)
Bronze
L. 5 1/4 in. (13.2 cm.)
Unearthed in 1982 at Maoling, Xingping County
Maoling Museum

This life-size mouse is a remarkable and rare example of Western Han dynasty bronze sculpture. It is posed with its body lowered to the ground as it holds and nibbles on a nut-like object in its mouth. It is alert with ears perked, eyes bulging, and its long, curved tail extended. There is little detail; only a few striations to suggest the joint between the paw and leg. It has a smooth surface, much like the earthenware animals from Yangling.

In the *Lun Heng*, Wang Chong (A.D. 27–ca. 97) reports that the appearance of a mouse (*shu*) was believed to foretell disaster of some kind:[16]

As long as people live in happiness and tranquillity, rats [/mice] do not stir, but scarcely is their felicity destroyed, and are dangers impending, when rats [/mice] by their agitation indicate an extraordinary calamity.

The meaning of this creature may be ominous, but on the other hand, the naturalistic and playful demeanor of this little mouse simply may have been planned to delight the viewer.

Literature

Zhong guo meishu quanji: gongyi meishu bian 5: qingtonqi, xia (Selections of Chinese art: art and crafts, vol. 5: Bronze objects, pt. 2), Beijing: Wenwu Chubanshe, 1986, pl. 213.

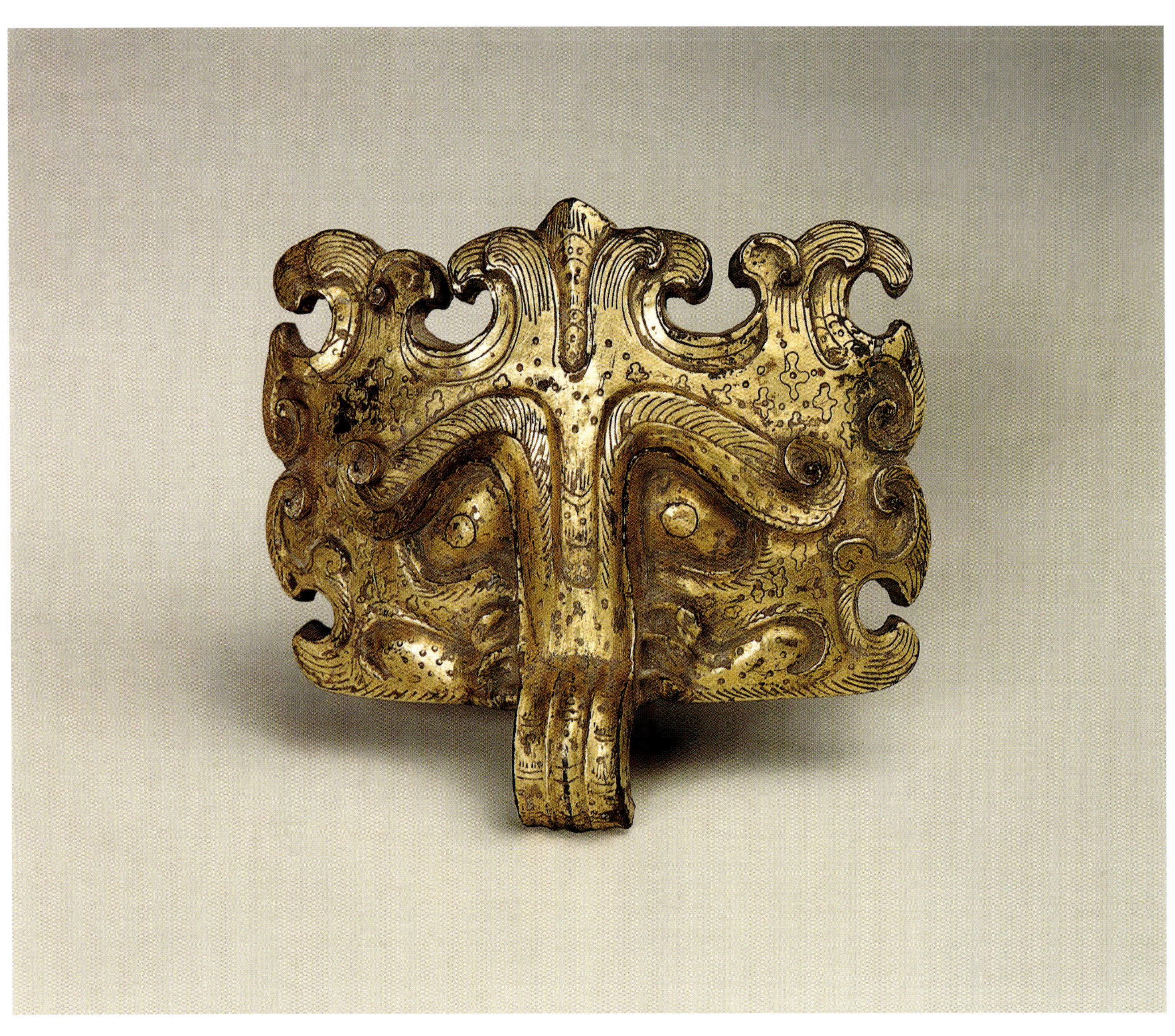

48 | RING-HOLDER MASK (*pushou*)
Western Han dynasty (206 B.C.–A.D. 9)
Gilded bronze
H. 3 1/2 in. (9 cm.); W. 4 3/8 in. (11 cm.)
Unearthed in 1973 at Yan'an
Shaanxi History Museum

The central motif of this fixture is a beast with large staring eyes, a broad nasal ridge, and horn-like forms at the top of the plaque. It was most likely used as decoration on a coffin. The inner and outer coffins of Liu Sheng at Mancheng featured this type of handle attached to the sides, the mask perhaps serving an apotropaic function (fig. 5.10).[17] The Yan'an fitting is missing a circular ring that would have hung from the mouth of the creature. Smaller versions of this kind of ring-holder mask were used as handles on bronze or lacquered vessels.[18]

Many fixtures like the one from Yan'an have been found at Han dynasty sites, but this one is special in the use of gilding on the surface and the unique characterization of the face of the creature. The brows are placed at an angle, nearly obscuring the eyes but lending a melancholy mood to the animal. The entire mask is finely rendered, with linear details and with high-relief curls that suggest a mane.

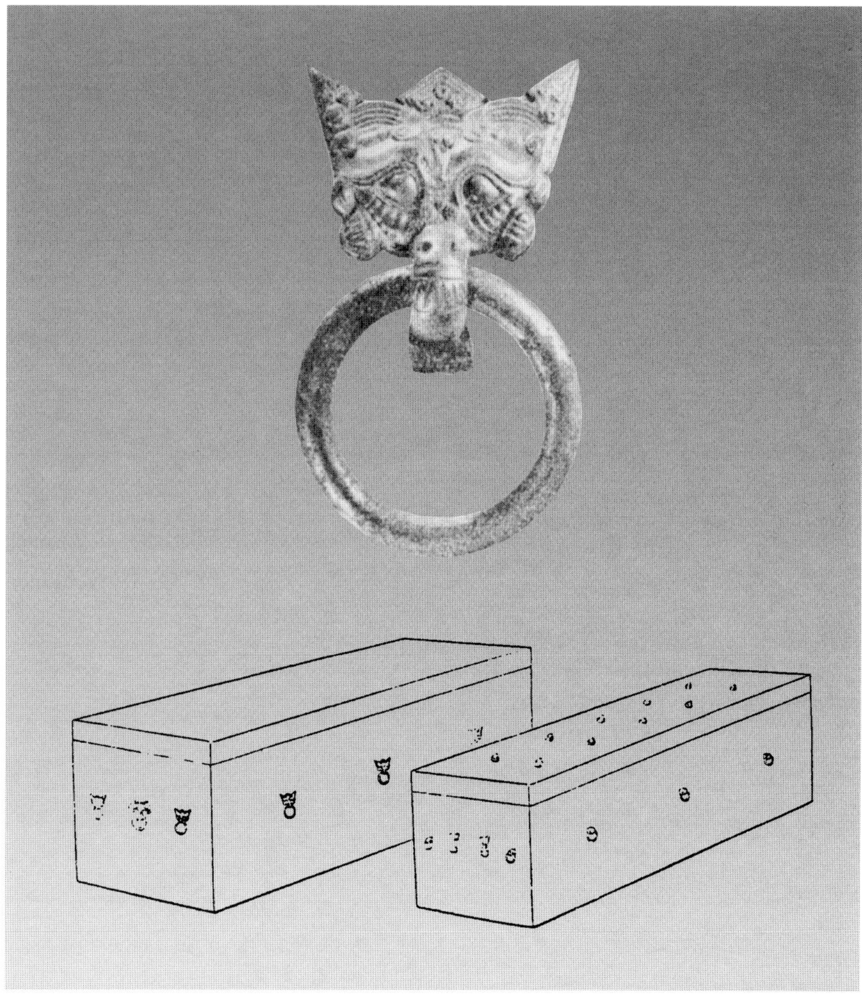

Fig. 5.10. Outer and inner coffins with ring-holder masks, Tomb of Liu Sheng, Mancheng. After *Mancheng Han mu fajue baogao*, shang, figs. 19–20.

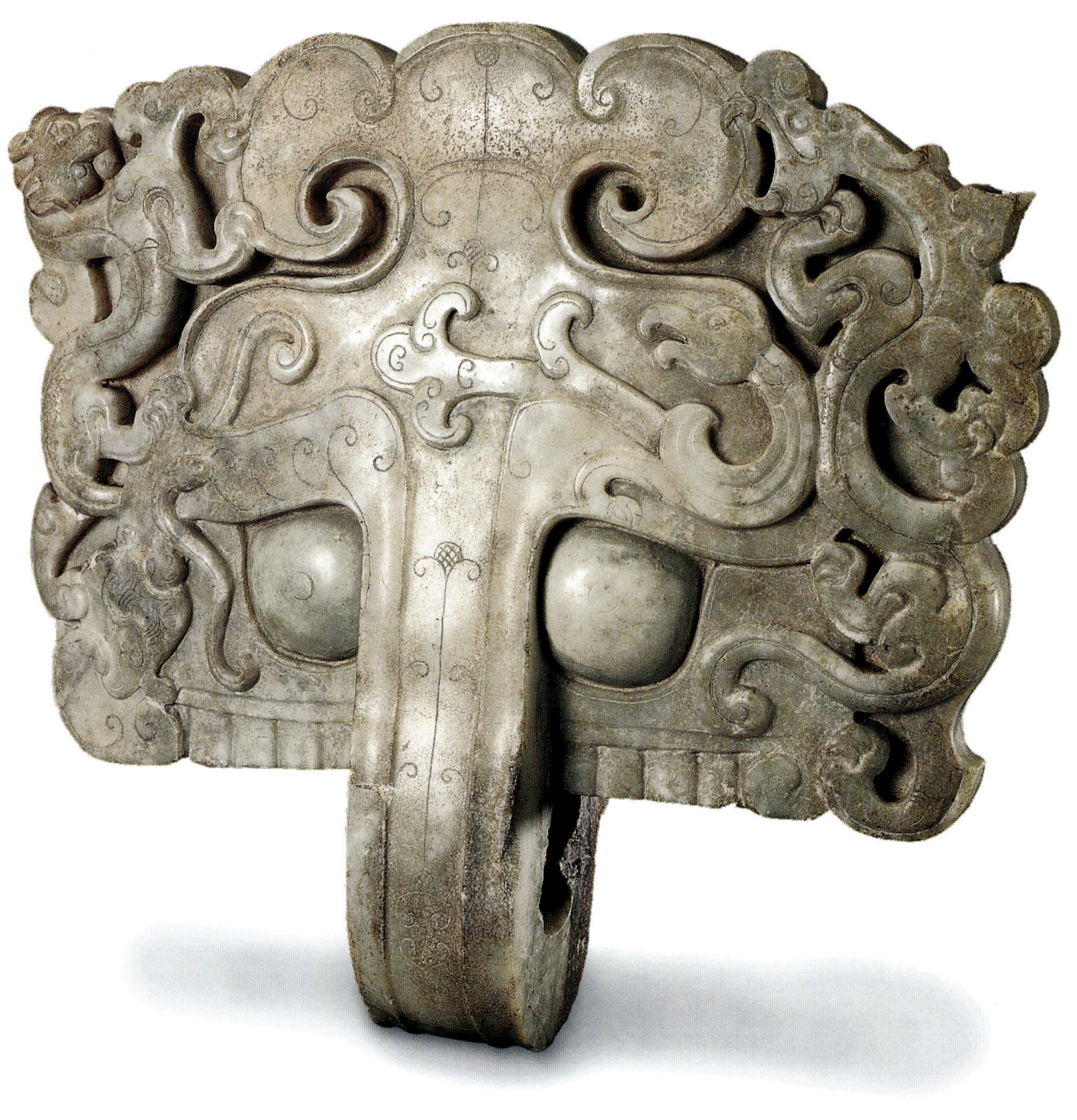

49 RING-HOLDER MASK (*pushou*)
Western Han dynasty (206 B.C.–A.D. 9)
Jade
H. 13 1/2 in. (34.2 cm.); W. 14 in. (35.6 cm.); D. 5 7/8 in. (14.7 cm.)
Unearthed in 1975 in the vicinity of Maoling, Xingping County
Maoling Museum

In general form, this jade object resembles mask fixtures that were used to hold ring handles on vessels or on coffins, and even on some tomb doors. For instance, the stone door of the tomb of Liu Sheng at Mancheng still had a bronze ring-holder mask in place upon excavation (fig. 5.11).[19] The large size and jade material of this image from Xingping County differentiate it from all others of this type. It is conjectured that it was once part of the furnishings of a ceremonial building at the site of the mausoleum of Emperor Wu, Maoling. On the reverse side there is a hole that presumably was used for mounting the mask, and at the edges of the hole, remnants of a metal fitting are still visible, with lead being the major component of this metalwork.

The principal image is a bestial mask with two large eyes that have finely incised lines indicating irises. A nasal ridge is placed between the eyes, and "teeth" are suggested along the lower edge.[20] Above and to the sides the creatures of the cardinal directions scale the surface of the mask. To the right the Green Dragon of the east stretches from top to bottom. The Vermilion Bird of the south rests on the right "eyebrow" of the mask. The Dark/Black Warrior of the north, comprised of a turtle and a snake, is situated on the lower left, and the White Tiger of the west is posed in the upper left corner. Enlivening the composition, the tiger tightly grasps part of the mask with its claws, and the dragon holds the top edge of the mask in its teeth.

Typical of the period, the carving technique includes low and high relief, sinuous designs, and soft, rounded edges. The bodies of the dragon and the tiger are made up of curving and countercurving forms, and the point of view varies from a profile to a bird's-eye perspective. The bird is reduced to a beaked head and a series of curling forms suggesting the body. The Dark/Black Warrior is most difficult to distinguish. The turtle is seen from a bird's-eye view, and its shell is partially obscured. In its mouth the turtle holds the snake, which is about to crawl unto the left eyebrow. Lightly incised curls and hatching enliven the surface of the mask and create the stripes on the tiger, the scales on the dragon, and the patterns on the carapace of the turtle.

Literature

Wang Zhijie and Zhu Jieyuan, "Han Maoling ji qi peizang zhong fujin xin faxian de zhongyao wenwu" (New discovery of important cultural relics: Han Maoling and its accompanying burial pits), *Wenwu* 7 (1976): 51–55.

Zhu Jieyuan, "Maoling faxian de Xi Han si shen wen yu pushou" (Discovery at Maoling of Western Han dynasty 'four deities' motif and the jade ring-holder mask), *Kaogu yu wenwu* 3 (1986): 9–10.

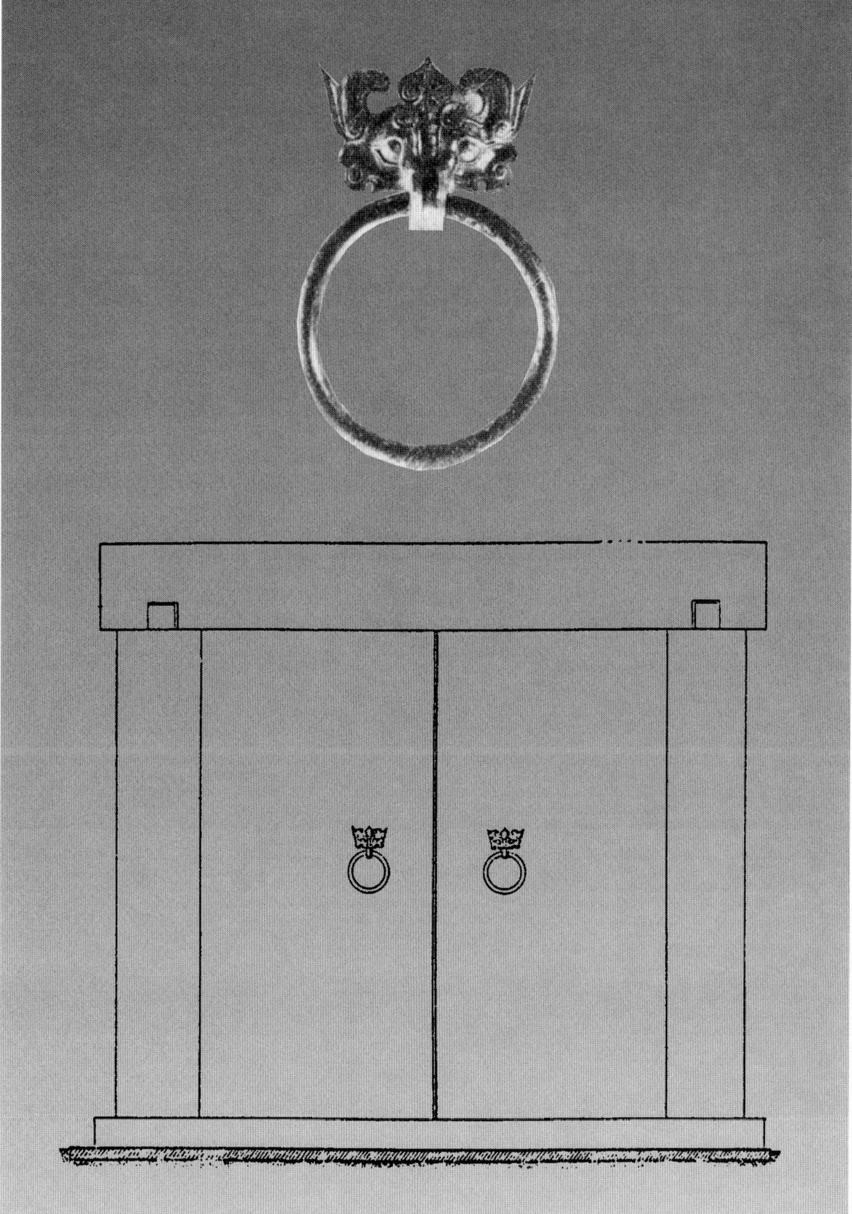

Fig. 5.11. Doors from the Tomb of Liu Sheng, Mancheng. After *Mancheng Han mu fajue baogao, shang*, fig. 8.

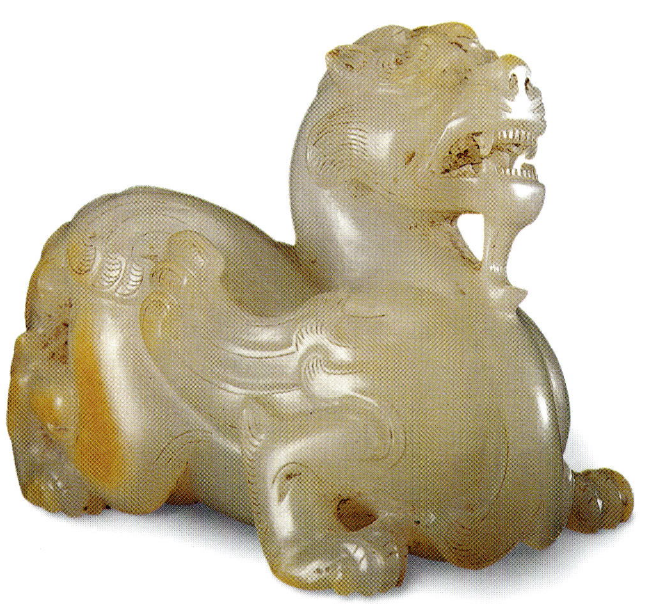

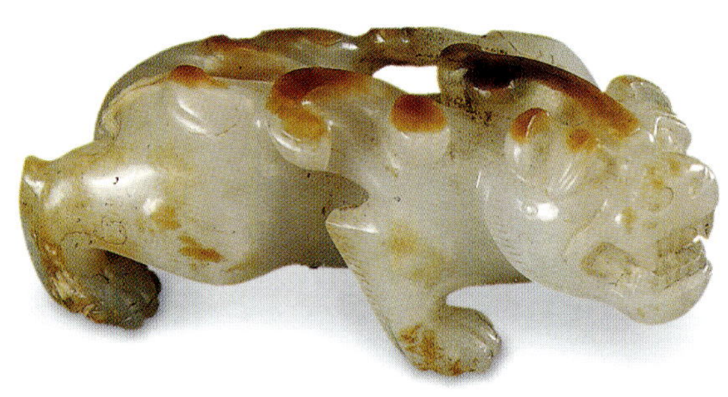

50 | CHIMERA (*bixie*)
Western Han dynasty (206 B.C.–A.D. 9)
Jade
L. 2 3/4 in. (7 cm.); H. 2 1/8 in. (5.5 cm.)
Unearthed in 1972 at Xinzhuang, Xianyang City, near Weiling, mausoleum
of Emperor Yuan (r. 48–33 B.C.)
Xianyang Museum

51 | CHIMERA (*bixie*)
Western Han dynasty (206 B.C.–A.D. 9)
Jade
L. 2 3/8 in. (5.8 cm.); H. 1 in. (2.5 cm.)
Unearthed in 1972 at Xinzhuang, Xianyang, near Weiling
Xianyang Museum

These small beasts represent the high level of miniature jade carving during the Western Han dynasty. The eminent archaeologist Xia Nai observed that, despite their size, "they are monumental in conception."[21] The surfaces are embellished with some low relief details and finished with a lustrous polish. Fine lines have been etched in the surface to suggest fur, but in other cases to create abstract patterns, which may be seen on many kinds of art produced during the Western Han period.

The animals are fantastic but have some vaguely feline characteristics, such as the form of the head and paws and the sharp, bared teeth. Both, however, do not look like identifiable animals. One has wings that lie back against its body and the other has raised, curling forms on its back, which could be read as a reptilian ruffle or abstracted wings. These creatures can probably be associated with the supernatural *bixie* or *qilin*, which is loosely translated as chimera. According to Wang Chong (A.D. 27–ca. 97) in his *Lun heng*, the *qilin* is considered auspicious.[22] The Chinese graphs "*bi xie*" mean to ward off evil.[23] Thus these creatures could serve auspicious as well as apotropaic functions. Both roar and tense their bodies as they prepare themselves against any adversity, and their wings would allow them to fly to the heavens, if necessary. A winged horse carved of jade was found in 1966 near Pingling, the mausoleum of Emperor Zhao (r. 87–74 B.C.). In that case the creature serves as a vehicle for an immortal riding on its back.[24]

Literature

Zhang Zibo, "Xianyang shi Xinzhuang chutu de si jian Han Dai yu diao qi" (Four Han dynasty jade carvings from Xinzhuang, Xianyang Municipality), *Wenwu* 2 (1979): 60.

Li Hongtao and Wang Pizhong, "Han Yuandi Weiling diaocha ji" (Investigation of the Han dynasty mausoleum of Emperor Yuan, Weiling), *Kaogu yu wenwu* 1 (1980): 38–41.

Zhang Xu, "Han dai yuandiao yuqi guibao" (Treasures of Han dynasty jade carving in the round). Yuqi yanjiu zhuankan (Special issue on jade research), *Wenbo* (1993): 59–62.

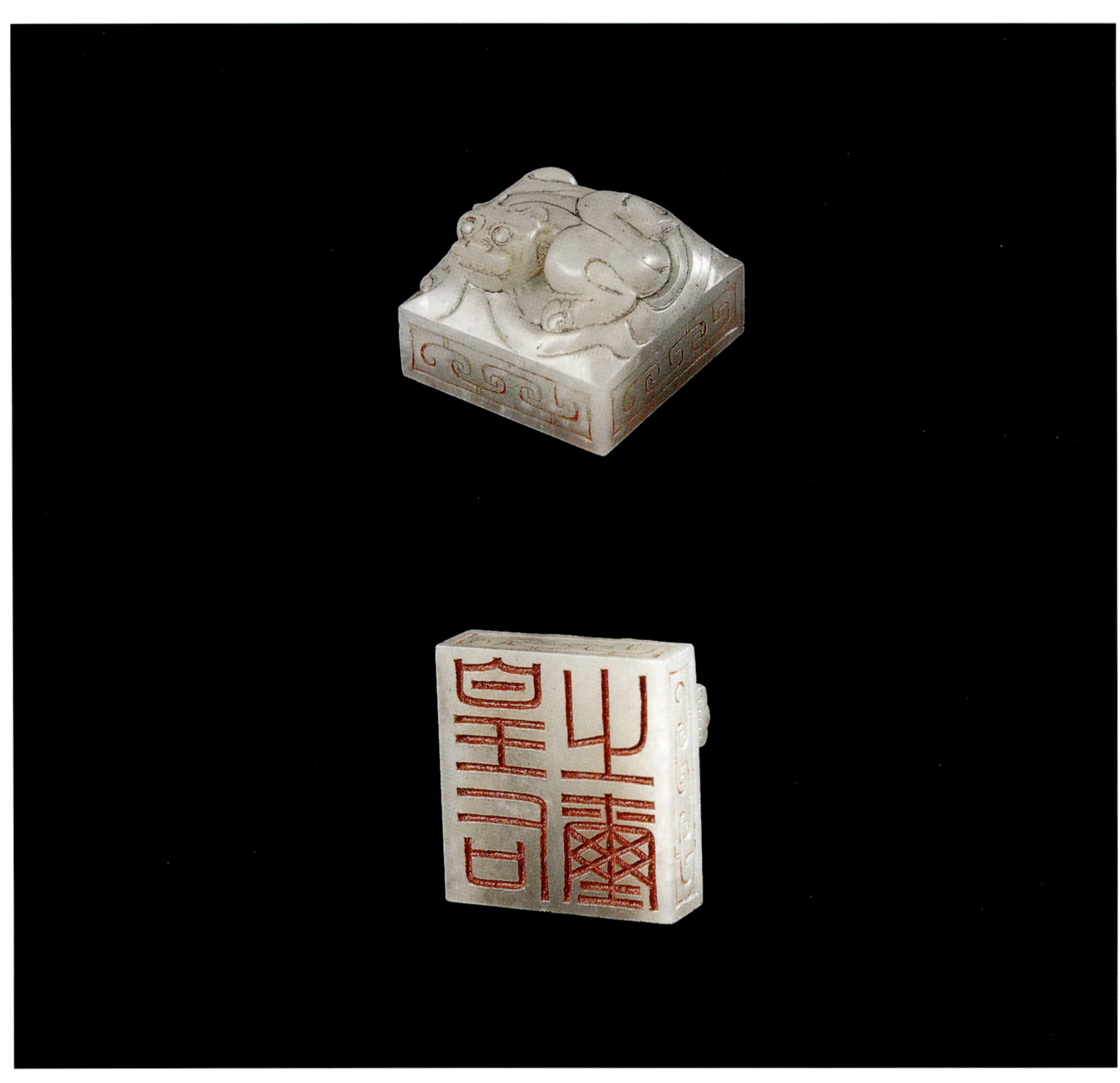

52 | SEAL OF EMPRESS
Western Han dynasty (206 B.C.–A.D. 9)
Jade
H. 3/4 in. (2 cm.); W. 1 1/8 in. (2.8 cm.)
Unearthed in 1968 in the vicinity of Changling, at Langjiagou, Xianyang City
Shaanxi History Museum

Found in the vicinity of Changling, this seal that bears the inscription "Seal of the Empress" (Huanghou zhi xi), most likely belonged to Lü Zhi (d. 180 B.C.), the empress of Emperor Gaozu. After Emperor Gaozu died in 195 B.C., their son, Liu Ying, became emperor, reigning until he died at the age of twenty-three. Two young puppet emperors followed, which gave Empress Lü the opportunity to rule as regent. She attempted to bolster her power by appointing members of her family, the Lü clan, as kings and generals. The historian, Sima Qian (ca. 145–90 B.C.) reported that she went even further and "eliminated" individuals who might disrupt her plan to give her family dominance over the clan of her deceased husband, the Liu family. Sima Qian also maintains that Empress Lü, like an emperor, issued decrees or edicts, which probably explains the existence of this kind of seal, which traditionally was reserved for the emperor and which is unique during the Western Han dynasty.

On the top of the seal a crouching creature functions as the knob. It has some feline characteristics but is really another fantastic beast. Its body is twisted and coiled like a ser-pent into an impossible but beautiful pose. It bares its teeth and stares out of two huge eyes. The sides of the seal are treated like panels with hook patterns within each frame. White jade seals of virtually the same size and composition, but without inscriptions, were found in the tomb of Liu Sheng, half-brother of Emperor Wu, at Mancheng in Hebei Province.[25]

Literature

Sima Qian, Records of the Grand Historian (Shi ji), juan 9, "The Basic Annals of Empress Lü" (Lü Taihou benji), *Records of the Grand Historian: Han Dynasty I*, trans. by Burton Watson. New York, Columbia University Press, 1993, 267–84.

Qin Bo, "Xi Han huanghou yuxi he 'Ganlu er nian' tongfanglu de faxian" (Discovery of the Western Han dynasty jade seal of an empress and the rectangular, bronze brazier inscribed 'Ganlu er nian [52 B.C.]'), *Wenwu* 5 (1973): 26–29.

An Jian, "Cong 'Huanghou zhu xi' tanqi" (On the inscription, 'Seal of the Empress'), *Wenwu* 11 (1976): 8–9.

Zhong guo meishu quanji: gongyi meishu bian 9: yu qi (Selections of Chinese art: arts and crafts no. 9; jade objects), Beijing: Wenwu Chubanshe, 1986, pls. 135–37.

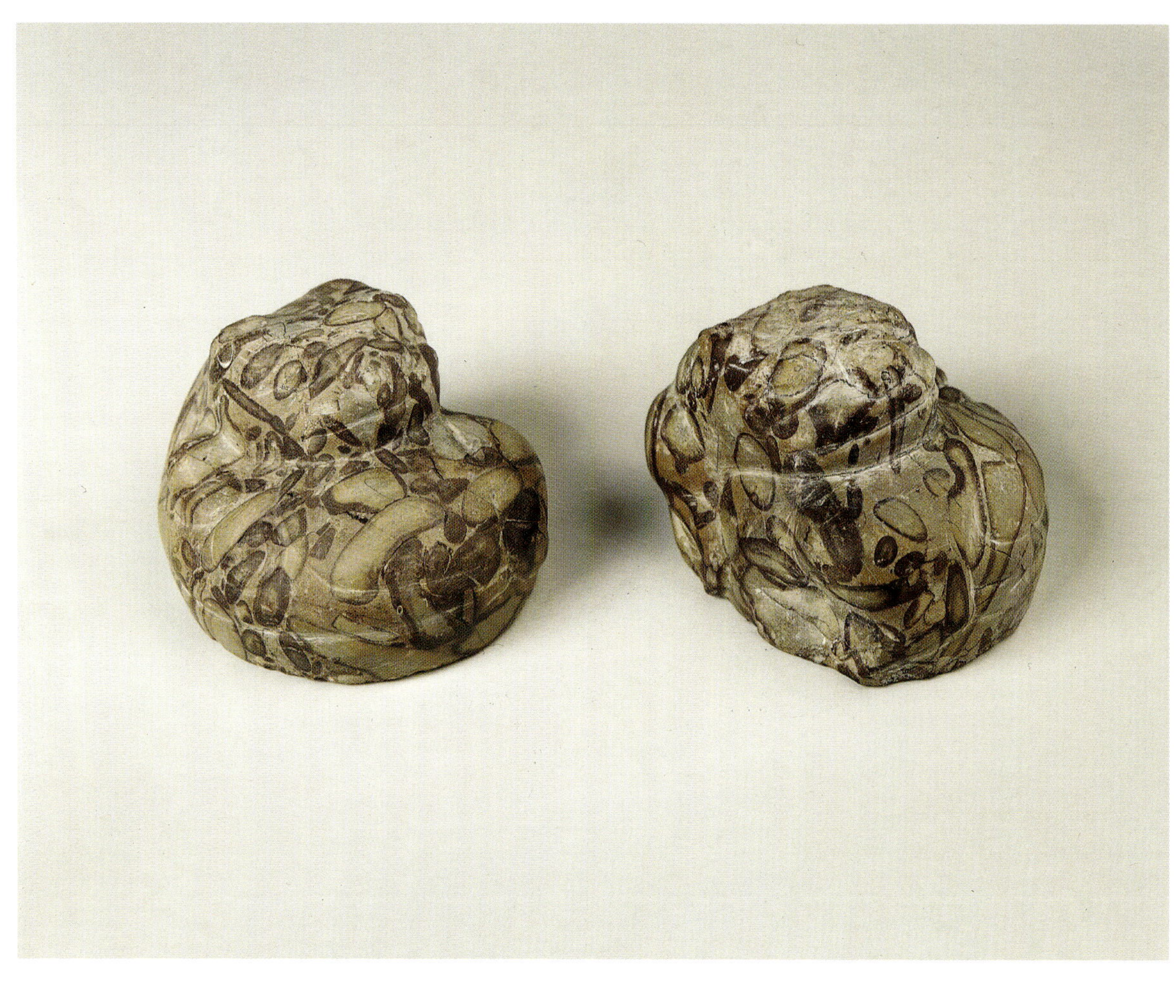

53 PAIR OF WEIGHTS
Western Han dynasty (206 B.C.–A.D. 9)
Stone
H. 2 1/4 in. (5.5 cm.); W. 3 1/8 in. (8 cm.)
Unearthed in Xingping County
Maoling Museum

This pair of weights is sculpted as crouching animals shaped into an
overall oval form. Like other animal
sculptures in this exhibition, the particular creatures being represented cannot be easily identified. They have
some feline characteristics, but the
sculptor has taken many liberties. The
features of the face are broadly carved,
with little detail. The type of stone is
called *zhuyeyan* (bamboo leaf stone)
and the pattern of the stone fabric facil-
itates an association with the fur of
tigers. Objects carved from this kind of
stone are quite rare, but a stemmed
bowl made of zhuyeyan was unearthed
in the environs of the Chang'an (fig.
5.12).[26] Archaeologists believe that the
bowl once supported the perforated lid
of a censer. Based on other objects
found with the stone vessel, the find
has been dated to the latter part of the
reign of Emperor Wu.

Weights made in the form of
crouching animals are common during
this period, but bronze, gilded bronze,
or bronze inlaid with gold and silver
are preferred media.[27] A set of four
gilded bronze weights comprised of
crouching animals was excavated from
a pit in the vicinity of Maoling mausoleum (fig. 5.13).[28]

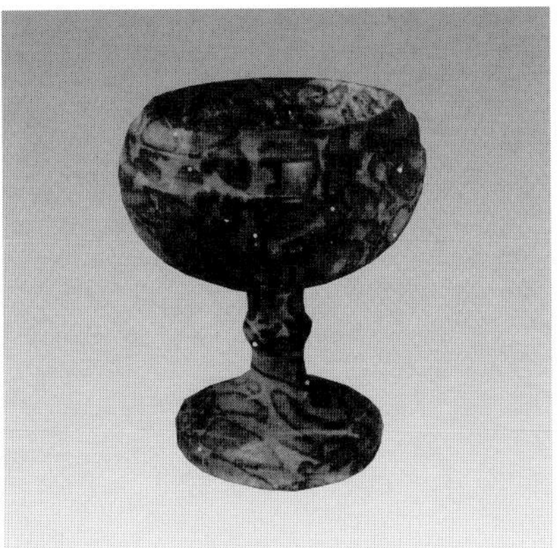

Fig. 5.12. Stemmed bowl, H. 4 9/16 in. After *Kaogu yu wenwu* 4 (1987): 39–41, pl. 1.1.

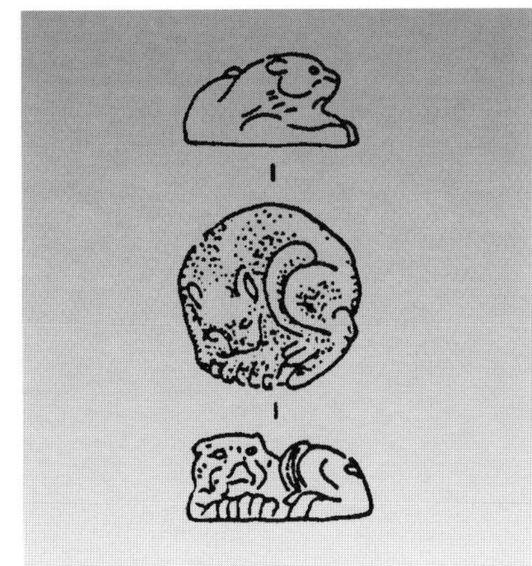

Fig. 5.13. Set of four gilded bronze weights, H. 9/16 in.; L. 1 1/8 in. After *Wenwu* 9 (1982): 1–17, fig. 28.

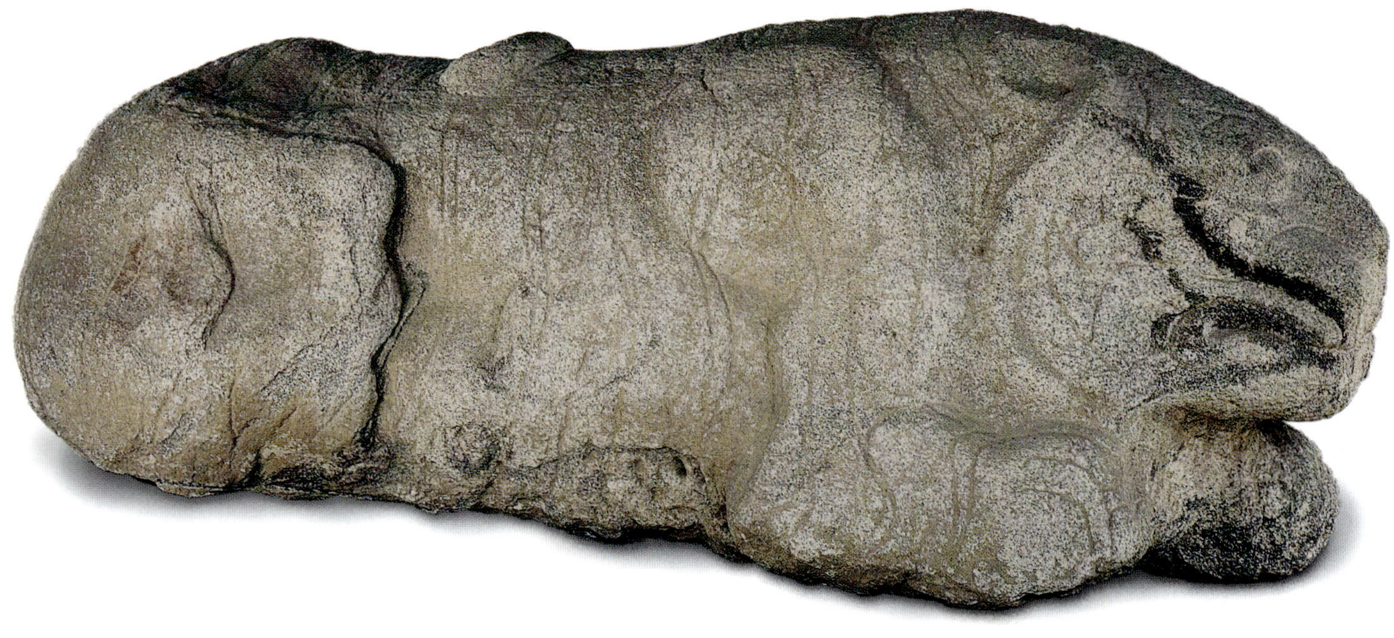

54 | RECUMBENT TIGER
Western Han dynasty (206 B.C.–A.D. 9)
Granite
L. 86 5/8 in. (220 cm.); W. 33 1/8 in. (84 cm.); Weight 2 1/2 tons
Outdoor Stone Sculpture from the tomb of Huo Qubing, near Maoling,
Xingping County
Maoling Museum

This large-scale stone sculpture is from the tomb of Huo Qubing (d. 116 B.C.), who was an important general during the reign of Emperor Wu. In fact, Huo's tomb is located in the vicinity of Wu's mausoleum, Maoling (fig. 5.14). According to Sima Qian, the historian during the reign of Wu:

> Huo Qubing died in the sixth year of yuanshou . . . . The emperor was deeply grieved and ordered soldiers from the tribes of Xiongnu who had submitted to Han rule to be called to the capital and ranged along the road from Chang'an to Maoling bearing iron weapons. At Maoling he had a grave mound constructed in the shape of then Qilian Mountains. In recognition of Huo Qubing's military achieve-

ments and his services in extending the borders of the empire, the emperor awarded him the double posthumous name of Jinghuan or "Righteous and Martial" marquis.[29]

Huo participated in six campaigns against the non-Chinese, Xiongnu. Part of the Huo's success was due to the fact that by this time a strong cavalry had been established, but there was an ever-growing demand for suitable horses. At Huo's tomb site three large stone horses are among the group of sculptures: a recumbent horse, a leaping horse, and a horse trampling a figure, often interpreted as a Xiongnu warrior. Other stone creatures found at the site include an elephant, a reclining ox, a tiger, a boar, a toad, a frog, and two fish. In addition sculptures of a man hugging a bear and a fantastic monster holding a small animal in its mouth were at the site. An interpretation of the whole program is problematic, since the original locations cannot be reconstructed. However, these images are distinguished from all other examples of funerary sculpture of this era in size and because they were made for the exterior of the tomb. They are not like the surrogate *mingqi* earthenware animals in this exhibition but should probably be considered commemorative monuments.

All of these sculptures feature a smooth surface with enough detail so that most of the figures can be recognized, but finer points of anatomical structure have been glossed over, as they are in the figures and animals from other Western Han dynasty sites. The tiger in this exhibition is in a recumbent position, but it is alert. Its head looks straight ahead, and its eyes are fixed on something in the distance. The closed mouth, however, lends a less ferocious nature to this beast. The limbs, ears, and tail of the tiger are rendered in slightly higher relief than the body, but the overall effect is a closed, compact work that appears to be little modified from the original stone. The

tiger's stripes are indicated by pairs of curving lines incised on the surface of the body. The representation of this stone tiger is comparable to a depiction of the White Tiger of the west on the face of a hollow architectural brick that was unearthed to the east of Maoling, Emperor Wu's mausoleum (fig. 5.15).[30] The representation of the head and of the stripes is similar to the stone example and may have been the model for Huo's tiger. Indeed, even though the stone tiger from Huo's tomb is sculpted in the round, it appears as if the sculptor has approached the stone as two relief surfaces melded together at the center.

Literature

Sima Qian, *Records of the Historian (Shi ji)*, juan 111, "Biography of General Wei Qing and Swift Cavalry General Huo Qubing" (Wei jiangjun piao-qi liechuan), in *Records of the Grand Historian: Han Dynasty*, trans. by Burton Watson. *Han Dynasty II*, New York: Columbia University Press, 1993, 163–84.

Liang Zuo, "Han Wudi Maoling yu Huo Qubing mu" (Maoling, the mausoleum of Emperor Wu and the tomb of Huo Qubing), *Wenbo* 3 (1985): 83–85.

"Maoling Huo Qubing mu" (The tomb of Huo Qubing at Maoling)," *Wenwu* 7 (1976): 87–89.

He Hannan, "Huo Qubing zhong ji shike" (Stone carvings from the tomb of Huo Qubing), *Wenbo* 2 (1988): 20–24.

Paludan, Ann, *The Chinese Spirit Road: The Classical Tradition of Stone Tomb Statuary*, New Haven: Yale University Press, 1991.

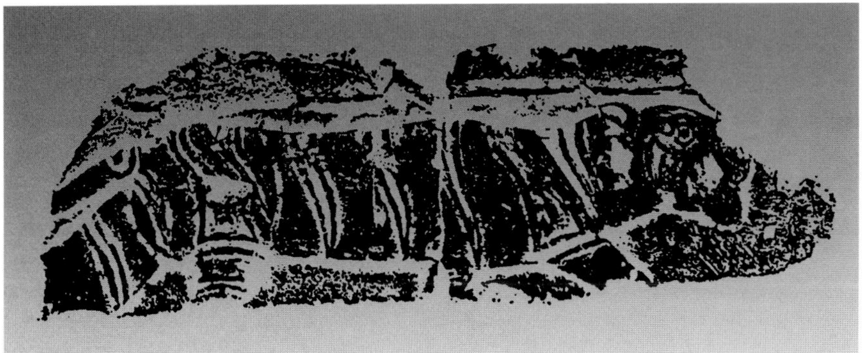

Fig. 5.14. Hollow tile with image of tiger (damaged L. 18 5/16 in.; W. 5 1/2 in.; damaged T. 5 1/2 in.). After *Wenwu* 7 (1976): 51–55, fig. 2.

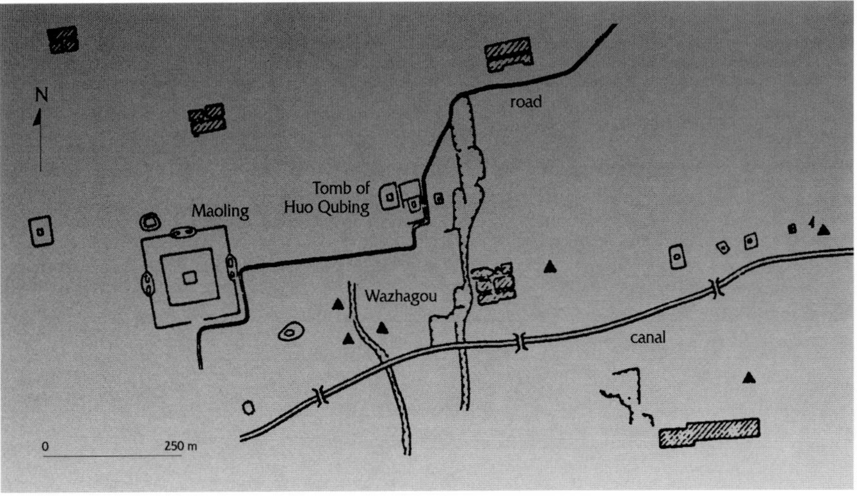

Fig. 5.15. Site of the Tomb of Huo Qubing. After *Wenwu* 7 (1976): 51–55, fig. 1.

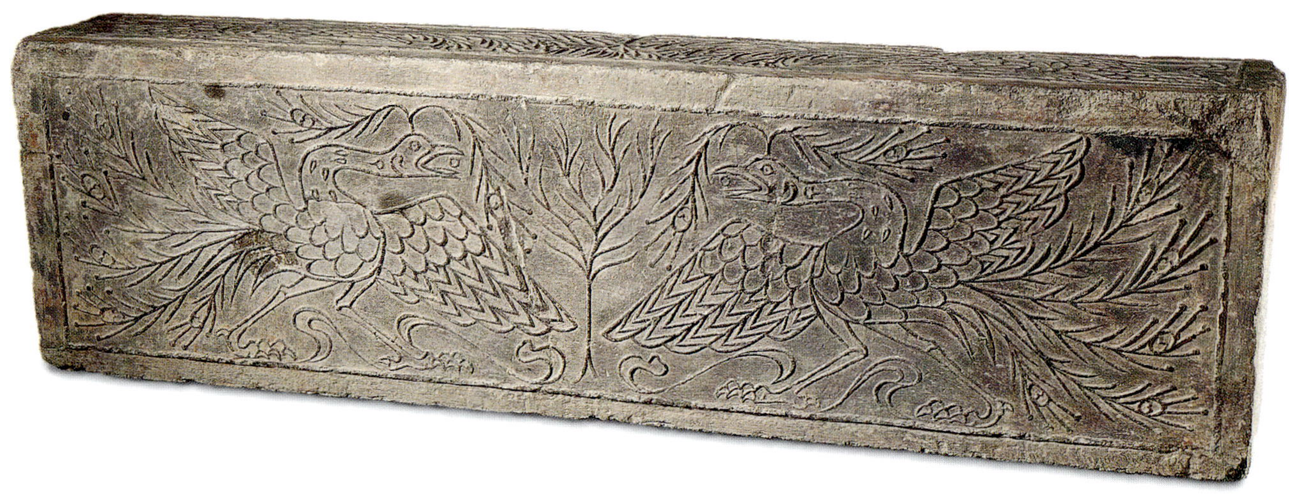

55 HOLLOW BRICK WITH PHOENIX AND TREE DECOR
Wang Mang Interregnum (A.D. 9–23)
Earthenware
L. 53 7/8 in. (137 cm.); W. 15 in. (38 cm.); D. 8 1/4 in. (21 cm.)
Excavated in 1980 at Taerpo, Xianyang
Xianyang Museum

The interior wall of Tomb 36 at Taerpo near Xianyang was the original location of this hollow earthenware brick. The tomb, which has been dated to the Wang Mang Interregnum, has a passageway, an entry door, and a chamber (fig. 5.16). The outer wall where the door is positioned and all walls inside the chamber are covered with this type of hollow brick, as well as some solid bricks. Many of the bricks are left undecorated, while others are elaborated with geometric patterns, including meanders. However, several of the hollow bricks are decorated with creatures that for the most part, represent the animals of the cardinal directions—the Vermilion Bird of the south, the White Tiger of the west, and the Green Dragon of the east—thus creating an auspicious setting in the tomb. The Black Warrior of the north is missing, but a phoenix (*feng*) has been added to the program. The creatures are not placed on the appropriate walls, that is, the tiger is located on the east and south walls rather than on the west, as would be expected. These bricks with animal decor seem randomly placed, although they occur most frequently within the tier closest to the floor.

A phoenix is represented on just one brick in this tomb, and this brick is placed in the center tier on the northwest sidewall. Images of pairs of phoenixes appear on the front, on the back, and on one side of the brick. The symmetrical composition is typical of all of the bricks ornamented with creatures. The birds are mirror images placed to either side of the center. In this case, they face one another, but in other instances the creatures have their backs to each other but turn their heads to look at one another. Many of the bricks have jade *bi* disks at the center, but a miniature tree is utilized in this example. The images of these creatures are rendered in relief, but the birds are depicted with very thin, raised lines. They have outstretched wings, and the tail and head plumage fills the space around the phoenix. The birds have pearls in their beaks, an attribute of both the Vermilion Bird of the south and the phoenix. The same motif, a bird with a pearl in its beak, also is visible on the surface of a broken brick from the Qin dynasty palace.[31] Other decorated architectural bricks (hollow and solid) dating to the reign of Emperor Wu, have been unearthed in the vicinity of Maoling.[32] They include the same repertoire of images: White Tiger, Vermilion Bird, phoenix, and the Black Warrior as well.

Literature

Sun Derun, "Xianyang shi kongxin zhuan Han mu qingli jianbao" (A brief report on the Han dynasty hollow brick tomb at Xianyang municipality), *Kaogu* 3 (1982): 225–35.

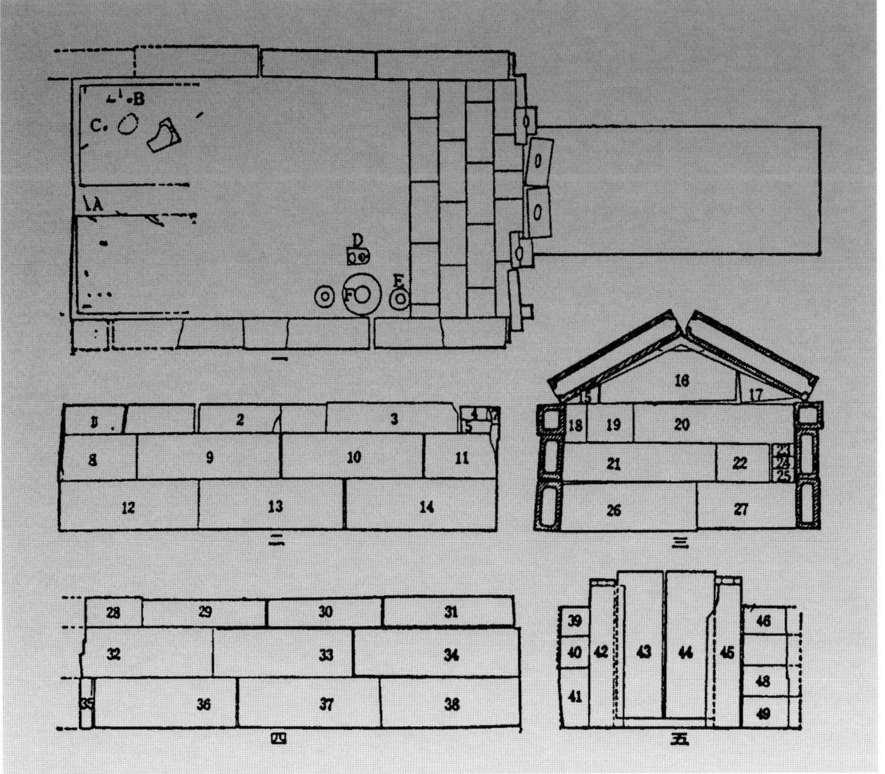

Fig. 5.16. Plan and elevation of Tomb 35, Taerpo. After *Kaogu* 3 (1982): 225–35, fig. 7.

56 | GREEN DRAGON OF THE EAST (*Cang* or *qing long*)
D. 7 3/8 in. (18.5 cm.)
Unearthed in the area of Xianyang, Shaanxi Province
Xianyang Museum

57 | WHITE TIGER OF THE WEST (*Bai hu*)
D. 7 in. (17.7 cm.)
Unearthed in 1958 in the northern suburb of Xi'an
Shaanxi History Museum

58 | VERMILION BIRD OF THE SOUTH (*Zhu que*)
D. 7 3/8 in. (18.8 cm.)
Unearthed in 1953 in the northern suburb of Xi'an
Shaanxi History Museum

59 | BLACK OR DARK WARRIOR OF THE NORTH (*Xuan wu*—serpent and tortoise)
D. 7 1/4 in. (18.3 cm.)
Unearthed in 1953 in the northern suburb of Xi'an
Shaanxi History Museum

Eave Titles (*wa dang*) with Four Divinities (*si shen*)
Western Han dynasty (206 B.C.–A.D. 9)
Earthenware

The faces of these earthenware eaves tiles are decorated with the animals symbolizing the four cardinal directions of the compass in the Five-Phase (*wu xing*) cosmology.[33] The creatures are molded in relief and fill the center of rondels that are framed by a smooth, raised border. The animals of the east and west—the dragon and the tiger—seem to be running, since their legs have been evenly spaced on the lower arc of the circle. In both cases the head of the creature fills the upper left quadrant. The heads of the dragon and tiger are balanced in the upper right by their tails that rise as elegant hooked forms. Although these tiles are relatively small and would have been placed on the roof of a building or gate, the creatures have been rendered with much detail. The stripes of the tiger are suggested with the use of irregular intaglio striations on the body. The scales, wings, and horns of the dragon also are carefully described. Both creatures have open mouths, as if roaring to alert everyone of their presence and to ward off the inauspicious.

The Vermilion Bird of the south extends its wings outward, but it has planted one leg solidly on the edge of the tile and has stretched the other forward, as if it could suddenly fly away. The long plumes to the rear and front are curled, and they fill the circular field. The feathers of its wings and the scales of its body are carefully detailed, and the bird holds a pearl in its mouth. John S. Major explains that the pearl is a symbol of *yin* and *yang*:[34] "Pearls are round (*yang*) in shape, and are luminous (*yang*) but are congealed from and found in water (*yin*)."

The Dark or Black Warrior of the north is comprised of a tortoise and a snake.[35] The tortoise lifts its head to look up at the snake, whose head is in the upper right quadrant of the tile. The snake has wound its body around the tortoise and raises its tail in the air.

At the center of each tile is a circular boss that may be related to the structure of earlier tiles that had lines dividing the format into four parts, with a boss where the lines intersected. This boss could be a reference to the fact that these creatures also symbolize the Celestial Palaces of the non-circumpolar stars; in fact, celestial bodies often are represented simply as dots in wall paintings of the period.[36]

These animals are part of the Five-Phase cosmology that flourished during the Western Han period and the Wang Mang Interregnum in Chang'an. Wang Zhongshu believes that this iconographic program can be associated with ceremonial architecture constructed by Wang Mang during his short reign.[37] In the south suburb of Chang'an, Wang Mang constructed several ritual structures, and excavations in this area during the late 1950s and 1960s revealed the foundations of structures that may be identified as his Ming tang or Pi yong. Eaves tiles like the ones in the exhibition were found at this site. When the tiles with these animals were placed according to the Five Phase theory, they would reinforce the ritual nature of these structures erected by Wang Mang to legitimize his rule. Inscriptions on Wang Mang interregnum bronze mirrors that feature these creatures as decoration suggest they also had an apotropaic function. An inscription on a mirror produced during Wang Mang's reign reads:[38]

> The Xin (dynasty) has excellent copper, it comes from Danyang. Refined and worked with silver and tin, it is clear and bright. The Shangfang [state workshops] have made (this) mirror, (which) is completely without flaw; To the left the Dragon and to the right the Tiger avert misfortune; the Vermilion Bird and the Dark Warrior are in accord with *yin* and *yang*. May your sons and grandsons be complete in number and dwell in the center; May you long preserve your two parents in happiness and good fortune. May your longevity be like that of metal and stone; May your lot be that of a prince.

Literature

Luo Zhongru, "Xi'an xijiao faxian Handai jianzhu yizhi" (Discovery of Han dynasty architectural sites in the western suburb of Xi'an), *Kaogu tongxun* 6 (1957): 26–30, pl. 8.

Wang Zhongshu, *Han Civilization*, New Haven: Yale University Press, 1982, 10 and 149.

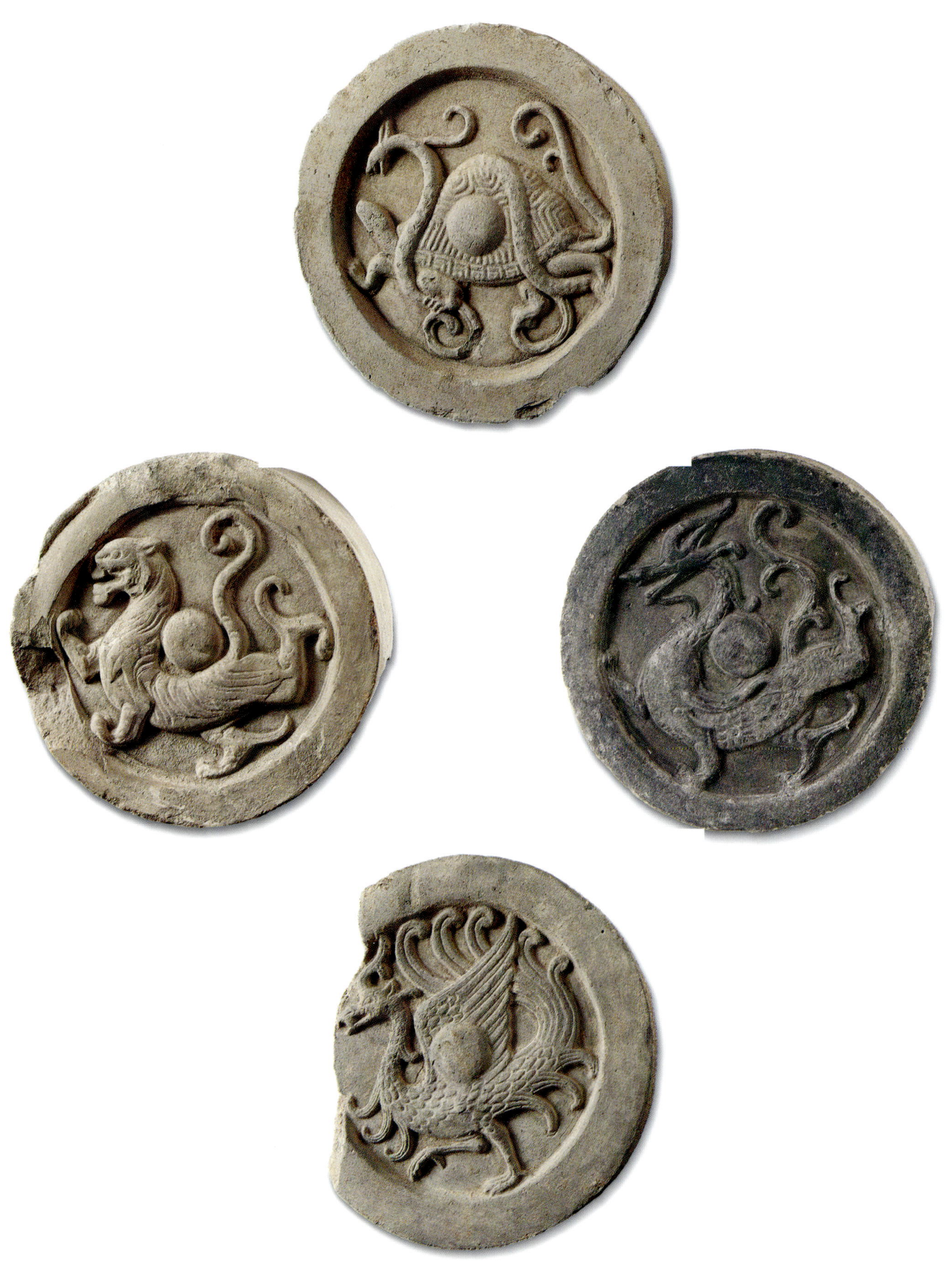

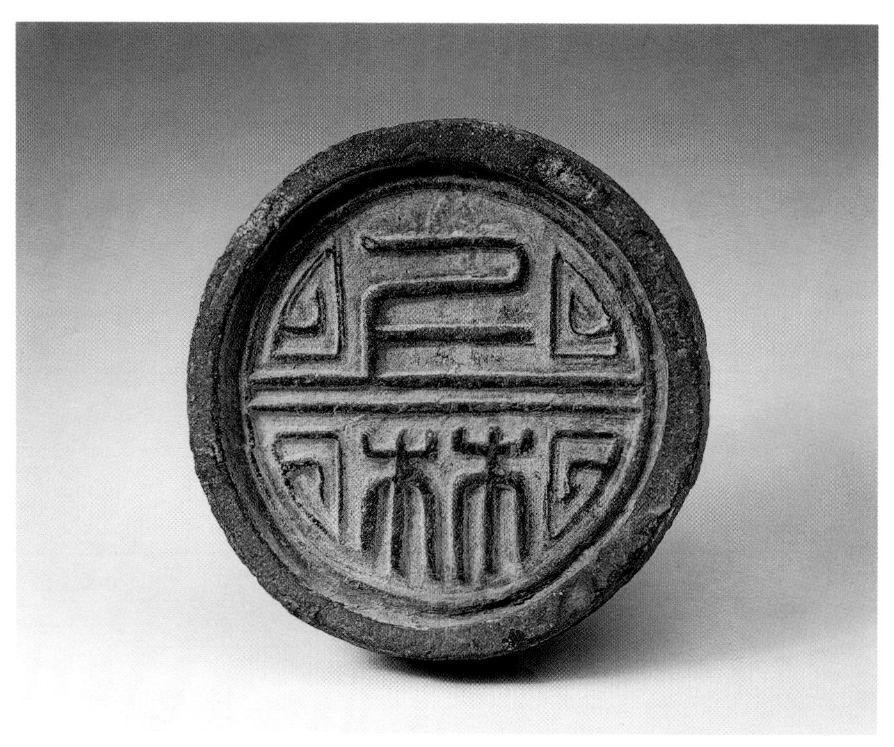

60 | TILE (*wadang*) WITH INSCRIPTION: "SUPREME FOREST (*Shanglin*)"
Western Han dynasty (206 B.C.–A.D. 9)
Earthenware
D. 5 3/8 in. (13.5 cm.)
Unearthed in 1954 in the northern suburb of Xi'an
Shaanxi History Museum

This tile is slightly smaller than the others in the exhibition, and its rondel shape has been divided into two semi-circles separated in the center by raised, parallel lines. In each half a single character is placed in the center of the field and geometric fill ornament is located in the awkwardly shaped side spaces. Using the style of calligraphy known as seal script, the top field is inscribed with the character "shang" and the bottom with "lin," which characters refer to the famous Shanglin or Supreme Forest imperial park used by the Western Han emperors and expanded by Emperor Wu (r. 141–87 B.C.).[39]

The Shanglin park was located southwest of Chang'an and included palaces, lodges, and pavilions that were roofed with this kind of tile. When Wudi expanded the park, he also had a pond dug, the Kunming pond, and he had the precinct filled with plants and animals from throughout China to create a microcosm of the empire. The park was the subject of a prose-poem entitled "The Imperial Park" (*Shanglin fu*) by Sima Xiangru (179–117 B.C.).[40] It is still questionable if Sima Xiangru had actually seen the park before writing the composition, but Emperor Wu was so pleased after reading it that he appointed Sima to the court. The following lines from "The Imperial Park" refer to the fabulous architectural structures in the Emperor Wu's park:[41]

> And then
> Detached palaces, separate
> lodges, Stretch over the
> mountains, straddle the valleys:
> Tall corridors pour out in four
> directions, With double decks
> and twisting passageways;
> Fitted with ornate rafters and
> jade finials, Carriage roads are
> laced and linked together.
> In the covered walkways to
> walk completely around,
> Long is the course and midway
> one must halt for the night.
>
> On leveled peaks they built the
> halls, With tiered terraces rising
> story upon story, And cavernous
> rooms in the crags and crannies.

Literature

Shaanxi gudai meishu xunli, 5: Qin Han wadang (Shaanxi ancient art series, no. 5: Eave tiles of the Qin And Han dynasties), Xi'an: Shaanxi Renmin Meishu Chubanshe, 1985.

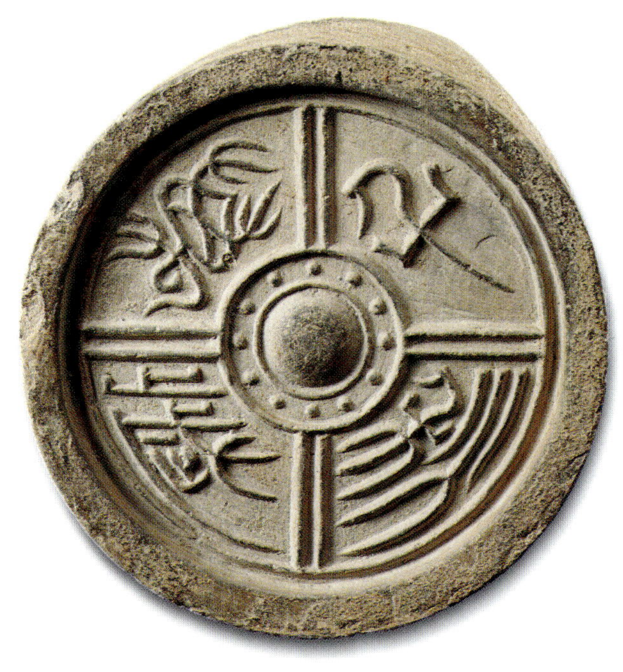

61 TILE (*wa dang*) WITH INSCRIPTION: "A THOUSAND AUTUMNS, TEN
THOUSAND YEARS (*Qianqiu wansui*)"
Western Han dynasty (206 B.C.–A.D. 9)
Earthenware
D. 6 3/4 in. (17.2 cm.)
Unearthed in 1974 in Daochang Village, Xingping County
Maoling Museum

The face of this tile is comprised of four quadrants with a large boss and twelve surrounding beads at the center. One character is placed in each section. The relief characters are rendered in a mannered style so that they fill the irregular spaces. The four-character inscription, which reads from right to left and top to bottom, is one of many used during this era and meant to impart blessings. This auspicious phrase, "A Thousand Autumns, Ten Thousand Years (*Qianqiu wansui*)," conveys the hope for everlasting life for the empire and for the emperor. According to Five-Phases Cosmology, the twelve circular beads surrounding the boss could symbolize the twelve months of the year and/or the Twelve Branches that represent the twelve divisions of heaven.[42]

Eastern Han dynasty
(A.D. 25–220)

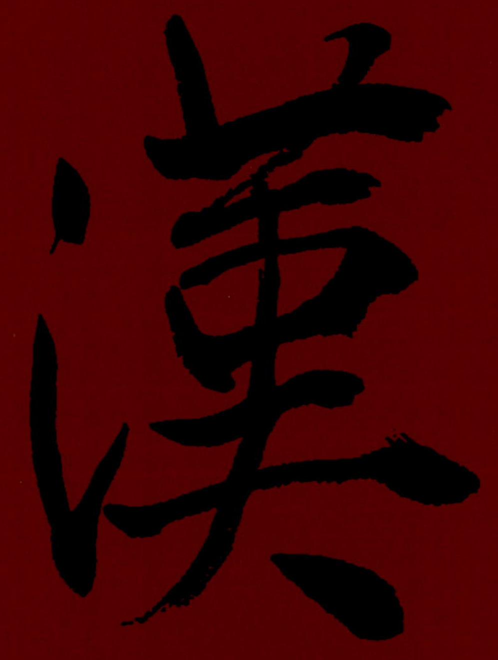

During the early first century A.D., Liu Xiu, a wealthy landowner of Nanyang, Henan Province, established the Eastern Han dynasty in Luoyang, Henan. During his reign (A.D. 25–57), Liu Xiu revitalized the government with a series of political systems of the Western Han and relaxed taxes on peasants' incomes. By the year A.D. 100, great progress had been made in agriculture and economy, and the population increased steadily. Agricultural techniques, such as the use of ox-pulled plows and iron tools, were widely spread over the country. However, changes occurred after the middle of the Eastern Han, when a large number of farmers lost their land and property due to heavy taxes and a change in court policies. When wealthy landowners began to purchase these farms, many large, privately owned manors emerged and the bankrupt farmers became tenant farmers or slaves of these new landowners.

Archaeological findings including pottery figures and architectural models, stone reliefs, and frescos from the tombs reflect these changes. Depicting human and spiritual scenes, this pictorial tomb art reflects not only the social reality and ideology, but also indicates a stylistic departure from non-realistic representation that had dominated ancient Chinese art since the Shang dynasty (ca. 1600–1050 B.C.). This tendency toward realism was enhanced by the ceramics produced at this time. Models of houses and household facilities such as wells and pigsties were made in such a genuine manner that they provide valuable sources for the study of Han architecture. The most notable achievement in the Han ceramics is the use of glaze, which made pottery more durable and appealing. Although the glazing technique appeared in the Western Han or even earlier, it was not until the Eastern Han that this technique became refined and widespread.

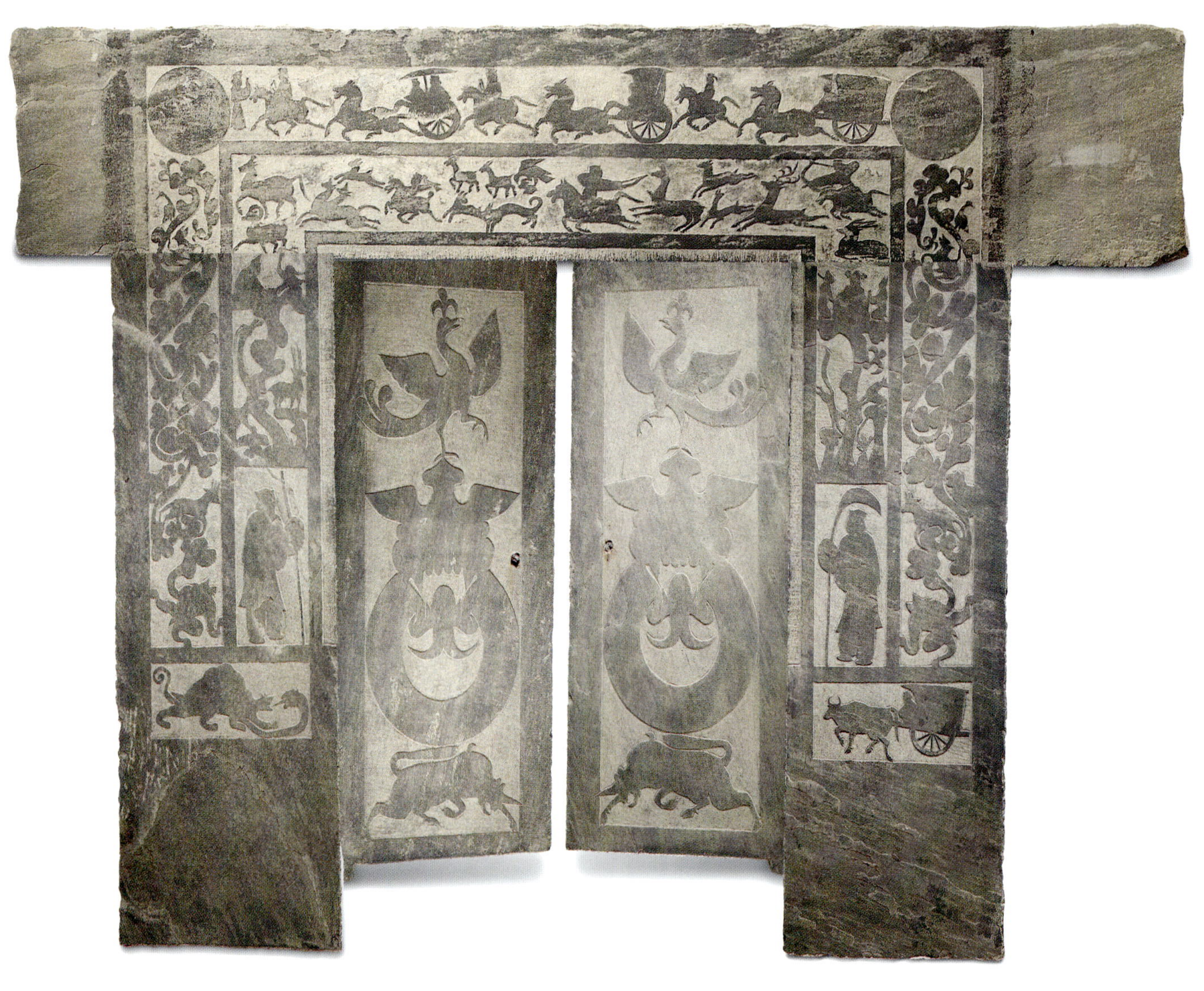

62

RELIEFS OF TOMB ENTRANCE
Eastern Han dynasty (A.D. 25–220)
Stone
Lintel: H. 16 in. (42 cm.); W. 86 5/8 in. (220 cm.)
Door panels: H. 46 in. (118 cm.); W. 19 3/4 in. (50 cm.)
Door posts: H. 48 in. (123 cm.); W. 16 in. (42 cm.)
Unearthed at Chenxingzhuang, Shangyanwan, Yulin, northern Shaanxi Province
Yulin Hongshixia Institute of Cultural Relics

Sets of stone entrances like this one have been found in Han tombs since the 1950s in Suide, Mizhi, and Yulin in northern Shaanxi Province. Archaeological finds indicate that using stone slabs with carved designs to build tomb chambers was a common practice of landowners and military officers during the Eastern Han dynasty. A stone chamber was not only durable, but it could also carry the carved images that convey symbolic meanings.

The stone reliefs, as seen in this set, convey two concepts of concern to the ancient Han people: the current life and the afterlife. On the door panels, legendary and sacred creatures such as red phoenixes, beast masks, and unicorns were carved as tomb guardians to warn off evil spirits. On the door posts, which are divided into compartments, are immortals seated on the divine trees: the King Father of the East on the left and the Queen Mother of the West on the right. The King Father, depicted in profile, is accompanied by an immortal with wings and by a deer under the tree. The Queen Mother, depicted in a frontal pose, is flanked by a divine rabbit and a winged immortal; she is also accompanied by a sacred fox and a bird under the tree. On the lower section of each post is a guardian with either a broom or a spear in his hand, signifying that the tomb chamber is secure. The lintel is divided into two secure. The lintel is divided into two sections. The lower section depicts a hunting scene and the upper a parade of riders and carriages that are greeted by a figure on the far left end, who makes a symbolic gesture. The human activities, such as processional and hunting scenes depicted on the reliefs, probably reflect the life of the tomb occupant and the events that occurred at the tomb site during the ritual ceremony. The entire scheme and imagery on this entrance stone emphasize the concept of immortality that became a favorite theme of tomb art during the Western Han.

These stone reliefs rank northern Shaanxi as one of four major stone relief centers of the Han dynasty, after Shandong, Henan, and Sichuan. As seen on this set, the Shaanxi reliefs are characterized by hunting and processional scenes on the lintel and by curling foliage and cloud motifs at the edge. With few images on silk or paper available from this period, these stone reliefs are valuable in terms of studying Han pictorial art, social life, economy, and ideology.

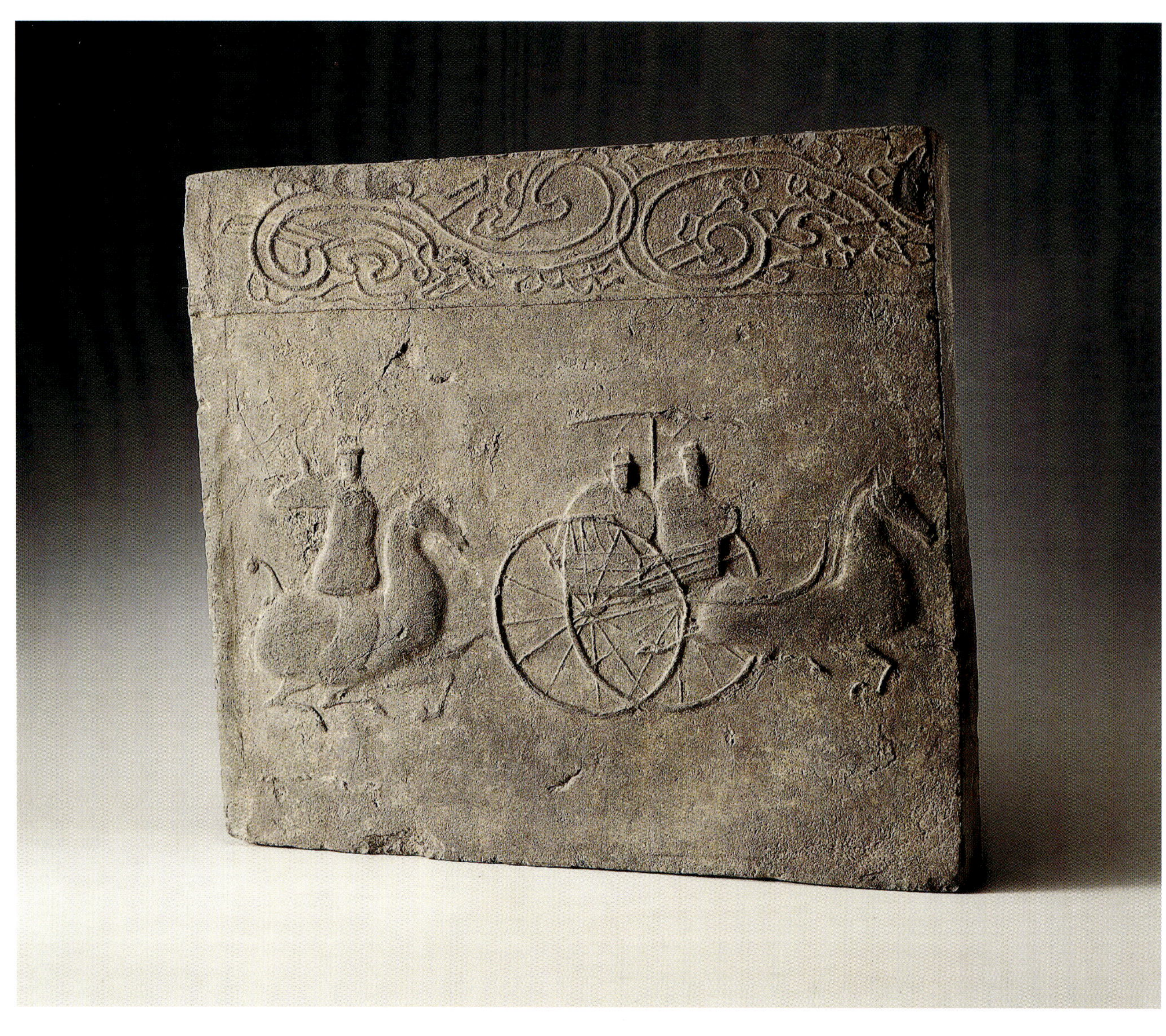

63 | BRICK WITH RIDING SCENE
Eastern Han dynasty (A.D. 25–220)
Earthenware
L. 18 1/2 in. (47 cm.); W. 15 1/8 in. (40.5 cm.); D: 1 1/8 in. (2.8 cm.)
Unearthed from Hanzhong, southwestern Shaanxi Province
Shaanxi History Museum

In ancient China, carriages were manufactured primarily for two purposes: fighting in war and as transportation vehicles. By the middle of the Western Han dynasty, many types of carriages were developed for use in daily transport. The most common type, depicted here, was a small, open carriage pulled by one and sometimes two horses and covered with an umbrella-shaped canopy decorated with tassels. This type of carriage could carry one passenger, usually an officer, and one driver, either in a seated position or standing to see into the distance.

In this solid brick relief, the riding scene is defined by flowing contours and a variety of molded elevations, which is not commonly seen in Shaanxi bricks of the Eastern Han period. However, its images of riders and a band of continuous cloud motifs on the upper border resemble the pictorial style shown in the stone and brick reliefs from Sichuan Province. The geographic connection of Hanzhong in southern Shaanxi and Sichuan may imply the stylistic influence of these two regions. Considering its size and composition, this piece was probably made as a construction element to decorate a tomb wall.

Literature

Lim, Lucy. *Stories from China's Past: Han Dynasty Pictorial Tomb Reliefs and Archaeological Objects from Sichuan Province, People's Republic of China*, San Francisco: Chinese Culture Foundation, 1987.

Sun Ji, *Handai wuzhi wenhua ziliao tushuo* (Illustrated comments on the material culture of the Han dynasty), Beijing: Wenwu Press, 1991.

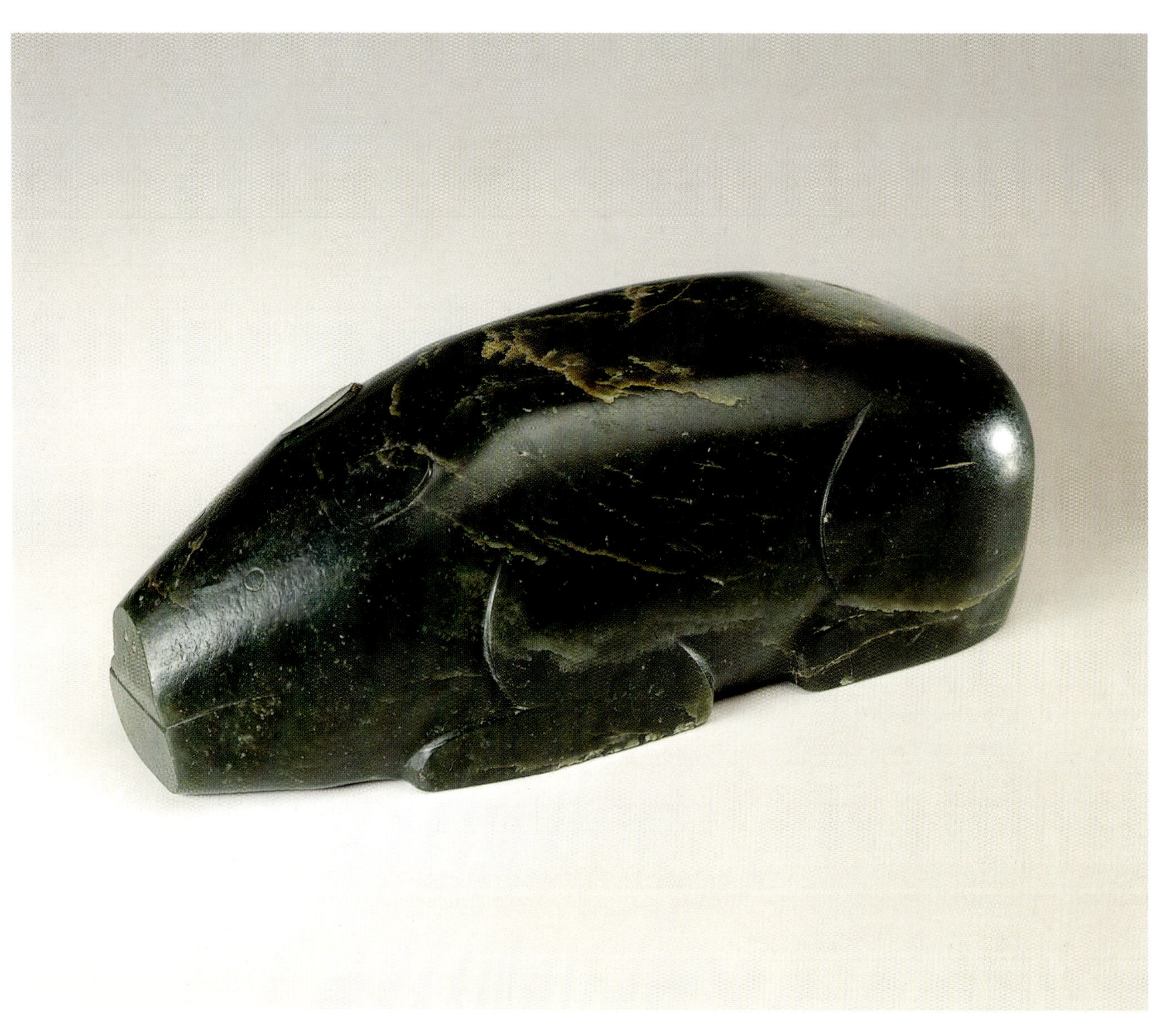

64 | PILLOW IN SHAPE OF A PIG
Han dynasty (206 B.C.–A.D. 220)
Jade
H. 3 1/2 in. (9 cm.); L. 9 5/8 in. (24.3 cm.); W. 4 3/8 in. (10.8 cm.)
Unearthed in 1979 at Xiwangcun, Xi'an
Xi'an Institute of Cultural Relics and Archaeology

Carved out of an oval-shaped piece of dark green jade, this pig is shown in a recumbent posture, with legs bent under the body, eyes incised as circles, and a deep, incised line indicating its mouth. Its ears are flattened against its head, and its tail is carved in low relief. Characterized by the economic use of knife work, this carving demonstrates the Han artisan's ability to handle the hardness of jade in a bold and abstract manner.

Although it was discovered at the site of a Han palace in a northern suburb of Xi'an, its actual function remains unclear. Small jade pigs have been found in the hands of the deceased in Han tombs, while a large pig like this one, which weighs seven pounds, is rarely encountered. Considering its shape, design, and dimensions, this piece was probably used as a burial pillow.

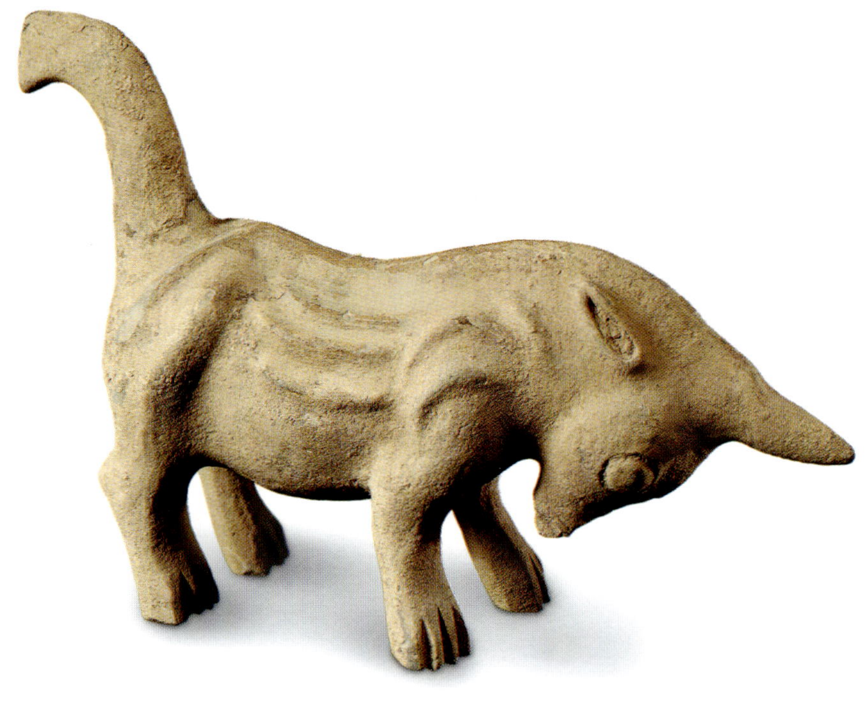

65 | UNICORN
Eastern Han dynasty (A.D. 25–220)
Earthenware
H. 11 in. (28 cm.); L. 16 1/2 in. (42 cm.)
Unearthed from Mianxian, southwestern Shaanxi Province
Shaanxi History Museum

The use of unicorn imagery might have derived from the rhinoceros, which was introduced from western Asia to China during the Western Han dynasty. Distinguished by its long horn, the unicorn was seen as a sacred creature for protection against evil spirits and was often carved on a tomb relief or sculpted as a free-standing statue.

Molded in grey clay, this figure is posed solidly on all four feet with its tail held up. Its head is lowered with its horn pointed, as if it is preparing to attack. Compared to most Han figurines, which are static, this unicorn is molded as if charged with power. The dynamic movement is indicated by its curved spine and exaggerated bone structures.

An almost identical statue was found from Tomb no. 5 in Hanzhong in southern Shaanxi in 1985. Among objects found with it was a bronze mirror that bears an inscription suggesting a date of the late Eastern Han dynasty.

Literature

Tang Jinyu and Guo Qinghua, "Shaanxi Mianxian Hongmiao Donghanmu qingli jianbao" (Brief excavation report on Eastern Han tombs at Hongmiao, Mianxian, Shaanxi), *Kaogu yu wenwu*, no. 4 (1983): 30–34.

Guo Qinghua, "Shaanxi Mianxian Laodaosi Hanmu" (Han Tombs excavated at Laodaosi in Mianxian, Shaanxi), *Kaogu*, no. 5 (1985): 432, 439.

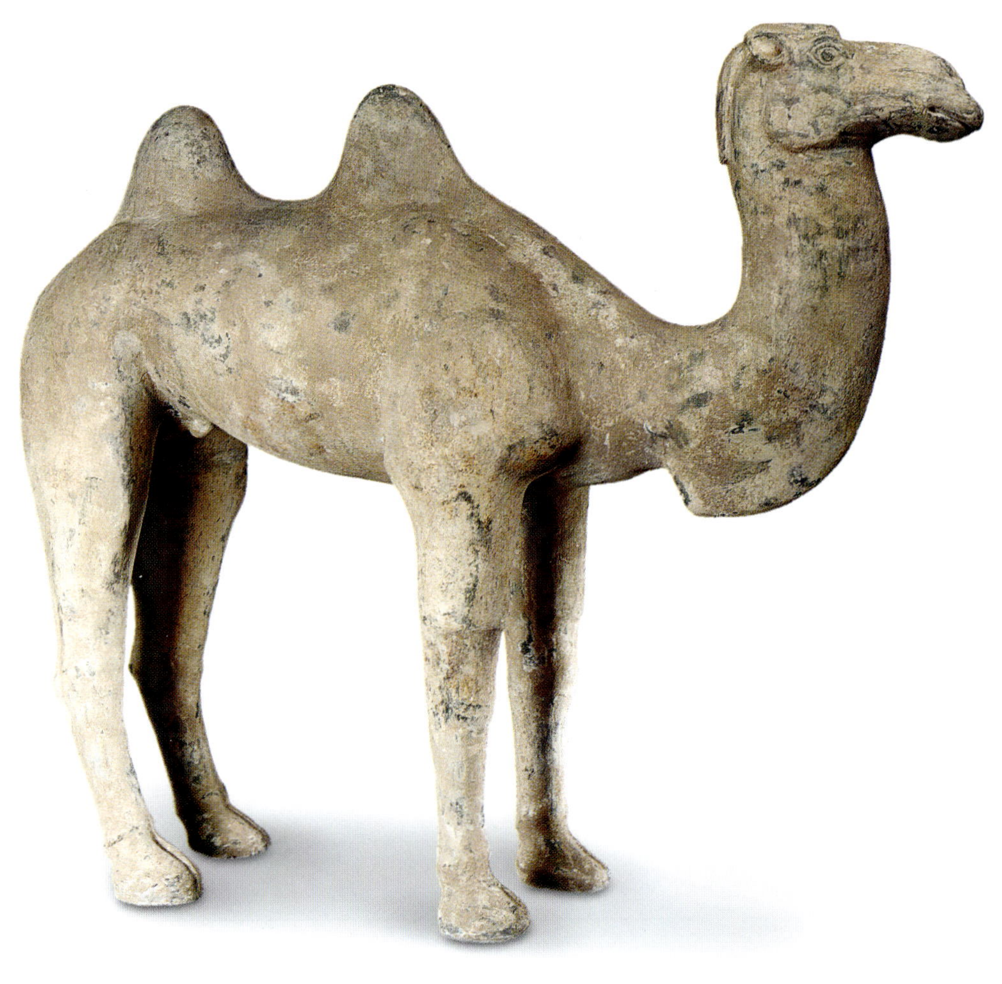

66 | CAMEL
Han dynasty (206 B.C.–A.D. 220)
Earthenware
H. 29 1/8 in. (74 cm.); L. 36 5/8 in. (93 cm.)
Unearthed in 1982 at Shapo, Xi'an
Xi'an Institute of Cutural Relics and Archaeology

This pottery camel is one of a pair unearthed from a tomb during a soil survey at a brick factory in a southern suburb of Xi'an. Because of the accidental nature of this discovery, accompanying objects and their locations in the tomb are not clear. Although historical texts indicate that camels were introduced by Westerners to the Han palace as early as the reign of Emperor Wu (141–87 B.C.), few free-standing camels have been unearthed from tombs of the Western Han in Shaanxi or other provinces. In order to date this camel to the Western Han period, more solid archaeological evidence is required.

As a rare exotic animal during the Han, the function of camels is not clear. A stone relief with a design of a camel was found in a tomb of the Eastern Han at Mamaozhuang in Lishi, Shanxi Province. This relief reveals a camel marching forward with a group of riders on horseback carrying spear-like weapons. This may suggest that the camel was used as transportation, or perhaps for hunting or fighting.

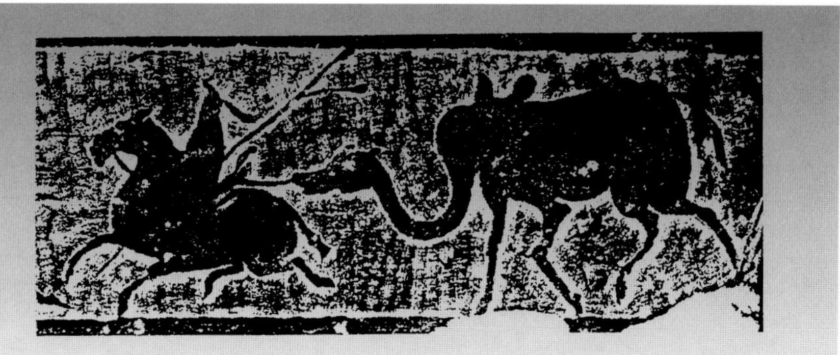

Fig. 6.1. Camel marching with riders. Eastern Han. Excavated at Mamaozhuang, Lishi. After Li Lin et al., fig. 654.

Literature

Wang Changqi, "Xi'an faxian de Han Sui shiqi taoyong" (Han and Sui period pottery figurines discovered in Xi'an), *Kaogu yu wenwu,* no. 2 (1992): 34–35.

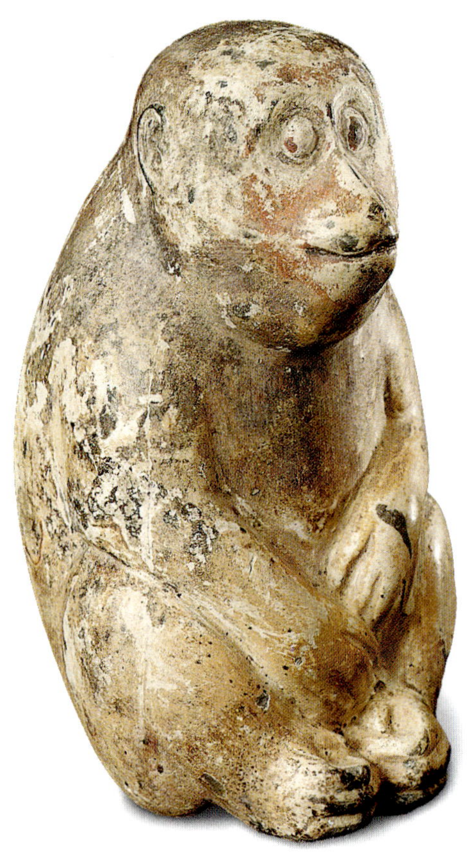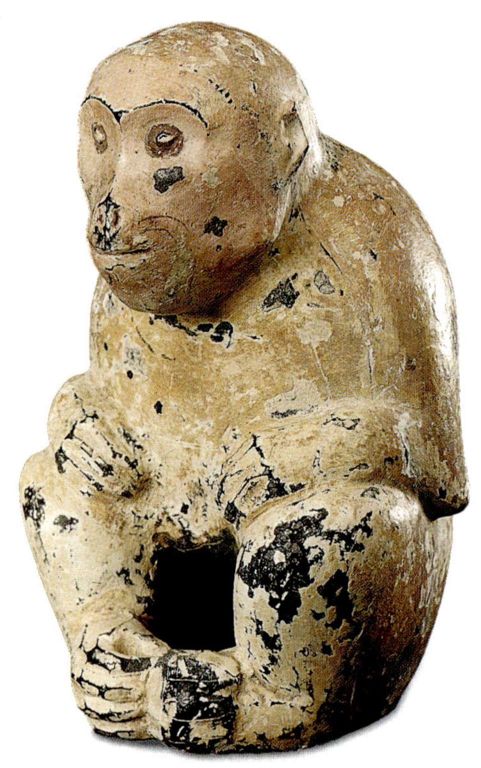

67 | PAIR OF MONKEYS
Han dynasty (206 B.C.–A.D. 220)
Earthenware with painted decoration
H. 5 3/8 in. (13.5 cm.); H. 5 7/8 in. (15 cm.)
Unearthed in 1982 at Shapo, Xi'an
Xi'an Institute of Cultural Relics and Archaeology

Molded in hollow gray clay, this pair of monkeys is depicted in a natural pose with their hands resting on their knees. Their backs are gently rounded and their faces detailed by arched eyebrows, circular eyes, straight noses, and closed mouths, originally painted in red over a coat of white slip. The subtle body language and vivid facial expression reflect a careful observation of genuine monkeys by the sculptor. Characteristic of realistic representation and free-standing forms, this unique pair has found no parallel elsewhere in China from the same period.

From ancient literature we know that monkeys, as a rare species from the West, were offered as tribute to emperors during the Western Han and were kept in the palace garden for the pleasure of the imperial family. Images of monkeys are revealed on Eastern Han stone carvings, often shown in pairs, seated on the roof of a ceremonial ower. The symbolic meaning of the scene tends to link it with the ritual concept of immortality, which grew increasingly popular during the Han dynasty.

Literature

Wang Changqi, "Xi'an faxian de Han Sui shiqi taoyong" (Han and Sui period pottery figurines discovered in Xi'an), *Kaogu yu wenwu*, no. 2 (1992): 34–35.

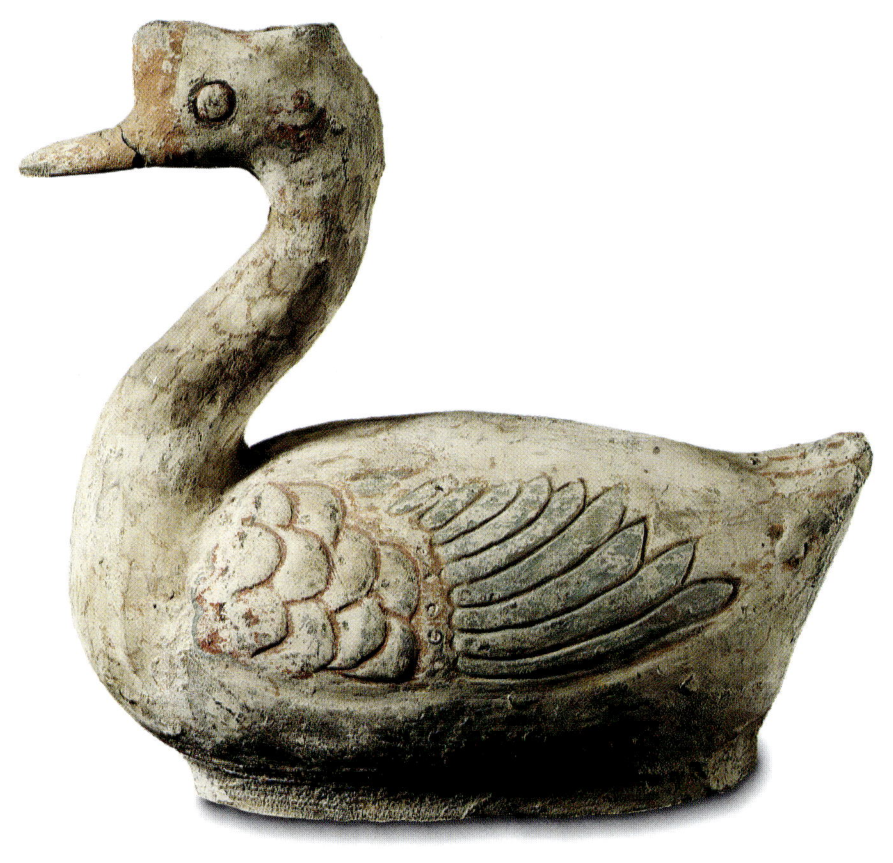

<table>
<tr><td>68</td><td>

GOOSE
Eastern Han dynasty (A.D. 25–220)
Earthenware with painted decoration
H. 9 5/8 in. (24.5 cm.); L. 10 5/8 (27 cm.)
Unearthed from a suburb of Xi'an
Shaanxi History Museum

</td></tr>
</table>

This sculpture depicts a seated goose with its head held erect forming an S-shape, as if the bird is floating on water. The well-proportioned form is enriched by painted details along the neck and over the wings and incised designs on the eyes and wings. The genuine representation of this goose exemplifies the realistic style of Han sculpture.

Burial figurines and pictorial stone reliefs unearthed from Shaanxi have revealed that domestic fowl and animals were raised in Shaanxi during the Han dynasty. The animals portrayed include horses, cows, sheep, pigs, dogs, chickens, and ducks, as well as geese. Geese are commonly seen in southern China, where water is prevalent, rather than Shaanxi, where it is relatively dry. The presence of figures of geese in Shaanxi may suggest that a climatic change occurred in this region, and that two thousand years ago the area may have been a grassland with many bodies of water.

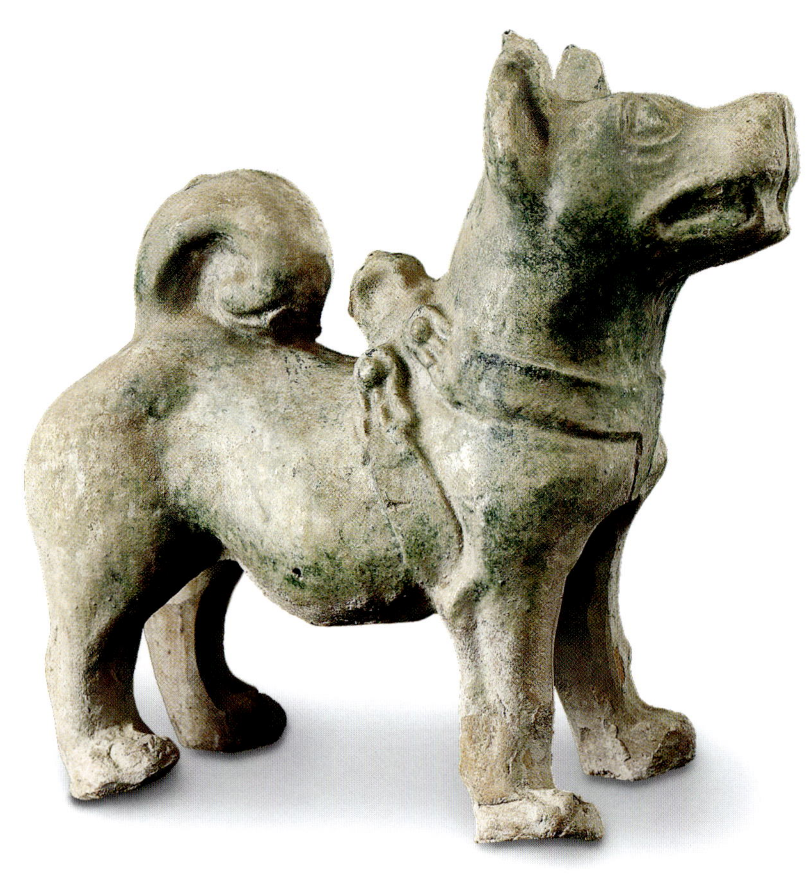

69 | DOG
Eastern Han dynasty (A.D. 25–220)
Earthenware with green glaze
H. 8 7/8 in. (22.5 cm.); L. 9 1/8 in. (23 cm.)
Unearthed in 1981 at Chengzhong School, Xingping, Shaanxi Province
Maoling Museum

Made of hollow molded red clay and covered with a green glaze, this dog is shown wearing a leather collar and standing in an alert posture, with erect ears, wide-open eyes and the tail curved upward. This animated and vigorous dog is an example of one of the domesticated animals of the Han dynasty. Frequently seen in Han stone reliefs, dogs served as watch dogs, as aids in hunting and grazing, and also as ceremonial offerings.

The most notable technique developed in pottery production during the Eastern Han period is the use of glaze. Early vessels with brown or green glazes appeared during the middle of the Western Han dynasty, mostly in Shaanxi and Henan provinces. By the Eastern Han dynasty, glazed pottery, especially green-glazed, had spread widely throughout the country. This type of glaze was called "lead glaze." It contained a large amount of oxidized lead, and it was fired at a temperature of eight hundred degrees centigrade. The origin of this type of glaze is not clear. Some scholars consider that it was invented in Egypt and introduced to China through West Asia at the beginning of the first century. Others believe that it had its origin in the primitive glaze created as early as the Shang and Zhou dynasties.

Literature

Feng Xianming et al., eds., *Zhongguo taoci shi* (History of Chinese ceramics), Beijing: Wenwu Press, 1987, 114–16.

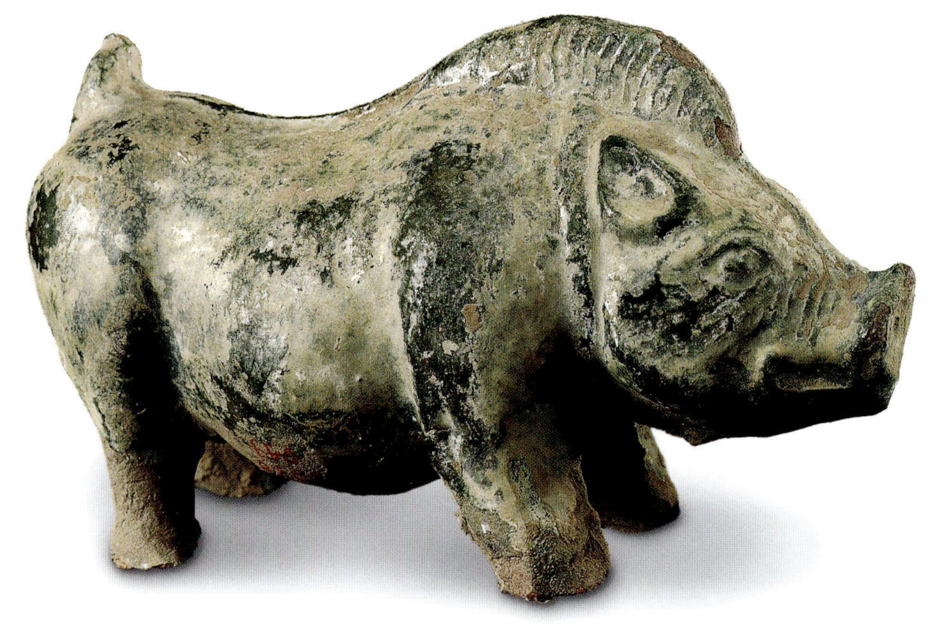

70 | PIG
Eastern Han dynasty (A.D. 25–220)
Earthenware with green glaze
H. 5 1/3 in. (14 cm.); L. 9 1/8 in. (23 cm.)
Unearthed in 1981 at Yikongcun, Xingping, Shaanxi Province
Maoling Museum

As a major domestic animal, the pig served as an important supplementary food source for the Han people. It could also be sold or exchanged for other products. To emphasize the tomb occupants' desire for prosperity during the afterlife, domestic animal figurines were buried with them in tombs, along with other daily utensils and architectural models. Based on burial finds, archaeological research has disclosed that one or two pigs, two chickens, and one dog seems to have been typical for the burial of an ordinary family member.

Early green glaze could provide a transparent jade color and smoothness to the surface of a ceramic work. However, the green-glazed objects for daily use are rarely found from Han tombs. Instead, most of the objects are vessels or figures made for burial purposes.

Literature

Zhu Tianshu, "Shixi Han tao jiaqin jiaxu muxing" (Commentary on Han pottery animals figurines), *Kaogu yu wenwu*, no. 1 (1996): 70–77.

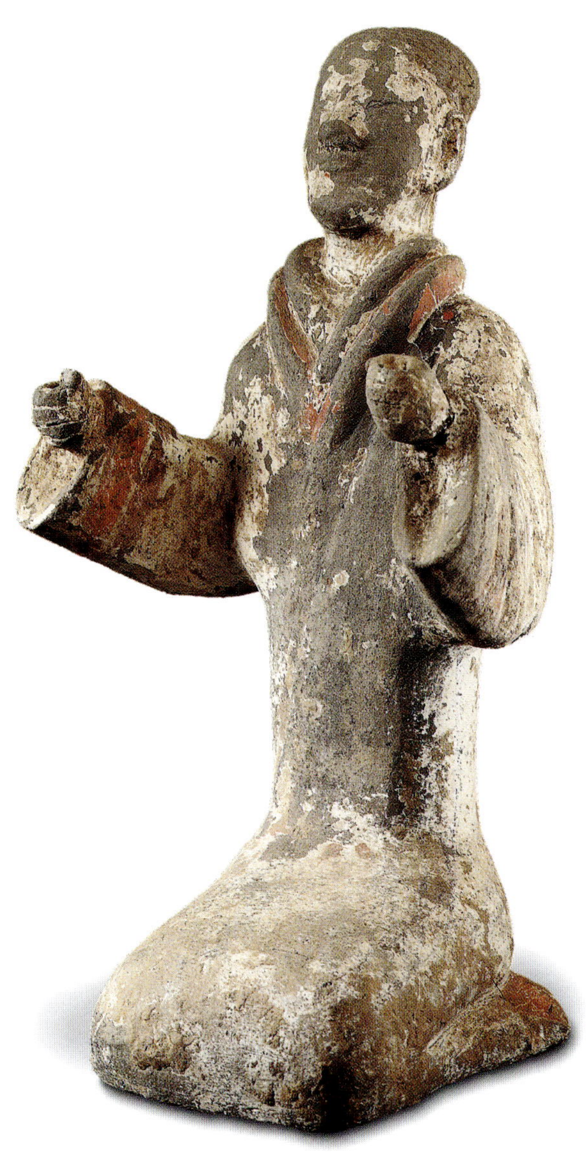

<table>
<tr><td>71</td><td>

PERFORMING FIGURE
Han dynasty (206 B.C.–A.D. 220)
Earthenware
H. 12 1/4 in. (31 cm.)
Unearthed in 1990 at Shilipu, Xi'an
Shaanxi History Museum

</td></tr>
</table>

This statue was unearthed from a tomb near Xi'an, along with more than twenty other objects, including pottery figures and bronze vessels. Although the tomb had been plundered earlier, by examining shapes and decorative motifs on the burial items, local scholars have found that the objects inherited the style of the late Warring States and Qin periods and have dated this tomb to the early Western Han.

This kneeling figure is shown with both arms raised, perhaps playing a musical instrument, such as a drum. With an elongated torso in a long garment and lively facial features, this female figure may represent one of the real performers who served the tomb occupant. This corresponds the fact that a variety of performances was developed during the Han period and a wealthy family would have maintained a group of performers at home.

Numerous performing figures were found in Han tombs, particularly in Henan and Sichuan provinces. This figure differs from Sichuan figures in the elongation of its torso and layers of garments; its large size and vivid facial expression distinguish it from Henan figures.

Literature

Wang Jiugang and Sun Jingyi, "Xi'an beijiao chutu de bixie deng Handai wenwu" (Bixie and other Han relics unearthed from the northern suburb of Xi'an), *Kaogu yu wenwu*, no. 5 (1992): 39–40.

Han Guohe and Cheng Linquan, "Youguan 92 hao Hanmu suizangpin de jige wenti" (A few concerns on the burial objects of Han tomb no. 92), *Kaogu yu wenwu*, no. 5 (1992): 84.

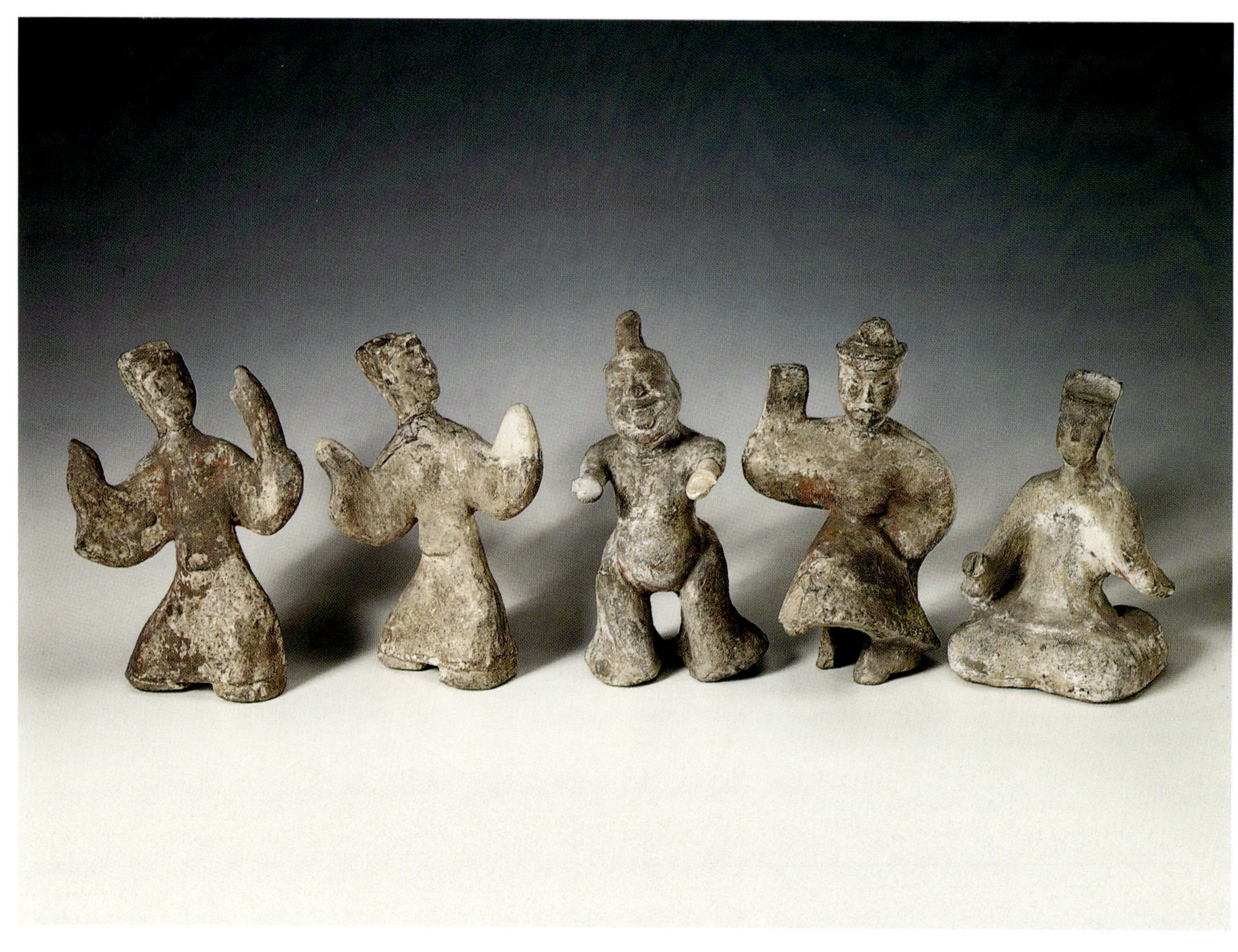

72 GROUP OF FIVE PERFORMING FIGURES
Eastern Han dynasty (A.D. 25–220)
Earthenware with traces of pigment
H. 6 3/4–8 1/8 in. (17–20.7 c m.)
Unearthed from a western suburb of Xi'an
Shaanxi History Museum

One of the major changes in funerary figurines during the Eastern Han was a transition from depicting military soldiers to depicting common people. This yielded many vigorous human figures, who not only represented the common people but also reflected the social life and activities of the time.

Sensitively molded, this group of five figures are dancing, singing, and performing music. The male figure with a bared torso in the center is an acrobat, who, with his arms stretched ahead and his mouth wide open, may be performing a magical act called "throwing flames." As recorded in the Hou Han shu (History of the later Han), this magic act was introduced from Rome and demonstrated by the Burmese at the Han palace during the Western Han dynasty. The acrobat is accompanied by three dancers. The last figure kneels, either singing or playing a musical instrument.

This group appears to be one of only a few Han performing figures discovered in Shaanxi. A nearly identical group of six figures was excavated in Luoyang in 1965, and their similarity suggests a regional influence between Chang'an and the new capital Luoyang during the Eastern Han dynasty. Another group of performing figures of the Western Han was unearthed in Tomb no. 8 in 1969 at Sijiangou near Jiyuan in Henan Province. Among the more than forty objects are seven performance figures, found in the center of the front chamber. This prominent position indicates the high status of the performing arts in Han society.

Literature

William Watson, *The Genius of China*, London: Times Newspapers, Ltd., 1973, 121.

Henan Provincial Museum, "Jiyuan Sijiangou sanzuo Hanmu de fajue" (Excavation of three Han tombs at Sijiangou, Jiyuan), *Wenwu*, no. 2 (1973): 46–54.

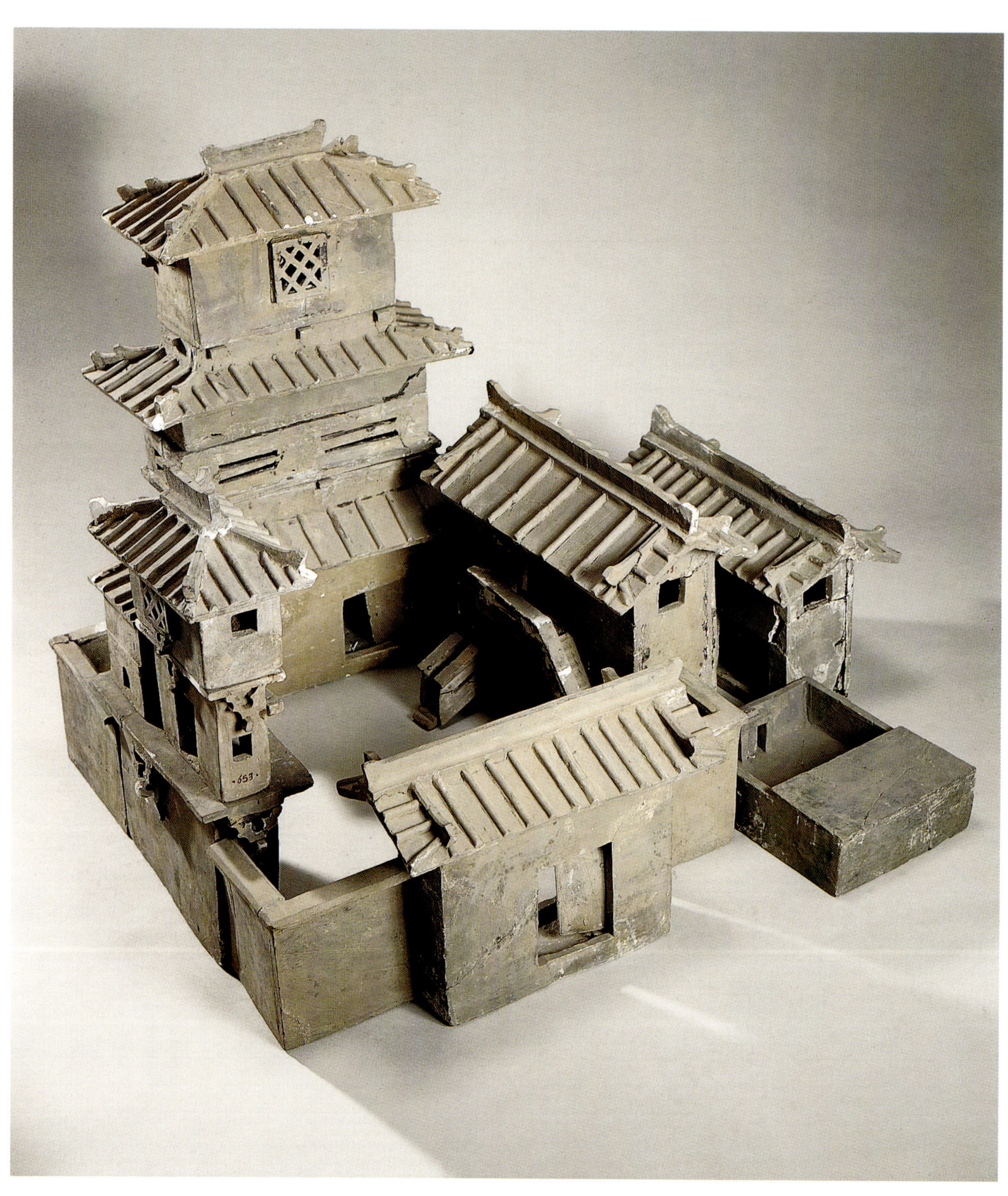

73 | SET OF BUILDINGS WITH COURTYARDS (19 units)
Eastern Han dynasty (A.D. 25–220)
Earthenware
H. 82 cm. (32 in.); W. 138 cm. (54 3/8 in.); D. 115 cm. (45 in.)
Unearthed in 1978 from Tomb no. 1, Laodaosi, Mianxian, Shaanxi Province
Mianxian Museum

As a rare Han residential complex from Shaanxi Province, this model consists of two courtyards of buildings connected by walls, a living quarter for the family, and a stable yard for livestock and other domestic animals. The main building in the front courtyard, which archaeologists believe is the residential chamber of the homeowner, is a three-story building with large, overhanging roofs. Another three-story building on one side has a watchtower, and opposite the tower is a two-story barn that has a railed stairway leading to the granary. The second courtyard consists of a livestock stable, a pigsty, a chicken coop, and a chamber that was probably used as a kitchen. The architectural details are highlighted by the presentation of various designs for roofs, eaves, brackets, doors, and windows. For instance, windows are decorated with a variety of lattice work. Based on the large number of bronze coins and other burial items found in the same tomb, this set of buildings is dated to around A.D. 100.

Han residential courtyards are primarily divided into two types: one-story and multi-story building complexes. The main residential buildings usually faced the south and the kitchen was located to the eastern side of the courtyard. The layout of this courtyard model largely fits into this prototype. Individual architectural models, such as wells and pigsties, have been found frequently in Han tombs, but an entire complex, especially with double courtyards, is extremely rare. Since little is known from existing textual sources on Han architecture, this set of buildings is significant for the study of Han architectural designs, structural modules, and construction materials.

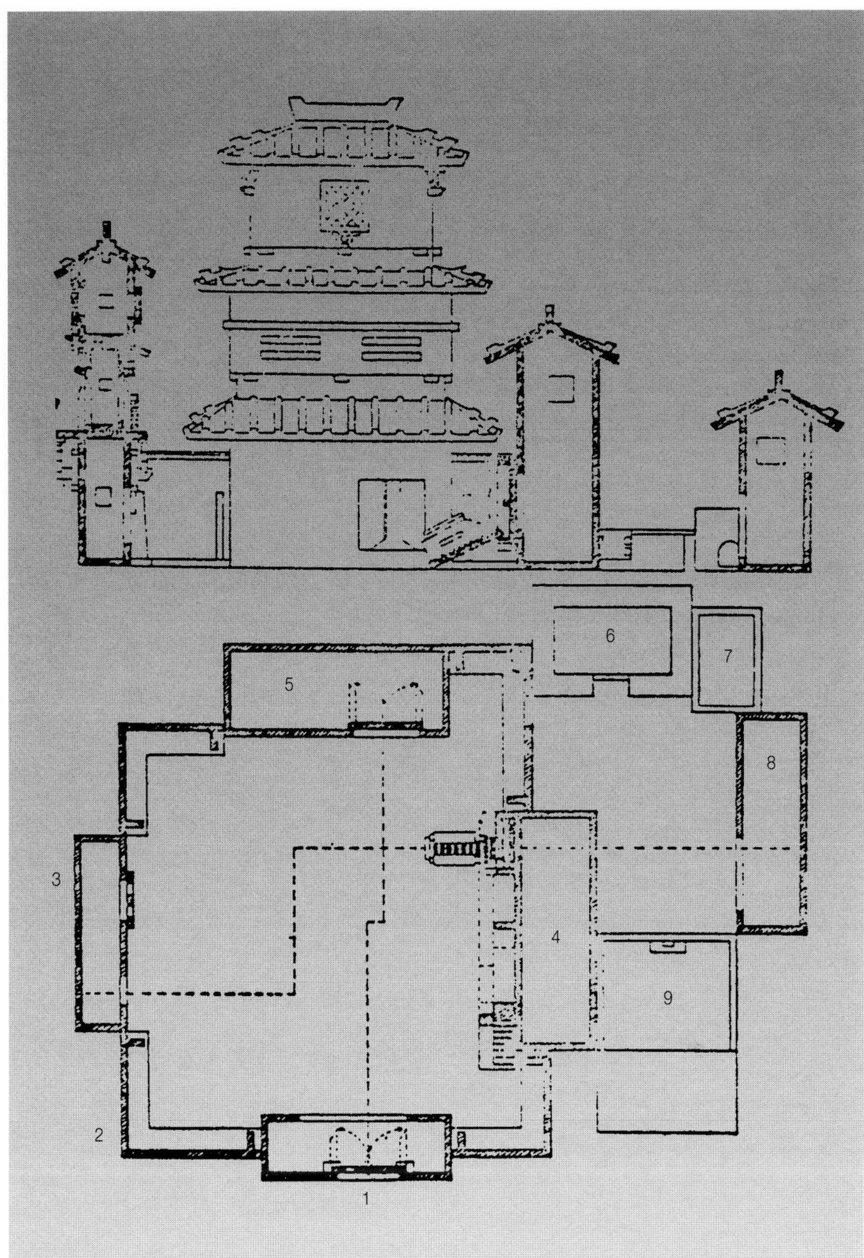

Fig. 6.2. Plan of the buildings with courtyards excavated in Laodaosi, Mianxian, Shaanxi. Based on Guo, fig. 6. 1. Entrance. 2. Courtyard Wall. 3. Chamber with a watertower. 4. Barn. 5. Main building. 6. Livestock pen. 7. Pigsty. 8. Kitchen. 9. Chicken coop.

Literature

Guo Qinghua, "Shaanxi Mianxian Laodaosi Hanmu" (Han tombs excavated from Laodaosi, Mianxian, Shaanxi), *Kaogu*, no. 5 (1985): 429–39.

Sun Ji, *Handai wuzhi wenhua ziliao tushuo* (Illustrated comments on the material culture of the Han dynasty), Beijing: Wenwu Press, 1991, 190.

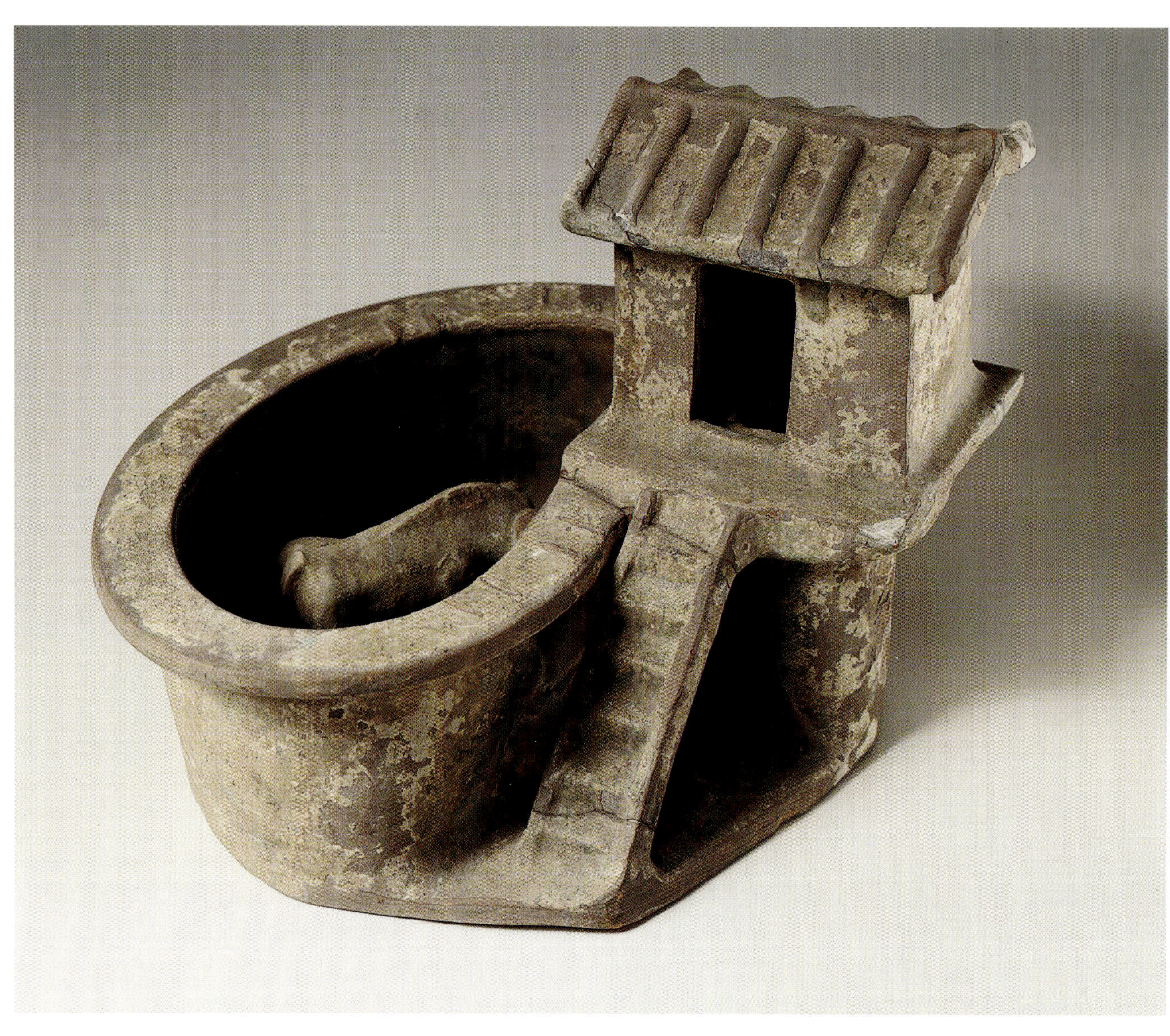

74 | MODEL OF A PIGSTY
Eastern Han dynasty (A.D. 25–220), ca. 168
Earthenware with green glaze
H. 7 1/2 (19 cm.); W. 9 1/2 (24 cm.)
Unearthed in 1959 from Tomb no. 6, Diaoqiao, Tongguan County
Shaanxi History Museum

During the Han period, family members were very close, due to traditional tenets as well as to the need for financial support. This family affiliation is demonstrated in the practice of the family cemetery, where generations of family members were buried. Exemplifying this funeral practice is the Yang family cemetery, excavated in 1959 at Diaoqiao, Tongguan County, Shaanxi. In this burial ground, a series of seven tombs, constructed during 125–225, were excavated. Among the burial items were a few architectural models, such as houses, wells, barns, and pigsties. This group remains significant in the study of Han architecture in Shaanxi.

Found in Tomb no. 6 the tomb of Yang Zhu (d. 168) at the Yang family cemetery, this pottery model exemplifies one of the distinctive pigsty styles of this region. It contains a pig enclosed by a semi-circular wall. Next to the wall is a stairway, which leads to a privy at the upper level. This type of arrangement indicates the Han people's concerns about circumventing pollution and the economical use of space.

Literature

Shaanxi Provincial Compiling Committee of Regional Chronicles, *Shaanxi sheng zhi* (Chronicles of Shaanxi province), *Wenwu zhi* (Chronicles of cultural relics), vol. 66, Xi'an: Sanqin Chubanshe, 1995, 98.

Wang Yuqing, "Tongguan Diaoqiao Handai Yangshi muqun fajue jianji" (Brief excavation records of Yang family tombs of Han dynasty, Diaoqiao, Tongguan), *Wenwu*, no. 1 (1961): 56–66.

Zhang Jianlin and Fan Peisong, "Qiantan Handai de ce" (Primary comments on Han privies), *Wenbo*, no. 4 (1987): 53–58.

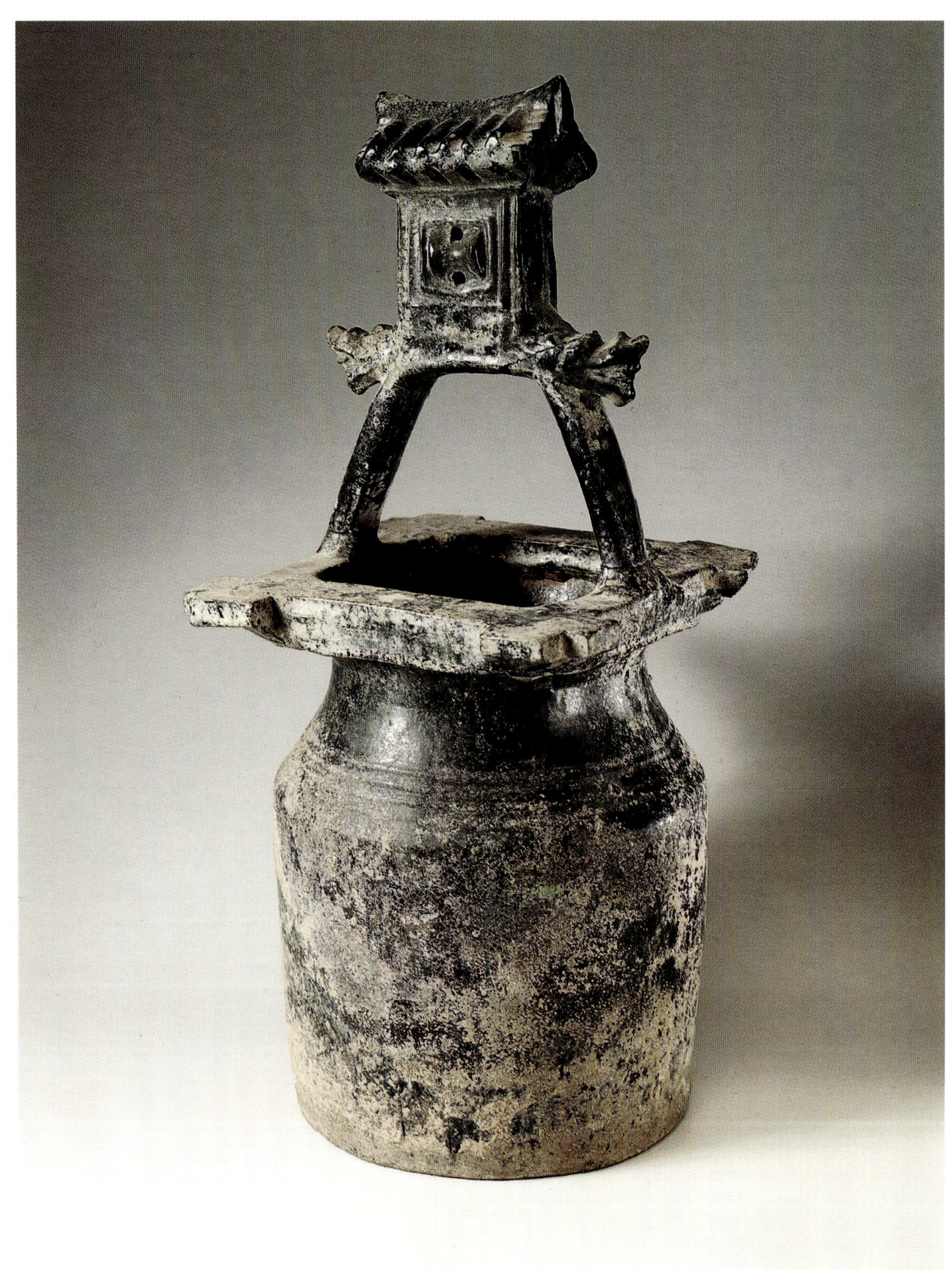

75 | WELL
Eastern Han dynasty (A.D. 25–220)
Earthenware with green glaze
H. 16 3/4 in. (42.5 cm.); W. 7 1/4 in. (18.5 cm.); Diam. at base 6 5/8 in. (17 cm.)
Unearthed from Chenggu, Shaanxi Province
Shaanxi History Museum

Molded in a cylinder and tapered at the upper portion, this well is covered with a tiled roof and equipped with a winch to pull up a bucket of water. The crossbar under the roof is decorated with a dragon head at each end, which suggests that this well was modeled after those built along an ancient canal, the Dragon Head Canal.

Built during the reign of Emperor Wu (141–87 B.C.), the Dragon Head Canal ran about fifteen miles from today's Chengcheng to Yongfeng, Shaanxi. Along the channel were wells about ninety-two feet deep, erected every 600 yards to irrigate nearby farm lands. A model of a pond with water plants and fish, dating to the Eastern Han, has been excavated from Tomb no. 1 in Laodaosi, less than 25 miles west of Chenggu, where this well model was found. All these discoveries manifest the spread of irrigation systems during the Eastern Han dynasty.

The earliest models of wells appeared between the second to the first century B.C. These early examples had a long cylinderical body secured with a frame at the mouth, either in a rounded shape or an oval. By the late Western Han, in the first century B.C., the body of the well disappeared and only the frame remained in either a squared or rectangular shape, often molded with images of mythological animals. By the early second century A.D., the body was added to the frame, and was elevated with a crossbar and a winch, as seen in this model, for efficient pulling.

Literature

Feng Xianming et al., eds, Zhongguo taoci shi (History of Chinese ceramics), Beijing: *Wenwu* Press, 1987, 110.

Guo Qinghua, "Shaanxi Mianxian Laodaosi Hanmu" (Han tombs excavated from Laodaosi, Mianxian, Shaanxi), *Kaogu*, no. 5 (1985): 438–39.

Zai Yonghua, "Shaanxi liang Han kaogu jicui" (Masterpieces of Shaanxi archaeology of the Western and Eastern Han), *Kaogu yu wenwu*, nos. 5–6 (1988): 90–91.

Notes

"Qin and Han Cities and Tombs"
by Lin Qingzhu and Yue Hongbin
pp. 15–25

1. Sima Qian, *Shi ji* (Records of the Grand Historian), *juan* 6, "Qin Shihuang benji" (Beijing: Zhonghua Shuju, 1959), 239.

2. Chen Zhi, ed., *Sanfu huangtu xiaozheng* (Xian: Shaanxi Renmin Chubanshe, 1980), 7.

3. For further information, see Han Wei, "Lueshu Shaanxi Chunqiu Zhanguo Qin mu," *Kaogu yu wenwu*, no. 1 (1986); Ye Xiaoyan, "Qin mu chutan," *Kaogu*, no. 1 (1982); Shang Zhiru, "Qin guo xiaoxing mu de fenxi yu fenqi," *Kaogu yu wenwu congkan*, 3 (1982); Teng Mingyu, "Guanzhong Qin mu yanjiu," *Kaogu xuebao*, no. 3 (1992).

4. For more information on these tombs, see Shaanxi Institute of Archaeology, "Qin Dongling diyihao lingyuan kanchaji," *Kaogu yu wenwu*, no. 4 (1987): 19–28 and "Qin Dongling dierhao lingyuan diaocha zuantan jianbao," *Kaogu yu wenwu*, no. 4 (1990): 22–30.

5. Ban Gu, *Han shu*, "Chu Yuanwang liechuan" (Beijing: Zhonghua Shuju, 1962), 1,954.

6. Sima Qian, *Shi ji*, 265.

7. Ibid.

8. Ban Gu, *Han shu*, 1,954.

9. Yinqueshan Hanmu zhujian zhengli xiaozu, *Sunbin bingfa*, "Bazheng" (Beijing: Wenwu Chubanshe, 1975), 60.

10. Xiao Tong, Wen Xuan, *juan* 1, "Xidu fu" (Beijing: Zhonghua Shuju, 1977), 23.

11. Du Yu, *Chunqiu jingzhuan jijie* (Shanghai: Shanghai Guji Chubanshe), 1986), 201.

12. Sun Zhirang, *Zhuzi jicheng*, *juan* 4, "Mozi jianyou" (Shanghai: Shanghai Shudian, 1986), 146.

13. Ban Gu, *Han shu*, "Wendi ji," 134.

14. Fang Xunling, *Jin shu*, "Suo Lin zhuan," (Beijing: Zhonghua shuju, 1979), 1,651.

"Legacy and Innovation"
by Susan N. Erickson
pp. 27–39

1. Ban Gu, *Han shu, juan* 4, "The Annals of [Emperor Hsiao] Wen" (Wendi ji), in *The History of the Former Han Dynasty*, trans. Homer Dubs (London: American Council of Learned Societies, 1938), 1: 267–72. On page 273 he writes: "He took advantage of [the rise of] the hill [where] his [grave was built], and did not raise a mound [upon his tomb]." For an in–depth discussion of the locations and structure of the imperial mausoleums see Robert L. Thorp, "The Qin and Han Imperial Tombs and the Development of Mortuary Architecture," in *The Quest for Eternity: Chinese Ceramic Sculptures from the People's Republic of China* (Los Angeles: Los Angeles County Museum of Art, 1987), 17–37. Also see Michael Loewe, "The Imperial Tombs of the Former Han Dynasty and Their Shrines," *T'oung Pao* 78 (1992): 302–40; and Wang Zhongshu, Han Civilization (New Haven: Yale University Press, 1982).

2. *Mancheng Han mu fajue baogao* (Beijing: Wenwu Chubanshe, 1980); also see the excellent study of the tombs at Mancheng by Robert L. Thorp, "Mountain Tombs and Jade Burial Suits: Preparations for Eternity in the Western Han," in *Ancient Mortuary Traditions of China: Papers on Chinese Ceramic Funerary Sculptures*, ed. George Kuwayama, (Los Angeles: Los Angeles County Museum of Art, 1991), 26–39.

3. Li Xueqin, "Some Problems Concerning Qin and Han Bronzes," *Early China* 11–12 (1985 87): 296 300.

4. The title of the Prince of Nanyue is more commonly translated as the King of Nanyue. *Xi Han Nanyue wang mu* (Beijing: Wenwu chubanshe, 1991); *Nanyue wang mu yuqi-Jades from the Tomb of the King of Nanyue* (Guangzhou and Hong Kong: The Museum of the Western Han Tomb of the Nanyue King, Guangzhou, and The Art Gallery, The Chinese University of Hong Kong, 1991); and Paula Swart, "The Tomb of the King of Nan Yue," *Orientations* 21 (June 1990): 56–66.

5. *Nanyue wang mu yuqi Jades from the Tomb of the King of Nanyue*, pl. 102.

6. For more about interpretations of the tomb and the perceptions of the afterlife during the Han dynasty see Wu Hung, "From Temple to Tomb: Ancient Chinese Art and Religion in Transition," *Early China* 13 (1988): 78–115; Yü Ying-shih, "Life and Immortality in the Mind of Han China," *Harvard Journal of Asiatic Studies* 25 (1964–65): 80–122; and " 'O Soul, Come Back!' A Study in the Changing Conceptions of the Soul and Afterlife in Pre-Buddhist China," *Harvard Journal of Asiatic Studies* 47, no. 2 (1987): 363–95.

7. "Baoji he Xi'an fujin kaogu fajue jianbao: 2. Xi'an Baijiakou," *Kaogu tongxun* 2 (1955): 37–38, pl. 2.1.

8. Two bronze phalluses were among the finds in a Western Han tomb in the eastern suburb of Xi'an at Sandian Village. They are hollow and are 5 15/16 inches and 6 7/8 inches in length. The tomb has been dated to the reigns of either Emperor Xuan or Zhao (87–49 B.C.). See Zhu Jieyuan and Li Yuzheng, "Xi'an dongjiao Sandiancun Xi Han mu," *Kaogu yu wenwu* 2 (1983): 22–25, pl. 7.5. Also see two bronze phalluses (actually V-shaped with a phallus on each end: 1:4018 and 1:4179) from the tomb of Liu Sheng at Mancheng in Hebei in Mancheng Han mu fajue baogao (Beijing: Wenwu chubanshe, 1980), *xia*, pl. 61.2 and shang, 100 (D. 15/16 inch and 1 3/8 inches). A third phallus of silver (1:4370) was also found (L. 6 1/2 inches). It was damaged when excavated. There is no illustration of this object in the report, but it is described as being hollow so it may resemble the one from Sandian Village (*shang*, 120).

9. Wang Kai, "Han Terra-cotta Army in Xuzhou," *Orientations* 22, no. 10 (October 1990): 62–66.

10. Li Yinde, "The 'Underground Palace' of a Chu Prince at Beidongshan," *Orientations* 22, no. 10 (October 1990): 57–61; and Qiu Yongsheng et al., "Xuzhou Beidongshan Xi Han mu fajue jianbao," *Wenwu* 2 (1988): 2–18, 68.

11. Princes who ruled during this period are: Liu Yingke, Liu Wu, Liu Li, and Liu Dao. See *Wenwu* 2 (1988): 2–18, 68.

12. Wu Hung, "The Art of Xuzhou: A Regional Approach," *Orientations* 21 (October 1990): 40–49. For more earthenware figures in the Xuzhou area but of limited quantities, see Meng Qiang and Geng Jianjun, "Xuzhou Xi Han Wanqu hou Liu Zhi mu," *Wenwu* 2 (1997): 4–21; Geng Jianjun, Meng Qiang, and Liang Yong, "Xuzhou Hanshan Xi Han mu," *Wenwu* 2 (1997): 26–43; and Geng Jianjun, "Jiangsu Tongshan xian Guishan er hao Xi Han yadong mu cailiao de zai buchong," *Kaogu* 2 (1997): 132–42.

13. Sima Qian, *Shi ji, juan* 6, "The Basic Annals of the First Emperor of Qin" (Qin Shihuangdi benji), in *Records of the Grand Historian*, trans. Burton Watson (New York: Columbia University Press, 1993), Qin Dynasty, 63–64.

14. Chen Anli and Ma Yongzhong, "Han Chang'an cheng yizhi chutu da xing taoyong," *Wenbo* 1 (1989): 33–36, figs. 2–3, frontispiece.

15. At sites such as Tomb 1 at Mashan, Jiangling, Hubei, four clothed female figures (H. 22 5/8 to 23 5/8 inches) and four male figures with "painted" clothes (H. 11 3/4 inches) were found, see *Jiangling Mashan yi hao Chu mu*

clothes (H. 11 3/4 inches) were found, see *Jiangling Mashan yi hao Chu mu* (Beijing: Wenwu Chubanshe, 1985), 80–82, figs. 66–67. At Baoshan, in Hubei, Tomb 1 had seven figures (H. 22 1/4 inches); Tomb 2 contained twelve figures (H. 20 7/8 to 44 1/16 inches); and Tomb 4 had three figures (H. approx. 28 5/16 inches), see *Baoshan Chu mu* (Beijing: Wenwu Chubanshe, 1991), *shang*, 38, fig. 24; 254–257, figs. 169–70; and 309, fig. 205. Also see *Yunmeng Shuihudi Qin mu* (Beijing: Wenwu Chubanshe, 1981), 52–54, figs. 97–100; *Jiangling Yutaishan Chu mu* (Beijing: Wenwu Chubanshe, 1984), 91–92, fig. 91; and *Xinyang Chu mu* (Beijing: Wenwu Chubanshe, 1986), 114–16, fig. 79.

16. Baoshan Tomb 1: two examples, (H. 26 7/8 and 25 inches); Xinyang Tomb 1: one example (H. 50 3/8 inches); Tomb 2: three examples (H. 60; 43 5/16; 34 1/16 inches); and Yutaishan sixty-seven examples (H. 22 1/4 to 46 5/8 inches).

17. *Changsha Mawangdui yi hao Han mu* (Beijing: Wenwu Chubanshe, 1973). Figures with actual clothing: two male attendant figures (H. 33 1/4 and 31 1/8 inches), and ten female attendants (H. 27 1/8 to 30 11/16 inches). Eight dancers (H. 18 7/8 to 19 5/16 inches) and kneeling singers (H. 12 3/4 inches) were similarly dressed. It also held five musicians (H. 12 3/4 to 15 inches) and 101 standing figures (H. 16 1/2 to 20 1/16 inches) with clothing painted on the wood surface. In addition, thirty-six much smaller and considerably more crudely made figures were part of the burial (H. 3 1/8 to 4 3/4 inches). Also see Tomb 168 at Fenghuangshan: "Hubei Jiangling Fenghuangshan 168 hao Han fajue jian bao," *Wenwu* 9 (1975): 1–8, 22; *Guangzhou Han mu* (Beijing: Wenwu Chubanshe, 1981), shang, 178–79; and Li Hongfu and Shi Xuewan, "[*Jiangsu*] Lianyun'gang diqu de ji zuo Han mu ji lingxing chutu de Han dai mu tong," *Wenwu* 4 (1990): 58, 80–93.

18. See *Shen Zhongchang*, "Chengdu Fenghuangshan Xi Han muguo mu," *Wenwu* 8 (1961): 413–18; He Zhiguo, "Sichuan Mianyang Yongxing Shuangbaoshan yi hao Xi Han muguo mu fajue jianbao," *Wenwu* 10 (1996): 4–12; and Zhao Shuzhong et al., "Mianyang Yongxing Shuangbaoshan er hao Xi Han muguo mu fajue jianbao," *Wenwu* 10 (1996): 13–29.

19. Zhao Shuzhong et al., *Wenwu* 10 (1996): 13–29. The occurrence of earth enware figurines in tombs of the Western Han dynasty throughout China is limited. For several examples see: *Shen Yi*, "Shandong Linyi Jinqueshan Zhou shi muqun fajue jianbao," *Wenwu* 11 (1984): 41–58; Wang Baolin, "[Henan] Sanmenxia shi li jiaoqiao Xi Han mu fajue jianbao," Huaxia kaogu 1 (1994): 12–21; and Jie Xigong, "Shanxi Xiaoyi Zhangjiazhuang Han mu fajue ji," *Kaogu* 7 (1960): 40–52.

20. Beijing Dabaotai Han mu (Beijing: Wenwu Chubanshe, 1989): 63, figs. 62–63.

21. Mancheng Han mu fajue baogao (Beijing: Wenwu Chubanshe, 1980): *xia*, pls. 146–48.

22. Yao Shengmin, "Guanyu Han Ganquan zhuti jianzhu weizhi wenti," Kaogu yu *wenwu* 2 (1992): 67, 93–98.

23. Fu Jiayi and Wang Hanzhen, "Xi'an shi wenguanhui suozang de si jian Han dai wenwu," *Kaogu yu wenwu* 4 (1981): 121–22, pl. 2.2 (H. 15.3).

24. Yang Xiong (zi: Ziyuan), "Sweet Springs Palace Rhapsody (Ganquan fu)," in *Wen xuan or Selections of Refined Literature*, trans. David Knechtges (Princeton: Princeton University Press, 1987), 2: 16–38.

25. The text known as the Daoyin tu illustrates various daoyin exercises. See *Daoyin tu Mawangdui Han mu bohua* (Beijing: Wenwu Chubanshe, 1979). Also see Catherine Despeux, "Gymnastics: The Ancient Tradition," in *Taoist Meditation and Longevity Techniques*, ed. Livia Kohn (Ann Arbor: Center for Chinese Studies, The University of Michigan, 1989), 225–27.

26. *Zhuang zi*, waipian, juan 2, no. 15, "Tormented mind" (Ke yi), in *The Complete Works of Chuang-tzu*, trans. Burton Watson (New York: Columbia University Press, 1968), 167–68.

27. Hei Guang, "Xi'an Han Taiyechi chutu yijian juxing shi yu," *Wenwu* 6 (1975): 91–92.

28. Sima Qian, *Shi ji, juan* 28, "The Treatise on the Feng and Shan Sacrifices" (Feng shan shu), in *Records of the Grand Historian*, Han Dynasty II: 49. Also see Ban Gu's "Western Capital Rhapsody" (Xidu fu), in *Wen xuan*, 1: 132–35.

29. Sima Qian, *Records*, Han Dynasty II: 49; also see the "Western Metropolis Rhapsody" (Xijing fu), by Zhang Heng (zi: Pingzi; A.D. 78–139), in *Wen xuan*, 1: 201, l. 299: "A whale washed ashore writhing desperately."

30. Tang Chi, "Xi Han she diao Qianniu Zhinü bian," *Wenwu* 2 (1979): 84, 87–88.

31. Ban Gu (zi: Mengjian), "Western Capital Rhapsody" (Xidu fu), in Wen xuan or *Selections of Refined Literature*, 1: 141, ll. 400–01.

32. Wu Hung, *Monumentality in Early Chinese Art and Architecture* (Stanford: Stanford University Press, 1995), 130.

33. See *Huai nan zi, juan* 6, "Peering into the Obscure" (Lan ming xun), in *Huai nan tzu: Philosophical Synthesis in Early Han Thought*, trans. Charles Le Blanc (Hong Kong: Hong Kong University Press, 1985), 184.

34. Li Yuzheng, "Shiquan xian shouci faxian Han liujin can," *Wenbo* 2 (1986): 93.

35. Li Yufang, "Shaanxi Xianyang Maquan Xi Han mu," *Kaogu* 2 (1979): 125–35, figs. 5.7 and 6 (H. 4 1/16 inches). For other examples see Hu Lingui, Sun Tieshan, and Li Gong, "Xi'an dong jiao guo mian wu guang Han mu fajue jianbao," *Wenbo* 4 (1991): 3–18, fig. 7 (H. 3 5/8 inches); and Wang Yongliang, "Yi jian tong 'wen jiu qi,'" *Wenbo* 3 (1993): 59, ill. on back cover .

36. Illustrated in *Shaanxi qingtongqi* (Xi'an: Shaanxi Renmin Meishu Chubanshe, 1994), pls. 319–20. Also see "Shenmu xian chutu yi jian tong caihui e yu deng," *Wenbo* 6 (1986): 64. The goose made of painted bronze is comparable to a similarly-sized, painted lamp found in Shuo County, Shanxi: see Lei Yungui, "Xi Han yan yu deng," *Wenwu* 6 (1987): 69–70.

37. For Qin dynasty tiles, see Wang Xueli, ed., *Qin wuzhi wenhua shi* (Xi'an: San Qin Chubanshe, 1994), 369 72, figs. 8.23–25.

38. Hu Lingui and Zhong Wanman, "Xi'an Jiaotong daxue Xi Han bihua mu fajue jianbao," Kaogu yu wenwu 4 (1990): 57–63; and Wang Guangyong, "Shaanxi sheng Qianyang xian Han mu fajue jianbao," *Kaogu* 3 (1975): 177, 178–81.

39. Sima Qian, *Shi ji, juan* 6, "The Basic Annals of the First Emperor of Qin" (Qin Shihuangdi benji), in *Records of the Grand Historian*, Qin Dynasty, 63: "Above were representations of all the heavenly bodies, below, the features of the earth."

40. Wu Hung, *Monumentality*, 107.

41. "Barn Found Underground at Emperor's Mausoleum," *China Daily*, 28 February, 1997.

"Classification of Han Pictorial Stone Carvings from
Northern Shaanxi"
by Li Jian
pp. 41–55

1. For the illustrations, see Shaanxi Provincial Museum, *Shanbei Donghan huaxiang shike xuanji* (Beijing: Wenwu Chubanshe, 1958).

2. Shih, Hsio-Yen, "Han Stone Reliefs From Shenxi Province," *Archives of the Chinese Art Society of America*, no. 14 (1960): 49–63.

3. Finsterbusch, Kate, *Verzeichnis und Motivindex der Han-Darstellungen* (Wiesbaden: Otto Harrassowitz, 1971).

4. Xin Lixiang, "Han huaxiangshi de fenqu yu fenqi de yanjiu," *Kaogu leixingxue de lilun yu shijian*, ed. Yu Weichao (Beijing: Wenwu Chubanshe, 1989): 234.

5. Li Lin, Kang Lanying, and Zhao Liguang, *Shanbei Handai huaxiangshi* (Xian: Shaanxi Renmin Chubanshe, 1995).

6. Xin Lixiang, "Han huaxiangshi de fenqu yu fenqi de yanjiu," 285–86.

7. Guo Qinghua, "Shaanxi Mianxian Laodaosi Hanmu," *Kaogu*, no. 5 (1985): 435–49.

8. Li Lin et al., *Shanbei*, 178.

9. Yan Genqi, Mi Jingzhou, and Li Junshan, *Shangqu Han huaxiangshi* (Luoyang: Henan Meishu Chubanshe, 1992): 37, fig. 47.

10. The inscription consists of twenty characters in the *zhuan* style. My translation is based on the reading by Chinese scholars and reads "In the ninth month of the first year of the Yongchu reign period [A.D. 107], Niu Wenming, at his chamber of longevity, let his descendents prosper in their livelihood." See the Chinese reading in Li Lin et al., *Shanbei*, 24.

11. Wu Lan and Xue Yong, "Shaanxi Mizhixian Guanzhuang Donghan huaxiangshimu," *Kaogu*, no. 11 (1987): 997.

12. Dai Yinxin and Li Zhongxuan, "Shaanxi Suidexian Yanjiacha Donghan huaxiangshimu," *Kaogu*, no. 3 (1983): 233–37.

13. For detailed legends and interpretation of the Queen Mother and the Kunlun mountain, see Wu Hung, *The Wu Liang Shrine: The Ideology of Early Chinese Pictorial Art* (CA: Stanford University Press, 1995): 108–41.

14. For more inscribed slabs, see Li Lin et al., *Shanbei*, 234.

15. Powers, Martin. *Art and Political Expression in Early China.* (New Haven: Yale University Press, 1991): 42.

16. The Team of Regional Records of Yulin, *Yulin Diquzhi* (Xian: Xibei Daxue Chubanshe, 1994): 11–12.

17. The inscription is translated as, "On the sixteenth day in the ninth month of the Yonghe reign period [a.d. 139], this chamber of longevity is completed for Niu Jiping, the Officer of Shanyang, Henei, who died in his hometown of Pingzhou, Hexi."

18. For more Lishi carvings, see Shih, Hsio-Yen, "Some Fragments from a Han Tomb in the Northwestern Relief Style," *Artibus Asiae* 25, no. 2–3 (1962): 149–62. See also Li Lin et al., *Shanbei*, 226, 228–29, 231.

Catalogue Entries
Western Han Dynasty
by Susan N. Erickson
pp. 102-153

1. For a detailed discussion of the Western Han and the Xin dynasties, see Denis Twitchett and Michael Loewe, eds., *The Cambridge History of China, vol. 1: The Ch'in and Han Empires (221 B.C.–A.D. 220)* (Cambridge: Cambridge University Press, 1986).

2. For information concerning the city of Chang'an during the Western Han dynasty and the Wang Mang interregnum, see Wu Hung, *Monumentality in Early Chinese Art and Architecture* (Stanford: Stanford University Press, 1995), 143–87.

3. Sima Qian, *Records of the Grand Historian (Shi ji), juan* 28, "The Treatise on the Feng and Shan Sacrifices" (Feng shan shu), in *Records of the Grand Historian*, trans. Burton Watson (New York: Columbia University Press, 1993), Han Dynasty II: 28.

4. Zhao Kangmin, "Lintong chutu de Han caihua taoyong," *Wenbo* 2 (1985), 94 (H. 54–59 cm.). Also see Yang Lingshan and Gu Fang, "Han Chang'an cheng yi hao yaozhi fajue jianbao," *Kaogu* 1 (1991): 18–22, fig. 3 (H. 57 cm.).

5. See Zheng Hongchun, "Shaanxi Xi'an ji zhuanchang Han chu jitan mu fajue baogao," *Kaogu yu wenwu* 4 (1990): 31–56, figs. 17 and 24.

6. *Mawangdui yi hao Han mu* (Beijing: Wenwu Chubanshe, 1973), *shang*, pls. 90 and 91; *xia*, pls. 198 and 201.

7. *Baoshan Chu mu* (Beijing: Wenwu Chubanshe, 1991), *shang*, fig. 169 (H. 44 1/8 in.) and fig. 170 (H. 44 in.).

8. See Liu Qingzhu and Li Yufang, "1982-1983 nian Xi Han Duling de kaogu gongzuo shouhuo," *Kaogu* 10 (1984): 887–94; or *Han Duling lingyuan yizhi* (Beijing: Kexue Chubanshe, 1993), 31 figures (H. 21 11/16 to 25 5/8 in.); *Tomb Treasures from China*, pls. 19 and 20, male and female figures unearthed at Sanyi Village, Xianyang, from attendant burial pits of Changling. Female figures have also been found at Zhangli Village, Xingping County, in the vicinity of Maoling, the mausoleum of Emperor Wu (*Zhong guo wenwu jinghua/Gems of China's Cultural Relics*). (Beijing: Wenwu Chubanshe, 1992), pl. 141 (H. 18 1/4 to 19 1/4 in.).

9. See Zhou Suping and Wang Zijin, "Han Chang'an cheng xibeiqu taoyong zuofang yizhi," *Wenbo* 3 (1985): 1–4 (fragments of male and female figurines); Bi Chu, "Han Chang'an cheng yizhi faxian luoti taoyong," *Wenwu* 4 (1985): 94–96 (fragments of male and female figurines); Yang Lingshan and Gu Fang, "Han Chang'an cheng yi hao yaozhi fajue jianbao," *Kaogu* 1 (1991): 18–22 (fragments); Gu Fang and Yang Lingshan, "Han Chang'an cheng 2–8 hao yaozhi fajue jianbao," *Kaogu* 2 (1992): 138–142 bao," *Kaogu* 2 (1992): 138–42 (males: H. 22 5/8 to 23 1/4 in.); Wang Changqi, "Xi'an faxian de Han, Suishiqi taoyong," *Kaogu yu wenwu* 2 (1992): 33–35 (30 male figurines, H. 19 11/16 to 22 1/16 in.; and 10 female figurines, H. 17 5/16 to 19 5/16 in.); Liu Qingzhu et al., "Han Chang'an cheng yaozhi fajue baogao," *Kaogu xuebao* 1 (1994): 99–129 (mostly male figures; H. 19 3/4 to 23 5/8 in.); and Liu Qingzhu et al., "Han Chang'an cheng 23–27 hao yaozhi fajue jianbao," *Kaogu* 11 (1994): 986–95 (heads and fragments; one intact figure stands 23 7/8 in. in height).

10. Liu Qingzhu et al., "Han Chang'an cheng yaozhi fajue baogao," *Kaogu xuebao* 1 (1994): 99–129, fig. 16.1–3 and pl. 15.1–3.

11. Forty-six oxen (H. 11 in.), 125 sheep (H. 8 1/4 to 9 1/16 in.), and 23 hogs (H. 5 1/8 in.) were found. See Zhang Zibo and Wang Pizhong, "Han Anling de kancha ji qi pei zang mu zhong de caihui taoyong," *Kaogu* 5 (1981): 422–45, fig. 6. Animals (eight oxen, six goats, nine sheep, two pigs, one chicken, and two pigeons) also were found in the tomb in the southeastern suburb of Xi'an that included the cavalry mentioned above. See *Kaogu yu wenwu* 4 (1990): 31–56.

12. Sun Derun, "Han Changling peizang mu you faxian tao ma," *Kaogu yu wenwu* 5 (1987): 102–103 (H. 65–68 cm.; L. 48 cm.).

13. Michéle Pirazzoli-t'Serstevens, trans, "Workshops, Patronage and Princely Collections during the Han Period," in *Proceedings of the International Colloqium on Chinese Art History, Taipei. Antiquities*, pt. 2. (Taipei: National Palace Museum, Taibei, 1991), 419.

14. A gilded bronze base in the Stocklet Collection has a composition similar to the base of this lamp. See Guiseppe Eskenazi, *Ancient Chinese Bronzes from the Stocklet and Wessén Collections, Exhibition June 11–July 12, 1975* (London, 1975), 51–52. A slightly larger, gilded bronze base in the Freer Gallery of Art (Freer 68.49) also is related to these bases (D. 6 1/4 in. or 16 cm.).

15. Sima Qian, *Shi ji, juan* 28, "The Treatise on the Feng and Shan Sacrifices" (Feng shan shu), trans. by Burton Watson, *Records of the Grand Historian: Han Dynasty II*, 3–52.

16. *Lun heng, juan* 16, no. 48, "The Tiger Trouble" (Zao hu), trans. by Alfred Forke, *Lun-heng* (New York: Paragon Book Gallery, 1962), pt. II, 360.

17. *Mancheng Han mu fajue baogao* (Beijing: Wenwu Chubanshe, 1980), *shang*, 35, figs. 19–20.

18. See *Mancheng Han mu fajue baogao, shang*, 152, fig. 108.1.

19. *Mancheng Han mu fajue baogao, shang*, 18, figs. 8–9.

20. A bronze mask with similar "teeth" was found in the Qin dynasty ruins of Xianyang. See Wu Zilin and Guo Changjiang, "Qindu Xianyang gucheng yizhi de diaocha he shi jue," *Kaogu* 6 (1962): 281–89, pl. 2.2 (W. 13 cm.; H. 8 cm.).

21. Xia Nai, *Jade and Silk of Han China* (Lawrence, KS: Helen Foresman Spencer Museum of Art, The University of Kansas, 1983), 39.

22. *Lun heng*, juan 16, no. 50, "Arguments on Ominous Creatures" (Jiang rui), trans. by Alfred Forke, *Lun-heng* (New York: Paragon Book Gallery, 1962), pt. 1, 359f. Wang discusses various creatures whose appearances were regarded by some as good omens.

23. The beast could also be related to the *juxu* mentioned in mirror inscriptions, where it served to eliminate baleful influences. See Bernard Karlgren, "Chinese Mirror Inscriptions," *Bulletin of the Museum of Far Eastern Antiquities*, 6 (1934): 27–29, and 50–51. Karlgren translates several of these inscriptions and states that the full name of this beast is *gonggong juxu*. Karlgren notes (p. 27) that in the *Er ya* and the *Lushi chunqiu*, the *juxu* allows another creature to ride on its back in times of danger.

24. See "Xianyang shi jin nian faxian de yi pi Qin Han yiwu," *Kaogu* 3 (1973): 167–70; and *Zhongguo yuqi quanji: #4: Qin Han—Nanbei chao* (Shijiazhuang: Hebei Meishu Chubanshe, 1993), 108, pl. 147 (H. 7 cm.; L. 8.9 cm.).

25. *Mancheng Han mu fajue baogao, shang*, 140–41; and *xia*, pls. 104.5 and 104.6. A similarly sized seal of green jade was found in the tomb of the King of Nanyue. It was inscribed "Seal of the Emperor (di yin)." See *Xi Han Nanyue wang mu* (Beijing: Wenwu Chubanshe, 1991), *shang*, 201–02; and *xia*, pl. 117.2.

26. See Wang Changqi and Kong Haojun, "Xi'an bei jiao faxian Han dai mu zang," *Kaogu yu wenwu* 4 (1987): 39–41, pl. 1.1 (H. 11.5 cm.; D. of mouth 9 cm.).

27. See Sun Ji, "Han zhen yishu," *Wenwu* 6 (1983): 69–72; and Wang Changqi, "Xi'an diqu faxian Chunqiu Zhanguo Qin Han shiqi de qingtongqi," *Kaogu yu wenwu* 5 (1992): 1–8, esp. section 3, pp. 3–6.

28. "Shaanxi Maoling yi hao wuming zhong yi hao congzangkeng de fajue." *Wenwu* 9 (1982): 1–17, fig. 28. Also see: Zhu Jieyuan and Li Yuzheng, "Xi'an dong jiao Sandiancun Xi Han mu," *Kaogu yu wenwu* 2 (1983): 22–25; four weights from a Western Han dynasty tomb in the eastern dynasty tomb in the eastern suburb of Xi'an at Sandian Village (H. 3.5 cm.; L. 9 cm.; and W. 6.8 cm.).

29. Sima Qian, *Shi ji, juan* 111, "Biography of General Wei Qing and Swift Cavalry General Huo Qubing" (Wei jiangjun piaoqi liechuan), trans. by Burton Watson, *Records of the Grand Historian: Han Dynasty II*, 178.

30. Wang Zhijie and Zhu Jieyuan, "Han Maoling ji qi peizang zhong fujin xin faxian de zhongyao wenwu," *Wenwu* 7 (1976): 51–55, fig. 2.

31. See Wang Xueli, ed., *Qin wuzhi wenhua shi* (Xi'an: San Qin Chubanshe, 1994), 370, fig. 8.23.

32. Wang Zhijie and Zhu Jieyuan, "Han Maoling ji qi peizang zhong fujin xin faxian de zhongyao wenwu," *Wenwu* 7 (1976): 51–55, figs. 2–4. In addition one of the hollow bricks that has primarily geometric decoration features a border consisting of immortals riding on the backs of dragons and one-horned chimeras.

33. See *Huai nan zi, juan* 3 "The Treatise on the Patterns of Heaven" (Tian wen xun), trans. by John S. Major, *Heaven and Earth in Early Han Thought, Chapters Three, Four, and Five of the Huai nan zi* (Albany: State University of New York, 1993), 70f.

34. John S. Major, *Heaven and Earth*, 168.

35. For an in-depth study see John S. Major, "New Light on the Dark Warrior," *Journal of Chinese Religions* 13 and 14 (Fall 1985 and 1986): 65–86.

36. John S. Major, "The Five Phases, Magic Squares, and Schematic Cosmography," in *Explorations in Early Chinese Cosmography*, ed. Henry Rosemont, Jr. JAAR Thematic Studies 50, no. 2 (Chico, CA: Scholars Press, c. 1984), 154. For a tomb painting with constellations from Qianyang County, Shaanxi Province, see Wang Guangyong, "Shaanxi sheng Qianyang xian Han mu fajue jianbao," *Kaogu* 3 (1975): 177–81.

37. Wang Zhongshu, *Han Civilization* (New Haven: Yale University Press, 1982), 10 and 149. Also see Nancy Shatzman Steinhardt, "The Mingtang of Wang Mang," *Orientations*, 15, no. 11 (1984): 42–48.

38. John S. Major, "The Five Phases," 157.

39. For a discussion of the Shanglin Park see: Wu Hung, *Monumentality in Early Chinese Art and Architecture* (Stanford: Stanford University Press, 1995), 165f.

40. For the "Shanglin fu" by Sima Xiangru (*zi* Zhangqing) see *Wen xuan, juan* 8, in *Wen xuan or Selections of Refined Literature*, trans. by David Knechtges, vol. 2, *Rhapsodies on Sacrifices, Hunting, Travel, Sightseeing, Palaces and Halls, Rivers and Seas* (Princeton: Princeton University Press, 1987), 72–113.

41. David Knechtges, *Wen xuan*, 88, ll. 168–78.

42. John S. Major, "The Five Phases," 157; and John S. Major, "Astrology in the Huai-nan-tzu and Some Related Texts," *Society for the Study of Chinese Religions Bulletin*, 8 (Fall 1980): 24.

List of Chinese Characters

Aidi 哀帝
Anling 安陵
Anyang 安阳
baihu 白虎
Baling 灞陵
Ban Gu 班固
ban liang 半两
Baoshan 包山
Bashui 灞水
Beidongshan 北洞山
bi 璧
bixie 辟邪
Bo (emperor dowager) 薄
Bohai 渤海
boshanlu 博山炉
Bushou (palace) 步寿
cang or qing long 苍或青龙
chang guan 长冠
Chang'an 长安
Changle (palace) 长乐
Changle gong 长乐宫
Changling 长陵
Changsha 长沙
changsheng 长生
Chengcheng (county) 澄城
Chengdi 成帝
Chenggu (county) 城固
Chengzhong 陈中
chenxingzhuan 陈兴庄
chidao 弛道
Chu 楚
Chunhua (county) 淳化
Chuyuanwang liezhuan 楚元王列传
Dabaotai 大葆台
dai 轪
Danyang 丹阳
daoyin 导引
Daoyin tu 导引图
Dayuan 大宛
Diaoqiao 吊桥
Dou 窦
Dou Wan 窦绾

Duling 杜陵
Epang (palace) 阿旁
fangshi 方士
fangzhang 方丈
feng 凤
Feng and Shan 封禅
fenghuang 凤凰
Fengxiang 凤翔
fu 赋
Fuxi 伏羲
Ganquan 甘泉
Ganquan fu 甘泉赋
Gaodi 高帝
Gaozu 高祖
guan 棺
Guanghan 广汉
Guangyang 广阳
Guanzhuang 官庄
Han (dynasty) 汉
Han shu 汉书
Hanzhong 汉中
Hebo 河伯
Hejiawan 贺家湾
Hengshan 横山
heqin 和亲
Hou Han shu 后汉书
hu 壶
Huainan zi 淮南子
huang 凰
Huang Lao 黄老
huanghou zhi xi 皇后之玺
Huangjiata 黄家塔
Huidi 惠帝
Huliang 壶梁
Huo Qubing 霍去病
ji 戟
jia 甲
jian 剑
Jiang rui 讲瑞
Jianzhang gong 建章宫
jin 斤
Jing (Han emperor) 景帝
Jingdo 景
jinghuan 景桓

Romanization	Characters
Renjiapo	任家坡
ri	日
Sanqiao	三桥
Sandian	三店
Sanzhao	三兆
Shang Yang	商鞅
Shangfang	尚方
Shanglin	上林
Shangyanwan	上盐湾
shao fu	少府
Shapo	沙坡
Shenmu	神木
Shi gong	寺工
Shi ji	史记
Shi jing	诗经
Shilipu	十里铺
Shiqu (palace)	石渠
Shizishan	狮子山
Shuangbaoshan	双包山
Sijiangou	泗涧沟
Sima Qian	司马迁
Sima Xiangru	司马相如
Sishipu	四十铺
Sui (county)	随
Suide (county)	绥德
Sun Bin	孙膑
Sunzi bingfa	孙子兵法
Taerpo	塔尔坡
Tai yi	太一
Taiye chi	太液池
tian ma	天马
Tianlu (palace)	天禄
tong tian tai	通天台
Tongguan (county)	潼关
tu	凸
wadang	瓦当
Wang Chong	王充
Wang Mang	王莽
Wangyi (palace)	望夷
Wei (river)	渭
Weiling	渭陵
Weiyang gong	未央宫
Wen (Han emperor)	文
Wen xuan	文选
Wendi	文帝
Wendi ji	文帝纪
Wu (Han emperor)	武
wu xing	五行
Wudi	武帝
Wuding (river)	无定
Wuwei	武威
Wuzhu	五株
Xi'an	西安
Xia (dynasty)	夏
xian	仙
Xiang Yu	项羽
Xiangong (Qin ruler)	献公
Xianyang	咸阳
Xiao He	萧何
Xiaogong (Qin ruler)	孝公
Xiaowen (Qin king)	孝文
Xiaoxuan	孝宣
Xidu fu	西都赋
Xijing fu	西京赋
Xin	新
Xingping (county)	兴平
Xinmang	新莽
Xinzhuang	新庄
xiong jing	熊经
Xiongnu	匈奴
Xiwangmu	西王母
Xuan (Han emperor)	宣
Xuandi	宣帝
Xuanwu	玄武
Xuzhou	徐州
ya	亚
yang	阳
Yang (surname)	杨
Yang Xiong	杨雄
Yang Zhen	杨震
Yang Zhu	杨著
Yangjiawan	杨家湾
Yangling	阳陵
Yangxin	阳信
Yanling	延陵
Yanshou	延寿
Yi (marquis)	乙
Yikongcun	义空村

Yiling 义 陵
yin 阴
Yingzhou 瀛 洲
Yishou 益 寿
Yong (Qin capital) 雍 城
Yongcheng 永 城 丰
Yougfeng (county) 永 丰
Yu 禹
Yu bu 禹 步
Yuandi 元 帝
Yuanshou 元 狩
Yuanzigou 园 子 沟
Yuchi 鱼 池 村
Yueyucun 岳 芋
Yulin 榆 林
Yushou 御 手
Zeng (state) 曾
zhang 丈
Zhang Heng 张 恒
Zhangcheng (gate) 章 城
Zhangtai (palace) 章 台
Zhao Mo 赵 眜 帝
Zhaodi 昭 帝
Zhaoxiang (Qin king) 昭 襄 女 阳
Zhi nü 织 女
Zhiyang 芷 阳
zhong 中
Zhongshan 中 山
Zhou Bo 周 勃
Zhou Yafu 周 亚 夫
zhuan 篆
Zhuang zi 庄 子
Zhuangtou 庄 头
Zhuangxiang (Qin king) 庄 襄 雀 岩
zhuque 朱 雀 叶
zhuyeyan 竹 叶 字
zi 字
zu 镞
Zuo Qiuming 左 丘 明
Zuo zhuan 左 传

Bibliography

Tomb Treasures from China: The Buried Art of Ancient Xi'an. San Francisco and Fort Worth: The Asian Art Museum of San Francisco and Kimbell Art Museum, 1994.

Ban Gu. *Han shu.* (The history of the former Han dynasty). Translated by Homer Dubs. London: American Council of Learned Societies, 1938.

Beijing Dabaotai Han mu (The Han tombs at Dabaotai, Beijing). Beijing: Wenwu Chubanshe, 1989.

Changsha Mawangdui yi hao Han mu (Han tomb no. 1 at Mawangdui, Changsha). Beijing: Wenwu Chubanshe, 1973.

Chang, Kwang-chih. *The Archaeology of Ancient China.* 4th rev. ed. New Haven: Yale University Press, 1986.

———. *Art, Myth, and Ritual.* Cambridge: Harvard University Press, 1983.

Dien, Albert. "A Study of Early Chinese Armor." *Artibus Asiae* 43, nos. 1–2 (1981–82): 5–67.

Doi Yoshiko. *Kōdai Chūgoku no gazō seki* (Stone engravings of ancient China). Kyoto, 1986.

Drake, F. S. "The Sculptured Stones of the Han Dynasty." *Monumenta Serica* 8 (1943): 280–318.

Du Baoren. "Xi-Han zhuling weizhi kao" (The location of the Western Han imperial mausoleums). *Kaogu yu wenwu,* no. 1 (1980): 29–33.

Erickson, Susan N. "Boshanlu—Mountain Censers of the Western Han Period: A Typological and Iconological Analysis." *Archives of Asian Art* 45 (1992): 6–28.

Fan Ye et al., comp. *Hou Han shu* (History of the Later Han). Beijing: Zhonghua shuju, 1965.

Feng Xianming et al., ed. *Zhongguo taoci shi* (History of Chinese ceramics). Beijing: Wenwu Press, 1987.

Finsterbusch, K. *Verzeichnis und Motivindex der Han-Darstellungen* (Catalogue and index to motifs of Han pictorial representation). 2 vols. Wiesbaden: Otto Harrassowitz, 1971.

Fong, Wen, ed. *Great Bronze Age of China.* New York: Metropolitan Museum of Art, 1980.

Fu Xihua. *Handai huaxiang quanji* (A complete collection of Han dynasty pictorial carvings). Beijing: Sinological Institute of the Chinese-French University, 1950.

The Genius of China. London: Times Newspapers, 1973.

Huang Zhanyue. "Zhongguo Xi'an Luoyang Han-Tang lingmu de diaocha yu fajue" (Survey and excavations of Han and Tang dynasty mausoleums in Xi'an and Luoyang). *Kaogu* 6 (1981): 531–38.

James, Jean. "A Provisional Iconology of Western Han Funerary Art." *Oriental Art* 25, no. 3 (1979): 347–57.

Jiang Yingju. "Handai de xiaocitang: Jiaxiang Songshan Han huaxiangshi de jianzhu fuyuan" (Han dynasty small shrines: an architectural reconstruction of Han pictorial stone carvings from Songshan in Jiaxiang). *Kaogu,* no. 8 (1983): 745–51.

Kesner, Ladislav. "Likeness of No One: (Re)presenting the First Emperor's Army." *Art Bulletin* 77 (1995): 115–32.

Laufer, Berthold. *Chinese Grave Sculptures of the Han Period.* London: E. L. Morice, E. C. Steshert, and E. Leronx, 1911.

Lawton, Thomas. *Chinese Art of the Warring States Period: Change and Continuity, 480–222 B.C.* Washington, D.C.: Freer Gallery of Art, 1983.

Ledderose, Lothar. "Module and Mass Production." In *Proceedings of the International Colloquium on Chinese Art History, Taipei. Antiquities,* pt. 1. Taipei: National Palace Museum, 1991, 826–47.

Li Lin, Kan Lanying, and Zhao Liguang. *Shanbei Handai huaxiangshi* (Han dynasty pictorial stone carvings of northern Shaanxi). Xian: Shaanxi Renmin Chubanshe, 1995.

Li Xueqin. "Some Problems Concerning Qin and Han Bronzes." *Early China* 11–12 (1985–87): 296–300.

Li Yinde, "The 'Underground Palace' of a Chu Prince at Beidongshan." *Orientations* 22, no. 10 (1990): 57–61.

Loewe, Michael. *Chinese Ideas of Life and Death.* London: George Allen and Unwin, 1982.

———. *Divination, Mythology and Monarchy in Han China.* Cambridge: Cambridge University Press, 1994.

———. *Everyday Life in Early Imperial China during the Han Dynasty 202 B.C.–A.D. 220.* New York: Putnam, 1968.

———. "The Imperial Tombs of the Former Han Dynasty and Their Shrines." *T'oung Pao* 78 (1992): 302–40.

———. *Ways to Paradise: The Chinese Quest for Immortality.* London: George Allen and Unwin, 1979.

Major, John S. "The Five Phases, Magic Squares, and Schematic Cosmography." In *Explorations in Early Chinese Cosmology,* edited by Henry Rosemont, Jr., 133–46. JAAR Thematic Studies, vol. 50, no. 2. Chico, CA: Scholars Press, 1984.

———. *Heaven and Earth in Early Han Thought: Chapters Three, Four, and Five of the Huainanzi.* Albany: State University of New York Press, 1993.

———. "Astrology in the Huai-nan-tzu and Some Related Texts," *Society for the Study of Chinese Religions Bulletin,* 8 (1980): 24.

Mancheng Han mu fajue baogao (Excavation report of the Han tombs at Mancheng). Beijing: Wenwu Chubanshe, 1980.

Mazzatenta, O. Louis. "A Chinese Emperor's Army for Eternity." *National Geographic* 182 (1992): 114–30.

Nanyue wang mu yuqi—Jades from the Tomb of the King of Nanyue. Guangzhou and Hong Kong: The Museum of the Western Han Tomb of the Nanyue King, Guangzhou, and The Art Gallery, The Chinese University of Hong Kong, 1991.

Paludan, Ann. *The Chinese Spirit Road: The Classical Tradition of Stone Tomb Statuary.* New Haven: Yale University Press, 1991.

Pirazzoli-t'Serstevens, Michèle. *The Han Dynasty.* Trans. by Janet Seligman. New York: Rizzoli, 1982.

———. "Workshops, Patronage and Princely Collections during the Han Period." In *Proceedings of the International Colloquium on Chinese Art History, Taipei. Antiquities,* pt. 2. Taipei: National Palace Museum, 1991, 415–30.

Powers, Martin Joseph. *Art and Political Expression in Early China.* New Haven: Yale University Press, 1991.

The Quest for Eternity: Chinese Ceramic Sculptures from the People's Republic of China. Los Angeles: Los Angeles County

Museum of Art; San Francisco: Chronicle Books, 1987.

Rawson, Jessica. *Ancient China: Art and Archaeology.* New York: Harper and Row, 1980.

———, ed. *Mysteries of Ancient China: New Discoveries from the Early Dynasties.* New York: George Braziller, 1996.

Rawson, Jessica, and Emma Bunker. *Ancient Chinese and Ordos Bronzes.* Hong Kong: The Oriental Ceramic Society of Hong Kong. 1990.

Rudolph, Richard C. *Han Tomb Art of West China: A Collection of First- and Second-Century Reliefs.* Berkeley: University of California Press, 1951.

Schloss, Ezekiel. *Art of the Han.* New York: China House Gallery/China Institute in America, 1979.

Segalen, Victor. *The Great Statuary of China.* Chicago: The University of Chicago Press, 1978.

Shaanxi Provincial Compiling Committee of Regional Chronicles. *Shaanxi sheng zhi* (Chronicles of Shaanxi province). *Wenwu zhi* (Chronicle of cultural relics), vol. 66. Xian: Sanqin Chubanshe, 1995.

Shaanxi Provincial Museum. *Shaanxi Dong-Han huaxiangshi xuanji* (Selected Eastern Han pictorial stone carvings from Shaanxi). Beijing: Wenwu Chubanshe, 1958.

Shenzhen Museum. *Zhongguo Handai huaxiang shihua xiangzhuan wenxian mulu* (Bibliography of Han dynasty pictorial stone carvings and bricks). Beijing: Wenwu Chubanshe, 1995.

Sima Qian. *Records of the Grand Historian* (*Shi ji*). Translated by Burton Watson. 3 vols. New York: Columbia University Press, 1993.

Steinhardt, Nancy Shatzman. "The Mingtang of Wang Mang." *Orientations* 15, no. 11 (1984): 42–48.

Stories from China's Past: Han Dynasty Pictorial Tomb Reliefs and Archaeological Objects from Sichuan Province, People's Republic of China. San Francisco: The Chinese Culture Center of San Francisco, 1987.

Sun Ji. *Handai wuzhi wenhua ziliao tushuo* (Illustrated commentary on the material culture of the Han dynasty). Beijing: Wenwu Chubanshe, 1991.

Swart, Paula. "The Tomb of the King of Nan Yue." *Orientations* 21 (1990): 56–66.

Thorp, Robert L. "Mountain Tombs and Jade Burial Suits: Preparations for Eternity in the Western Han." In *Ancient Mortuary Traditions of China: Papers on Chinese Ceramic Funerary Sculptures*, ed. by George Kuwayama. (Los Angeles: Los Angeles County Museum of Art, 1991): 26–39.

Till, Barry and Paula Swart. *Images from the Tomb: Chinese Burial Figurines.* Victoria, B.C.: Morriss Printing Co., Ltd., 1988.

Twitchett, Denis and Michael Loewe, eds. *The Cambridge History of China.* Vol. 1, *The Ch'in and Han Empires* (221 B.C.–A.D. 220). Cambridge: Cambridge University Press, 1986.

Wang Kai. "Han Terra-Cotta Army in Xuzhou." *Orientations* 22, no. 10 (1990): 62–66.

Wang Wenqing, ed. *Ten Major Museums of Shaanxi.* Hong Kong: Polyspring Co., Ltd., 1994.

Wang Xueli. *Qin yong zuanti yanjiu* (Special studies on Qin terracotta figures). Xian: Sanqin Chubanshe, 1994.

———. *Zhongguo Han Yangling caiyong* (The colored figurines in Yangling mausoleum of Han China). Hong Kong: Shaanxi Travel and Tourism Press, 1992.

Wang Zhongshu. *Han Civilization.* Translated by K. C. Chang et al. New Haven: Yale University Press, 1982.

Wu Hung. "The Art of Xuzhou: A Regional Approach." *Orientations* 21 (1990): 40–49.

———. "From Temple to Tomb: Ancient Chinese Art and Religion in Transition." *Early China* 13 (1988): 78–115.

———. *Monumentality in Early Chinese Art and Architecture.* Stanford: Stanford University Press, 1995.

———. *The Wu Liang Shrine: The Ideology of Early Chinese Pictorial Art.* Stanford: Stanford University Press, 1989.

Xi-Han Nanyue wang mu (The Western Han dynasty tomb of the King of Nanyue). Beijing: Wenwu Chubanshe, 1991.

Xia Nai. *Jade and Silk of Han China.* Lawrence: Helen Foresman Spencer Museum of Art, University of Kansas, 1983.

Xiao Tong. *Wen xuan* (Selections of refined literature). Translated by David Knechtges. 3 vols. Princeton: Princeton University Press, 1987.

Yin Shengping and Li Xixing, eds. *Shaanxi History Museum: Selected Treasures.* Hong Kong: Educational and Cultural Press, Ltd., 1992.

Yu Ying-shih. "Life and Immortality in the Mind of Han China." *Harvard Journal of Asiatic Studies* 25 (1964–65): 80–122.

———. "'O Soul, Come Back!' A Study in the Changing Conceptions of the Soul and Afterlife in Pre-Buddhist China." *Harvard Journal of Asiatic Studies* 47, no. 2 (1987): 363–95.